From Keynes to Piketty

Peter de Haan

From Keynes to Piketty

The Century that Shook Up Economics

Peter de Haan

ISBN 978-1-349-95605-0   ISBN 978-1-137-60002-8   (eBook)
DOI 10.1057/978-1-137-60002-8

© The Editor(s) (if applicable) and The Author(s) 2016
Softcover reprint of the hardcover 1st edition 2016
The author(s) has/have asserted their right(s) to be identified as the author(s) of this work in accordance with the Copyright, Designs and Patents Act 1988.
This work is subject to copyright. All rights are solely and exclusively licensed by the Publisher, whether the whole or part of the material is concerned, specifically the rights of translation, reprinting, reuse of illustrations, recitation, broadcasting, reproduction on microfilms or in any other physical way, and transmission or information storage and retrieval, electronic adaptation, computer software, or by similar or dissimilar methodology now known or hereafter developed.
The use of general descriptive names, registered names, trademarks, service marks, etc. in this publication does not imply, even in the absence of a specific statement, that such names are exempt from the relevant protective laws and regulations and therefore free for general use.
The publisher, the authors and the editors are safe to assume that the advice and information in this book are believed to be true and accurate at the date of publication. Neither the publisher nor the authors or the editors give a warranty, express or implied, with respect to the material contained herein or for any errors or omissions that may have been made.

Printed on acid-free paper

This Palgrave Macmillan imprint is published by Springer Nature
The registered company is Macmillan Publishers Ltd. London

To Marisales

Preface

Sometime ago I read an obituary about the American sociologist Daniel Bell. It said that two of his books were included in the *Times Literary Supplement List of the 100 Most Influential Books since World War II*. To satisfy my curiosity, I compared the *Times Literary Supplement* (*TLS*) list with my own list of books written by economists. To my delight I discovered that most of the books on my list were also included in the *TLS* list. However, there are also differences. This is partly explained by the fact that the *TLS* list ends in the 1990s, while my list ends in 2014. And, surely, the criteria applied by the ones who put together the *TLS* list were different from mine. The first criterion I applied was that the selected books should best reflect the often turbulent political and economic developments since the early part of the twentieth century. The second criterion was that the selected works should be reflective of the ups and downs of mainstream economic theories (in particular Keynesianism and neoclassical theory) and how these theories influenced public opinion and policymaking in the political domain. The third selection criterion was that the books should explain the factors behind these economic ups and downs.

To put a bit of historical order in my list, I cut it into seven distinct periods and brought the selected books that represented the political, economic, and intellectual 'signs of the times' under the period concerned. Two books written by John Maynard Keynes fitted the first period, spanning the time between the start of the First World War and the end of the Great Depression. *The Economic Consequences of Peace* (1919) pretty much predicted what would happen after the ill-fated Treaty of Versailles, while *The General Theory of Employment, Interest, and Money* (1936) ushered in the Keynesian revolution.

During the second period, encompassing the 1940s, economists like Joseph Schumpeter and Karl Polanyi struggled with the question whether socialism would not be a better option than capitalism. After all, capitalism had not brought much improved economic life after the 'Gilded Age' had abruptly ended. In *Capitalism, Socialism and Democracy* (1942) Schumpeter investigated whether socialism could eclipse capitalism. He concluded that it very well could. The main theme of Karl Polanyi's *The Great Transformation* (1944) is that self-regulating markets required subordinating society to the market. It means no less than the running of society as an adjunct to the market, instead of the economy embedded in social relations. Unchecked, they lead to excesses as confirmed by the endless—and sometimes extreme—ups and downs of entire economies.

After the end of the Second World War a third period—this time of affluence—started which was enjoyed by the industrialised countries. Pent-up demand, reconstruction, and Keynesian policies resulted in robust growth, full employment, higher incomes for all and social security formed the constituent parts of affluence. John Kenneth Galbraith epitomised the period in *The Affluent Society* (1958). And so did Tibor Scitovsky, zooming in on affluence's troubling aspects in *The Joyless Economy* (1976). But the 'Golden Age', as this postwar period was called, didn't last.

The fourth period began in the first half of the 1970s when wages and prices in industrialised countries spun out of control. Growth sputtered, inflation soared, and so did unemployment. This lethal mix became known as stagflation. Keynesians wrung their hands; they couldn't explain, nor redress, what was happening. Neoclassical economists maintained that they knew how to solve the problems. Milton Friedman and Friedrich Hayek were the intellectual leaders of the neoclassical counter-revolution, discarding Keynesianism. Hayek's *The Constitution of Liberty* (1960) and Milton Friedman's *Capital and Freedom* (1962) wielded enormous influence, not only in economics but also in terms of economic policy. Nonetheless, there were economists who questioned the neoclassical assumptions. Albert Hirschman, for example, argued in *Exit, Voice and Loyalty* (1970) that when the market fails to achieve an optimal state, society will recognise the gap, and non-market social institutions will arise and attempt to bridge it.

After the 'Lost Decade' of the 1980s (and for many developing countries well into the 1990s), period number five started. The study of economic growth again flourished, with a particular focus on developing countries. Douglass North's *Institutions, Institutional Change and Economic Performance* (1990) is a classic work in which he demonstrates the importance of institutions in explaining economic growth or stagnation. His book greatly influenced development economics and development practitioners. Before North, Peter Berger had published *The Capitalist Revolution* at the right time, that is, in 1986 when capitalism was riding high. He presented 50 propositions about prosperity, equality, and liberty. He concluded that capitalism was to be preferred to a socialist order. After the dragon of stagflation had been slain, a fairly long period of stability followed. Neoclassical economists believed that 'The Great Moderation', as this period was coined, would last forever. Even Nobel Prize laureates made statements that the economic science had developed the instruments to fine tune the economy. But they should have known better. Surely there were economists who sent out warnings about instabilities in the system, but they were not heard.

And then, in 2007, the housing bubble burst, not only in America, but also in countries such as Ireland and Spain. Period number six, a dark period, began. Banks started to have trouble. A year later, credit dried up all of a sudden. Banks and insurance companies failed. The process was contagious; the entire financial sector nearly collapsed. Governments intervened with unprecedented emergency rescue operations, but they could not prevent the Great Recession and the Euro-zone crisis from happening. In taming the crisis, Keynes was re-appreciated by economists and policymakers alike. Neoclassical economics was blamed for what had gone wrong. Not all recession-ridden countries applied Keynesian anti-depression policies; some resorted to austerity. John Cassidy in his book *How Markets Fail: The Logic of Economic Calamities* (2009) describes what went wrong and what was done about it.

After the Great Recession the seventh period started. Just like after the Great Depression, a host of critical books appeared. Some of them passionately advocated Keynesian policies, others focused on the downside of unfettered capitalism. A favourite subject was inequality; an issue that is not new, but that regained relevance given the widening gap between the wealthy and the rest. In 2014 the English translation of Thomas Piketty's *Capital in the Twenty-First Century* was published. The book was a bestseller. Piketty—like Keynes almost a century before him—gained world fame.

These seven periods constitute seven chapters of this book. Each chapter contains a summary of the books I mentioned, which—to my mind—best represent the particular period at hand, preceded by a biography of the author concerned. The introductory chapter sketches the political and economic context in which the books were written, starting with the aftermath of the First World War up to the Great Recession, subsequent Euro-zone crisis and ending with serious concerns about the economic system at large.

I believe that this book gives the reader an insight into the main developments of the economic science of the past and current century. It will also aid in understanding the debate on major economic challenges. After all, the authors and their works presented are the ones who provided the theoretical groundwork for the economic policies applied today.

Milton Friedman once said that Marx and Keynes may have been the best-known economists, but their works were the least read. I hope that the biographies and summaries presented in this book give the reader a handy guide to what the authors proposed.

The Hague
May 2015

Peter de Haan

Acknowledgments

Writing seems a lonely business, but it is not so. I received a great deal of help from other people. They took a genuine interest in what I was trying to accomplish and—to my great delight—were indeed willing to help.

My good friend and former colleague Kees Beemsterboer thoroughly analysed my text and provided solid advice, which improved the text considerably. The same applies to retired banker Dr Thom van de Burgt. His critical eye spotted inconsistencies, which I quickly removed. My friend and retired publisher, Leo van Grunsven, consistently told me to keep the text brief. He was not very successful in getting his message through, I admit. Yet, he managed to have me limit the introductory chapter from the original 50 pages to some 20 pages.

Alfonso Garcia, my former Bolivian colleague, also helped me in sorting out the wheat from the chaff and putting order in the build-up of the argument. Peter Kardoes, a retired lawyer, went through all the versions of the manuscript, and—again—helped me a great deal with his suggestions. He even confessed, after having read the manuscript, that he started to take an interest in economics, which is a rare compliment coming from a lawyer.

I also want to thank Professor Bert Helmsing who gave me helpful comments, like he did with earlier manuscripts of mine. Professor Arie Kuyvenhoven analysed the text as well. I am particularly grateful for the critical, yet constructive, manner in which he provided me with comments and suggestions, which I gladly took on board. The same applies to Dr Auke Leen, who has been a strong supporter, right from the start, of this book's idea and purpose.

Michiel Vergeer, former spokesman of the Netherlands Bureau of Statistics, was very helpful in sorting out unemployment and economic growth data for the Netherlands during the difficult time of stagflation and Dutch Disease. Dr Marein van Schaaijk, director of Micro-Macro Consultants, acted as sparring partner in understanding the mathematical intricacies of Piketty's formula: $r > g$, which we discussed aboard his ship. It was in various ways a dizzying experience.

All of them regularly sent me copies of articles they felt that might interest me, which they certainly did. As a positive side-effect (as economists would say, an externality) I got to know Dorothy Parker, who characterised the Bloomsbury Group in a funny way (her quote is in the section on Keynes). I also got to know Dorothy's two favourite words: 'cheque' and 'enclosed'. Needless to say, Ms Parker was a professional writer.

My sister, Simone Whittemore, who took American citizenship some 60 years ago, did a sterling job in editing my English, assisted by her daughter-in-law, Genanne Walsh, who is a writer. Thank you Simone and Genanne!

My wife, Marisales Ramón-Chordá, read the entire text, and—as always—made critical comments, which, at times, I found hard to swallow. But, as always, I accepted them with deep gratitude, as she was right.

Finally, the unwavering support of Palgrave Macmillan's Rachel Sangster and Gemma Leigh helped me through the stages of the publishing process. I thank them and all other Palgrave Macmillan staff for their solid and often charming assistance.

Contents

1	**Political and Economic Developments, 1914–2014**	1
	A Bird's-Eye View	1
	Capitalism or Socialism? That's the Question	9
	Affluence	13
	The Return of Neoclassical Economics	14
	Capitalism Riding High	18
	The Great Recession	22
	Challenges	34
2	**The Great War and the Great Depression**	37
	Introduction	37
	Biography: John Maynard Keynes (1883–1946)	38
	The Economic Consequences of Peace	57
	The General Theory of Employment, Interest, and Money	69
3	**Capitalism or Socialism? That's the Question**	109
	Introduction	109
	Biography: Joseph Alois Schumpeter (1883–1950)	110
	Capitalism, Socialism and Democracy	120

	Biography: Karl Polanyi (1886–1964)	158
	The Great Transformation: The Political and Economic Origins of Our Time	164
4	**Affluence**	**173**
	Introduction	173
	Biography: John Kenneth Galbraith (1908–2006)	174
	The Affluent Society	181
	Biography: Tibor Scitovsky (1910–2002)	201
	The Joyless Economy: The Psychology of Human Satisfaction	206
5	**The Return of Neoclassical Economics**	**225**
	Introduction	225
	Biography: Friedrich August Hayek (1899–1992)	226
	The Constitution of Liberty	237
	Biography: Milton Friedman (1912–2006)	277
	Capitalism and Freedom	292
	Biography: Albert Otto Hirschman (1915–2012)	308
	Exit, Voice and Loyalty: Response to the Decline in Firms, Organizations and States	317
6	**Capitalism Riding High**	**351**
	Introduction	351
	Biography: Peter Ludwig Berger (1929–)	352
	The Capitalist Revolution: Fifty Propositions About Prosperity, Equality, and Liberty	354
	Biography: Douglass Cecil North (1920–2015)	386
	Institutions, Institutional Change and Economic Performance	395
7	**The Great Recession**	**425**
	Introduction	425
	How Markets Fail: The Logic of Economic Calamities	426
	Conclusion	469

8 Inequality Revisited	471
Introduction	471
Biography: Thomas Piketty (1971–)	473
Capital in the Twenty-First Century	479
Erratum to: From Keynes to Piketty	E1
Epilogue	495
References	499
Index	507

List of Figures

Fig. 1.1   GDP levels, 1928–1942   6
Fig. 1.2   Unemployment development, 1928–1938   7

List of Tables

Table 1.1	GDP levels, 1921–1927	3
Table 1.2	Per capita growth rates of stagnating African economies, 1980–2002	21
Table 5.1	Organisational reactions to exit and voice	347
Table 5.2	Organisational decline in relation to exit and voice	347

1

Political and Economic Developments, 1914–2014

A Bird's-Eye View

The past century was extreme and turbulent. It was extreme in its destructive brutality: two World Wars, many civil wars, and historically unprecedented oppression in the Soviet Union and China in which millions of people were killed and entire cities, infrastructures, and transport systems were destroyed. The past century was also turbulent from an economic perspective. Europe—in particular the United Kingdom and runner-up Germany—called the shots until 1914. Since then, the United States of America eclipsed the UK as the world's new economic hegemon.

Other fundamental shifts in the world economy took place. The October Revolution of 1917 in Russia ushered in an entirely new central-planning model under autocratic rule. The Soviet Union evolved into a formidable political opponent of the 'free world' until the Soviet Empire imploded in 1991. Meanwhile, the free world, in particular high-income countries, became affluent. In the East, Japan had started its stunning economic ascent after the Meji Restoration in 1867. The Four Asian Tigers (South Korea, Taiwan, Singapore, and Hong Kong) experienced rapid economic growth after World War II (WWII), followed by China and India towards the end of the past century. After a period of relative economic stability, the Great Recession broke out in 2008. It took the biblical 7 years before solid signs of recuperation emerged.

The Great War and the Great Depression

When the Great War (1914–1918) broke out, the gold standard was suspended. The belle époque, a long period of free international trade and prosperity, came to an abrupt end and Europe's economic decline began. World War I (WWI) also marked the breakdown of nineteenth-century western civilisation. Winston Churchill captured in *My Early Life* (1930) what was to be lost for Britain:

> I was a child of the Victorian era, when the structure of our country seemed firmly set, when its position in trade and on the seas was unrivalled, and when the realisation of the greatness of our Empire and of our duty to preserve it was ever growing stronger. In those days the dominant forces in Great Britain were very sure of themselves and of their doctrines. They thought they could teach the world the art of government, and the science of economics.[1]

The Treaty of Versailles, which was concluded on 28 June 1919, did not particularly reverse Europe's political and economic fate; on the contrary. John Maynard Keynes, who participated in the Treaty's negotiations as a member of the British delegation, had warned in *The Economic Consequences of Peace* (1919) that what the victorious Allies demanded from defeated Germany in the form of an enormous amount of war reparations (132 billion goldmarks), loss of coal and iron ore-rich territory and overseas possessions, would lead to political instability and economic collapse. Keynes was right, and ill-conceived monetary policies, such as the return to the gold standard after the end of the war, combined with protectionist trade policies contributed to a dramatic drop in international trade which led to the Great Depression.

---

[1] Churchill, W. (2000) *My Early Life*. London: Eland, ix.

The Roaring Twenties

After a brief post-WWI recession, a period of progress followed, particularly in America: the Roaring Twenties. Pent-up demand triggered a spectacular increase in the production of consumer goods. Cars, radios and electrical household appliances found their way to millions of consumers. Charlie Chaplin's movie *Modern Times* was a humorous critique of business progressivism, emphasising production efficiency, as practised by, for example, Henry Ford's assembly lines pouring out millions of Model T Fords.

Art Deco, jazz, surrealism, new dances and women's fashion flourished and underscored the upbeat mood. New York became a hotbed of artistic innovation: the Harlem Renaissance catapulted Duke Ellington and his orchestra to fame. The mood was optimistic. More and more Americans speculated on the soaring stock market. Credit was cheap, thanks to the Federal Reserve System's (Fed) expanding credit policy.

The Gross Domestic Products of the USA, Australia, Canada, the Netherlands, Sweden and the UK registered robust economic growth, as Table 1.1 shows.

The Great Depression

The booming 1920s—a period of innovation, creativity and prosperity—abruptly ended with the Wall Street crash on 29 October 1929, when the stocks at the New York Stock Exchange took a nosedive. Black Tuesday

Table 1.1 GDP levels, 1921–1927

Country Year	USA	UK	Australia	Canada	The Netherlands	Sweden
1921	579,986	195,642	26,818	30,307	30,670	15,854
1922	612,064	205,750	28,225	34,741	32,342	17,351
1923	692,776	212,264	29,579	36,801	33,140	18,273
1924	713,989	221,024	31,524	37,360	35,561	18,847
1925	730,545	231,806	33,002	41,445	37,058	19,544
1926	778,144	223,270	33,792	43,680	40,028	20,640
1927	785,905	241,240	34,305	48,010	41,700	21,284

Source: Maddison, A. (2003) *The World Economy: Historical Statistics.* Paris: OECD Development Centre Studies

came as a shock; $14 billion in share prices was lost. Few expected the collapse. Two weeks before the crash, Irving Fisher, one of America's foremost economists, declared that 'stock prices had reached what looked like a permanently high plateau'.

Two years later the Great Depression hit Britain and continental Europe in full force. In the autumn of 1931 one of Austria's largest banks, Kreditanstalt, collapsed. This started a financial crisis. European investors, who had their money deposited in London-based banks, withdrew their sterling deposits in a frantic attempt to cash them. The pound devalued, and Britain—which had returned to the gold standard in 1925—ended the pound–gold convertibility in September 1931.

Mainstream economics had no adequate response to the crisis; in fact, traditional economic recipes deepened the crisis. Bank runs and a scramble for gold led to declines in national money supplies. Many Marxists viewed the depression as the final crisis of capitalism. After all, had not Marx written in the *Communist Manifesto* that commercial crises, by their periodical return, put the existence of the entire bourgeois society on trial? Great Depression expert and former Fed chairman Ben Bernanke quoted in his *Essays on the Great Depression* (2000) Barry Eichengreen's analysis of the depression's causes:

> Monetary contractions in turn were strongly associated with falling prices, output and employment. Effective international cooperation could in principle have permitted a worldwide monetary expansion despite gold standard constraints, but disputes over World War I reparations and war debts, and the insularity and inexperience of the Federal Reserve, among other factors, prevented this outcome. As a result, individual countries were able to escape the deflationary vortex only by unilaterally abandoning the gold standard and re-establishing domestic monetary stability, a process that dragged on in a halting and uncoordinated manner until France and other gold bloc countries finally left gold in 1936.[2]

Germany had to pay back their citizens who had invested in German war bonds, as well as large amounts of war reparations to the Allies.

---

[2] Bernanke, B. (2000) *Essays on the Great Depression*. Princeton University Press, 276–7.

The German Reichsbank printed more and more money. The result was hyperinflation. Frederick Taylor's *The Downfall of Money* (2013) presented the spectacular plunge of the mark–dollar exchange rate from 4.19 marks to the dollar (August 1914) to approximately 2.5 trillion marks to the dollar (December 1923).[3]

Sebastian Haffner, the son of a Berlin-based senior civil servant, described the consequences of inflation for his family in *Geschichte Eines Deutschen* (2000):

> On the 31st or the first of the month, my father received his monthly salary, which represented all we had to live on—bank deposits and savings certificates had long since become worthless … In any case, my father would try to acquire a monthly season ticket for the underground railway as fast as he could, so that during the next month he could at least travel to work and back … Then cheques were written for the rent and school fees, and in the afternoon the whole family would go to the hairdresser. What money remained was handed over to my mother—and the next day the entire family, even the housemaid, though not my father, got up at four or five a.m., and took a taxi to the central market. There a big shopping session was organised, and in the course of an hour the monthly salary of a Senior Government Councillor was spent on non-perishable food … At around eight o'clock, just before school time, we would return home, more or less supplied with enough to see us through a month's siege. And that was not the end. For another month there was no more money.[4]

In fact, Germany's hyperinflation was preceded by inflation in Austria immediately after the end of the Great War. Austria had lost its empire status, the country was broke, there was a shortage of almost everything, and government's coffers were empty. Austrian author Stefan Zweig describes the desperate situation in *The World of Yesterday* (1945). Despite all the misery, he also observed a rather ironical phenomenon

---

[3] Taylor, F. (2013) *The Downfall of Money*. New York: Bloomsbury Press, 361–70.
[4] Haffner, S. (2000) *Geschichte eines Deutschen: Die Erinnerungen 1914–1933*. Stuttgart/München: Deutsche Verlags, 216–17.

at the time resulting from the fact that the Austrian krone had then lost heavily against the German mark:

> Bavarians from neighbouring villages and cities poured into the little town by hundreds and by thousands. They patronised the tailor, they had their cars repaired, they consulted physicians and bought their drugs ... Then, a border control was established to stop Germans from buying their supplies in Salzburg ... One article, however, that could not be confiscated remained free of duty: the beer in one's stomach ... No more superb enticement could be imagined and so they would come in hordes with their wives and children ... to enjoy the luxury of gulping down as much beer as belly and stomach would hold. Every night the railway station was a veritable pandemonium of drunken, bawling, belching humanity; some of them, helpless from overindulgence, had to be carried to the train on hand-trucks and then, with bacchanalian yelling and singing, they were transported back to their home country.[5]

There was one economist who shook up the economic conventional wisdom. He demonstrated that the economy's self-correcting mechanism, as prescribed by the neoclassical theory, didn't work. He argued that government had to actively intervene to pull the economy out of the depression and restore full employment (see Fig. 1.1). He analysed the economy in aggregate terms: aggregate demand, aggregate savings and investment; thereby inventing macroeconomics. His name was

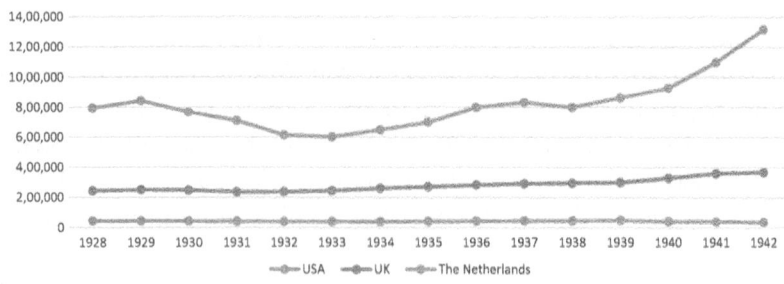

Fig. 1.1 GDP levels, 1928–1942 (million 1990 international Geary-Khamis dollars)

---

[5] Zweig, S. (1945) *The World of Yesterday*. New York: The Viking Press, 293–4.

John Maynard Keynes. He published *The General Theory of Employment, Interest, and Money* in 1936, triggering the Keynesian revolution.

Keynes demonstrated in *The General Theory* that an economic equilibrium could go together with permanent unemployment (see Fig. 1.2). He argued that to counter this, traditional deflation policies made matters worse. Instead, aggregate demand had to be boosted by fiscal measures (i.e., tax cuts and government spending) and by monetary measures (lowering interest rates and printing money by the central bank). The Keynesian revolution eclipsed neoclassical economics, but not forever as future economic and political developments would demonstrate.

Even before Keynes's *General Theory* came out, some governments already applied a Keynesian approach to the Depression. The best-known is President Roosevelt's New Deal, launched immediately after Roosevelt's inauguration in March 1933. Roosevelt was at heart a balanced-budget supporter. However, the newly elected president instinctively understood that the government must 'spend money when no one else had money left to spend'.[6] The New Deal was intended to prevent financial collapse, stimulate demand and provide work and relief for millions of unemployed people through increased government spending, financial reforms and job-creation programmes.

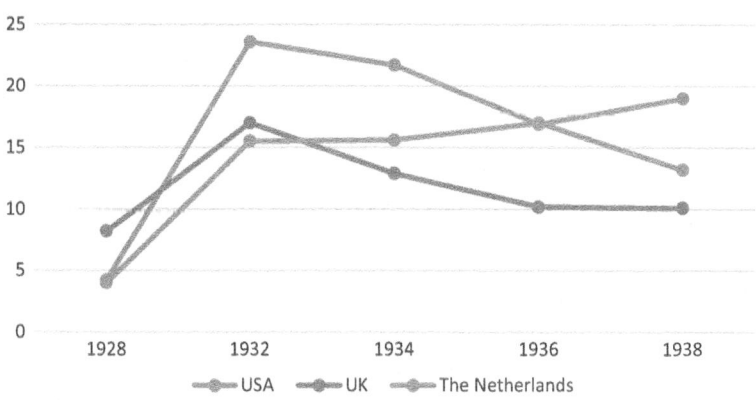

Fig. 1.2 Unemployment development, 1928–1938

---

[6] Eichengreen, B. (2015) *Hall of Mirrors: The Great Depression, the Great Recession, and the Uses—and Misuses—of History.* New York: Oxford University Press, 352.

Roosevelt took a variety of measures, such as the establishment of the Tennessee Valley Authority (a regional economic development agency and electricity provider), the enactment of social security and the Works Progress Administration, which managed the Civilian Conservation Corps (a temporary facility providing jobs to 2.5 million young unemployed Americans). The Glass–Steagall Act of 1933 separated investment from commercial banking.

Roosevelt's stimulus initiatives—and his personal resolve—had a positive effect on the nation's confidence, boosted by his fireside radio talks. For example, he stressed during his talk on 22 October 1933 that, 'If we cannot do this one way, we will do it another. Do it, we will.'

A Keynesian *avant la lettre* was Adolf Hitler. The more powerless the Weimar Republic was in quelling Germany's hyperinflation and in creating jobs, the more popularity Hitler's National Socialist party gained. Hitler was elected German Chancellor in January 1933. Hitler put the unemployed back to work through massive public works (such as Germany's *Autobahnen*) and he started to prepare for war. In 1938, Germany's unemployment rate was down to only 3 %.

Another pre-Keynesian, so to speak, was Japan's finance minister Korekiyo Takahashi who, upon being appointed as finance minister in 1931, reversed Japan's earlier decision to return to the gold standard. Takahashi applied policies to get the Japanese economy going again. He pushed down the yen's rate in order to strengthen Japan's exports. In March 1932, he proposed that Japan's central bank directly purchase all new issued government bonds, which helped to expand the money supply. And in June of that same year, Takahashi submitted a supplementary budget involving fresh spending on rural relief and on Japan's military operations in Manchuria.[7]

The Outbreak of World War II

Nazi Germany wanted to create a Greater Germany (more *Lebensraum*— space to grow) and access to raw materials. Germany remilitarised coal-rich Rhineland, which had been administered by France, as stipulated

---

[7] Detailed information on Japan's response to the Great Depression can be found in *Hall of Mirrors*, chapter 17, 'Takahashi's Revenge', 253–65.

in the Treaty of Versailles. Hitler also wanted to reunite all German-speaking people by taking back the territories that Germany had lost after the Great War. The Austrian *Anschluss* of 1938 started a process which led to WWII. Germany invaded Czechoslovakia in early 1939. The UK and France didn't interfere, in a vain attempt to preserve their policy of appeasement. But when Germany invaded Poland in September 1939, France and Britain declared war. Germany violated the 1939 Molotov–Ribbentrop Pact by invading the Soviet Union in June 1941, whereupon Stalin declared war. Germany's Axis ally, Italy, had already occupied Ethiopia in 1935, and had started occupying Mediterranean countries such as Albania and Greece in 1939.

In the East, the third Axis partner, Japan, had—as noted—occupied Manchuria on mainland China. Manchuria was rich in natural resources. As Japan didn't have access to the Asian colonies of European imperial powers, it was unable to get raw materials from these colonies and was barred from selling its products to them. In its search for raw materials and markets, Japan occupied French, British and Dutch colonies, thereby underscoring its ambition to drive the colonial powers from Asia: *Asia for the Asians*. The Japanese air raid of 7 December 1941 on America's naval base at Pearl Harbor prompted President Roosevelt to declare war.

Capitalism or Socialism? That's the Question

The Great Depression shattered belief in the capitalist system. The sense during the 1940s was that something was fundamentally wrong with it. Apart from fascism, which had gained wide popularity in Germany and Italy, an alternative political and economic system was drawing attention: central planning applied by the Soviet Union, where all property belonged to the state. After all, the Soviet Union's economy wasn't plagued by depressions and unemployment.

Was central planning under autocratic rule perhaps a better way to run an economy than a capitalist system as applied by Western democracies? This question occupied the minds of politicians and scholars alike. Joseph Schumpeter dealt with this question extensively in *Capitalism, Socialism and Democracy*, which came out in 1942. Schumpeter argued that capitalism can't survive, as—in the course of time—it would be killing its own roots. He thought that socialism could work if a requisite stage of industrial development had been reached. Schumpeter had a socialist society in mind, characterised by an institutional pattern in which control over the means of production, and production itself, was vested with a central authority.

Schumpeter maintained that a socialist system is perfectly manageable. It should be borne in mind, however, that a socialist economy requires a large bureaucracy, and at least social conditions favourable to its emergence and functioning. He argued that in such a system it is easier to handle uncertainties that business leaders in capitalist economies encounter. There are no uncertainties, as the managers of socialised industries would know exactly what they are supposed to produce.

Karl Polanyi's *The Great Transformation* (1944) criticised capitalism in its annihilating influence on societies. Friedrich Hayek's bestseller *The Road to Serfdom* (1944) warned against government intervention, as this would put a society on the slippery slope down to despotic rule; people wouldn't be free to make their own choices any longer.

The Soviet Union gradually caught up with America in technological achievements, symbolised by putting her first *Sputnik* as well as the first cosmonaut (Yuri Gagarin) into space before the United States was able to do so. This triggered concern and a competitive spirit in 'the land of unbound possibilities'. As John Kenneth Galbraith observed in *The New Industrial State* (1967),

> The competition in space exploration is largely ... devoid of military implication ... It is held to be of the utmost importance to the international prestige of the United States that its vehicles be first to the moon, the other parts of the solar system and the less convenient reaches of the universe.[8]

The concern wasn't limited to technological progress. Paul Samuelson even predicted in his famous textbook *Economics* that the Soviet Union's GDP might outstrip that of America between 1990 and 2000.[9]

---

[8] Galbraith, J.K. (1967) *The New Industrial State*. Boston: Houghton Mifflin Company, 340–1.
[9] Samuelson, P. (1970) *Economics: An Introductory Analysis*. New York: McGraw-Hill, 831.

The Soviet Union had drawn its Iron Curtain after WWII; the Cold War began. The Soviets spread their political and ideological influence throughout the world. In particular, newly independent nations were sensitive to its ideology. The 'free world' under America's leadership did the same. The stand-off between the two superpowers came to an end when the Soviet Union collapsed on 26 December 1991; the Cold War ended. John Cassidy explained its collapse from an economic vantage point:

> Economics ... is largely about incentives. Communism collapsed because it failed to encourage innovation, enterprise, and hard work; capitalism has thrived, broadly speaking, because it rewarded these things, while punishing conservatism and dawdling. The market system is heartless and unforgiving, but, as even Marx and Engels pointed out, it is uniquely productive.[10]

But let's take a step back in time.

Preparing for the Postwar Period: Marshall Plan

Even before WWII ended, measures had been taken to prevent the mistakes of the Treaty of Versailles. Keynes had already proposed something comparable to the Marshall Plan in *The Economic Consequences of Peace*:

> But if America recalls for a moment what Europe meant to her and still means to her, what Europe, the mother of art and knowledge, in spite of everything, still is and still will be, will she not reject these counsels of indifference and isolation, and interest herself in what may prove decisive issues for the progress and civilisation of all mankind? ... [A]nd for the greater portion of the sum required, the United States, must provide foreign purchasing credits for all the belligerent countries of continental Europe, allied and ex-enemy alike.[11]

---

[10] Cassidy, J. (2009) *How Markets Fail: The Logic of Economic Calamities*. London: Allen Lane, 285.
[11] Keynes, J.M. (2005) *The Economic Consequences of Peace*. New York: Cosimo Classics, 286–7.

The lessons of Versailles had indeed been learned by policymakers. A combination of American magnanimity and self-interest came together in the Marshall Plan, whose US$13 billion financial support greatly helped put Western Europe on its feet again after the war. The aid also made the beneficiaries less vulnerable to Soviet influence. Marshall Plan aid had initially been offered to the Soviet Union and her allies. However, Stalin declined and forced Czechoslovakia and Poland to decline as well. The Soviets launched their own Molotov Plan.

The Marshall Plan laid the basis for Europe's economic integration. Thanks to the Plan's emphasis on productivity improvement, Europe caught up with America over the next two decades. Europe's economic recovery was spectacular: between 1947 and 1951 Western Europe's GDP rose by 30 %.

The Allies did not bleed Germany economically like the war reparations did after WWI. West Germany received US$1.4 billion Marshall aid. The Americans realised that without Germany's recovery, the recovery of other European countries would be problematic. In 1952 West Germany joined the European Coal and Steel Community (ECSC). The ECSC was the predecessor of the European Economic Community formed by France, Germany, Italy, Belgium, the Netherlands and Luxemburg, in Rome, Italy, in 1957.

Apart from praise, the Marshall Plan also met with criticism. Not surprisingly, it mainly came from neoclassical economists, such as former Fed Chairman Alan Greenspan, who observed that aid had the tendency to be wasteful and interfered in the free functioning of markets. Greenspan downplayed the Plan's significance in his memoirs *The Age of Turbulence*:

> Conventional wisdom credits the Marshall Plan for Europe's recovery. I do not doubt that the Marshall Plan helped, but it was too small to account for the remarkable dynamics of postwar recovery. I would regard the freeing of product and financial markets in 1948 by West German economics director Ludwig Erhard as by far the more important spur to the postwar recovery of Western Europe.[12]

---

[12] Greenspan, A. (2007) *The Age of Turbulence*. London: Allen Lane, 281.

Japan was defeated by the Allies in early September 1945. Douglas MacArthur, Supreme Commander for the Allied Powers, was tasked with overseeing the recovery of Japan. Japan received American reconstruction support of $2.4 billion with the goal of establishing democratic self-government, economic stability and Japan's peaceful co-existence with the world. Japan's economy recovered very rapidly; it was back on its feet in 1953 when it reached its pre-WWII level.

Bretton Woods and the UN

International monetary stability was ensured through the Bretton Woods agreements, negotiated by all 44 allied nations in July 1944 in Bretton Woods, New Hampshire. The disruptive volatility in the value of international currencies before WWII was replaced by a system of fixed exchange rates. Bretton Woods included the establishment of the International Monetary Fund and the World Bank. Another Bretton Woods objective was free trade. To this effect the General Agreement on Tariffs and Trade was eventually established in 1956. And in 1995 the Uruguay Round of the GATT was concluded, which resulted in the creation of the World Trade Organization.

After the establishment in 1943 of the United Nations Relief and Rehabilitation Administration, on 24 October 1945 the United Nations Organisation was created, which—unlike the short-lived League of Nations, established after WWI—still plays an important role in diplomatic and military peacekeeping, in emergency and development aid, as well as attending to global concerns such as human rights, care for refugees, food, health and climate change.

Affluence

The postwar period up to the first oil shock of 1973 is known as the Golden Age. America, Canada, Western Europe, Australia, New Zealand and Japan all registered robust economic growth. The economies of the four Asian Tigers (Hong Kong, Singapore, South Korea and Taiwan) were taking off. This wasn't the case for the former colonies of the European imperial powers that had gained independence after WWII. They were not successful in promoting economic growth and in eradicating poverty. These new countries were grouped together under the term Third World.

During the Golden Age—as the French say *les trentes glorieuses*—scarcity made way for affluence in the developed world. Incomes converged to some extent; people even felt that capitalism was something of the past. In 1958, John Kenneth Galbraith wrote a bestseller about this new phenomenon in America: *The Affluent Society*. It was the contrast between the affluent and the poor that triggered the book's idea. He was critical of the way firms manipulated consumer behaviour and lamented the neglect of public services resulting in private opulence and public squalor.

Another economist followed suit. In 1976, Tibor Scitovsky, a Hungarian immigrant in the USA, published *The Joyless Economy*, in which he analysed the question why affluence hadn't brought more joy and happiness to the American people. Scitovsky summarised what physiological psychologists had discovered about human behaviour. In so doing, he paved the way for behavioural economics—a new branch of the economic science.

The Return of Neoclassical Economics

Stagflation

The economic growth engine started to sputter in the early 1970s due to stagflation. This stagflation is a combination of inflation and unemployment. There are various explanations for this phenomenon: inflation reached double digits in the early 1970s as monetary authorities paid little attention to inflation in their zeal to boost employment. The rapid growth in welfare state benefits had contributed to soaring budget deficits. Working conditions had improved and labour costs risen, resulting in inflexible labour markets. Many firms lost their competitive edge and had to lay off personnel; unemployment started to rise. In 1973, and again in 1979, OPEC, the cartel of oil exporting countries, decided to raise the price of oil. These factors—put together—triggered stagflation.

During the 1960s and the early 1970s many Keynesians believed that a bit of inflation would keep unemployment down. This belief was based on the so-called Phillips Curve. This curve shows that a bit of inflation promotes employment, while cutting inflation would push unemployment up. The Keynesians downplayed inflation expectations, but towards the end of the 1970s inflation spun out of control, and unemployment rose worryingly.

Keynesians couldn't explain this stagflation phenomenon.[13] Milton Friedman, however, could. He introduced the notion of a natural rate of unemployment. He argued that if government brought unemployment down to below its natural rate, workers would claim higher wages and businesses would increase prices, triggering a wage–price spiral. Friedman had also observed that too much money in circulation triggers too much demand for goods, leading to inflation. To do something about inflation was to limit the supply of money; this was Friedman's monetary policy advice.

The result was that Friedman left Keynesians behind in embarrassment, while taking the opportunity to promote his neoclassical convictions. His timing was perfect as around that time Ronald Reagan had won the American presidential elections and Margaret Thatcher became Britain's prime minister. Both embraced Friedman's political and economic philosophies. This also applied to, among others, General Pinochet, who was Chile's president at the time.

Slaying the Inflation Dragon

The approaches taken by the USA and the Netherlands provide telling examples of anti-stagflation drives. As regards the USA, Friedman's advice wasn't wasted on Fed chairman Paul Volcker, who had been appointed by President Carter to 'slay the inflationary dragon', in Volcker's own words.

---

[13] This is what Galbraith had to say about the issue in *Economics in Perspective*: 'Wage and price determination was a microeconomic phenomenon, and microeconomics had been separated off by Keynes and left to the classical market orthodoxy. In orthodox microeconomics the wage–price spiral could not occur; producers of goods and the wages they paid their workers were still subject to market forces that the producers did not control. And if, as with monopoly or oligopoly, they did control them, it was in order to maximise profits, not to retrieve increases in wage costs forced by the unions. The separation of microeconomics from the purview of Keynesian economics and policy thus prevented a microeconomic model that could not be accorded an inflationary role. This separation was important; it was at the very heart of the great compromise of Keynes with the classical tradition, the compromise that preserved the market nexus' (268).

The US Congress had passed a law in 1977 establishing the Fed's *dual mandate* of promoting stable prices and full employment. During Volcker's tenure, the Fed's objective of full employment made way for its second objective: keeping inflation in check. Volcker slowed the money supply in the period 1980–1982. Initially, the American economy went into recession. But by 1983 inflation rates began to fall. Growth resumed, and unemployment dropped to 6.2 % in 1987. Volcker's successor at the Fed, Alan Greenspan, wrote about this episode in his memoirs:

> The consequences of his policy were even more severe than Volcker had expected. In April 1980, interest rates on Main Street USA climbed to more than 20 percent. Cars went unsold, houses went unbuilt, and millions of people lost their jobs—unemployment rose to near 9 percent in mid-1980s, on its way to near 11 percent by late 1982 ... But by the middle of the year, after peaking at nearly 15 percent, inflation began gradually to decline. Long-term interest rates inched down too. Still, it would take three years before inflation was fully in check.[14]

The Dutch faced a double challenge: stagflation and the Dutch disease. The economy had initially been hit by the oil price hike of 1973, as the Netherlands was boycotted by OPEC because of its pro-Israel stance. At the same time the value of the Dutch natural gas exports soared as the price of gas and oil are linked. Inflation picked up, and so did prices and wages; the Netherlands was plagued by a wage–price spiral.

In 1978 the Dutch coalition government had launched its anti-stagflation policy in *Bestek 81* (Roadmap 1981). Its objective was to curb public expenditures, which had been spinning out of control due to steeply increased costs of public benefits. This had been largely financed by proceeds from Dutch natural gas exports. The steep increase in natural gas exports had led to the appreciation of the Dutch guilder, making Dutch exports expensive and imports competing with domestic industry cheaper. The result was a decline in the Dutch manufacturing sector and, consequently, a loss of jobs. This chain reaction was coined Dutch disease.

Bestek 81 met with large public protests. The coalition government resigned in 1981. The economy was in recession, inflation ran high and

---

[14] *The Age of Turbulence*, 85–6.

unemployment shot up from 4.8 % in 1980 to 10.7 % in 1983. A new coalition government undertook a fresh attempt to address the problems. It received support from employers and labour unions: the Wassenaar Agreement was signed in 1982 between employers' organisations and the labour unions. It included a cap on wages to lower labour costs, in exchange for a reduction of weekly working hours, and the expansion of part-time employment. It worked: the economy started to grow again, and unemployment gradually came down to 8.6 % in 1986, after its peak of 10.7 % in 1983.

Neoclassical Economics Takes Centre Stage

Milton Friedman was already preparing an attack on the reigning Keynesian paradigm in the early 1960s. His *Capitalism and Freedom* came out in 1962, in which Friedman challenged the Keynesian proposition that government had a crucial role to play in managing the negative effects of business cycles. Instead, Friedman wrote that the Great Depression, like most other periods of severe unemployment, was produced by government mismanagement rather than by any inherent instability of the private economy. However, *Capitalism and Freedom* neither drew the attention from critics nor from readers, as—at the time—they were 'into Keynes', so to speak.

Regarding freedom, Friedman's book was inspired by Friedrich Hayek's neoclassical philosophy as described in his *The Constitution of Liberty* (1960). Friedman confessed that he was more impressed with Hayek's philosophical and political thinking than with his economic deliberations. *The Constitution of Liberty* is indeed more a philosophical than an economic treatise.

After the outbreak of stagflation, neoclassical economics became the dominant school of thought. Friedman and Hayek became the new *masters of the universe*, as one author quipped.[15] Their neoclassical philosophy was widely communicated by a transatlantic network of think tanks, journalists and politicians. Ha-Joon Chang summarised the essence of the neoclassical school in one sentence: 'Individuals know what they are doing, so leave them alone—except when markets malfunction.'[16]

---

[15] Stedman Jones, D. (2012) *Masters of the Universe: Hayek, Friedman, and the Birth of Neoliberal Politics.* Princeton University Press.
[16] Ha-Joon Chang (2014) *Economics: The User's Guide.* London: Pelican Books, 120.

Neoclassical economics studies the optimising economic behaviour of rational and perfectly informed individuals. It focuses on the efficient allocation of resources through the unfettered functioning of the market. It assumes that markets, including the effects of transaction costs, always reach a point at which supply equals demand. Unemployment will disappear once the labour market will have adjusted through the upward or downward movement of wages. The economy will always reach a situation of general equilibrium. In short, neoclassical economics is an elegant, comprehensive and appealing theoretical structure. Moreover, the functioning of markets allows individuals, firms and countries to specialise in what they are best at and so contributing to an economy's productivity, which—in turn—improves living standards.

However, the neoclassics' Achilles heel is their assumptions, as stripped bare by later events. Even before those events, neoclassical economics didn't fare unchallenged. Economics Nobel laureate Joseph Stiglitz, for example, questioned the neoclassical assumption of the functioning of markets, in that not all participants involved in the exchange of goods or services are equally informed, resulting in market failures. And Albert Hirschman's *Exit, Voice and Loyalty* (1970) rejected the suggestion that markets take human beings as they are, with their inevitable self-interest, as professed by the father of economics Adam Smith.

Keynes gained prominence because unemployment was the problem in the 1930s; however, Friedman and Hayek became popular because inflation and big government were the main problems of the 1970s. In short, neoclassical economics was calling the shots again, as it did before Keynesianism became mainstream thinking.

Capitalism Riding High

The Great Moderation

The 1970s and early 1980s were turbulent times: stagflation had to be controlled at the cost of rising unemployment and firms filing for bankruptcy. The costs of the Vietnam War resulted in ever larger US budget deficits. Countries, especially France, wanted to change their US dollar reserves into gold. The pressure on the dollar became so high that the fixed dollar–gold exchange rate, as stipulated in the Bretton Woods agreements, could no longer be maintained. President Nixon ended the fixed dollar–gold exchange rate on 15 August 1971.

In the mid-1980s it seemed as if the economic tide changed for the better. A long period of steady growth started in the Western world, also known as the period of the *Great Moderation*. This was the favourable environment in which Peter Berger's *The Capitalist Revolution* (1986) was welcomed by many readers. He argued that capitalism had become an international system determining the economic fate of most of humankind and, at least indirectly, its social, political and cultural fate.

Top-ranking economists believed that they had found the way to fine-tune economies to the extent that recessions were over. As Robert Lucas, in his 2003 Presidential Address to the prestigious American Economic Association (AEA), emphasised,

> Macroeconomics was born as a distinct field in the 1940s, as a part of the intellectual response to the Great Depression. The term then referred to the body of knowledge and expertise that we hoped would prevent the recurrence of that economic disaster. My thesis in this lecture is that macroeconomics in this original sense has succeeded: its central problem of depression-prevention has been solved, for all practical purposes, and has in fact been solved for many decades.[17]

However, Lucas apparently overlooked Nordic countries' banking crisis of 1991–1992, Mexico's financial crisis in 1995, and the Asian crisis 2 years later when the exchange rates of some South-East Asian countries took a nosedive in 1997. Russia was near-bankrupt and had to be supported by a joint American–IMF financial injection in 1998. Brazil (1999) and Argentina (2001–2002) also had their financial crises. That wasn't all. During the Great Moderation period there were other hiccups like the bursting of three speculative bubbles: in technology stocks, real estate and in oil. An IMF Working Paper of June 2012 estimated that there were 147 banking crises between 1970 and 2011.

---

[17] Krugman, P. (2013) *End This Depression Now.* New York: Norton & Company, 91.

Yet, the economies of the advanced capitalist world were humming along, boosted by cheap credit and by the rise of globalised trade. After a long period of converging incomes and wealth, the gap started to widen again. Japan was the odd man out; its economy was in a deflationary deadlock which the political leadership seemed unable to address.

Anybody with a bit of common sense could know that the Great Moderation couldn't last forever. After all, economic ups and downs are reflective of human nature. And sure enough, the Great Moderation came to an abrupt end in 2008 when the financial crisis broke out in America. However, before dealing with the Great Recession, let's have a look at how other countries fared.

New Institutional Economics

During the Great Moderation period many developing countries, particularly in Latin America and Africa, did not enjoy prosperity. On the contrary, for them the 1980s and 1990s were *lost decades*. Structural reforms were needed to repair the damage done by ill-conceived economic policies, overspending, market distortion, incompetence and corruption. Table 1.2 shows negative growth over the period 1980–2002 of a number of African countries. Structural reform was required in those Latin American and African countries which were near bankrupt. The so-called Washington Consensus recommended ten reform measures to get these countries back on track.[18]

Meanwhile, as mentioned before, most Asian developing countries—including the four Asian Tigers and the emerging economies of China and India—proved that growth could be achieved. The question was, Why was stagnation, rather than growth, the rule in many Latin American and

---

[18] The ten policy recommendations were: (1) Fiscal policy discipline; (2) redirection of public spending from subsidies toward broad-based provision of key pro-growth, pro-poor services such as primary education and health; (3) tax reform; (4) market-determined interest rates; (5) competitive exchange rates; (6) trade liberalisation; (7) liberalisation of foreign direct investment; (8) privatisation of state enterprises; (9) deregulation; (10) legal security for property rights.

Table 1.2 Per capita growth rates of stagnating African economies, 1980–2002

Country	Per capita growth rate (%)
Nigeria	−1.6
Niger	−1.7
Togo	−1.8
Zambia	−1.8
Madagascar	−1.9
Cote d'Ivoire	−1.9
Liberia	−3.9
Congo, Dem. Rep.	−5.0
Sierra Leone	−5.8

Source: Easterly, W. (2006) The White Man's Burden: Why The West's Efforts to Aid The Rest Have Done So Much Ill and So Little Good. New York: Penguin, 347

African countries? Economists and other social scientists renewed their interest in the factors explaining growth. Initially, assumptions about the quality and capacity of the main actors in society, and their interplay, as manifest in developed societies, were projected on developing countries. These assumptions were clearly wrong as demonstrated by the lack of growth in most developing countries.

Researchers recognised that developing countries had different political, cultural, technological and institutional environments. Therefore, the old growth theories, based on simple capital accumulation and the exogenous factor of technical progress, had to be amplified by endogenous environmental factors, like the ones just mentioned. Hence, explaining development involved understanding and mapping of the institutional setting of developing societies. Institutions are the rules of the game in a society. They are important in explaining growth or stagnation because they structure incentives for exchange: good incentives promote growth, while bad ones result in stagnation.

Towards the end of the 1980s, new institutional economics gained recognition by economic historians, development economists and policymakers alike. In 1990, economic historian Douglass North published *Institutions, Institutional Change and Economic Performance*, wherein he identified which institutions promoted or hindered economic growth in various development settings.

The Great Recession

Fed chairman Greenspan retired in 2006. He published his memoirs *The Age of Turbulence* in 2007; 1 year before the American financial crisis broke out.[19] He must have sensed that something was boiling over in the American economy, as he wrote,

> Economists cannot avoid being students of human nature, particularly of exuberance and fear. Exuberance is a celebration of life ... Regrettably, a surge of exuberance sometimes also causes people to reach beyond the possible; when reality strikes home, exuberance turns to fear ... It is also the basis of many of our economic responses, the risk aversion that limits our willingness to invest and to trade, especially far from home, and that, in the extreme, induces us to disengage from markets, precipitating a severe falloff of economic activity.[20]

It wasn't surprising that Greenspan saw trouble looming, as in August 2007 the European Central Bank (ECB) had to inject close to €95 billion into the markets, in part in response to the announcement on 9 August 2007 of BNP Paribas, a large French bank, that it couldn't repay investors of three of its investment funds. Later in his memoirs, Greenspan even broadened 'exuberance' to 'irrational exuberance', a term he borrowed from Economics Nobel Laureate, Robert Shiller.[21] Greenspan wrote that we would never be able to identify irrational exuberance with certainty until *after* the fact.

In 2007, the housing bubble burst in America; the subprime mortgage market collapsed in the middle of that year and the recession started at the end of 2007. Wall Street's financial crisis followed in September 2008, immediately after the failure of Lehman Brothers, an investment bank, quickly deepening Europe's banking troubles, ushering in the global *Great Recession* of 2008.

---

[19] In fact, the subprime financial crisis began to unfold in 2007. Events took a massive turn for the worse in the fall of 2008.
[20] *The Age of Turbulence*, 17.
[21] Shiller, R. (2000) *Irrational Exuberance*. Princeton University Press.

> In late August (2007, PdH), Countrywide Financial secured a $2 billion capital injection from Bank of America. Northern Rock, Britain's fifth biggest mortgage lender wasn't so lucky. The bank … didn't have any direct connection to the U.S. subprime market, but its practice of raising large amounts of money from other financial institutions had prompted questions about its viability. In the middle of September, many of Northern Rock's depositors started queuing up to withdraw their savings. The British government, fearing the depositors' panic would spread, agreed to rescue the bank.[22]

Lucas was wrong after all, when he declared during his AEA speech in 2003 that economists had found the way to fine-tune economies. He apparently had not paid attention to the work of economists, such as Joseph Stiglitz, who had already done work on aspects that did not fit the neoclassical philosophy, ranging from information problems, monopoly power and herd behaviour. Also the behavioural sciences undertook studies to find out whether the *homo economicus* really acted in an economically rational manner. Psychologists Amos Tversky and Daniel Kahneman, for example, found that the neoclassical assumption of rational behaviour did not always apply to human beings faced with complicated choices.

Lucas should also have listened to Hyman Minsky, a Keynesian, who quite accurately predicted in his book *Stabilizing an Unstable Economy* (1986) what eventually happened. Minsky argued that periods of economic stability (such as the Great Moderation) lead to an expansion of debt financing, triggered by new financial assets. An investment boom is the result. During the boom, competition between lenders increases, while their sense of caution diminishes. Many lenders make loans to borrowers who barely can pay the principal and interest. These types of loans have to be rolled over regularly. In time, banks start extending credit to people and firms that are not able to pay even the interest and the credit system becomes unstable. This is precisely what happened 22 years after Minsky formulated his financial instability hypothesis. His warning was ignored because Keynesians weren't listened to at the time.

---

[22] Cassidy, *How Markets Fail*, 303.

When the financial crisis broke out in 2008, first in America and then spreading throughout Europe as well as other high-income countries, neo-classical economists were at a loss. They hadn't predicted what had happened; their assumptions were apparently not universally applicable.[23] The US Congressional Oversight Committee summoned Greenspan (aka The Maestro), then 82 years old, to the Hill to share his thoughts on the financial crisis. British newspaper *The Guardian* reported this on 24 October 2008:

> The Committee's chairman, the Democrat Henry Waxman, asked Greenspan: 'You found that your view of the world, your ideology, was not right, it was not working?' Greenspan's response was: 'That's precisely the reason I was shocked because I'd been going for forty years or so with considerable evidence that it was working exceptionally well.' Waxman then pressed on: 'My question is simple. Were you wrong?' Greenspan: 'Partially ... I made a mistake in presuming that the self-interest of organisations, specifically banks, is such that they were best capable of protecting shareholders and equity in firms ... I discovered a flaw in the model that I perceived is the critical functioning structure that defines how the world works. I had been going for 40 years with considerable evidence that it was working exceptionally well.'

Cassidy's *How Markets Fail* (2009) presents a comprehensive account of the failure of what he called utopian economics, which hadn't prevented the calamities from happening. Cassidy wrote this on Greenspan's role in the unfolding of the financial crisis:

> For almost two decades, Greenspan had headed an institution that was designed to save financial capitalism from itself. For him to claim that the market economy is innately stable wasn't merely contentious; it was an absurdity ... The combination of a Fed that can print money, deposit insurance, and a Congress that can authorise bailouts provides an extensive safety net for big financial firms. In such an environment, pursuing a policy of easy money plus deregulation doesn't amount to free market economics; it is a form of crony capitalism.[24]

---

[23] As for predicting, John Kenneth Galbraith once quipped that the only function of economic forecasting is to make astrology respectable.
[24] *How Markets Fail*, 234.

The process of deregulation had already begun under President Ford, and was continued in the late 1970s by the Carter Administration, when the airlines were deregulated. The same applied to trucking, and to the deregulation of oil and gas. In 1999, President Clinton signed into law the Financial Modernization Act, which allowed commercial and investment banks to merge and create vast financial institutions.[25] Since 1992, Clinton's Democratic Party moved in a business-friendly direction so as to regain the political middle ground. President Clinton's Third Way policies consisted of balanced budgets, private–public partnerships and finance for growth, including financial deregulation.

Why was it that, apart from Minsky and a handful others, economists didn't predict the financial crisis of 2008 and the subsequent Great Recession? One answer is that the neoclassical assumption of self-regulating markets didn't apply. Another answer is that economics had evolved into a variety of specialised, compartmentalised fields which didn't see eye-to-eye. Neither macroeconomics nor financial economics—unlike Minsky—had paid much attention to the workings of financial institutions such as banks. This was obviously a serious omission, the reason being that the dominant theories had been developed at the time of the Great Moderation, when there were no major economic shocks in advanced capitalist economies. And—let's face it—economics is not a science like chemistry and physics. Ha-Joon Chang formulated it accurately: 'there are no objective truths in economics that can be established independently of political, and frequently moral, judgments'.[26]

Behavioural economists are sceptical about markets' rationality. Their argument is that human beings tend to be too confident of their abilities, and they tend to extrapolate recent trends into the future. These two characteristics explain bubbles. Furthermore, losses can make investors irrationally risk-averse, which would explain dramatic price falls when a bubble

---

[25] Carmen Reinhart and Kenneth Rogoff noted in *This Time is Different*, 'In eighteen of the twenty-six banking crises they (Obstfeld and Taylor; PdH) studied, the financial sector had been liberalised within the preceding five years, usually less' (155).

[26] *Economics: The User's Guide*, 451.

bursts. Their insights led to a new branch of specialised economics: neuro-economics, which makes use of progress made in brain science, opening up possibilities to study consumer behaviour through the identification of reward structures which are fed by neurotransmitters in the brain.[27]

How the Recession Was Countered

The US authorities took a Keynesian approach. Both monetary and fiscal stimuli were applied. The Bush Administration introduced a $150 billion stimulus package, consisting of $100 billion worth of tax cuts and $50 billion of extra spending. The Federal Home Loan Mortgage Corporation (Freddie Mac) and the Federal National Mortgage Association (Fannie Mae), two large government-sponsored mortgage companies, were bailed out by the American government. Letting them go under was unacceptable, as foreign countries—in particular China—were large holders of their bonds. After all, these countries could start doubting America's creditworthiness.

Bear Stearns, an investment bank, was taken over by JP Morgan Chase for a fire-sale price.[28] This happened 6 months before Lehman Brothers' demise. As mentioned, Lehman Brothers collapsed in September 2008. Lehman was not a commercial bank, so it did not have depositors. Money market mutual funds held Lehman's short-term notes. When Lehman failed, the mutual funds' shareholders panicked and these funds suffered runs. This in turn triggered runs by large investors on the money funds' investment-bank parents. Finally this then led to the collapse of the securitisation market.

The federal government did not rescue Lehman; neither did Lehman—not being a commercial bank—have access to the Fed's lending facility. This is what Barry Eichengreen concluded:

> Officials from the US Treasury Secretary Henry Paulson on down would insist that they had lacked the authority to lend to an insolvent institution like Lehman Brothers, as well as a mechanism to smoothly shut it down.

---

[27] McFadden, D.L. (2013) The New Science of Pleasure. *NBER Working Paper 18687*. Cambridge: National Bureau of Economic Research.

[28] Bear Stearns wasn't the only bank that was taken over. For example, Merrill Lynch was bought up by Bank of America, and Wachovia by Wells Fargo Bank.

Uncontrolled bankruptcy was the only option. But it is not as if Lehman's troubles were a surprise. Regulators had been watching it ever since the rescue of Bear Stearns, another important member of the investment-banking fraternity six months earlier. The failure to endow Treasury and the Fed with the authority to deal with insolvency of a nonbank financial institution was the single most important policy failure of the crisis.[29]

American International Group (AIG), an insurance company, was supported by the US government. AIG received a rescue package of $150 billion. AIG's total financial problems amounted to some $400 billion in credit protection provided to banks and other financial institutions. Most of this credit protection was by way of credit default swaps on subprime mortgage bonds.

There were rumours that Goldman Sachs and Morgan Stanley were also in trouble. Their stock prices plunged; clients started to withdraw their deposits. Then Fed chairman Bernanke and Secretary of the Treasury Henry Paulson requested Congress to approve a huge rescue plan to the tune of some $700 billion, to recapitalise the banks through the purchase of preference shares. The Troubled Asset Relief Program (TARP) was established. The government also launched a Temporary Liquidity Guarantee Program to prop up the financial system.

Acts were adopted as well; a prominent one being the Dodd–Frank Act of 2010. This act, in full the Dodd–Rank Wall Street Reform and Consumer Protection Act, includes measures ranging from limiting speculative trading by financial institutions, raising capital and liquidity requirements, creating a regulatory entity responsible for systemic stability, to the creation of a Consumer Financial Protection Bureau. What the act didn't do, however, was to limit the size of banks; they could still grow 'too big to fail'.

The Fed—while keeping its interest rate close to zero—pumped $3 trillion into the American economy by buying government and mortgage bonds. In addition, the Fed widened its Quantitative Easing (QE) measures by monthly injections of $60 billion into the economy. Chairman Bernanke declared that this would be continued as long as the economy

---

[29] Eichengreen, *Hall of Mirrors*, 5.

needed it.³⁰ In March 2014, Janet Yellen, Bernanke's successor at the Fed, announced tapering the monthly 'monetary morphine', a term coined by *The Economist*. Yellen's announcement led to some unrest in the financial markets of Brazil, Russia, India, China and South Africa (the BRICS countries) and in other economies such as Argentina and Turkey that had gotten used to low international interest rates.

The Obama Administration bailed out General Motors (GM) and Chrysler, two of the Big Three American carmakers—both were practically bankrupt. President Obama—à la Roosevelt—also launched a fiscal stimulus programme, embodied in the Recovery and Reinvestment Act, which he signed on 17 February 2009, within 1 month from taking office. The Recovery Act included tax cuts, social safety net expenditures, financial support to states, investments in renewable energy, health care, education, infrastructure and transportation. Its 2-year budget was $787 billion, the equivalent of 5 % of the GDP. In comparison, the New Deal's investments were equivalent to 1.5 % of the GDP.

The question is whether all these fiscal and monetary stimuli helped to quell the recession and created enough jobs to bring unemployment down. Economists agree that the Great Recession ended in America in June 2009. *Time* magazine reporter Michael Grunwald concluded in his book *The New New Deal* (2012),

> The Recovery Act didn't end the recession by itself. TARP stopped the financial meltdown, and Obama's stress tests helped restore confidence in the banking system. His auto rescue provided vital anti anti-stimulus by bringing GM and Chrysler back from the dead, preventing the collapse of the industrial Midwest.³¹

The Recovery Act, despite creating 2.5 million jobs, didn't cut unemployment below the president's target of 8 % by the end of 2010.

---

³⁰ *The Economist* of 21 December 2013 reported the following: 'Not everybody is happy with this. Many fret that the Fed's bond-buying has done more to inflate asset bubbles than boost employment. Mr. Volcker worries that the Fed has "got so much authority, used so much authority, made up some authority … To exaggerate, everything that happens in the economy is because of the Federal Reserve. I think it's a little dangerous and too much of a burden"' (98).

³¹ Grunwald, M. (2012) *The New New Deal*. New York: Simon & Schuster, 297.

The unemployment rate was then still 9.6 %. As of 2010 the economy was beginning to improve. The US economy was growing again and unemployment started dropping. In 2013 the American economy grew 1.8 % and the unemployment rate was 6.7 % at the end of that year. Grunwald emphasised positive results. But economists like Joseph Stiglitz and Paul Krugman, both New Keynesians, argued that the act's budget was inadequate. Krugman felt that the Obama Administration should have proposed much higher funding for fiscal stimulus, as one instrument of monetary policy, cutting interest rates, wasn't possible since it was already close to zero. He argued that fiscal stimulus—propelled by the income multiplier—was the appropriate policy to boost overall spending and create jobs.[32] He pitted the $787 billion stimulus package against the $13 trillion drop in household net wealth resulting from the slump in house and stock prices, to show that the stimulus package was far too small to fill the demand gap.[33]

The Recovery Act met with fierce resistance from Republican lawmakers. Most of them argued in favour of classical austerity, saying that 'the immediate pain would produce long-term gain'. America's economic growth slowed again, as a result of $1.2 trillion in federal spending cuts. In 2013, this was followed by the expiry of tax cuts for top incomes (introduced at the time by the Bush Administration). In the same year the reduction of employee contributions to the Social Security Trust Fund ended. The so-called Sequester, involving 8.5 % cut in federal spending, also affected aggregate demand and economic growth. Nonetheless, the American economy is forecasted to grow 3 % in 2015. The unemployment rate is down to 5.4 %.

European Union member countries and eurozone members in particular reacted to the Great Recession as follows. After an initial period of fiscal stimulus, the eurozone countries, and other EU members such as the UK, introduced structural reform measures. A combination of insufficient

---

[32] Stiglitz proposed applying the balanced-budget multiplier. Stiglitz argues in *The Price of Inequality* (2012) that 'If the government simultaneously increases taxes and increases expenditure—so that the *current* deficit remains unchanged—the economy is stimulated. Of course, the taxes by themselves dampen the economy, but the expenditures stimulate it.' *The Price of Inequality: How Today's Divided Society Endangers Our Future*. New York: W.W. Norton & Company, 217–18.
[33] Krugman, *End This Depression Now*, 117.

fiscal stimulus and structural reform led in 2010 to a double-dip recession in Europe, deepening the euro crisis. A prominent reason why the eurozone was in particular trouble is that economies as diverse as Germany and Greece were brought under one monetary set of rules. As Eichengreen observed,

> The single greatest failure to learn appropriate lessons … was surely the decision to adopt the euro. The 1920s and 1930s illustrated nothing better than the dangers of tying a diverse set of countries to a single monetary policy. Experience under the interwar gold standard highlighted the tendency for large amounts of capital to flow from countries where interest rates were low to where they were high, and the destabilising consequences that would follow when those flows came to a stop. It highlighted the economic pain and political turmoil that would result when the only available response was austerity. That history should have given European leaders pause before moving ahead with the euro.[34]

From a fiscal point of view, the focus was on bringing budget deficits down. On the monetary front the ECB injected two shots of emergency credit to the tune of €156 billion into European economies. The ECB kept its interest rate low. A temporary European Financial Stability Facility (EFSF) and European Financial Stability Mechanism (EFSM) were established in 2010 to help member-countries in financial difficulties with loans—often together with IMF credits—in exchange for tough structural reforms by borrowing countries to bring their finances under control. It should be mentioned that at the beginning of the financial crisis in Europe, the Fed helped European banks in overcoming their US dollar shortages.

ECB President Draghi introduced two Long-Term Refinancing Operations (LTROs); one in December 2011 and the second one in February 2012. The first LTRO—involving 3-year loans at an interest rate of 1 %—supplied €489 billion, while the second LTRO relaxed the rules on eligible collateral, prompting banks to borrow €529.5 billion. On 26 July 2012, President Draghi delivered a remarkable speech in London in which he stated, 'Within our mandate, the ECB is ready to do whatever it takes to preserve the euro. And believe me, it will be enough.' Draghi's speech had a positive impact. European stock exchanges registered a

---

[34] *Hall of Mirrors*, 382.

sudden increase in share prices, and the interest on bonds of Southern European governments dropped.

The ECB was prepared to buy the bonds of vulnerable states. This facility became known as Outright Monetary Transactions. In October 2012, both the EFSF and EFSM were replaced by the Permanent European Stability Mechanism (ESM) with a lending capacity of €500 billion. In the run-up to the creation of a banking union, the ECB conducted stress tests of major European banks in 2014. The Asset Quality Review, as the stress tests are officially called, involved 130 eurozone banks. Twenty-five of them failed the test.[35] In most eurozone countries budget deficits have come down to the 3 % norm, or close to it. Yet, unemployment in the eurozone area still ran high: 11.1 % of the workforce at the end of May 2015. But in Greece (25.4 %) and in Spain (22.7 %) the unemployment rate was much higher. Worse, in Southern Europe unemployment among the 18–35 age group is higher still, hovering around 50 %.

Economic growth of the eurozone countries is picking up again. The growth forecast for 2015 is 1.5 %. Although ECB's inflation target is 2 %, the actual inflation rate is much lower (though there are signs that it may be growing). Both are harbingers of deflation, which prompted the ECB to introduce a large quantitative-easing programme, thereby stretching its mandate. Germany and some other Northern eurozone countries were not in favour of injecting €1.1 trillion into the eurozone economies; they fear that this injection may create new 'bubbles', and it would take away the pressure on governments to implement necessary structural reforms.

Most commentators argue that fiscal stimulus measures were—and still are—necessary to help prevent deflation which would result in less aggregate demand, less investment, and more unemployment. People will be inclined to save more, which would add to the global savings glut.[36]

---

[35] Meanwhile, out of these 25 banks, 12 increased their capital buffers sufficiently; the remaining 13 other banks should have their respective buffers increased to 8 per cent of outstanding loans by the end of November 2014.

[36] Martin Wolf refers to Keynes in *The Shifts and the Shocks*: 'Keynes introduced the second alternative to economic theory—adjustment via the level of output and incomes in a slump when short-term interest rates are zero and long-term rates are as low as they can go, because of "liquidity preference"—the point at which people prefer to hold cash to bonds because the yield on the latter is too low to make holding them attractive ... The immediate impact of higher desired savings, he noted, is then to lower demand and so lower output and incomes.' (2014) *The Shifts and the Shocks: What We've Learned—and Have Still to Learn—from the Financial Crisis*. London: Allen Lane, 152.

> According to Martin Wolf the villain of the eurozone drama is Germany: 'Under German influence, the Eurozone's policy doctrine borders on liquidationism, though Eurozone's central bank has been relatively aggressive and some fiscal support has also been granted ... the chosen policies consist of fiscal austerity, asymmetric adjustment of competitiveness (with virtually all the adjustment falling on deficit countries), and limited assistance with recapitalisation of banks in crisis-hit countries. The ECB is handcuffed by exaggerated fears of inflation, notably in Germany, and so is resistant to the idea of quantitative easing or other controversial policies, such as significantly negative interest rates.'[37]

China wasn't much affected by the Great Recession. True, its growth percentage dropped from 11.9 % in 2007 to 6.2 % in 2009. Thanks to a massive $586 billion local demand stimulus injection by the Chinese authorities, economic growth bounced back to 11.9 % in 2010. As a percentage of GDP, the Chinese stimulus was more than double the size of President Obama's $787 billion package. However, China's growth rate is very likely to come down to around 7 %. China is also confronted with other challenges.

There is overcapacity in the housing sector and in some industrial sectors, such as steel, shipbuilding and mining. On the other hand, China's service sector is growing; it contributed 46 % of China's GDP in 2013, having eclipsed the output of industry (44 %). State-run companies will be increasingly exposed to the free functioning of the market. Income inequality constitutes a potential threat to political stability. Corruption and an underdeveloped legal system could prompt foreign investors to withdraw from China. Consumption represents just 35 % of China's GDP. This is reflective of the fact that China's economy is still driven by investment. The challenge is to transform China's economy into one that is mainly driven by the service sector and consumption.

The challenge for the Chinese authorities isn't limited to the economic domain; air, water and soil pollution will have to be addressed, as well as China's shrinking population of working age. The question is also

---

[37] *The Shifts and the Shocks*, 329.

whether the growing middle class will put forward demands which may threaten China's political stability.

Japan's Prime Minster, Shinzō Abe, launched a Keynesian-style stimulus programme after his re-election in December 2012. His programme included 'three arrows' aimed at Japan's long-time stagnant economy. Arrow number one involved a massive fiscal stimulus package; the second consisted of monetary easing from the Bank of Japan, and pushing the inflation percentage up to 2 %. The third arrow constituted structural reforms to boost Japan's competitiveness. The three arrows together are known as 'Abenomics'.

The Central Bank established Japan's inflation target at 2 % in combination with pumping yens into the economy (i.e. quantitative easing) and setting a de facto negative interest rate. Inflation hovered around 0.6 % by the middle of 2015. Fresh fiscal spending increased Japan's already large budget deficit. In the course of 2014 a rise in the consumption tax helped tip the economy back into recession. Inflation dropped to 0 %. Japanese GDP is forecast to rise by only 0.8 % in 2015. The good news is that as a result of the Bank of Japan's quantitative easing policy, the yen weakened against other currencies, making Japan's exports more competitive.

Lessons Learned

The Great Depression provided lessons about what to do to pull economies away from the abyss of a total financial collapse. Have these lessons been applied when the Great Recession broke out?

Eichengreen, for example, concluded that policymakers did just enough to prevent another Great Depression. But this 'just enough' implies that too little was done to make the world a safer place. Sure, banks are now required to have higher capital and liquidity buffers. Yet, there still are banks that are too big to fail. The Europeans, having avoided their own Great Depression, have to tackle thorny issues, such as the creation of a banking union for the eurozone, and preventing a *Grexit*. Given the fact that the deeper-lying causes of the Great Recession have not been sufficiently addressed, Eichengreen concludes that future deep recessions cannot be ruled out.

Challenges

The world economy is undergoing rapid changes. Martin Wolf observed the following:

> These three underlying drivers—liberalisation, technology and ageing—proceeded to shift the world economy into a new shape, one that created huge gross and net capital flows across borders, growing inequality within countries, radical shifts in the location of investment and the rise of liberalised credit. These shifts led high-income economies into 'secular stagnation'—a world of structurally deficient aggregate demand, identified by Lawrence Summers, the former US treasury secretary.[38]

The capitalist system almost collapsed after the outbreak of the financial crisis. Massive bank rescue operations (paid for by tax payers), unorthodox monetary policies, but also austerity measures (leading to massive job losses and plunging millions of people into poverty) prompted quite a few economists to write about the shadier sides of capitalism.[39] One book stood out; in fact it became a bestseller after it was published in English in 2014: Thomas Piketty's *Capitalism in the Twenty-First Century*.[40] Like Keynes, after publishing *The Economic Consequences of Peace* in 1919, Piketty became a superstar after his *Capital in the Twenty-First Century* came out.

He wasn't the first one to draw attention to the dangers of income and wealth inequality.[41] Joseph Stiglitz had done so 2 years earlier in *The Price of Inequality: How Today's Divided Society Endangers Our Future*.

---

[38] *The Shifts and the Shocks*, 184.

[39] Just a few examples: Ha-Joon Chang (2010) *23 Things They Don't Tell You about Capitalism*. London: Penguin; Sedlacek, T. (2011) *Economics of Good and Evil: The Quest for Economic Meaning from Gilgamesh to Wall Street*. New York: Oxford University Press; Skidelsky, R. and Skidelsky, E. (2012) *How Much is Enough? Money and the Good Life*. New York: Other Press; Stiglitz, *The Price of Inequality*.

[40] Piketty, T. (2014) *Capitalism in the Twenty-First Century*. Cambridge: Belknap Press of Harvard University Press.

[41] Ha-Joon Chang also wrote about inequality in *23 Things They Don't Tell You about Capitalism*: 'Despite the usual dichotomy of "growth enhancing pro-rich policy", pro-rich policies have failed to accelerate growth in the last three decades. So the first step in this argument—that is, the view that giving a bigger slice of pie to the rich will make the pie bigger—does not hold. The second part of the argument—the view that greater wealth created at the top will eventually trickle down to the poor—does not work either' (137–8).

The difference between the two books is that Stiglitz limited his analysis to America, while Piketty took a much broader scope. He assembled income and wealth data over the last three centuries, wherever available in as many countries as possible. Piketty concluded that there is no such thing as the Kuznets Curve, which says that economic growth first leads to increasing inequality in income and wealth after which a converging process will take place. True, convergence did indeed happen between 1920 and 1973 in the developed world. This was possible thanks to a combination of shrinking wealth, as a result of economic shocks caused by two World Wars, the Great Depression, progressive tax policies, and rising wages thanks to strong labour unions. Piketty considers the period 1920–1973 a historical exception; the income and wealth gap is now widening again. Unions have lost some of their negotiating power; in many developed countries wages remained stagnant. He concludes that the widening gap between the rich and the rest is a politically, economically and morally disturbing development.

What can be done about it? Piketty suggests that more should be invested in education, as better-educated people can get better-paid jobs. His main proposal, however, is taxing high incomes very highly and introducing a global wealth tax. As this isn't easy to achieve, he proposes a gradual approach towards limiting the gap between the rich and the rest.

2

The Great War and the Great Depression

Introduction

Before the war, Europe was benefitting from globalised trade. Life was good; that is, for those who could afford it. John Maynard Keynes once depicted an attractive image of a Londoner at the time who would be sipping his morning tea in bed and ordering the various products of the whole of the earth to his door.

When WWI broke out on 28 July 1914, a fairly long period of prosperity and stability abruptly ended. One after the other European nation was drawn into the war, which would cost 9.4 million people their lives and wound 17.7 million others. Only after the Americans joined the Allies in 1917 was the war brought to an end. The peace negotiations took 1 year before the Treaty of Versailles was signed by the parties involved on 28 June 1919.

Keynes foresaw in *The Economic Consequences of Peace*, which was published in December 1919, that the Treaty could only lead to more misery. He had hoped that US President Wilson could enforce a reasonable and implementable arrangement, but Wilson was outwitted by his co-negotiators French President Clemenceau and British Prime Minister

Lloyd George. Meanwhile the 1917 October Revolution in Russia had brought the Bolsheviks to power, and in the 1920s Fascism rose—most prominently—in Germany, Austria and Italy.

The Great Depression worsened the already volatile political situation in Europe. Adverse economic policies only deepened the economic crisis. It was again Keynes who explained in his *General Theory of Employment, Interest, and Money* (1936) what should be done to counter the depression, and why.

This chapter includes a biography of John Maynard Keynes, followed by summaries of *The Economic Consequences of Peace* and *The General Theory of Employment, Interest, and Money*.

Biography: John Maynard Keynes (1883–1946)

In 2011 the British newspaper *The Economist* asked the members of Economics by Invitation (its forum of some 50 prominent economists) to nominate the most influential economists over the past decade. Former Fed chairman Ben Bernanke won the vote, while Keynes came in second. So, 65 years after his death, Keynes still wielded enormous influence. Now, why is that? It is because Keynes was exceptional in many ways. During his entire professional life he challenged political and economic conventional wisdom, revolutionised economic theory, proposed government interventions in pursuit of full employment, and was involved in the design and establishment of the Bretton Woods monetary system. Apart from all this, he speculated in currencies and shares; he was a successful Bursar of King's College, a Director of the Bank of England, a patron of the arts, established a theatre in Cambridge, saved Covent Garden Opera House from demolition and collected rare books as well as paintings.

Great Individuals Make a Difference

Great individuals change the outlook, even the basic principles, of their academic discipline. Keynes certainly changed—some say revolutionised—economics. In the year that Karl Marx died, John Maynard was born on

5 June 1883 in Cambridge. Milton Friedman once said that these two men, Marx and Keynes, influenced humankind the most. However, in their respective objectives they were far apart: Marx projected a doomed capitalism, while Keynes tried to rescue capitalism from crises.

Keynes's father, John Neville Keynes, was a Cambridge don and his mother, Florence Ada Brown, pursued a political career; she became mayor of Cambridge in 1932. Cambridge at the time provided a truly inspiring intellectual environment. Alfred Marshall, author of *The Principles of Economics* (1890), *the* standard work on neoclassical economics, taught at Cambridge. The philosopher G.E. Moore also taught there. Both had a great influence on Keynes.

Eton

Young Maynard was a bright pupil, excelling in mathematics and the classics. He won a scholarship to Eton, where his intellectual abilities came to fruition. It was also at Eton where his sexual preference for men dawned. Keynes was very successful and happy at Eton. He won prizes, acted in plays and—at the end of his Eton days—was elected President of the Eton Literary Society. And that was not all. In 1901, as Richard Davenport-Hines noted, he achieved his biggest triumph as he was elected into the most exclusive Eton society by the name of 'Pop'. After his election, Keynes started to dress differently, wearing white duck trousers with a highly decorated waistcoat. He daily ordered a flower to put it in his buttonhole. As Keynes's mother noted,

> This costume was the outward mark of a position which entitled the wearer to certain privileges, such as the right to stand in front row to watch matches, and to a carry a small cane with which to castigate the ankles of unauthorised intruders, also to walk with other boys of similar standing arm in arm in the street.[1]

---

[1] Davenport-Hines, R. (2015) *Universal Man; The Seven Lives of John Maynard Keynes.* London: William Collins.

King's College

Tutored by his father, he gained a scholarship to King's College at Cambridge. It was there that Maynard underwent his emotional and spiritual development. His brilliance and interest in many subjects, ranging from science to the arts, was soon discovered by Leonard Woolf (Virginia Woolf's husband-to-be) and Lytton Strachey (an eccentric, who became a central figure of the Bloomsbury Group),[2] who invited 'embryo' Keynes to join the secretive, yet prestigious, Apostles also known as the Cambridge Conversazione Group. Keynes's biographers noted that being an Apostle strengthened his self-awareness and strong sense of superiority. He was equipped with an 'indestructible superiority complex', a characteristic coined by philosopher Isaiah Berlin. And Joan Robinson, one of Keynes's favourite students, observed that Keynes was singularly free and generous because he valued no one's opinion above his own. If someone disagreed with him, it was they who were being silly; he had no cause to get peevish about it. But Keynes wasn't only generous; he could also be rude and egocentric. Keynes's biographer Robert Skidelsky provided two examples:

> As for his rudeness, this was laid upon those he thought ought to know better. On one occasion at the board meeting of the National Mutual, an insurance company of which he was the chairman, he broke out to Francis Curzon, brother of the marquess, Vice-Roy of India: 'Really Curzon, you have all the pomposity of your brother and none of his intelligence.' Keynes was by no means easy company for the slower-witted. He was almost invariably the cleverest person in any gathering, knew it and showed it. Kenneth Clark, who served with him on the Council for the Encouragement of Music and the Arts during the Second World War, complained that he used his brilliance 'too unsparingly ... he never dimmed his headlights'.[3]

Keynes studied mathematics during his undergraduate years at King's College. Later, he was tutored by Alfred Marshall, who wrote flattering

---

[2] Strachey, who was gay, liked to shock people, albeit with a dry sense of humour. He once discussed sex differences with a Victorian dowager at a dinner party explaining that 'The whole matter turns, as in golf, on the question of holes and balls.'

[3] Skidelsky, R. (2004) *John Maynard Keynes 1883–1946: Economist, Philosopher, Statesman*. London: Pan Books, 471.

remarks on Maynard's papers and wanted him to pursue the study of economics, in particular money and banking. However, Keynes didn't take Marshall's advice. Skidelsky rightly concluded that Keynes never took an economics degree; his doctoral thesis was about mathematical probability. Nonetheless, Keynes wrote in an essay on Alfred Marshall that economics was an easy subject, at which yet few excelled. He explained this paradox by noting that

> the master economist must possess a rare combination of gifts. He must reach a high standard in several different directions and must combine talents not often found together. He must be a mathematician, historian, statesman, philosopher—in some degree. He must understand symbols and speak in words. He must contemplate the particular in terms of the general, and touch the abstract and concrete in the same flight of thought. He must study the present in the light of the past for the purpose of the future. No part of man's nature or his institutions must lie entirely outside his regard. He must be purposeful and disinterested in a simultaneous mood; as aloof and incorruptible as an artist, yet sometimes as near the earth as a politician.[4]

As for the use of mathematics in economics, Keynes's scepticism grew rather than diminished with age, though it was present from the start. Skidelsky felt that this had to do with Keynes's growing understanding of the complexity and reflexive nature of social life.

It was Moore's *Principia Ethica* which influenced Maynard's philosophical outlook. Important aspects in Moore's philosophy were the notion of good which couldn't really be defined; the only things valuable in themselves are 'states of mind' of which the most valuable are the pleasures of human intercourse and the enjoyment of beautiful objects. This sounds rather vague, but the point is that Keynes and his contemporaries were trying to shed Victorian values and faith (God was dead, according to Nietzsche); they were looking for an alternative 'religion' that was more akin to their feelings and opinions.

---

[4] Davenport-Hines, *Universal Man*, 137.

The India Office and Back to Cambridge

Keynes intended to pursue moral sciences during his postgraduate studies. His father had already projected an academic path for Maynard to prepare him for the Civil Service Examinations. Keynes passed successfully in 1906; he came second after Otto Niemeyer whose scores on economics were better than Maynard's. He went to the India Office, which was then one of the best destinations for young civil servants. The India Office didn't excite him much. Yet, the 2 years spent there were not wasted; Keynes published in 1913 a well-reviewed book: *Indian Currency and Finance*.

Keynes wrote another book on monetary issues: *A Tract on Monetary Reform* (1923), which pointed at the dangers of inflation. It doesn't subside in the long run, argued Keynes. Corrective measures were necessary to redress the situation. The sad experience of Germany and Austria with hyperinflation underscored Keynes's warnings. After his time at the India Office, Keynes came back to Cambridge in 1909, where he started to lecture and was given the editorship of the *Economic Journal* (an offer which his father had refused at the time). He edited the *Economic Journal* for 33 years. At the dinner marking his retirement from the editorship he proposed a toast to 'Economists, who are the trustees, not of civilisation, but of the possibility of civilisation.'

Meanwhile the Bloomsbury Group beckoned. Both Leonard Woolf and Lytton Strachey, who earlier had invited Maynard to become an Apostle, now belonged to that small coterie of influential intellectuals and artists. They invited Pozzo (as Keynes was called among them) to become a member of the Bloomsbury Group, of which the American poet and satirist Dorothy Parker said lived in squares, painted in circles and loved in triangles.

The Economic Consequences of Peace

It was after the Great War (1914–1918) when Keynes's name was made. He had joined the Treasury at the beginning of the war and worked there in the department of Britain's overseas finances. This did not go down well with his Bloomsbury friends as they all opposed it. Keynes, who had no great anti-war feeling, countered them by saying that while the war was bad his presence in the Treasury would make it less so.

After the war, Keynes represented the Treasury in the British delegation to negotiate the Treaty of Versailles, which proved to be a highly frustrating experience for him. Keynes was the first one to note that the Treaty was unfair to Germany and the economic and political consequences would be disastrous, as it would rob Germany and other defeated countries from any means to economically recover from the war. The implementation of the Treaty would—as Keynes rightly predicted—only result in famine, poverty and political and economic chaos in Europe. What he had hoped to bring about was the promotion of economic recovery and the resumption of growth, which would help restore political stability and smother revolutionary tendencies. His initial intentions were to have the Germans pay much less than the Allies had stipulated, and to ask the Americans to provide financial assistance to the indebted Allies and Germany alike.

Exhausted and disgusted with the unforgiving attitude of the Allies (in particular France and Great Britain), Keynes resigned from the Treasury and wrote an angry book: *The Economic Consequences of Peace*, which was published a few months after the Treaty of Versailles was concluded on 28 June 1919. The book was a bestseller in England and the USA.

Keynes stated that the reparation payments, which Germany had to pay, were far too high and the demand that Germany was to hand over to the Allies a sizeable portion of its iron and coal production facilities, all its ships beyond 1600 tons, and 5000 locomotives plus 150,000 wagons, would only lead to misery and disaster. The defeated Germans were helpless; they had no choice but to accept the Treaty's draconian conditions. The book revealed here and there compassion for the defeated enemy; some critics found it too pro-German. Robert Skidelsky suggested that it may have been the pleasant time young Maynard spent with his German governess that may have made him sensitive to Germany's plight, which was in stark contrast with British, French and American public opinion at the time.

After his resignation from the Treasury and the successful publication of his book, the question was, What to do next? He lectured in Cambridge, wrote for the *Manchester Guardian*, the *Evening Standard* and the American *New Republic*. Keynes became the publisher of the *New Statesman*. He also became a successful investor—although with a few ups and downs. He also became Bursar of King's College and guided the finances of a life insurance company. He collected paintings of French Impressionists, and rare books (a hobby he shared with Friedrich Hayek).

To the great surprise of his Bloomsbury friends, he married the Russian former ballerina of Diaghilev's troupe, Lydia Lopokova, in 1925.[5] The marriage was childless; there is a suggestion—as Skidelsky mentions—that she miscarried in 1927. Before the wedding Keynes had bought Tilton, a country estate in Surrey, where he would write articles and books, and where he rested from his ever more demanding tasks.

> Historian Niall Ferguson said during a May 2013 investment conference in Carlsbad, California that Keynes's famous quote 'in the long run we are all dead' was inspired by his indifference to the future because he was gay and childless. Should he have known more about Keynes's life, Ferguson couldn't have made this embarrassing statement. The remarks were widely criticised for being offensive, factually inaccurate, and a distortion of Keynes's ideas. Ferguson posted an apology for these statements shortly after reports of his words were disseminated, saying his comments were 'as stupid as they were insensitive'. In the apology, Ferguson stated, 'My disagreements with Keynes's economic philosophy have never had anything to do with his sexual orientation. It is simply false to suggest, as I did, that his approach to economic policy was inspired by any aspect of his personal life.'

A Treatise on Money

Keynes published *A Treatise on Money* in 1930. It was in fact the precursor to *The General Theory of Employment, Interest, and Money*, which appeared 6 years later. The *Treatise* emphasised the role of investment and saving.

---

[5] The Bloomsbury friends' surprise isn't strange as Keynes did have quite a few homosexual relationships before falling in love with Lydia Lopokova. Davenport-Hines devotes an entire chapter to Keynes as a persuasive lover. Keynes kept a score of his brief sexual encounters with other men, ranging from a 'Stable boy of Park Lane', 'the Shoemaker of the Hague', to the 'Grand Duke Cyril of the Paris Baths' (*Universal Man*, 215–16).

The book's central theme is that there is no automatic mechanism in a credit-money economy to keep savings and investments in equilibrium. It is the duty of the monetary authority to regulate the stock of money to keep savings equal to investments in order to control economic fluctuations. Moreover, decisions on savings are made by people other than those who decide on investments. The quantity of money is to be controlled by the banking system, while the demand for it, in the short term, is unstable. The only short-term instrument that can keep a credit economy in balance is the central bank, which should keep savings and investments in equilibrium. But under Britain's restored gold standard in 1925, the Bank of England was prevented from setting bank rates low enough to allow a level of investment equal to what the community wanted to save; the result was mass unemployment. Keynes had already predicted this in his 1925 essay 'The Economic Consequences of Mr Churchill'. Winston Churchill was then Chancellor of the Exchequer and reintroduced the gold standard at its pre-WWI level.

So it was the insufficiency of spending on investment relative to the rate of saving which caused both the price level to fall *and* people to be unemployed. Hence Keynes observed that the engine which drives enterprise (via investment) is not thrift (saving), but profit. This insight was, as we will see, further elaborated in *The General Theory*. Skidelsky noted that Keynes's break from the classical view of saving as providing an automatic fund for investment was a fundamental new insight in economic psychology.

Friedrich Hayek wrote a critical review of *A Treatise on Money* in the London School of Economics journal *Economica*. Initially, Keynes responded himself in a fierce counter-attack, but he left the ensuing polemic to the Cambridge Circus, consisting of his 'lieutenants' Richard Kahn and Piero Sraffa. Hayek's Austrian School theory was pro-saving, since the Austrians believed—unlike Keynes—that it was out of the savings of individuals that the wealth of nations was built. The price which coordinates the intertemporal plans of consumers and producers is the rate of interest. However, interest rates can do this job efficiently only if money is kept 'neutral' (that is, in the absence of inflation or deflation) by the monetary authority.

Hayek was *the* antipode to Keynes. Hayek was of the opinion that the economy can only be understood by considering the interaction of individuals; the microeconomic perception, so to speak. Keynes, on the other hand, believed that an economy could best be understood by grasping the big picture, so looking down from the top to aggregate demand and supply, aggregate savings and investment; the macroeconomics approach, which Keynes invented.

While life-long intellectual adversaries, Keynes and Hayek yet maintained a friendship. They collected rare books; a recurring topic of their conversations. Nicholas Wapshott recalls in *Keynes–Hayek: The Clash That Defined Modern Economics* (2011) that

> During World War II, John Maynard Keynes and Friedrich Hayek spent all night together, alone, on the roof of King's College, Cambridge. Their task was to gaze at the skies and watch German bombers aiming to pour incendiary bombs on the small picturesque cities of England.[6]

After *The Treatise*, Keynes started work on *The General Theory of Employment, Interest, and Money* in 1932. That book would become one of the most influential books on economics of the twentieth century.

The General Theory of Employment, Interest, and Money

The economy is self-regulating, according to neoclassical economics. Wrong said Keynes: the economy isn't self-regulating; it has to be managed to redress or prevent imbalances so as to ensure full employment. That is what, in essence, *The General Theory* is about. Keynes started circulating—and lecturing on—the manuscript of *The General Theory* in 1935. He wrote to his friend and playwright George Bernard Shaw:

> ... you have to know that I believe myself to be writing a book on economic theory which will largely revolutionize—not, I suppose at once, but in the course of the next ten years—the way the world thinks about economic problems.[7]

---

[6] Wapshott, N. (2011) *Keynes–Hayek: The Clash That Defined Modern Economics*. New York: Norton & Company, xi.

[7] Heilbroner, R. (1995) *The Worldly Philosopher: The Lives, Times and Ideas of the Great Economic Thinkers*. London: Penguin, 269.

He proved to be right. *The General Theory*'s publication in 1936 triggered the Keynesian Revolution. This book—while accepting some aspects of the classical doctrine—exposed the weaknesses of the neoclassical theory, which stipulated that any economic disturbance will be corrected by the functioning of market forces so that, in due course, economic equilibrium is restored with full employment. Keynes criticised it for using models which assumed full employment instead of constructing models which tried to explain why persisting unemployment occurred. Keynes demonstrated that an economy could be in equilibrium with underemployment as a result of a drop in aggregate demand. This happened during the Great Depression, which broke out towards the end of 1929.

The central question of the *General Theory* is to discover what determines the volume of employment. The level of employment depends on what consumers want to buy and what investors want to invest in. Once we know what a community will consume (which does not change much in case of a mild contraction or growth of the economy), the amount of employment depends on its rate of investment (see the biography of Milton Friedman in Chap. 5 for his criticism of Keynes's consumption function). And investment will rise whenever the expected rate of return on the investment is higher than the cost of borrowing. However, investment is less stable than consumption. This investment instability emerges as the crucial cause of fluctuations in employment. The reason is the volatile *expectations* of the future yield of these investments: in a depressed economy there isn't enough investment to make use of available savings. This has a negative effect on economic growth. People will lose their job and unemployment rises, triggering a downward spiral. Keynes concluded that, at the end of the day, it is aggregate demand that determines the level of economic activity and employment.

In the neoclassical doctrine the explanation is different: should the propensity to invest drop, the interest rate and wages will drop as a result, triggering fresh investments. Thus equilibrium is being restored thanks to the self-regulating functioning of the market. Keynes wrote that in case of a recession, if one can measure in money terms what the population is buying and how much extra output the unemployed would add if they worked, one can calculate how much extra 'demand' or spending power has to be injected into an economy by the government to close the output gap and return to full employment.

Keynes introduced the investment multiplier (which was inspired by his pupil Richard Kahn's employment multiplier). The investment multiplier plays its part in situations where there is a gap between saving and investment. In simple terms, the idea is that increasing government spending by, for example, $1 generates more than $1 of private spending, since the initial increase in consumption by the recipients of this $1 increase leads to more hiring and income and another—if smaller—increase in spending, and so on.

At the new equilibrium level of income there will be more investment spending and, in addition, more consumer spending, triggered by the higher level of income. The investment multiplier thus shows by how much investment has to rise to eliminate any gap between intended saving and actual investment. It also establishes income–output adjustment as the main mechanism by which an economy reaches a new position of equilibrium. The multiplier tells a government how much extra spending is needed to eliminate unemployment. The question then arises, On what is the injected money to be spent so as to stimulate employment? Keynes doesn't give a clear answer; he makes a rather outlandish proposal:

> If the Treasury were to fill old bottles with bank-notes, bury them at suitable depths in disused coal-mines which are then filled up to the surface with town rubbish, and leave it to private enterprise on well-tried principles of laissez-faire to dig the notes up again … there need be no more unemployment and with the help of the repercussions, the real income of the community would probably become a good deal larger than it is. It would, indeed, be more sensible to build houses and the like; but if there are practical difficulties in the way of doing this, the above would be better than nothing.[8]

As for monetary policy, the authorities (i.e., the central bank) concerned can lower the interest rate to make investments cheaper, broaden credit facilities or increase this rate, and tighten credit in case the economy is getting overheated. As for this latter aspect, Keynes noted that the right remedy for the trade cycle is not to be found in abolishing booms,

---

[8] *The General Theory*, 129.

and thus keeping us permanently in a semi-slump, but in abolishing slumps and thus keeping us permanently in a quasi-boom. Throughout history there has been a chronic tendency for the propensity to save to be stronger than the inducement to invest, creating the condition for a semi-slump. This has been at all times the key to economic problems, concluded Keynes.

What about the other famous term coined by Keynes: animal spirits, being 'a spontaneous urge to action rather than inaction'? His point of departure is the shaky knowledge on which our estimates of prospective investment have to be made. Share prices, for example, are not dependent on real investment prospects, but on sentiment, which can fluctuate up and down with the day's news. It is the flimsiness of knowledge supporting conventional share valuations which makes the investment function peculiarly dependent on these animal spirits. When entrepreneurs are optimistic about the future, they will invest more and the economy will grow fast; the economy could even develop into a boom. On the other hand, when their mood is pessimistic, they will not invest, incomes will drop and unemployment will rise.

The government plays an important role in mitigating both optimistic and pessimistic moods, by either taking money out of circulation, through selling bonds—that is, bond buyers pay government for these bonds—so their payments together lower the money in circulation for the same amount. In the case of a depression, the government should pump money into the economy to boost aggregate demand and create employment though public works.

The *General Theory* includes a general theory of interest. Again, Keynes deviates from the neoclassical school which argues that through the invisible hand of the capital market, savings will be turned into investments. Their reasoning is that income will always lead to consumption; be it directly through consumption or indirectly through investment in shares which enable firms to invest in machines and other capital goods. Keynes denies the automatic relationship between savings and investment. It isn't saving that determines the rate of interest and—partly through it—investment; partly, since investment also depends on the expected rate of return on investment. If that rate of return would be higher than the interest rate, investment would ensue.

Keynes introduced another term: *liquidity trap*. He argued that the greater people's preference for holding their savings in money, the higher the rate of interest they will demand to put it to other uses. From an investment point of view, Skidelsky explains,

> A collapse in the expected profitability tends to lead to an increase in liquidity-preference, thus pushing interest rates up when they need to come down. The chain of logic of the *General Theory* is thus completed by showing that the rate of interest can remain above the 'rate of return to capital' necessary to secure full employment.[9]

Keynes's major policy concern was unemployment. Once demand-deficiency is removed, full employment could be attained, which was a top government priority at the time. Keynes's departure from the neoclassical doctrine, with their counterproductive policy prescriptions, led the way to more effective measures to counter recessions and unemployment.

This was Keynes's great contribution to policymakers and humanity at large. He developed macroeconomics; at that time an entirely new way of analysing economic interrelationships. Surely, his theory has its flaws, in that technological progress, triggering new capital investments, isn't considered. Keynes assumed a given stock of capital equipment. His model is too static and it isn't suited to the analysis of problems of long-term growth.

Another critical observation is that Keynes's model is too aggregative. For example, disaggregation of income distribution would be required. The model distinguishes two income shares: wages and profits. The savings of large corporations aren't included. It is assumed that wages and profits either have identical consumption patterns or that the distribution of income between them is stable, or a stable function of aggregate income. Nonetheless, the model is in itself consistent and complete.

Keynes always insisted that the vulnerability of the capitalist system isn't its inequities or injustices; it is its instability. Keynes's thinking formed the basis for further elaboration by New Keynesians.

---

[9] Ibid., 534.

After The General Theory

After the publication of *The General Theory* a fierce polemic ensued between defenders of the neoclassical school and Keynesians. Joan Robinson wrote about the former in *Economic Philosophy*:

> What made the *General Theory* so hard to accept was not its intellectual content, which in a calm mood can be easily mastered, but its shocking implications. Worse than private vices being public benefits, it seemed that the new doctrine was the still more disconcerting proposition that private virtues (of thriftiness and careful husbandry) were public vices.[10]

> Economists of the Stockholm School had in fact anticipated Keynes. One of them was Gunnar Myrdal (1898–1987) who accused Keynes of his 'unnecessary originality'. Myrdal had already explained how an increase in investment over *ex ante* savings would lead to additional savings through higher profits and other incomes, so that *ex post* savings would equal investment. In the same vein, greater savings, *ex ante*, would lead to fewer sales, layoffs and lower profits. So, firms would reduce investment, so that *ex post* savings would equal investment. In the *General Theory* investment and saving are always equal; so in Myrdal's *ex post* sense. As Galbraith noted in his memoirs, the economists of the Stockholm School had substantially anticipated Keynes. They had urged with success that the government budget be balanced only with the revenues that accrued at full employment and high levels of output. When employment and output fell and therewith tax revenues, the excess of public expenditures over receipts was a useful and necessary stimulant. That the state should provide the purchasing power needed to keep people employed was common ground. Keynes, accordingly, was a source of little excitement in Sweden.[11]

Robinson underscored that Keynes brought back the *moral problem* into economics by destroying the neoclassical reconciliation of private egoism and public service. The neoclassical school received a devastating

---

[10] Robinson, J. (1974) *Economic Philosophy*. Harmondsworth: Penguin, 73.
[11] Galbraith, J.K. (1983) *A Life in Our Times: Memoirs*. London: Corgi, 94.

blow from Keynes who demonstrated that the invisible hand didn't work and that their doctrine was no use in solving the problems at hand. His charge fitted the intellectual and popular mood of the day.

Friedrich Hayek who, as noted, had written an acid review of *The Treatise* in *Economica*, was advised by his publisher not to review *The General Theory*. Yet, Hayek found Keynes's remedy for the Great Depression nothing more than a temporary solution, as any artificial rise in aggregate demand would distort the productive structure and can only generate unstable employment. Milton Friedman was critical of Keynes's consumption function, in that, according to Friedman, there is no declining average propensity to consume as economies grow. He also pointed to the fact that Keynesians couldn't explain stagflation. He proposed a monetarist approach to economic instabilities rather than Keynes's interventionist recipes. His critique is elaborated in the biographical section on Friedman in Chap. 5. One interviewer once asked Friedman whether he thought that Keynes tried to save capitalism. Friedman replied as follows:

> No. Keynes's … objective like my objective was to contribute to the well being of society. I am a great admirer of Keynes. I think he was a great human being and a great economist. I don't agree with the particular hypothesis he offered about the depression, but advances in every science come from people offering hypotheses that turn out to be wrong.[12]

Other critics include Robert Lucas and James Buchanan. Lucas is identified with the rational expectations approach to macroeconomics, providing a microeconomic foundation to macroeconomics: new classical macroeconomics. What it boils down to is that macroeconomic actors, like the *homo economicus*, are rational human beings, serving their self-interest, unlike Keynes's opinion, who introduced his animal spirits element in the behaviour of economic actors. Lucas maintained that people act in a rational manner in forming their expectations about the future.

---

[12] Ebenstein, L. (2007) *Milton Friedman*. New York: Palgrave Macmillan, 107.

One of the implications of Lucas's insight is that there is no involuntary unemployment as a result of inadequate demand, as Keynes suggested. Unemployment is the consequence of wages having risen too high. So, if workers would be willing to accept a lower wage, they would find a job, and the labour supply would equal demand again; Lucas concluded that equilibrium would be restored.

James Buchanan made his name by developing the public choice theory, which studies exchange in the political domain. Political exchange is made with the expectation of gain (i.e., what's in it for me? is it in my interest?). Buchanan opposes Keynes's view that government can redress imbalances in the economy, assuming that bureaucrats and policymakers act in the public interest. Buchanan's ideological position is that nobody (including governments and civil servants) but people themselves can decide what is good for themselves. Bureaucrats are not able to promote the public good. The more they try, the more individual freedom will be affected, according to Buchanan. His solution is twofold: (1) amending the constitution with a view to limit the ability of politicians to act in their own interest, and (2) amend the constitution to ensure balanced budgets.

> The polemic that Keynes had with the Dutch economist Jan Tinbergen is noteworthy. Keynes—unlike Tinbergen—doubted the relevance of correlations. The League of Nations had sponsored a book by Tinbergen to test various hypotheses about the trade cycle. Keynes's main point in his article in the *Economic Journal* of September 1939 was that economics is a 'moral science', thus requiring the constant exercise of judgment by the economist in applying models. He queried Tinbergen's logic in applying the method of multiple correlations to non-homogenous material and his assumption of fixed coefficients for long series. Keynes asked, 'Is it claimed that there is a likelihood that the equations will work approximately *next* time?' Keynes shot the following deadly rhetorical question at Tinbergen: 'It will be remembered that the seventy translators of the Septuagint were shut up in seventy separate rooms with the Hebrew text and brought out with them, when they emerged, seventy identical translations. Would the same miracle be vouchsafed if seventy multiple correlators were shut up with the same statistical material?'[13]

---

[13] Verbon, H. (2013) De Late Erkenning van de Zwarte Zwaan door Paul Samuelson. In: *ESB, Jaargang 98* (4664m, 4665) 12 July 2013, 463.

The supporters of *The General Theory* saw it primarily as an engine of policy, capable of, as one reviewer put it, 'Restoring and maintaining prosperity without the support of prison camps and executions.' Whatever the causes of unemployment might have been, *The General Theory* provided convincing arguments why and how aggregate demand should be increased in order to get the unemployed back to work.

The General Theory made a big impression in America's academic and political circles. Even before its publication, Keynes had urged President Roosevelt in a letter in *The New York Times* of 31 December 1933 to pump government money into the economy financed by loans to counter the depression. *The General Theory* was praised by Harvard economists. As John Kenneth Galbraith wrote in an essay for *The New York Times Book Review* (1965), Harvard was the principal avenue by which Keynes's ideas passed to the United States. Paul Samuelson, who was to teach whole generations of economists, was the acknowledged leader of the younger Keynesian community. Samuelson even expanded Keynes's proposal with the so-called accelerator, showing that in an expanding economy business owners would become more optimistic and this would lead to accelerate their investments. Combined with Keynes's multiplier, output would be even more expanded, triggering even more expectations and investments, and a renewed multiplier effect.

Alvin Hansen, who initially had reservations about *The General Theory*, once he saw its relevance, turned into a strong defender of it. He wrote scores of articles and books to explain in clear terms what the master himself had meant. After all, *The General Theory* is not an easy book to read. Gradually, senior positions within the American Executive were held by Keynesians. All this did not happen without opposition from conservatives. Yet, as Galbraith noted, those who objected to Keynes were also invariably handicapped by the fact that they hadn't read the book. Galbraith quipped that it was like attacking the original *Kama Sutra* for pornography without being able to read Sanskrit.

Keynes was to pay a high price. He lost friends as a result of differences of opinion and interpretation. After all the strain following *The General Theory*'s publication, Keynes was felled by a heart attack in 1937, which forced him to slow down. Yet he couldn't sit still. Even while writing *The General Theory* he was establishing a theatre in Cambridge.

Robert Heilbroner, the author of *The Worldly Philosophers* (1995), wrote that Keynes attached a restaurant to the theatre and watched its recipes, graphing them against different types of entertainment to ascertain how food consumption varied with the state of one's humour. There was a bar, too, where champagne was sold at an especially low discount to promote its wider consumption.

The Bretton Woods Agreement

At the outbreak of war in 1939 Keynes was given a room in the Treasury so that government could benefit from his advice, mainly regarding financing Britain's war investments, and the question how to organise an appropriate international financial and trade system after the war. Keynes wanted to help prevent a repeat of the mistakes made by the Allies after WWI. He was in favour of an international clearing union, including the establishment of a new international reserve currency: the *bancor*. This clearing union would help countries with trade deficits with temporary credits and penalise countries running trade surpluses in order to prevent the international economic system sinking into another depression.

President Roosevelt invited 43 nations to attend the Bretton Woods conference in New Hampshire to formulate definite proposals for a stable international monetary system, the establishment of an International Monetary Fund (IMF) and, possibly—as the invitation stated—a Bank for Reconstruction and Development, better known as the World Bank. The idea behind it was to revive world trade and to stabilise currencies (which the IMF was to ensure), as well as to deal with war debts and frozen credit markets. Sylvia Nasar captured the mood in her monumental *Grand Pursuit* (2011):

> The war had left much of the world dramatically poorer, and countries had to be able to earn their way back to prosperity. In the broadest sense, salvage meant rebuilding and reconstruction, moving back toward pre-1913 globalisation, but without reviving the pre-World War I assumption that the economic machinery worked automatically.[14]

---

[14] Nasar, S. (2011) *Grand Pursuit: The Story of Economic Genius*. London: Fourth Estate, 393.

Keynes's American counterpart, Harry Dexter White, presided over the negotiations regarding the IMF. Keynes led the negotiations on the establishment of the World Bank. Keynes represented a near-bankrupt empire in decline, while the Americans were swimming in their money, so to speak. The Americans got an amendment through, which boiled down to allowing member states to fix their currency either to gold or to the dollar. This made the dollar the only gold-convertible currency (instead of Keynes's *bancor*) and key currency in the system. America, which was running a huge trade surplus at the time, didn't like Keynes's idea of surplus countries paying penalties; the proposal for his international clearing union was shot down. Keynes gave the final speech at the closing banquet at Bretton Woods. His arrival (a bit late) prompted the entire meeting to stand up, silently, until he made his way to the dais and set down.

The End

During the first half of the 1940s Keynes was appointed Director of the Bank of England, and as Chairman of a new government committee to promote classical music and the arts. He also became a member of the National Gallery's Board of Trustees. On top of it all, he was elevated to the peerage: he became Lord Keynes, Baron of Tilton. The final war years, involving tough negotiations with the Americans and many trips across the Atlantic, took their toll. Keynes died of a second heart attack on 21 April 1946.

John Maynard Keynes, more than 60 years after his death, again wields enormous influence. But was he a revolutionary, a genius who dramatically changed economics? No, he wasn't, although he certainly had insights of genius. He can be best honoured, I believe, by what Jan Pen, a Dutch economics professor, wrote about him:

> As soon as anyone accepts the *common sense* of the income and consumption analysis, has an open eye for the instability of the market sector, understands how unemployment occurs as a consequence of insufficient aggregate demand, as soon as all that is understood, we may reserve the word 'Keynes' for that special person, who lived from 1883 to 1946.[15]

---

[15] Pen J. (1983) Keynes, Keynes, Keynes. *Intermediair*, 3 June 1983, 9.

The Economic Consequences of Peace

John Maynard Keynes gained world fame with the publication of *The Economic Consequences of Peace*, which came out in December 1919; 1 year after the end of the Great War's brutal hostilities.[16] The book is a mixture of a passionate political pamphlet and a sharp economic analysis.

It was a bombshell of a book, as it reflected an opinion that was contrary to public opinion at the time. Keynes was one of the few to criticise the Treaty of Versailles, which was signed on 28 June 1919 between the victorious Allies (the USA, Great Britain and France) and the defeated enemy Germany. Keynes had been involved in the negotiations as a representative of the British Treasury. He also sat as deputy for the Chancellor of the Exchequer on the Supreme Economic Council. Even before the Treaty was signed, Keynes resigned, exhausted and disappointed about its contents, which, he believed, would plunge Europe into more misery and instability, and which he had tried to help prevent during the negotiations.

General Smuts, who represented South Africa during the negotiations, and with whom Keynes had rapport, told him towards the end of the negotiations that political and territorial questions could not be solved in a satisfactory manner if economic problems would not have been resolved beforehand. According to Keynes's biographer, Robert Skidelsky, Keynes would have remarked how true it was and that he had never thought of it that way. This insight, Skidelsky wrote, formed perhaps the origin of the main theme of *The Economic Consequence of Peace*.[17]

The book consists of seven chapters, starting with 'Introductory' and ending with 'Remedies'. In-between Keynes describes the rapid transformation Europe underwent after 1870. He then describes the negotiations about the Treaty and their contents, leading to a possible projection of what Europe could look like after the Treaty. The book was hailed for its lucid style, but some critics found that Keynes was pro-Germany, and that his characterisations of the statesmen, in particular of President Wilson, were too harsh.

---

[16] The Cosimo Classics edition (New York, 2005) formed the basis of this summary.

[17] Skidelsky, R. (2003) *John Maynard Keynes 1883–1946: Economist, Philosopher, Statesman*, 232.

Chapter 1: Introductory

The negotiators at Paris ran the risk of completing the ruin which Germany began, by a peace which must impair further the delicate political and economic situation already shaken by the Great War. Keynes warned that an age was over. He feared that the continent was facing 'the fearful convulsions of a dying civilization'.

The Supreme Economic Council received regular reports of misery, disorder and decaying organisation of Central and Eastern Europe, while the negotiators seemed to be dissociated from the real events, which would eventually lead to the destruction of great institutions, but—as Keynes added—may also create a new world. Keynes describes the setting as follows:

> A sense of impending catastrophe overhung the frivolous scene; the futility and smallness of man before the great events confronting him; the mingled significance and unreality of the decisions; levity, blindness, insolence, confused cries from without—all elements of ancient tragedy were there.[18]

Chapter 2: Europe Before the War

Since 1870 Europe rapidly evolved from an agricultural into an industrial continent, in parallel with a rapidly growing population as well as economic interdependency. In 1890 Europe had a population three times that of North and South America put together. Germany had eclipsed France in economic terms and Germany had grown into one of the world's economic superpowers. Germany was Britain's second largest customer. Germany was Britain's second most prominent supplier of goods.

This transformation process was facilitated by almost completely free international trade in raw materials and final products. Keynes called it an economic Eldorado, which was partly possible thanks to an unequal distribution of income and wealth. This wealth was invested in more productive modes of production. Society, wrote Keynes, was not working for the small pleasures of today but for the future security and improvement of the race, in fact for progress.

---

[18] *The Economic Consequences of Peace*, 6.

The Great War put an end to it; free trade made way for protectionist policies. Most of the countries involved in the war were near-bankrupt. While their populations had grown in numbers, their agricultural sectors and transport systems had been destroyed. Keynes pointed at a few instabilities of Europe before 1914: (1) the instability of an excessive population dependent for its livelihood on food imports, especially from America, and (2) the psychological instability of the labouring and capitalist classes.

Chapter 3: The Conference

The Allied victors seemed to be blind to the deplorable economic conditions on the Continent. Each of the victorious chief negotiators had his own political agenda. French President Clemenceau wanted to bring Germany to its knees by breaking its economic prowess and, thus, to prevent an eventual German revenge. Clemenceau had, according to Keynes, 'One illusion—France; and one disillusion—mankind, including Frenchmen, and his colleagues not least.'[19]

US President Wilson, a reconciliatory force at the negotiation table, wanted his Fourteen Points agreed, ranging from the freedom of the seas, via the restoration of invaded territories, adequate guarantees that national armaments would be reduced, to the establishment of the League of Nations. The League was indeed established (America didn't become a member as the League failed to win Senate approval) but the President was outwitted by his colleagues at the negotiation table. Before the negotiations, President Wilson enjoyed a prestige and influence unequal in history, wrote Keynes, yet the President was neither a hero nor a prophet,

> but a generously intentioned man, with many of the weaknesses of other human beings, and lacking that dominating intellectual equipment, which would have been necessary to cope with the subtle and dangerous spellbinders whom a tremendous clash of forces and personalities had brought to the top as triumphant masters in the swift game of give and take, face to face in Council—a game of which he had no experience at all.[20]

---

[19] Ibid., 32.
[20] Ibid., 39.

British Prime Minister Lloyd George, who initially had a reconciliatory stance, hardened his position in view of upcoming elections in Britain.

The chapter ends with an explanation of the book's purpose: it was to demonstrate that the Treaty overlooked the deeper economic forces which were to govern Europe's future. The Treaty would let loose human and spiritual forces that would overwhelm the institutions and the existing order of society.

Chapter 4: The Treaty

President Wilson wanted to create the League of Nations, and was prepared to make concessions as long as the League's establishment would remain intact. Although the German delegation accepted Wilson's Fourteen Points, the French and British objected to the 'freedom of the seas' clause, in that it should not apply to German merchant marine ships. Objection number two was that the French and British wanted Germany to also pay for the pensions of war widows. The end result of the negotiations was a Treaty which was insincere and unrealistic. The book then provides an analysis as to why the Treaty was 'insincere' (read: immoral) and that, from an economic vantage point, it was bound to fail.

Germany's economic force was based on three factors: (1) her income from exports, (2) the exploitation of coal mines and steel mills and (3) Germany's transport system combined with low excise duties.

The Treaty was intent on breaking down these three economic 'pillars', so to speak. Germany had to transfer all her ships beyond 1600 tons to the Allies, and half the number of ships between 1000 and 1600 tons. The German colonies, including private German investments there, had to be handed over to the Allies as well. The proceeds would be used to meet private debts to Allied nationals from German, Austrian, Hungarian, Bulgarian or Turkish nationals.

The Alsace-Lorraine region, rich in coal and iron ore mines, came into French hands, including the large German corporations located there. The coal-rich Saar Basin would fall under the administration of the League of Nations. Upper Silesia's fate, where more than 20 % of coal for Germany's consumption came from, would depend on a plebiscite.

Germany also had to deliver a large tonnage of coal to the Allies, partly to compensate for damage done to coal mines of the Allies, and partly to pay in kind for War Reparations. Keynes calculated that should Germany comply, it would run a coal deficit of 50 million tons per annum for its own consumption. So, the result was that, in the end, Germany had to *import* coal in order to get its own industrial production running again. Austria, Northern Europe and Switzerland would be affected as well, since they drew their coal from Germany in large part.

As for Germany's tariff systems, the country would bind herself for 5 years to accord favoured-nation treatment to the Allies. However, Germany was not entitled herself to receive such a treatment. There were other measures, but they all boiled down to benefitting the victors, while the reciprocal benefits would not be granted to Germany. As for transport, Germany had to surrender 5000 locomotives and 150,000 wagons to the Allies. As regards the river systems, the Allies' demands included an unprecedented interference with Germany's domestic arrangements, and were capable of taking from Germany all effective control over her own waterways. The Treaty stipulated that the administration of Germany's main rivers, such as the Rhine and the Danube, would be run by an International Commissions, in which Germany would occupy a minority position.

Chapter 5: Reparation

The damages done by Germany during the war had to be compensated to the Allies. The question arose whether Germany could be made contingently liable for damage done by co-belligerents, such as Austria-Hungary, Bulgaria and Turkey. Wilson's Fourteen Points gave no clear answer. Keynes noted that Germany's capacity to pay would be exhausted by the direct and legitimate claims which the Allies held against it; hence, the question of Germany's contingent liability for its allies became academic.

Some claims were irresponsible, according to Keynes: Belgian claims, amounting to a sum in excess of the total estimated pre-war wealth of the whole country, were simply absurd. France, which was affected most by the war among the Allies, claimed an exorbitant reparation sum of

US$26.8 billion. Keynes had calculated that a fair amount would have been around US$4 billion. Britain claimed US$2.85 billion, mainly based on the enormous losses of its merchant marine fleet. All told, Keynes calculated that a fair amount of war reparation claims on the part of the Allies would be US$10.6 billion. He concluded,

> I believe that it would have been a wise and just act to have asked the German Government at the Peace negotiations to agree to a sum of $10,000,000,000 in final settlement, without further examination of particulars. This would have provided an immediate and certain solution, and would have required from Germany a sum which, if she were granted certain indulgences, might not have proved entirely impossible for her to pay.[21]

Although Lloyd George initially agreed with Wilson's Fourteen Points, he later realised that, if he wished to be re-elected, he had to take a tougher stance against Germany, which he did. It was widely recognised at the time that this was an act of political immorality. Germany had to pay up to the limit of her capacity, according to a statement of the prime minister briefly before polling day. Lloyd George won the elections and with this promise he set off to the negotiations in Paris. Keynes then observed,

> To what a different future Europe might have looked forward if either Mr. Lloyd George or Mr. Wilson had apprehended that the most serious of the problems which claimed their attention were not political or territorial but financial and economic, and that the perils of the future lay not in frontiers or sovereignties but in food, coal, and transport. Neither of them paid adequate attention to these problems at any stage of the conference.[22]

There was a financial interest on the part of those Allies who had incurred large war debts, especially France and Italy, but that problem was best solved through American magnanimity, according to Keynes. He also proposed that the former enemy Powers should be allowed, with a view to their economic restoration, to issue a moderate amount of

---

[21] Ibid., 135.
[22] Ibid., 146.

bonds. These proposals implied an appeal to the generosity of the United States, being the only nation that was able to buy these bonds.

As regards the exact amount of the war reparations to be paid up by Germany, no figure was mentioned in the Articles of the Treaty; this was left to the Reparation Chapter. The Reparation Commission was to manage the reparations; more precisely, it was to establish the bill of claim to be paid within 30 years, to fix the mode of payment and to approve necessary abatements and delays. The Commission could also determine how much of the resources stripped from Germany could be returned to keep enough life in Germany's economic organisation to enable it to continue to make reparation payments in future. In short, the Commission was the arbiter of Germany's economic life.

Keynes made his own rough calculations. He arrived at a total figure of US$25 billion, this time including pensions and allowances. However, including the claims other than those for pensions, of US$15 billion (Keynes's upper-limit estimate), the total amount would be US$40 billion. The question was, Would Germany have the capacity to pay this sum? Keynes calculated that it didn't. Germany's sources of payment were: (1) immediately transferable wealth in the form of gold, ships and foreign securities, (2) the value of property in ceded territory and (3) annual payments partly in cash and partly in kind (e.g. coal). Keynes estimated for each of the three sources what Germany's potential to pay was based on available data and documents. He concluded that only Belgium would probably be able, at best, to receive US$500 million by May 1921 (the first deadline) as Belgium had agreed with the other Allies that it should be paid first to repair the enormous damage done there. All in all, the expectations should be tempered, concluded Keynes, also when one takes into consideration the sorry state of Germany after the war:

> It is evident that Germany's pre-war capacity to pay an annual foreign tribute has not been unaffected by the almost total loss of her colonies, her overseas connections, her mercantile marine, and her foreign properties, by the cession of ten percent of her territory and population, of one-third of her coal and of three-quarters of her iron ore, by two million casualties amongst men in the prime of their life, by the starvation of her people for four years, by the burden of a vast war debt, by the depreciation of her

currency to less than one-seventh of its former value, by the disruption of her allies and their territories, by Revolution at home and Bolshevism on her borders, and by all the unmeasured ruin in strength and hope of four years of all-swallowing war and final defeat.[23]

Germany could only make payments when over a series of years it could diminish its imports and increase its exports. Since Germany was at the time a net-importing country, its first task would be to readjust consumption and production to cover this trade deficit. Most of Germany's exports went to the Allied countries. Unless the Allies would be prepared to encourage the importation of German products, a substantial increase in total volume could only be achieved by the wholesale swamping of neutral markets. Imports could be diminished a bit; however, the best guess as to an annual trade surplus would be US$500 million. But given the political, economic and human factors obtaining in Germany, Keynes doubted whether this amount could indeed be paid to the Allies. Keynes's overall conclusion? A capacity of US$40 billion, or even US$25 billion, is not within the limits of reasonable possibility. Should the surplus be taken away from Germany in conjunction with a lowering of the standard of life, Keynes made the following observation:

> It cannot be overlooked ... that in its results on a country's surplus productivity a lowering of the standard of life acts both ways. Moreover, we are without experience of the psychology of a white race under conditions little short of servitude. It is, however, generally supposed that if the whole of a man's surplus production is taken from him, his efficiency and his industry are diminished. The entrepreneur and the inventor will not contrive, the trader and the shopkeeper will not save, the labourer will not toil, if the fruits of their industry are set aside, not for the benefit of their children, their old age, their pride, or their position, but for the enjoyment of a foreign conqueror.[24]

What was Germany's counter-proposal? Germany offered to pay US$25 billion under various conditions ranging from retention of its territorial

---

[23] Ibid., 187.
[24] Ibid., 207.

integrity, keeping its colonial possessions, to reciprocity in trade relations. The first instalment would be paid by May 1926. Keynes then introduced a point hitherto unmentioned: the Allies recognised the inconvenience of the indeterminacy of the burden on Germany and they proposed a method by which the final total claim might be established before 1 May 1921. This offer, however, didn't include any opening up of the problem of Germany's capacity to indeed pay. The chapter ends as follows:

> The policy of reducing Germany to servitude for a generation, of degrading the lives of millions of human beings, and of depriving a whole nation of happiness should be abhorrent and detestable ... even if it did not sow the decay of the whole civilized life of Europe. Some preach it in the name of Justice. In the great events of man's history, in the unwinding of the complex fates of nations Justice is not so simple. And if it were, nations are not authorized ... to visit on children of their enemies the misdoings of parents or of rulers.[25]

Chapter 6: Europe After the Treaty

The Treaty included no provisions for the economic rehabilitation of Europe. No arrangement was made in Paris for restoring the finances of France and Italy, or to adjust the system of the Old World to the New. Clemenceau, Wilson and Lloyd George had no eye for these challenges.

Europe was densely populated, with a relatively high standard of life. Europe wasn't self-sufficient; it could not feed itself. The population secured its livelihood by means of a delicate and complicated organisation of which the foundations were supported by coal, iron, transport and the unbroken supply of imported food and raw materials from other continents. The rapid deterioration of the standard of life would mean starvation for some, a point which had already been reached in Russia (Austria was close to it). If food aid would not be provided to Germany, it was expected that many Germans would die of hunger.

---

[25] Ibid., 225.

But there were other considerations which had to be taken into account: the drop in productivity, the breakdown of transport and exchange, and the inability of Europe to purchase its usual supplies from overseas. Unemployment was on the rise, and so was inflation.

Agricultural production in Germany had fallen as a result of lower productivity of the soil, and livestock quality had diminished by 55 %. Former providers of grains and beef to Germany, such as Russia, Austria and Hungary, had their own problems. Even if they would have been able to export some of their produce to Germany, that wouldn't have been possible, as the European railway system was broken. A Malthusian situation ensued, in that Europe's food production fell short of feeding 100 million people. Without food imports, starvation was unavoidable, as Herbert Hoover of the American Commission of Relief reported at the time.

The values of the German mark, Italian lira, the French franc and even the British pound had dropped. Keynes concluded that there were three obstacles to the revival of trade: (1) a maladjustment between internal prices and international prices; (2) a lack of individual credit abroad wherewith to buy the raw materials needed to secure the working capital and to restart the circle of exchange; and (3) a disordered currency system which renders credit operations hazardous or impossible.

All these influences not only prevented Europe from supplying immediately a sufficient stream of exports to pay for the goods it needed to import, but they impaired its credit for securing the working capital required to restart the circle of exchange and also, by swinging the forces of economic law further from equilibrium, they favoured a continuance of the present conditions instead of a recovery from them. The miseries in Russia, Austria and Hungary might lead to a disintegration of society, Keynes feared.

Chapter 7: Remedies

The economic situation in Britain was not as bad as that on the Continent. England's problems were more fundamental, observed Keynes: the forces of the nineteenth century had run their course and were exhausted.

England must suffer the pangs of a new industrial birth. However, in countries such as Turkey, Austria, Russia and Hungary the situation was very bad. What could be done? For those who believed that the Treaty of Versailles could not stand, Keynes proposed three programmes: (1) the revision of the Treaty, (2) the settlement of inter-Ally indebtedness and (3) the relations of Central Europe to Russia.

As regards the revision of the Treaty, Keynes suggested establishing the amount of war reparation to be paid by Germany at US$10 billion; the Reparation Commission should be dissolved. As for coal, France should be compensated by Germany for the damage done to France's coal mines. The delivery of German coal should not exceed 20 million tons per annum during the first 5 years, and 8 million tons during the succeeding 5 years. The Saar Basin should be returned to Germany after 10 years. But this should be conditional on France's entering into an agreement to supply Germany during that period with 50 % of the iron ore which was carried from Lorraine into Germany before the war, in return for an undertaking from Germany to supply Lorraine with an amount of coal equal to the whole amount formerly sent to Lorraine from Germany. In Upper Silesia a plebiscite should be held on its future status.

As regards tariffs, a free trade union should be established under the auspices of the League of Nations of countries undertaking to impose no protectionist tariffs. Economic frontiers were tolerable so long as an immense territory was included in a few great empires; but they wouldn't be tolerable when the empires of Germany, Austria-Hungary, Russia and Turkey had been partitioned between some twenty independent authorities.

Settlement of inter-Ally indebtedness would be required as well. Britain should waive altogether its claims for cash payment in favour of Belgium, Serbia and France. Payments made by Germany would then be subject to the prior charge of repairing the material damage done to those countries.

Another proposal concerned an appeal to the generosity of the United States. America should cancel the debts which the Allies incurred for the purpose of the war. In return, Europe would vouch not to engage in war again, but to reconstruct its broken economies and infrastructure. At any event, Keynes didn't believe that the debts would continue to be paid. He predicted that for a few years payments would be made, but after that, they would stop.

It would be very difficult for European production to get started again without a temporary measure of external assistance. Keynes was therefore a supporter of an international loan, and the burden offering the immediate resources must, in major part, come from the United States. Keynes also proposed support for Germany. His proposal was preceded by a rhetorical question:

> And as for assistance to Germany, is it reasonable or at all tolerable that the European Allies, having stripped Germany of her last vestige of working capital, in opposition to the arguments and appeals of the American financial representatives at Paris, should then turn to the United Sates for funds to rehabilitate the victim in sufficient measure to allow the spoliation to recommence in a year or two?[26]

The proposed international loan should be provided by countries in a position to lend: the United Kingdom, the United States and the neutral countries. This loan would provide foreign purchasing credits for all belligerent countries of continental Europe, allied and ex-enemy alike. Keynes calculated that much could be done with a sum of US$1 billion in the first instance. Expenditure out of that loan should be subject to general supervision by the lending countries. Keynes realised that his proposal would only have a chance if and when public opinion would undergo a great change.

Regarding the relations between Central Europe and Russia, first the blockade of Russia should be suspended. Europe can't do without Russia's grain and other agricultural products; however, it should be remembered that Russia's export will only gradually grow since its present productivity is low. The transport system in the region could be repaired and improved with the help of German technical expertise. Keynes ended his book as follows:

> The events of the coming year will not be shaped by the deliberate acts of statesmen, but by the hidden currents, flowing continually beneath the

---

[26] Ibid., 284.

surface of political history, of which no one can predict the outcome. In one way only can we influence those hidden currents—by setting in motion those forces of instruction and imagination which change *opinion* ... Never in the lifetime of men now living has the universal element in the soul of man burnt so dimly. For these reasons the true voice of the new generation has not yet spoken, and silent opinion is not yet formed. To the formation of the general opinion of the future I dedicate this book.[27]

The General Theory of Employment, Interest, and Money

The General Theory of Employment, Interest, and Money (1936) triggered the Keynesian Revolution.[28] Keynes confessed that the composition of the book was 'a struggle of escape from habitual modes of thought'. The book is difficult to fully comprehend, as it contains inadequacies (as elaborated in the biographical chapter) and Keynes's presentation of many interdependencies from time to time blur the reader's understanding. Yet, Keynes wrote in the preface that he hoped that *The General Theory* would be intelligible to other than economists as well. He explained that the book primarily was a study of the forces which determine changes in the scale of output and employment as a whole; so already foreshadowing that Keynes analysed society from a macroeconomic vantage point.

This summary intends to give the reader as accurate as possible a reflection of Keynes's text. It doesn't include formulas nor mathematical equations; it describes in words what they represent.

The Great Depression inspired Keynes to deviate from the lessons from his tutor Alfred Marshall, the godfather of the neoclassical school.[29] *The General Theory* exposes the disastrous consequences of the failings of the policies based on the principles of neoclassical economics during the Great Depression.

---

[27] Ibid., 297–8.
[28] The edition used is the Harvest Book edition of 1964 published by Harcourt Brace & Company.
[29] Marshall's *Principles of Economics* (1890) was *the* standard book on neoclassical economics. A well-known expression at the time was: It is all in Marshall!

The General Theory's point of departure is that an economy can be in equilibrium with underemployment. The economic system is not self-adjusting. In a situation of declining demand, Keynes prescribed that: (1) the monetary authorities stimulate investments by lowering the interest rate, and (2) government borrow money and use the funds to finance public works and, hence, raise incomes and create jobs. For Keynes the government had to be prepared to act as *spender* of last resort, just as the central bank acted as *lender* of last resort. This Keynesian pump-priming prescription has again been widely applied since the commencement of the Great Recession in 2008.

The analytical essence of *The General Theory* is to discover what determines the volume of employment. In order to establish this, the interrelationships between consumption, saving, investment, interest and money had to be unravelled. The level of employment depends on what consumers want to buy and what investors want to invest. But investors and consumers aren't purely rational; they are influenced by all kinds of psychological factors. Keynes called them 'animal spirits'. Whilst the classics believed a person to behave rationally, as a *homo economicus*, Keynes maintained that people are generally concerned about the future (i.e., the good life might be over soon) and, therefore, save money to prepare for leaner years. There is thus the tendency to spend less, resulting in economic underperformance combined with underemployment. Now, Keynes said that in case of a recession, if one can measure in money terms what the population is buying and how much extra output the unemployed would add if they worked, one can calculate how much extra 'demand' or spending power has to be 'injected' into an economy to close the output gap.

The General Theory consists of six books, each divided up in chapters. This summary presents in essence the contents of these six books.

Book I: Introduction

Keynes argues that the postulates of the classical theory are applicable to a special case only, and not to the general case; the situation which it assumes being a limiting point of the possible positions of equilibrium. Moreover, the characteristics of the special case assumed by the classical theory happen not to be realistic, with the result that its teaching is misleading and disastrous if one attempts to apply it to real situations.

The Postulates of Classical Economics

The classical theory assumes a given volume of employed available resources. The pure theory of what determines the actual employment of the available resources has seldom been examined. The classical theory of employment was based on two fundamental postulates: (1) the wage is equal to the marginal product of labour, and (2) the utility of the wage when a given volume of labour is employed is equal to the marginal disutility of that amount of employment. The classical postulates don't admit the possibility of involuntary unemployment; they do recognise though frictional and voluntary unemployment. Subject to these qualifications, the volume of employed resources is duly determined by these two postulates. There are then only four means of increasing employment: (1) an improvement in the organisation or in foresight which diminishes 'frictional' unemployment; (2) a decrease in the marginal disutility of labour, as expressed by the real-wage for which additional labour is available, so as to diminish 'voluntary' unemployment; (3) an increase in the marginal physical productivity of labour in the wage-goods industries; or (4) an increase in the price of non-wage goods compared with the price of wage goods.

Experience tells us that a situation where labour stipulates for a money-wage, rather than a real-wage, that is the normal case. Workers will resist a reduction in money-wages, but it is not their practice to withdraw from labour when prices of wage goods rise.

The neoclassical contention that the unemployment which characterises a depression is due to a refusal by labour to accept a reduction of money-wages is not supported by the facts. If it were true that the existing real-wage is a minimum below which more labour than now is employed will not be forthcoming in any circumstances, involuntary unemployment would be non-existent. The traditional theory maintains that the wage bargains between the entrepreneurs and the workers determine the real-wage, so that the latter can bring their real-wage into conformity with the marginal disutility of the amount of employment offered by the employers at that wage. If this is not true, then there is no longer any reason to expect a tendency towards equality between the real-wage and the marginal disutility of labour.

If money-wages change, one would have expected the classical school to argue that prices would change in almost the same proportion, leaving the real-wage and the level of unemployment practically the same as before. This is not realistic, according to Keynes. He will show that it is other forces which determine the general level of real-wages.

The struggle about money-wages affects the distribution of the aggregate real-wage between different labour groups, and not its average amount per unit of employment, which depends on a different set of forces. The effect of combination on the part of a group of workers is to protect their relative wage. The general level of real-wages depends on other forces of the economic system. Every trade union will put up some resistance to a cut in money-wages. However, no union will strike on every occasion when the costs of living rise.

Involuntary unemployment occurs when a small rise in the price of wage goods, relative to the money-wage, both the aggregate supply of labour willing to work for the current money-wage and the aggregate demand for it at the that wage would be greater than the existing volume of employment. So long as the classical postulates hold good, unemployment can't occur. Apparent unemployment must therefore be the result either of temporary loss of work of the between-jobs type of intermittent demand for highly specialised resources, or of the effect of a trade union's 'closed shop' on the employment of free labour.

If the neoclassical theory is only applicable to the case of full employment, it is fallacious to apply it to the problems of involuntary unemployment. Keynes then concludes that we need to throw over the second postulate of this doctrine and, instead, to work out the behaviour of a system in which involuntary unemployment can happen. Yet, Keynes agrees to the first postulate, in that with a given organisation, equipment and technique, real-wages and the volume of output (and hence employment) are uniquely correlated, so that an increase in employment can only occur when real-wages decline. Thus, if employment increases, then—in the short run—the reward per unit of labour in terms of wage goods must decline and profits increase.

Jean Baptiste Say said that every supply creates its own demand, meaning that the whole of the costs of production must necessarily be spent in the aggregate on purchasing the product. Abstaining from consumption leads to causing the labour and commodities thus released to be invested in the production of capital wealth. In other words, an act of individual saving inevitably leads to a parallel act of investment. People who think along these lines are deceived. They are supposing that there is a nexus which unites decisions to abstain from present consumption with decisions to provide for future consumption; whereas the motives which determine the latter are not linked in any way with the motives which determine the former.

It is then the assumption of equality between the demand price of output as a whole and its supply price which is to be regarded as the classical theory's 'axiom of parallels'. Granted this, all the rest follows—the social advantages of private and national thrift, the traditional attitude towards the rate of interest, the classical theory of unemployment, the quantity theory of money, the unqualified advantages of laissez-faire in respect of foreign trade, and much else which one has to question.

The Principle of Effective Demand

Factor costs are the costs which the entrepreneur pays to the factors of production for their current services. The costs paid to other entrepreneurs for what one has to purchase from them, together with the sacrifice incurred by employing the equipment instead of leaving it idle; these are the user costs.[30] The excess of value of the resulting output over the sum of its factor costs is the profit, or the income of the entrepreneur. Thus the factor costs and the entrepreneur's profit make up between them total income.

In a given situation of technique, resources and factor cost per unit of employment, the amount of employment, both in each individual firm and industry in the aggregate, depend on the amount of the proceeds which the entrepreneurs expect to receive from the corresponding output. Entrepreneurs will endeavour to fix the amount of employment at the level which they expect to maximise the excess of the proceeds

---

[30] An appendix on user cost is included in pp. 66–73 of the book.

over the factor costs. If these proceeds which entrepreneurs expect to receive from the employment of a number of workers are greater than the aggregate supply price of the output employing that number of workers, there will be an incentive to increase employment beyond that number of workers up to a point where total supply becomes equal to aggregate demand. This is called the effective demand.

Since this is the substance of *The General Theory*, the succeeding chapters will be largely occupied with examining the various factors upon which these two functions depend.

In the classical understanding that supply creates its own demand, it means that there is always an equilibrium in supply and demand for the number of workers; there is always full employment. Effective demand, instead of having a unique equilibrium value, is an infinite range of values all equally admissible; and the amount of employment is indeterminate except in so far as the marginal disutility of labour sets an upper limit. Say's law implies that there is no obstacle to full employment.

What does the theory of employment tell us? It is assumed that the money-wage and other factor costs are constant per unit of labour employed. When employment increases, income increases as well but not by as much as income. Hence, employers would make a loss if the whole of the increased employment were to be devoted to satisfying the increased demand for immediate consumption. There must be an amount of current investment sufficient to absorb the excess of total output over what the community chooses to consume when employment is at a given level.

Given the community's propensity to consume, the equilibrium level of employment, that is, the level at which there is no inducement to employers either to expand or to contract employment, will depend on the amount of current investment. And the amount of current investment depends, in turn, on the inducement to invest, and that depends on the relation between the schedule of the marginal efficiency of capital (mec) and the complex of rates of interest on loans of various maturities and risks.

Thus, the conclusion is that given the propensity to consume and the rate of new investment, there will be only *one* level of employment consistent with equilibrium; since any other level will lead to inequality between aggregate supply price of output as a whole and its aggregate demand price. This is in essence *The General Theory of Employment*. The effective demand associated with full employment is a special case, only realised when the propensity to consume and the inducement to invest stand in particular relationship to one another; this is an optimum relationship.

The economic system may find itself in stable equilibrium with the number of workers at a level below full employment, namely at the level given by the intersection of the aggregate demand function with the aggregate supply function.

The propensity to consume and the rate of new investment determine between them the volume of employment, and the volume of employment is uniquely related to a given level of real-wages—not the other way around. If in a potentially wealthy community the inducement to invest is weak, then the working of the principle of effective demand will compel it to reduce its actual output, until, in spite of its potential wealth, it has become so poor that its surplus over its consumption is sufficiently diminished to correspond to the weakness of the inducement to invest. Not only is the marginal propensity to consume weaker in a wealthy community, but, owing to its accumulation of capital being already larger, the opportunities for further investment are less attractive, unless the rate of interest falls at a sufficiently rapid rate. This brings us to the theory of the rate of interest and to the reasons why it does not automatically fall to the appropriate level. Thus the analysis of the propensity to consume, the definition of the mec and the theory of the rate of interest are the three main gaps in the existing knowledge which will have to be filled, concluded Keynes.

The idea that we can neglect the aggregate demand function is fundamental to Ricardian economics—Ricardo was triumphant. The puzzle of effective demand wasn't even mentioned in the works of Marshall, Edgeworth and Pigou. That it was adapted to carry a vast and consistent logical superstructure gave it beauty. But it failed for purposes of scientific prediction; a discrepancy, Keynes wrote,

> which the ordinary man has not failed to observe, with the result of his growing unwillingness to accord to economists that measure of respect which he gives to other groups of scientists whose theoretical results are confirmed by observation when they are applied to the facts.[31]

---

[31] *The General Theory*, 33.

Book II: Definitions and Ideas

The Choice of Units

There were three perplexities which impeded Keynes's progress in writing his book: (1) the choice of units appropriate to the problems of the economic system as a whole, (2) the part played by expectation in economic analysis and (3) the definition of income. That the units, in terms of which economists normally work, are unsatisfactory can be illustrated by the concept of the National Dividend, the stock of real capital and the general price level, is explained by the fact that they cannot be properly measured in terms of value; it is better to do without them.

In dealing with the theory of employment, Keynes proposed to make use of only two fundamental units: quantities of money and quantities of employment. The unit in which the quantity of employment is measured is the 'labour unit', and the money-wage of a labour unit is called 'the wage unit'. Much unnecessary perplexity can be avoided if one was to limit oneself to these two units, money and labour, when one is dealing with the behaviour of the economic system as a *whole*; reserving the use of units of particular outputs and equipment to instances when one is dealing with individual firms in isolation.

Expectation as Determining Output and Employment

All production is for the purpose of ultimately satisfying a consumer. Meanwhile, the entrepreneur is guided by expectations: short-term and long-term. The short-term ones are related to as 'finished' output. The long-term ones are concerned with what the entrepreneur can hope to earn in the shape of future returns if he or she purchases finished output as an addition to capital equipment. It is upon these expectations that the amount of employment which the firms offer will depend.

Now, in general, a change in expectations will only produce its full effect on employment over a considerable period of time. Every state of expectation has its definite level of long-period employment. Suppose that the change is of such a character that the new long-period employment will be greater than the old. The initial increase in employment will be modest. However, employment will gradually increase. Thus a change in expectation is capable of producing an oscillation of the same kind of shape as a cyclical movement in the course of working itself out. The level of employment at any time depends not merely on the existing state of expectation but on the states of expectation which have existed over a certain period of time.

The Definition of Income, Saving and Investment

The entrepreneur's income is the excess of the value of finished output sold during the period of prime cost. The entrepreneur's income is taken as being equal to the quantity, depending on scale of production, which one endeavours to maximise, that is, to gross profit in the ordinary sense of this term.

Effective demand is simply the aggregate income which the entrepreneurs expect to receive, inclusive of the incomes which they hand on to the other factors of production, from the amount of current employment which they decide to give. The effective demand is the point of the aggregate demand function which becomes effective because, taken in conjunction with the conditions of supply, it corresponds to the level of employment which maximises the entrepreneur's expectation of profit. In calculating the net income and the net profit of the entrepreneur it is usual to deduct the estimated amount of the supplementary cost (the excess of the expected depreciation over the user cost) from income and gross profit as defined above. In one's capacity as *producer* deciding whether or not to use the equipment, prime cost and gross profit are the two significant concepts. But in one's capacity as *consumer* the amount of supplementary cost works on one's mind in the same way as if it were a part of the prime cost.

Saving and Investment

Saving means the excess of entrepreneurs' income over expenditure on consumption. Expenditure on consumption can be defined as the total sales made minus the sales made from one entrepreneur to another.

Current investment is the current addition to the value of the capital equipment. And this is equal to how savings were defined, for it is that part of income that hasn't gone into consumption.

Each consumer's income is spent partly in consumption and partly in savings. Investors spend their income on their own consumption plus investment. As Income = value of output = consumption + investment, and since saving = income—consumption, therefore, saving = investment. The amounts of aggregate income and of aggregate saving are the results of the free choices of individuals whether or not to consume and whether or not to invest; but they are neither of them capable of assuming an independent value resulting from a separate set of decisions taken irrespective of the decisions concerning consumption and investment. In accordance with this principle, the conception of the propensity to consume will take the place of the propensity to save.

The Meaning of Saving and Investment Further Considered

Investment includes the increment of capital equipment whether it consists of fixed capital, working capital or liquid capital; and the significant differences of definition are due to the exclusion from investment of one or more of these categories. The volume of employment (and consequently of output and real income) is fixed by entrepreneurs under the motive of seeking to maximise their present and prospective profits; whilst the volume of employment which will maximise their profits depends on the aggregate demand function given by their expectations of the sum of the proceeds resulting from consumption and investment respectively on various hypotheses.

There can't be a buyer without a seller, or a seller without a buyer. Though an individual whose transactions are small in relation to the market can safely neglect the fact that demand isn't a one-sided transaction, it makes no sense to neglect it when we come to aggregate demand. This is the vital difference between the theory of economic behaviour of the aggregate and the theory of the behaviour of the individual unit, which assumes that changes in the individual's demand don't affect his or her income.

Book III: The Propensity to Consume

The volume of employment is determined by the point of intersection of the aggregate supply function with the aggregate demand function. It is the part played by the aggregate demand function which has been overlooked. This function relates any given level of employment to the 'proceeds' which that level of employment is expected to attain. The amount that the community spends on consumption depends partly on the amount of its income, partly on the other objective attendant circumstances, partly on the subjective needs and the psychological propensities and habits of the individuals composing it, and the principles on which the income is divided between them.

The principle objective factors which influence the propensity to consume are: (1) a change in the wage unit (consumption is much more a function of real income than of money-income); (2) a change in the difference between income and net income; (3) windfall changes in capital values not allowed for in calculating net income; (4) changes in the rate of time-discounting, that is, in the ratio of exchange between present goods and future goods; (5) changes in fiscal policy. If fiscal policy is used as a deliberate instrument for the more equal distribution of incomes, its effect in increasing the propensity to consume is all the greater. A changeover from a policy of government borrowing to the opposite policy of providing sinking funds (or vice versa) is capable of causing a severe contraction or marked expansion of effective demand; and (6) changes in expectations of the relation between the present and the future level of income. We are left with the conclusion that in a given situation the propensity to consume may be considered a fairly stable function, provided that we have eliminated changes in the wage unit in terms of money. While the other factors are capable of varying, the aggregate income, measured in terms of the wage unit is *the* principal variable upon which the consumption-constituent of the aggregate demand function will depend.

When an individual's real income rises, it will not increase its consumption by an equal absolute amount, so that a greater absolute amount must be saved. This means that, if employment and hence aggregate income increases, not all additional employment will be required to satisfy the needs of additional consumption. On the other hand, a decline in income, due to a decline in employment, may even cause consumption to exceed income not only of some individuals, but also by government, which will be liable to run into a budgetary deficit or will provide unemployment relief out of borrowed money. Employment can only increase *pari passu* with an increase in investment; unless there is a change in the propensity to consume. For since consumers will spend less than the increase in aggregate supply price when employment is increased, the increased employment will prove unprofitable unless there is an increase in investment to fill the gap.

Sinking funds are apt to withdraw spending power from the consumer long before the demand for expenditure on replacements comes into play. By 1929, in the US, for example, the rapid capital expansion of the previous 5 years had led cumulatively to the setting up of sinking funds and depreciation allowances in respect to plant which did not need replacement, on so huge a scale that an enormous volume of entirely new investment was required merely to absorb these financial provisions; and it became almost hopeless to find still more new investment on a sufficient scale to provide for such new saving as a wealthy community in full employment would be disposed to set aside. This factor alone was probably sufficient to cause a slump. And since financial prudence of this kind continued to be exercised through the slump by great corporations, which were still in a position to afford it, it offered a serious obstacle to early recovery.

The problem of new capital investment always outrunning capital disinvestment sufficiently to fill the gap between net income and consumption presents a problem which is increasingly difficult as capital increases. New capital investment can only take place in excess of current capital disinvestment if *future* expenditure on consumption is expected to increase. Capital is not a self-subsistent entity existing apart from consumption. On the contrary, every weakening in the propensity to consume regarded as a permanent habit weakens the demand for capital and for consumption.

The Propensity to Consume II: The Subjective Factors

There are subjective and social incentives which determine how much is spent, given the aggregate of income in terms of wage units and given the relevant objective factors as already discussed. There are eight motives of a subjective character which lead individuals to refrain from spending out of their income: (1) to build up a reserve against unforeseen contingencies; (2) to provide for an anticipated future relation between income and the needs of the individual (e.g. old age); (3) to enjoy interest and appreciation, as a larger real consumption at a later date is preferred to a smaller immediate consumption; (4) to enjoy a gradually increasing expenditure; (5) to enjoy a sense of independence and the power to do things; (6) to reserve money to speculate; (7) to bequeath a fortune; and (8) to satisfy pure miserliness, that is, unreasonable but insistent inhibitions against acts of expenditure as such.

Businesses and government also have their motives to withhold, for example, to keep money for further investment—to have money in cash; to secure a gradually increasing income; and the motive of financial prudence. However, there are also motives which lead to an *excess* of consumption over income. It depends on the culture and institutional setting, how strong positive or negative motives work out.

Short-period changes in consumption largely depend on changes in the rate at which income (measured in wage units) is being earned and not on changes in the propensity to consume out of a given income. The influence of changes in the rate of interest on the amount actually saved is of paramount importance, but it is in the opposite direction to that usually supposed. For aggregate savings is governed by aggregate investment; a rise in the rate of interest will diminish investment; hence a rise in the rate of interest must have the effect of reducing incomes to a level at which saving is decreased in the same measure as investment.

Since incomes will decrease by a greater absolute amount than investment, it is true that, when the rate of interest rises, the rate of consumption will decrease. But this doesn't mean that there will be a wider margin for saving. On the contrary, saving and spending will *both* decrease. The rise in the rate of interest might induce us to save more, if our incomes were unchanged. But if the higher rate of interest retards investment, our incomes will necessarily fall. The more virtuous we are, the more our incomes will have to fall when interest rises relatively to the marginal efficiency of capital.

The Marginal Propensity to Consume and the Multiplier

Keynes's pupil, Richard Kahn, invented the employment multiplier, in that the change in the amount of employment will be a function of the net change in investment. A change in income will trigger a smaller change in consumption. The marginal propensity to consume can be described as defining how the next change in output will be divided in consumption and in investment.

Keynes then introduced the investment multiplier, which tells us that when there is an increment of aggregate investment, income will increase by an amount which is equal to the multiplier coefficient times the increase in investment. If a community wants to consume the whole of any increment of income, there will be no point of stability and prices will rise without limit. An increment of investment cannot occur unless the public are prepared to increase their savings. The public will not do this unless their aggregate income is increasing. Thus their effort to consume a part of their increased incomes will stimulate output until the new level of incomes provides a margin of saving sufficient to induce to correspond to the increased investment.

The multiplier tells us by how much their employment has to be increased to yield an increase in real income sufficient to induce them to do the necessary extra saving, and is a function of their psychological propensities.

If the marginal propensity to consume is not much above zero, small fluctuations in investment will lead to correspondingly small fluctuations in employment. At the same time, it may require a large increment of investment to produce full employment. Some of the multiplier effect may leak to foreign countries in case the extra consumption is in imported goods. However, it is to the general principle of the multiplier to which we have to look for an explanation of how fluctuations in the amount of investment, which form a comparatively small proportion of the national income, are capable of generating fluctuations in aggregate employment and incomes so much greater in amplitude than themselves. In some cases, for example in an unforeseen expansion of capital-goods industries, the effects will only be over a period of time, which is important in the analysis of the trade cycle.

The greater the marginal propensity to consume is, the greater the multiplier and the greater the disturbance to employment corresponding to a given change in investment. One would expect that a poor community, in which saving is a very small proportion of income, will be more subject to violent fluctuations than a wealthy community where saving is a larger proportion of income and the multiplier consequently smaller. This would overlook the distinction between the effects of the marginal propensity to consume and those of the average propensity. For whilst a high marginal propensity to consume involves a larger proportionate effect from a given percentage change in investment, the absolute effect will, nevertheless, be small if the average propensity to consume is high. Whilst the multiplier is larger in a poor country, the effect on employment of fluctuations in investment will be much greater in a wealthy community, assuming that in the latter current investment represents a much larger proportion of current output.

Employment of a given number of men on public works will have a much larger effect on aggregate employment than it will have later on when full employment is approached. Keynes concluded that public works, even of doubtful utility, may pay for themselves over and over again at a time of severe unemployment, if only from the diminished cost of relief expenditure, provided that we can assume that a smaller proportion of income is saved when unemployment is greater. Keynes then proposed a much-quoted approach to public works:

> If the Treasury were to fill old bottles with bank-notes, bury them at suitable depths in disused coal-mines which are then filled up to the surface with town rubbish, and leave it to private enterprise on well-tried principles of laissez-faire to dig the notes up again ... there need be no more unemployment and with the help of the repercussions, the real income of the community

would probably become a good deal larger than it is. It would, indeed, be more sensible to build houses and the like; but if there are practical difficulties in the way of doing this, the above would be better than nothing.[32]

If the marginal propensity to consume falls off steadily as we approach full employment, it follows that it will become more and more troublesome to secure a further increase of employment by further increasing investment.

Book IV: The Inducement to Invest

The Marginal Efficiency of Capital

The relation between the prospective yield of a capital asset and its supply price or replacement cost, that is, the relation between the prospective yield of one more unit of that type of capital and the cost of producing that unit, furnishes us with the *marginal efficiency of capital* (mec) of that type. Keynes defined the mec more precisely, as being equal to that rate of discount which would make the present value of the series of annuities, given by the returns expected from the capital-asset during its life just equal to its supply price. This gives us the marginal efficiencies of *particular* types of capital assets. The greatest one of them can be regarded as the mec in general. For each type of capital we can build up a schedule showing by how much investment in it will have to increase within the period in order that the marginal efficiency should fall to any given figure. Aggregating these schedules results in the investment demand schedule; or the schedule of the mec.

It is obvious that the actual rate of current investment will be pushed to the point where there is no longer any class of capital asset of which the marginal efficiency exceeds the current rate of interest. In other words, the rate of investment will be pushed to the point on the investment demand schedule where the marginal efficiency of capital in general is equal to the market rate of interest.

---

[32] Ibid., 129.

The most important confusion concerning the meaning and significance of the mec had ensued on the failure to see that it depends on the *prospective* yields of capital, and not merely on its current yield. The expectation of a fall in the value of money stimulates investment, and hence employment, because it raises the schedule of the mec.

Often the mistake is made in supposing that it is the rate of interest on which prospective changes in the value of money will directly react, instead of the marginal efficiency of a given stock of capital. The prices of existing assets will always adjust themselves to changes in expectation concerning the prospective value of money. The stimulus to output depends on the marginal efficiency of a given stock of capital, rising *relatively* to the rate of interest. An expectation of a future fall in the rate of interest will have the effect of lowering the schedule of the mec; since it means that the output from equipment produced today will have to compete during part of its life with the output from equipment which is content with a lower return.

It is important to understand the dependence of the mec of a given stock of capital on changes in *expectation*, because it is chiefly this dependence which renders the mec subject to the somewhat violent fluctuations that are the explanation of the trade cycle. The succession of booms and busts can be described and analysed in terms of fluctuations of the mec relative to the rate of interest.

In concluding, the schedule of the mec is of fundamental importance because it is mainly through this factor (much more than through the rate of interest) that the expectation of the future influences the present. Even if the rate of interest is virtually a current phenomenon, and if we reduce the mec to the same status, we cut ourselves off from taking any direct account of the influence of the future in our analysis of the existing equilibrium.

The State of Long-Term Expectations

Long-term expectations are not based only on the most probable forecasts we can make. They are also based on the confidence with which we make them. The state of confidence is relevant because it is one of the major factors determining the schedule of the mec, which is the same thing as the investment demand schedule.

A collapse in the price of equities which has had disastrous reactions on the mec may have been due to the weakening either of speculative confidence or of the state of credit. As for speculation, the situation becomes serious when enterprise becomes the bubble on a whirlpool of speculation.

Apart from the instability due to speculation, there is the instability due to the characteristic of human nature that a large proportion of our positive activities depend on spontaneous optimism rather than on a mathematical expectation, whether moral or hedonistic or economic. Most of our decisions to do something positive, the full consequences of which will be drawn out over many days to come, can only be taken as a result of *animal spirits*—of a spontaneous urge to action over inaction, and not as the outcome of a weighted average of quantitative benefits multiplied by quantitative probabilities.

If the animal spirits are dimmed and the spontaneous optimism falters, leaving us to depend on nothing but a mathematical expectation, enterprise will fade and die; though fears of loss may have a basis no more reasonable than hopes of profit had before. Individual initiative will only be adequate when reasonable calculation is supplemented and supported by animal spirits, so that the thought of ultimate loss which often overtakes pioneers, as experience undoubtedly tells us (and them), is put aside as a healthy man puts aside the expectation of death. This means, unfortunately, not only that slumps and depressions are exaggerated in degree, but that economic prosperity is excessively dependent on a political atmosphere which is congenial to the average business man.

One should not conclude, however, that everything depends on waves of irrational psychology. On the contrary, the state of long-term expectation is often steady, and even when it is not, the other factors exert compensating effects. Yet, it is the innate urge to activity which makes the wheels go round, our rational selves choosing between the alternatives as best we are able, calculating where we can, but often falling back for our motive on whim or sentiment or chance.

The General Theory of the Rate of Interest

What factors determine the rate of interest?[33] We shall find that they make the rate of interest to depend on the interaction of the schedule of the mec with the psychological propensity to save. One has to consider individuals' liquidity preference. This is where an individual's liquidity preference is given by a schedule of the amount of one's resources, valued in terms of money, which that person will wish to retain in the form of cash in different circumstances.

The rate of interest can be defined as the reward for parting with liquidity for a special period. Another factor influencing the rate of interest is the quantity of money, which, in conjunction with the liquidity preference, determines the actual rate of interest in given circumstances.

Liquidity preference exists because of uncertainty as to the future rate of interest; that is, as to the complex of rates of interest for varying maturities which will rule at future dates. Keynes distinguished between three divisions of liquidity preference: (1) the transaction motive, that is, the need for cash for current transactions; (2) the precautionary motive, that is, the desire for security as to the future cash equivalent of a certain proportion of total resources; and (3) the speculative motive. As a rule, we can suppose that the schedule of liquidity preference relating the quantity of money to the rate of interest is given by a smooth curve which shows the rate of interest falling as the quantity of money is increased.

However, while an increase in the quantity of money may be expected to reduce the rate of interest, this will not happen if the liquidity preferences of the public are increasing more than the quantity of money; and while a decline in the rate of interest may be expected to increase the volume of investment, this will not happen if the schedule of the mec is falling more rapidly than the rate of interest. While an increase in the volume of investment may be expected to increase employment, this may not happen if the propensity to consume is falling off. Finally, if employment increases, prices will rise in a degree partly governed by the shapes of the physical supply functions, and partly by the liability of the wage-units

---

[33] In an appendix (pp. 186–93) Keynes provides an overview of past answers to this question.

to rise in terms of money. When output has increased and prices have risen, the effect of this on the liquidity preference will be to increase the quantity of money necessary to maintain a given rate of interest.

Hoarding may be regarded as a first approximation to the concept of liquidity preference. The habit of overlooking the relation of the rate of interest to hoarding may be a part of the explanation why interest has usually been regarded as the reward of not-spending, whereas in fact it is the reward of not-hoarding.

The Classical Theory of the Rate of Interest

The neoclassical economic principle on which the practical advice of economists has been almost invariably based has assumed that a decrease in spending will tend to lower the rate of interest and an increase in investment raise it. But if what these two quantities determine is not the rate of interest as proposed by the classical theory of interest but the aggregate volume of employment (as Keynes proposed), then the outlook on the mechanism of the economic system will be profoundly changed: a decreased readiness to spend will be looked on in quite a different light if, instead of being regarded as a factor which will increase investment, it is seen as a factor which will diminish employment. The traditional analysis has overlooked the fact that income depends on investment in such fashion that, when investment changes, income must necessarily change in just that degree which is necessary to make the change in saving equal to the change in investment.

The Psychological and Business Incentives to Liquidity

People have different motives to have liquidity: (1) the income motive (to bridge the time between the receipt of income and its disbursement); (2) the business motive (to bridge the interval between the time of incurring business costs and that of the receipt of sale proceeds); (3) the precautionary motive (to provide for contingencies); and (4) the speculative motive (this one is important in transmitting the effects of a change in the quantity of money). The aggregate demand for money to satisfy this speculative motive usually shows a continuous response to gradual changes in the rate of interest; that is, there is a continuous curve relating changes in the demand for money to satisfy the speculative motive and changes in the rate of interest, as given by changes in the prices of bonds and debts of various maturities.

Changes in the liquidity function itself, due to a change in the news which causes revision of expectations, will often be discontinuous, and will give rise to a corresponding discontinuity of change in the rate of interest. It is the change in the rate of interest, rather than the redistribution of cash, which is usually the most prominent part of the reaction to a change in the news.

The wish to hold cash to satisfy the transaction and the precautionary motives: these motives are different from the speculative motive, and are largely independent of one another. The former depend on the level of income, while the latter depends on the current rate of interest and the state of expectation. The rate of interest is a highly psychological phenomenon. It cannot be in equilibrium at a level below the rate which corresponds to full employment because at such a level a state of true inflation will be produced, with the result that the amount of cash held for transaction and precautionary motives will absorb ever-increasing quantities of cash. But at a level *above* the rate which corresponds to full employment, the long-term market rate of interest will depend not only on the current policy of the monetary authority, but also on market expectations concerning its future policy.

There is a special direct connection between changes in the quantity of money and changes in the rate of interest. This arises from the fact that the banking system and the monetary authority are dealers in money and debts and not in assets or consumables. The monetary authority's ability to establish any given complex of rates of interest for debts of different terms and of risk is limited by: (1) those limitations which arise out of the monetary authority's own practices in limiting its willingness to deal in debts of a particular type; (2) there is the possibility that after the rate of interest has fallen to a certain level, liquidity preference may become virtually absolute in the sense that almost everyone prefers cash to holding a debt which yields so low a rate of interest; and (3) a complete breakdown of stability in the rate of interest; this happened in cases of currency crises, leading to capital flight.

The great fault in the quantity theory is that it doesn't distinguish between changes in prices which are a function of changes in output, and those which are a function of changes in wages. The explanation of this omission is to be found in the assumptions that there is no propensity to hoard and that there is always full employment.

Sundry Observations on the Nature of Capital

The expectation of consumption is the only *raison d'être* of employment. There should be nothing paradoxical in the conclusion that a diminished propensity to consume has a depressing effect on employment. A person who saves does it in connection with his wish to have a prospective yield. Now, a prospective yield wholly depends on the expectation of future effective demand in relation to future conditions of supply. If an act of saving does nothing to improve prospective yields, it does nothing to stimulate investment. The prospective yield with which the producers of new investment have to be content cannot fall below the standard set by the current rate of interest. And the current rate of interest depends on the strengths of the desire to hold it in liquid and illiquid forms respectively, coupled with the amount of the supply of wealth in the one form relative to the supply of it in the other.

Capital has to be kept scarce enough in the long run to have a marginal efficiency which is at least equal to the rate of interest for a period equal to the life of the capital, as determined by psychological and institutional conditions. The postwar experiences of Great Britain and America are actual examples of how an accumulation of wealth, so large that its marginal efficiency has fallen more rapidly that the rate of interest can fall in the face of the prevailing institutional and psychological factors, can interfere in conditions mainly of laissez-faire, with a reasonable level of employment and with the standard of life which the technical conditions of production are capable of furnishing. Keynes then wrote the following memorable paragraph:

> In so far as millionaires find their satisfaction in building mighty mansions to contain their bodies when alive and pyramids to shelter them after death, or, repenting of their sins, erect cathedrals and endow monasteries

or foreign missions, the day when abundance of capital will interfere with the abundance of output may be postponed. 'To dig holes in the ground', paid for out of savings, will increase, not only employment, but the real national dividend of useful goods and services.[34]

Let's assume that steps are taken to ensure that the rate of interest is consistent with the rate of investment which corresponds to full employment. Let's also assume that state action enters as a balancing factor to ensure that the growth of capital equipment shall be such as to approach saturation point at a rate which does not put a disproportionate burden on the standard of life of the present generation. On such assumptions, Keynes argued that a properly run community, equipped with modern technical resources, and of which the population is not increasing rapidly, ought to be able to bring down the mec in equilibrium approximately to zero within a single generation. That should attain the conditions of a quasi-stationary community where change and progress would result only from changes in technique, taste, population and institutions.

Keynes concluded that, supposing that it is comparatively easy to make capital goods so abundant that the mec is zero, this may be the most sensible way of gradually getting rid of many of the objectionable features of capitalism. Reflection will show what enormous social changes would result from a gradual disappearance of a rate of return on accumulated wealth. A man would still be free to accumulate his earned income with a view to spending it at a later date, but his accumulation would not grow.

The Essential Properties of Interest and Money

Why should the volume of output and employment be more intimately bound up with the money-rate of interest than with that of other commodities? Keynes formulated it as follows:

> It seems ... that *the rate of interest on money* plays a peculiar part in setting a limit to the level of employment, since it sets a standard to which the marginal efficiency of a capital-asset must attain if it is to be newly produced.[35]

---

[34] Ibid., 220.
[35] Ibid., 222.

The money-rate of interest, as explained, is nothing more than the percentage excess of a sum of money contracted for forward delivery; this is called the spot (or cash) price of the sum contracted for delivery in the future. Now, for every durable commodity (e.g. wheat) there is a rate of interest in terms of itself (e.g. a wheat-rate of interest). The difference between the future and spot contracts for a commodity, such as wheat, bears a definite relation to the wheat-rate of interest. However, since the future contract is quoted in terms of money for forward delivery, and not in terms of wheat for spot delivery, it also brings in the money-rate of interest.

The rates of interest for different commodities (their own rates) are typically not the same as the relation between the spot and future contracts for different commodities. It turns out, however, that the money-rate of interest is more bound up with the volume of output and employment. The money-rate of interest in terms of itself as standard being more reluctant to fall as output increases than the 'own rates' of interest of any other asset in terms of themselves, justifies the question at the start of this section. This is so because money has in the short and in the long run a zero or very small elasticity of production; money cannot be readily produced. Hence, its own rate of interest will be relatively reluctant to fall. Second, money has an elasticity of substitution equal, or nearly equal, to zero. This means that as the exchange value of money rises, there is no tendency to substitute some other factor for it. Third, in an economy of the type to which we are accustomed it is very probable that the money-rate of interest will often prove reluctant to decline adequately.

Money-wages tend to be *sticky*; money-wages are more stable than real-wages. This tends to limit the readiness of the wages to fall in terms of money. Then there is the liquidity preference. In certain circumstances these will cause the rate of interest to be insensitive to a substantial increase in the quantity of money in proportion to other forms of wealth. In other words, beyond a certain point money's yield from liquidity does not fall in response to an increase in its quantity to anything approaching the extent to which the yields from other types of assets fall when their quantity is comparably increased.

The significance of the money-rate of interest arises out of the combination of the characteristics that, through the working of the liquidity motive, this rate of interest may be somewhat unresponsive to a change in the proportion which the quantity of money bears to other forms of wealth measured in money, and that money has (or may have) zero (or negligible) elasticities both of production and of substitution.

No further increase in the rate of investment is possible when the greatest among the own rates of own interest of all available assets is equal to the greatest among the marginal efficiencies of all assets, measured in terms of the asset whose own interest is greatest. In a position of full employment this condition is necessarily satisfied. But it may be satisfied *before* full employment is reached, if there exists some asset, having zero (or relatively small) elasticities of production and substitution, whose rate of interest declines more slowly as output increases than the marginal efficiencies of capital assets measured in terms of it.

The fact that contracts are fixed, and wages are usually somewhat stable in terms of money, unquestionably plays a large part in attracting to money so high a liquidity premium. This, however, is insufficient by itself to produce the observed characteristics of the money-rate of interest. It is not probable that there exists a commodity of which the value of output is expected to be more stable than in terms of money. Thus, the expectation of a relative *stickiness of wages* in terms of money is a corollary of the excess of liquidity premium over carrying costs being greater for money than for any other asset.

For every rate of interest there is a level of employment for which that rate is the 'natural' rate, in the sense that the system will be in equilibrium with that rate of interest and that level of employment. In a situation of full employment, it is better to speak of an optimum rate of interest.

The General Theory of Employment Restated

In this chapter the general theory will be presented in a succinct manner. Keynes considered the following elements as given: the existing skill and quantity of available labour, the existing quality and quantity of available equipment, the existing technique, the degree of competition, the tastes and habits of the consumer, the disutility of different intensities of labour and of the activities of supervision and organisation, as well as the social structures which determine the distribution of the national income.

The independent variables are: the propensity to consume, the schedule of the mec and the rate of interest. The dependent variables are the volume of employment and the national income.

The schedule of the mec depends partly on the given factors and partly on the prospective yield of capital assets of different kinds, while the rate of interest depends partly on the state of liquidity preference and partly on the quantity of money. Thus, concluded Keynes, we can sometimes regard the ultimate independent variables as consisting of: (1) the three fundamental psychological factors: the propensity to consume, the attitude to liquidity and the expectation of future yields from capital assets; (2) wages as determined by the bargains between employers and employed; and (3) the quantity of money as determined by the action of the central bank. These factors combined determine the national income and the quantity of employment. As stated before, the objective is to discover what determines at any time the national income of a given economic system and the amount of its employment. The final task is to select those variables which can be deliberately controlled or managed by central authority in the kind of system in which we actually live.

The General Theory in Summary

> There will be an inducement to push the rate of new investment to the point which forces the supply price of each type of capital asset to a figure which, taken in conjunction with its prospective yields, brings the mec in general to approximate equality with the rate of interest. The physical conditions of supply in the capital-goods industries, the state of confidence concerning the prospective yield, the psychological attitude to liquidity and the quantity of money determine, between them, the rate of new investment. But an increase (or decrease) in the rate of investment will have to carry with it an increase (or decrease) in the rate of consumption; because the behaviour of the public is of such a character that they are only willing to widen (or narrow) the gap between their income and their consumption if their income is being increased (or diminished). Changes in the rate of consumption are in the same direction (though smaller in amount) as changes in the rate of income. The relation between the increment of consumption which has to accompany a given increment of saving is given by the marginal propensity to consume. The ratio between an increment of investment and the corresponding increment of aggregate income,

> measured in wages, is given by the investment multiplier. If we assume that the employment multiplier is equal to the investment multiplier, we can, by applying the multiplier to the increment (or decrement) in the rate of investment brought about by the factors first described, infer the increment of employment. An increment (or decrement) of employment is liable to raise (or lower) the schedule of liquidity preference; there being three ways in which it will tend to increase the demand for money, inasmuch as the value of output will rise when employment increases even if the wages and prices are unchanged. But the wages themselves will tend to rise as employment improves, and the increase in output will be accompanied by a rise in prices (in terms of wages) owing to increasing cost in the short run. Thus, the position of equilibrium will be influenced by these repercussions; there are other repercussions also. Moreover, there is not one of the above factors which is not liable to change without much warning, and sometimes substantially; hence, the extreme complexity of the actual course of events. Nevertheless, these seem to be the factors which it is useful to isolate. If we examine any actual problem along the lines of the above schematism, we shall find it more manageable—and our practical intuition will be offered a less intractable material upon which to work.

A characteristic of the economic system in which we live is that, while it is subject to severe fluctuations in respect of output and employment, it is not violently unstable. It seems capable of maintaining, for considerable periods, a chronic condition of subnormal activity without any marked tendency either towards recovery or towards complete collapse. Full employment is the exception rather than the rule. Keynes then wondered what the psychological propensities would be which lead to a stable system, and whether they could be ascribed to the world we live in.

The conditions of stability which the above analysis suggests are the following: (1) the marginal propensity to consume is such that the multiplier is greater than unity, but not very large; (2) moderate changes in the prospective yield of capital or in the rate of interest will not be associated with very great changes in the rate of investment; (3) changes in employment will not trigger equal changes in money-wages in the same direction (this is a condition of the stability of prices rather than of employment); and (4) a rate of investment higher (or lower) than prevailed formerly begins to react unfavourably (or favourably) on the mec if it is continued for a period which isn't very large.

These four conditions are adequate to explain the outstanding features of our actual experience, namely that we oscillate round an intermediate position appreciably below full employment and appreciably above the minimum employment; a decline below which would endanger life.

Book V: Money-Wages and Prices

The neoclassical theory professes the self-adjusting character of the economic system on an assumed fluidity of money-wages; and when there is rigidity, to lay on this rigidity the blame of maladjustment. The classical theory has it that a reduction in money-wages is capable, in certain circumstances, to stimulate output by diminishing the price of the finished product. Keynes's critique of this theory is that as it is not allowed to extend by analogy its conclusions in respect of a particular industry to industry as a whole, it is unable to answer the question of what effect on employment a reduction in money-wages will have. Pigou's summary of the classical theory on unemployment[36] reveals that this theory 'has nothing to offer', in Keynes's words.

Keynes then posed two questions: (1) does a reduction in money-wages have a direct tendency to increase employment, being taken to mean that the propensity to consume, the schedule of the mec and the rate of interest are the same as before for the community as a whole; and (2) does a reduction in money-wages have a certain probable tendency to affect employment in a particular direction through its certain probable repercussions on these three factors?

As for question 1, the volume of employment is uniquely correlated with the volume of effective demand (the sum of the expected consumption and expected investment) measured in wages and the effective demand can't change if the propensity to consume, the schedule of the mec and the rate of interest are all unchanged. If, without any change in these factors, the entrepreneurs were to increase employment as a whole, their proceeds will necessarily fall short of their supply price.

---

[36] Summarised in an appendix: ibid., 272–9.

There is no method of analysing the effect of a reduction in money-wages, except by following up its possible effects on the three factors: (1) a reduction of money-wages will somewhat reduce prices, and will thus involve some redistribution of real income; (2) from wage earners to other factors entering into marginal prime cost whose remuneration has not been reduced; and (3) from entrepreneurs to rentiers to whom a certain income fixed in terms of money has been guaranteed. The net effect of both will probably be negative. (4) If we are dealing with an unclosed system, and the reduction in money-wages is a reduction relative to money-wages abroad, when both are reduced to a common unit, it is evident that the change will be favourable to investment, since it will tend to increase the balance of trade. (5) In the case of an unclosed system, a reduction of money-wages, though it increases the favourable balance of trade, is likely to worsen the terms of trade. Thus there will be a decrease in real income. (6) If the reduction of money-wages is expected to be a reduction relative to money-wages in the future, the change will be favourable to investment, because it will increase the mec; whilst for the same reason it may be favourable to consumption. If on the other hand the reduction leads to the expectation of a further wage reduction, it will have precisely the opposite effect. (7) The reduction in the wage bills, accompanied by some reduction in prices and in money incomes, will diminish the need for cash for income and business purposes as a whole. This will reduce the rate of interest and thus prove favourable to investment. In this case, the effect of expectation concerning the future will be of an opposite tendency to those under 6 above. (8) Since a special reduction of money-wages is always advantageous to an individual entrepreneur or industry, a general reduction may also produce an optimistic sentiment in the minds of entrepreneurs, which may break through a vicious circle of unduly pessimistic estimates of the mec, and set things moving again. (9) The depressing influence on entrepreneurs of their greater burden of debt may partly offset any cheerful reactions from the reduction of wages.

There is no ground for the belief that a flexible wage policy is capable of maintaining a state of continuous full employment; any more than for the belief that an open market monetary policy is capable, unaided, of achieving this result. The economic system cannot be made self-adjusting along these lines.

There is a world of difference between a flexible wage policy and a flexible money policy. Keynes elaborated this point by going back to the three outstanding considerations above: (1) there is no means of securing uniform wage reductions for every class of labour. A change in the quantity of money is already within the power of most governments; (2) if money-wages are inflexible, such changes in prices as occur will mainly correspond to the diminishing marginal productivity of existing equipment as the output from it is increased; (3) the method of increasing the quantity of money by decreasing the wages increases proportionally the burden of debt; whereas the method of producing the same result by increasing the quantity of money, whilst leaving the wages unchanged, has the opposite effect; and (4) if a sagging rate of interest has to be brought about by a sagging wage level, there is a double drag on the mec and a double reason for putting off investment and thus postponing recovery.

It follows, therefore, that if labour were to respond to conditions of gradually diminishing employment by offering its services at a gradually diminishing money-wage, this would not have the effect of reducing real-wages and might even have the effect of increasing them, through its adverse effect on the volume of output. The main result would be a great instability of prices.

In light of these considerations, Keynes was of the opinion that the maintenance of a stable general level of money-wages is the most advisable policy for a closed system; whilst the same conclusion will hold good for an open system, provided that equilibrium with the rest of the world can be secured by means of fluctuating exchanges. For the long run, taking into consideration technical progress, wages should be allowed to rise slowly whilst keeping prices stable.

The Employment Function

The employment function only differs from the aggregate supply function in that it is, in effect, its inverse function and is defined in terms of the wage unit; the object of the employment function being to relate the amount of the effective demand, measured in terms of the wage unit, directed to a given firm or industry or to industry as a whole with the amount of employment, the supply price of the output of which will compare to that amount of effective demand.

The way in which we assume the increase in aggregate demand will be distributed between different commodities considerably influences the volume of employment. If, for example, the increased demand is largely directed towards products which have a high elasticity of employment, the aggregate increase in employment will be greater than if it is largely directed towards products which have a low elasticity of employment. Employment may diminish without there having been any change in aggregate demand, if the direction of demand is changed in favour of products having a low elasticity of employment. If the increased demand is directed to products with a relatively low elasticity of employment, a larger proportion of it will go to swell the incomes of entrepreneurs and a smaller to wage earners, with the possible result that the repercussions may be somewhat less favourable to expenditure, owing to the likelihood of entrepreneurs saving more of their increment of income than wage earners would.

When effective demand is deficient, there is under-employment of labour in the sense that there are men unemployed who would be willing to work at less than the existing real-wage. Consequently, as effective demand increases, employment increases, though at a real-wage equal or less than the existing one, until a point comes at which there is no surplus of labour available at the then existing real-wage.

What would happen next when this point has been reached, and expenditure continues to increase? The conditions of strict equilibrium require that wages and prices, and consequently profits as well, should all rise in the same proportion as expenditure, the 'real' position, including the volume of output and employment, being left unchanged in all respects. Then we have reached a situation in which the crude theory of money is fully satisfied.

However, there are qualifications to this conclusion: (1) rising prices may delude entrepreneurs into increasing employment beyond the level which maximises their individual profits measured in terms of the product, and (2) since the part of his profit which the entrepreneur has to hand on to the rentier is *fixed* in terms of money, rising prices will redistribute incomes to the advantage of the entrepreneur. After full employment will have been reached, a further rise in prices will mean that the rate of interest will have to rise somewhat to prevent prices from rising indefinitely, and that the increase in the quantity of money will be less than in proportion to the increase in expenditure.

A deflation of effective demand below the level required for full employment will diminish employment as well as prices. Inflation above this level will merely affect prices. This asymmetry is merely a reflection of the fact that labour is not in a position to insist on being offered work on a scale involving a real-wage which is not greater than the marginal disutility of that amount of employment.

The Theory of Prices

The effect of changes in the quantity of money on the price level can be considered as being compounded of the effect of the level of wages and the effect on employment. Further it is assumed that: (1) all unemployed resources are homogeneous and interchangeable in their efficiency to produce what is wanted, and (2) the factors of production entering into marginal cost are content with the same money-wage so long as there is a surplus of them unemployed. In this case we have constant returns and a rigid level of wages, so long as there is unemployment. It follows that an increase in the quantity of money will have no effect whatever on prices so long as there is any unemployment, and that employment will increase in exact proportion of any increase in the quantity of money. As soon as full employment is reached, it will thenceforward be the level of wages and prices which will increase in exact proportion to the increase in effective demand.

The quantity theory of money can be described as follows: so long as there is unemployment, employment will change in the same proportion as the quantity of money; and when there is full employment prices will change in the same proportion as the quantity of money. This is the tradition on the basis of the assumption as mentioned. Keynes then introduced possible complications which will influence events, such as: (1) the effective demand will not change in exact proportion to the quantity of money; (2) since resources are not homogeneous, there will be diminishing—and not constant—returns as employment gradually increases; and (3) wages will tend to rise before full employment is reached.

One must then first consider the effect of changes in the quantity of money on the quantity of effective demand; and the increase in effective demand will spend itself partly in increasing the quantity of employment and partly in raising the level of prices. Thus instead of constant prices in conditions of unemployment, we have in fact a condition of prices rising gradually as employment increases. Thus, the theory of prices must direct itself to the complications mentioned above.

1. The primary effect of a change in the quantity of money on the quantity of effective demand is through the rate of interest. Given the interdependence of various elements at play, one needs to take them into account. For example, the liquidity preference (which partly influences the quantity of effective demand), in turn depends on how much of the new money is absorbed into the income and industrial circulations, which depends—in turn—on how much effective demand increases and how the increase is divided between the rise of prices, the rise of wages and the volume of output and employment. Once we have all the facts before us, we shall have enough simultaneous equations to give us a determinate result. In any event, only in exceptional circumstances will an increase in the quantity of money be associated with a decrease in the quantity of effective demand. The ratio between the quantity of effective demand and the quantity of money closely corresponds to what is called the 'income velocity of money'. This ratio depends on many complex and variable factors.
2. The supply price will increase as output from a given equipment is increased; increasing output will be associated with rising prices.
3. As output increases a series of bottlenecks will be reached, where the supply of particular commodities ceases to be elastic and their prices have to rise to whatever level is necessary to divert demand into other directions. A moderate change in effective demand, coming on a situation where there is widespread unemployment, may spend itself very little in raising prices and mainly in increasing employment; whilst a larger change which, being unforeseen, causes some temporary

bottlenecks to be reached, will spend itself in raising prices to a greater extent at first than subsequently.
4. We have a succession of earlier semi-critical points (before the final critical one of full employment) at which increasing effective demand tends to raise money-wages, though not fully in proportion to the rise of the price of goods; and similarly in the case of decreasing demand.
5. The rates of remuneration of different factors in terms of money will show varying degrees of rigidity and they may also have varying degrees of elasticities of supply in response to changes in the money reward offered.

Perhaps the most important element in marginal cost which is likely to change in a different proportion from the wages, and also to fluctuate within much wider limits, is marginal user cost. For this cost may increase sharply when employment begins to improve, if the increase in effective demand brings a rapid change in the prevailing expectation as to the date when the replacement of equipment will be necessary.

When a further increase in the quantity of effective demand produces no further increase in output and entirely spends itself on an increase in the cost unit fully proportionate to the increase in effective demand, we have reached a condition of true inflation. The view that any increase in the quantity of money is inflationary is bound up with the underlying assumption of the classical theory that we are always in a condition where the reduction in the real rewards of the factors of production will lead to a curtailment in their supply.

What about changes in the quantity of money and its consequences in the long run for prices? The very long-run course of prices has almost always been upward. For when money is relatively abundant, wages rise; and when money is relatively scarce, some means is found to increase the effective quantity of money.

The long-run relationship between the national income and the quantity of money will depend on liquidity preferences. And the long-run stability or instability of prices will depend on the strength of the upward trend of the aggregate of wages compared with the rate of increase in the efficiency of the productive system.

Book VI: Short Notes Suggested by *The General Theory*

Notes on the Trade Cycle

Fluctuations in the propensity to consume and in the state of liquidity preference and in the mec, all play their part in explaining trade cycles. The regularity of the time sequence and duration of the cycle is mainly due to the way in which the mec fluctuates, however, aggravated by associated changes in the other significant short-period variables of the economic system.

A crisis starts when there is a sudden collapse in the mec. Liquidity preference only starts after the collapse in the mec. This collapse may be so complete that no reduction in the rate of interest will be enough. The return of confidence helps the recovery. A fall in the mec also tends to affect adversely the propensity to consume, as it involves a severe decline in stock prices, exerting a depressing influence on the propensity to consume, precisely in a situation when it is needed to increase.

Keynes then dealt with a situation in which capital is not so abundant that the community as a whole has no reasonable use for it anymore, but where investment is being made in conditions which are unstable and cannot endure, because it is prompted by (speculative) expectations which are destined to disappoint. This is a case in which investment is misdirected. Once this is discovered, the optimistic mood will be replaced by one of pessimism, that is, by overreacting in the negative sense. The right remedy for the trade cycle is then not to be found in abolishing booms and thus keeping us permanently in a semi-slump, but in abolishing slumps and thus keeping us permanently in a quasi-boom.

Except during the war, Keynes doubted if there is recent experience of booms so strong that they led to full employment. A state of full investment in the strict sense has never yet occurred. Hence, higher rates of interest would be the wrong remedy to redress the boom. For in this case those who attribute the disease to under-consumption would be wholly established. The remedy would lie in various measures designed to increase the propensity to consume by the redistribution of incomes or otherwise; so that a given level of employment would require a smaller volume of current investment to support it.

In cases where it is impracticable materially to increase investment, there is no means of securing a higher level of employment except by increasing consumption. There are two ways to expand output: (1) through increasing capital and (2) through increasing the propensity to consume.

Keynes finally pointed at Jevons's insight that trade cycles can be explained by fluctuations in agricultural prices. However, they are less important than in the past as agricultural output is now much smaller as a percentage of GDP, and globalised trade in agricultural products average out differences between good and bad harvests.

Notes on Mercantilism, the Usury Laws, Stamped Money and Theories of Under-Consumption

Keynes explained in this chapter that protection might increase domestic employment. Mercantilism promotes national advantages. The rate of interest and the volume of investment are not self-regulating. Keynes hoped that the technique of bank rates will never be used again to protect foreign balance in conditions in which it is likely to cause unemployment at home. Mercantilist thought never supposed that there was a self-adjusting tendency by which the rate of interest would be established at the appropriate level. On the contrary, they are empathic that an unduly high rate of interest depended on liquidity preference and the quantity of money. They were concerned both with the diminishing liquidity preference and the quantity of money. The mercantilists were aware of the fallacy of cheapness and the danger that excessive competition may turn the terms of trade against a country. They were also aware of the 'fear of goods' (i.e. prohibition of imports to protect employment at home) and the scarcity of money as causes of unemployment, which the classicals were to denounce two centuries later. Mercantilists killed two birds with one stone: on the one hand a country got rid of an unwelcome surplus of goods, which was believed to result in unemployment, while on the other hand the total stock of money in that country was increased with the resulting advantages of a fall in the rate of interest.

Throughout history, Keynes noted, there has been a chronic tendency for the propensity to save to be stronger than the inducement to invest. This latter aspect has been at all times the key to economic problems.

Never in history was there a method devised of such efficacy for setting each country's advantage at variance with its neighbour's advantage as the international gold standard. For it made domestic prosperity directly dependent on a competitive pursuit of markets and a competitive appetite for the precious metal. It is the policy of an autonomous rate of interest, unimpeded by international preoccupations, and of a national investment programme directed to an optimum level of domestic employment which is twice blessed in the sense that it helps us and our neighbours at the same time. And it is the simultaneous pursuit of these policies by all countries together which is capable of restoring economic health and strength internationally, whether we measure it by the level of domestic employment or by the volume of international trade. Keynes pointed to the constant tendency of the rate of interest to be too high.

He quoted with appreciation Bernard Mandeville's *Fable of the Bees*. Mandeville maintained that prosperity was increased by expenditure rather than by saving; an opinion which didn't go down well at the time. Malthus, in his later years, discovered that it was insufficiency of effective demand that could explain unemployment.

Concluding Notes on the Social Philosophy Towards Which *The General Theory* Might Lead

The outstanding faults of the economic society in which we live are its failure to provide for full employment and its arbitrary and inequitable distribution of wealth and incomes.

We have seen that the growth of capital doesn't depend on a low propensity to consume but is held back by it; only in conditions of full employment would a low propensity to consume be conducive to the growth of capital. Experience suggests that in existing conditions, saving by institutions and through sinking funds is more than adequate, and measures for the redistribution of incomes in a way likely to raise the propensity to consume may prove favourable to the growth of capital.

Keyes has shown that the extent of effective saving is necessarily determined by the scale of investment and that scale is promoted by a low rate of interest. It is in our best interest to reduce the rate of interest to that point relative to the schedule of the mec at which there is full employment.

Thus we might aim in practice at an increase in the volume of capital until it ceases to be scarce, so that the functionless investor will no longer receive a bonus; Keynes foresaw the 'euthanasia of the rentier'. It seems unlikely that the influence of the banking policy on the rate of interest will be sufficient by itself to determine an optimum rate of investment. Keynes conceived, therefore, that a somewhat comprehensive socialisation of investment will prove the only means of securing an approximation to full employment; though this need not exclude all manner of compromises and devices by which public authority will cooperate with private initiative.

It was Keynes's intention to indicate the nature of the environment which the free play of economic forces requires if it is to realise the full potentialities of production. The central controls necessary to ensure full employment will involve a large extension of the traditional functions of government. Keynes defended it both as the only practicable means to avoid the destruction of existing economic forms in their entirety, and as the condition of the successful functioning of individual initiative.

The authoritarian state systems of today seem to solve the problem of unemployment at the expense of efficiency and of freedom. It is certain that the world is associated with present-day capitalist individualism. But it may be possible by a right analysis of the problem to cure the disease whilst preserving efficiency and freedom.

Keynes brought to mind that laissez-faire and the gold standard forced governments in mitigating economic distress at home by the competitive struggle for markets abroad. Indeed, all measures helpful to a state of chronic underemployment were ruled out, except measures to improve the balance of trade. If nations learn to provide themselves with full employment by their domestic policy, there need be no economic forces to set the interest of one country against that of its neighbours.

In concluding, Keynes predicted that if his ideas are correct, their potency would not be disputed over a period of time. He concluded the book with a much-quoted text:

> … the ideas of economists and political philosophers … are more powerful than is commonly understood. Indeed the world is ruled by little else. Practical men, who believe themselves to be quite exempt from any intellectual influences, are usually the slaves of some defunct economist. Madmen in authority, who hear voices in the air, are distilling their frenzy from some academic scribbler of a few years back. Not, indeed, immediately, but after a certain interval; for in the field of economic and political philosophy there are not many who are influenced by new theories after they are twenty-five or thirty years of age, so that the ideas which civil servants and politicians and even agitators apply to current events are not likely to be the newest. But, soon or late, it is ideas, not vested interests, which are dangerous for good or evil.[37]

---

[37] Ibid., 383–4.

3

Capitalism or Socialism? That's the Question

Introduction

Winston Churchill once said that the inherent vice of capitalism was the unequal sharing of blessings, and the inherent virtue of socialism was the equal sharing of miseries. Churchill's observation may not have gone down well during the 1930s and 1940s when the fate of capitalism was hanging in the balance. The Great Depression, which in fact spanned more than a decade, wasn't particularly flattering for the capitalist system, while socialism as practised in the Soviet Union pretended not to have capitalist vices of extreme economic ups and downs, nor was there unemployment, according to the Soviets. Keynes's efforts were directed at helping to restore capitalism. In one of his essays he wrote,

> For my part, I think that Capitalism wisely managed, can probably be made more efficient for attaining economic ends than any alternative system yet in sight, but that in itself is in many ways extremely objectionable. Our problem is to work out a social organisation which shall be as efficient as possible without offending our notions of a satisfactory way of life.[1]

---

[1] Keynes, J.M. (1931) *Essays in Persuasion: Politics.* London: MacMillan & Co., 321.

His contemporary Joseph Schumpeter had a fascination for Marx. He investigated whether socialism could eclipse capitalism. The result Schumpeter arrived at was that it very well could, as he elaborately explained in *Capitalism, Socialism and Democracy*, which was published in 1942, during WWII. Two years later, another émigré to the USA, Karl Polanyi (1886–1964), also took a critical look at the prevailing capitalist system in *The Great Transformation*. Both works are classics and haven't been out of print since their first publication.

The biographies of Schumpeter and Polanyi are included in this chapter followed by summaries of *Capitalism, Socialism and Democracy* and *The Great Transformation*.

Biography: Joseph Alois Schumpeter (1883–1950)

The fame and academic reputation of Joseph Schumpeter, the prophet of innovation and analyst of short-term and long-term business cycles, has grown over the years. He certainly is one of the most influential economists who ever lived. One of his pupils, Robert Heilbroner, wrote a chapter about him in *The Worldly Philosophers* (1995), in which he said that Schumpeter carried his economic analysis of capitalism to its final optimistic conclusion, and then—ironically—pronounced doom on the system for noneconomic reasons. Other well-known pupils of Schumpeter are former Fed chairman Alan Greenspan, who said about Schumpeter's term 'creative destruction', that like many powerful ideas, it was simple. It became a buzzword during the dot-com craze. Other Schumpeter pupils were economics Nobel laureates Paul Samuelson and Robert Solow. Hyman Minsky, who in 1986 predicted the financial crisis of 2008, was another one. Marxist economist Paul Sweezy was also one of Schumpeter's pupils. Sweezy said about Schumpeter that he did not care what his pupils thought, as long as they did think.

The Economist's qualification of economists is that most of them live pretty dull lives. Schumpeter was anything but dull. Some observers characterised him as an *enfant terrible*. His best-remembered bon mot is that he had three wishes in life: to become a great lover, a great horseman and a great economist. He quipped that two of the three had already been granted to him, and added that there were already too many fine horsemen in Austria.

He maintained an aristocratic lifestyle, including—in his younger days—showing up late for classes in riding pants. At times he could afford living the good life. While Austria's Minister of Finance in 1919, he rented various houses and apartments in Vienna. He had himself driven to the ministry in a horse-drawn carriage, from time to time accompanied by sophisticated call girls. When he lost his money in 1924, he had to write articles and give lectures while in Germany and the United States to pay back the debts incurred, which he eventually did in full.

His Life

The year 1883 proved to be a fertile year for economics, as Joseph Alois Schumpeter and John Maynard Keynes were both born in that year. Schumpeter was born in February 1883 in Triesch (now Trest, Czech Republic), a small town in Moravia, then part of the Austro-Hungarian Empire to Catholic ethnic German parents. His father was a textile factory owner. Joseph hardly knew his father as he died when Joseph was 4 years old. His mother, Johanna, and young Joseph moved to Graz, Austria, as she wanted her son *Jozsi* to get the best education possible. Johanna married a retired general when Joseph was 11 years old. She convinced her new husband to move to Vienna. The capital city attracted many people, among them intellectual and artistic talents. By the time Schumpeter came to Vienna, Austria was economically progressing; it had the fourth largest concentration of commerce and industry in Europe.

Thanks to his stepfather's aristocratic connections, Schumpeter could attend the *Theresianum*, where the sons of nobles and other aristocrats were educated. There he learned the arts of riding and fencing. Language classes included instruction in two classical and three foreign languages. At the *Theresianum* he developed his aristocratic manners, promiscuous habits and elegant tastes. But that was one side of Joseph's personality. The other one was that of a curious scholar who, besides law, read philosophy, economics and sociology.

Schumpeter studied law at the University of Vienna. The famous Austrian School economist, Eugen von Böhm-Bawerk, oversaw his PhD thesis which he completed in 1906, when Schumpeter was only 23 years old. He then took off on an intellectual grand tour of Germany, France and England. While in Britain he divided his time between an aristocratic and an austere life. His aristocratic lifestyle included tailor-made suits, hunting, attending plays, dinner parties and weekends in countryside estates.

In Britain he fell in love with an upper-class English woman, Gladys Ricarde-Seaver, 12 years his senior. After having married in 1907, the couple left for Egypt which had a boom economy at the time. Schumpeter worked for an Italian law firm in Cairo, and managed the finances of an Egyptian princess. There he made a good deal of money. In-between his business affairs, he wrote a book: *The Nature and Essence of Theoretical Economics* (1908). Schumpeter fell ill in Egypt, after which the couple returned to Europe in 1909.

Schumpeter took up the position of associate professor of economics and government at the University of Czernowitz, now Chernivtsi, Ukraine. He was then only 26 years old, the youngest professor in the entire Austro-Hungarian Empire. He wrote during his time at Czernowitz *The Theory of Economic Development* (1911), in which the constant change under capitalism played a central role. He moved from Czernowitz to the University of Graz 3 years later where he taught political economy. He stayed in Graz until he received an invitation from Columbia University in New York to teach there during the academic year 1913–1914.

When the Great War broke out in 1914 he returned to Austria. After the war the Austro-Hungarian Empire was split up; the Emperor went into exile. Vienna was cut off from its hinterland which used to provide the necessary foodstuffs to feed its population, fuel and raw materials for industrial production. In short, Austria was broke, the Viennese were starving and Austria had a huge war debt to pay.

Schumpeter was invited to join a group of German and Austrian socialist politicians to discuss the question how privately owned factories and businesses could be nationalised. Word has it that a young economist asked Schumpeter how someone who had extolled enterprise could possibly take part in a commission whose aim was to nationalise it. Schumpeter replied that if somebody wants to commit suicide, it is a good thing if a doctor is present. A member of that group was Otto Bauer, then Austria's Minister of Foreign Affairs. He was urged to include Schumpeter in the Cabinet. Chancellor Karl Renner gave Schumpeter the near impossible position of Minister of Finance. After all, Austria had hardly any gold and other financial reserves left, food had to be bought abroad and there were no funds to finance the government's budget; most funding had to come from the victorious Allies.

Schumpeter presented his *Finanzplan* in 1919 to save his country from sinking even deeper. One of its primary aims was to prevent the Austrian currency's exchange rate from dropping, let alone collapsing. He was also convinced, as he later described in *Capitalism, Socialism and Democracy* (1942), that a nation's resources and landmass mean less than what was done with them by *entrepreneurs* who should be allowed to create new enterprises, supported by a functioning financial sector and as few trade barriers as possible. Another aspect of his plan was to impose a one-time tax on property, the proceeds of which could be used to pay off government bond holders. He also proposed the creation of a central bank.

Despite all his plans, the value of the Austrian krone started to drop in value. There was no help from the Allies. So, the government had no option but to print money. And once the very harsh war reparation conditions of the St Germain Treaty (the Versailles Treaty addressed the German Empire) became known for the Austro-Hungarian Empire, the krone went into a free-fall. Schumpeter's position became untenable. He was sacked at the end of 1919 when he challenged the government's plans of an *Anschluss* (Union) with Germany. As a farewell present, parliament granted him a banking license.

Schumpeter went back for a brief stint to the University of Graz until he was appointed president of the Biedermann Bank in 1921. He held that position until the bank collapsed in 1924 after the Viennese stock market crash. Schumpeter lost his job and his fortune, which he had assembled during the previous years.

He divorced Gladys and married Annie Reisinger, a young woman whom he had known since her infancy, as she was the daughter of the concierge of the building where he and his mother lived when they came to Vienna.

Schumpeter returned to Academia in 1925 when he was appointed to the University of Bonn, Germany, to teach public finance. The Schumpeters were happy in Bonn, but happiness was short-lived. His mother, to whom he was very much attached, died in the same year. Briefly after that sad loss, his wife Annie died while giving birth to their child who also died. These were deeply tragic losses which he never really overcame. He plunged himself into frantic work, interrupted with guest lectureships at Harvard in 1927–1928 and 1930. In 1931 he went to Japan where he lectured at the Tokyo College of Commerce. He started the habit of grading himself from 0 to 1 for his accomplishments in his diary. The low scores during those years reflected that he was seldom happy with his daily accomplishments.

Like so many other Central European scholars, Schumpeter moved to the United States to take up a professorship at Harvard University in 1932. He became a US citizen in 1939. Schumpeter married the American scholar Elizabeth Boody. She helped him to popularise his writings. Schumpeter stayed at Harvard until his death on 8 January 1950.

Schumpeter's Academic Work

During Schumpeter's first visit to Britain in 1908 he attended classes at the London School of Economics and he studied in the British Museum's library, making sure always to study at the same table where Karl Marx wrote *The Capital*. Schumpeter became fascinated by Darwin's theory of natural selection. It seemed to him as if economic theory had overlooked the evolutionary character of economic development. Economic theory was basically static: the economy revolved around its equilibrium. The dynamic dimension was missing in the theory, which Marx had recognised. Schumpeter was the first economist to talk about the dynamics of capitalism. He concluded that the whole idea of equilibrium became problematical, as continual disruption was the basis for economic development; it embodied the essence of capitalism.

Schumpeter discovered that what Darwin had done for biology, Marx had done for economics. Two questions stood out: (1) Can one prove the existence of economic development in the sense that growth can be traced to economic rather than external causes, such as political developments or population growth?, and (2) Can capitalism and democracy persist? For Schumpeter the process of growth and development was not only an *endogenous* process, it also implied that the economy was getting bigger, development resulted in rising living standards and that the economy's structure also changed. He wrote in *Capitalism, Socialism and Democracy*, 'The cumulative power of capitalism doesn't typically consist in "providing more silk stockings for queens" but in bringing them within the reach of factory girls in return for decreasing amounts of effort.'[2]

There was no stationary state of the economy and no law of diminishing returns; no, it was the perennial gale of creative destruction, innovation, entrepreneurship and productivity growth that propelled development. With innovation Schumpeter meant the profitable application of new ideas rather than invention per se. It could involve many types of change: a new product, production process, supply source, market or type of organisation. And innovation triggers disruptive discontinuous leaps and bounds. Innovation is *the* driving force behind business cycles. The entrepreneur—supported by accessible and cheap credit—was the one to revolutionise the production process by exploiting an invention while destroying old patterns of production and organisation, driven by a will to establish a private empire and to fight and earn others' respect. And there was of course also the simple joy of creating, getting things done by simply exercising one's ingenuity. Schumpeter observed about the important role of credit that the headquarters of capitalism is the money market—the place where credit is allocated.

At Harvard he was a popular teacher. He relished lecturing and debating with his students. Strangely enough, he never lectured about his own academic work. He was a bit of an outsider among his colleagues. Schumpeter was not a Keynesian, unlike most of his colleagues at Harvard. They were the ones to introduce Keynesianism in America. While at Harvard, Schumpeter published his classic *Capitalism, Socialism and Democracy* in 1942, preceded by *Business Cycles: A Theoretical and Statistical Analysis of the Capitalist Process* (1939).

In his *Business Cycles*, Schumpeter maintains that it is the entrepreneur who disturbs the classical equilibrium. The entrepreneur creates economic waves through the application of innovations. Schumpeter identified three cycles along various time scales: the longest being the Kondratiev cycle,

---

[2] *Capitalism, Socialism and Democracy*, 67. The edition used is the 12th impression of Unwin University Books (1970).

spanning a period of 45–60 years. Great innovations drive the Kondratiev cycle, starting with the Industrial Revolution, followed by railroad construction, the introduction of motor cars, electricity and chemical products, and the dot.com revolution. Within the Kondratiev cycle, there are two Juglar ones ranging from 7 to 11 years, comparable to the business cycle people normally refer to. Within the Juglar wave there are two (or three) Kitchin waves, caused by changes in inventories held by businesses. Schumpeter left out the Kuznets wave (15–25 years), as he didn't recognise it as a valid cycle. If each of these waves is in phase, especially in the downward movement, it would explain disastrous slumps and consequent depressions. *Business Cycles* represented Schumpeter's interpretation of the history of capitalism, characterised by rapid growth and instability. This book also contained elements which would be elaborated in full force a few years later in *Capitalism, Socialism and Democracy*. He projected at the end of *Business Cycles* that capitalism would continue to flourish for a couple of decades more. He underscored that, despite the economic success of the system, faith in the values and virtues of the civilisation that capitalism produced was losing its mobilising force.

The publication of *Business Cycles* in 1939 was overshadowed by Keynes's *General Theory* that had appeared 3 years earlier, and had attracted a lot of international attention and admiration. Moreover, *The General Theory* provided a prescription to cure the Great Depression, while Schumpeter's *Business Cycles* didn't.

> Schumpeter reviewed *The General Theory*, probably inspired by professional jealousy and certainly by intellectual disagreement. He noted that Keynes's theory is not really a general theory, as it applies to a specific situation: a particular kind of capitalist economy in depression.
> He accused Keynes of having designed a theory which fits his proposed policy of deficit spending by government. Schumpeter concluded that Keynes's argument confuses practical issues with scientific ones and divides economists along lines of political preference rather than analytical ability. Keynes believed that there could be prolonged equilibrium at low levels of investment and employment. Schumpeter's vision of capitalism rejected the possibility of long-term stagnation.

> Schumpeter didn't give Keynes sufficient credit for ideas that were to become part and parcel of economists' vocabulary such as the multiplier, the propensity to consume, the liquidity preference and for his invention of macroeconomics. Yet, Schumpeter himself made a Keynesian proposal during the early 1930s to inject US$9 billion of emergency public spending into the US economy. This proposed huge sum was larger than anything put into the New Deal.
> The mutual distaste they felt towards each other's work was a pity as Schumpeter's writings provided a good corrective to Keynes's omission of the importance of innovation in capitalist evolution; Schumpeter broke the spell of the static approach to economic problems. And Schumpeter's own shortcomings lay in the areas that Keynes's theory illuminated: where consumption and investment could be considered as aggregates, and where analysts could think in macroeconomic terms.

In *Capitalism, Socialism and Democracy* Schumpeter—like Marx—applies a sociological, political and historical approach to economics. He poses the question, 'Can capitalism survive?' And he responded: 'No. I do not think it can.' The entrepreneurs of innovative businesses will gradually be replaced by salaried managers of bureaucratised corporations, resulting in a loss of innovative vitality. These large firms help to socialise the bourgeois mind, and, compounded by the growing number of intellectuals critical of the capitalist system, limit the scope of capitalist motivation and eventually kill its roots. So, like Marx, he predicted the demise of capitalism. Heilbroner concluded in *The Worldly Philosophers*, 'But he has bested Marx by demonstrating—or at least arguing—that capitalism will give way to socialism for Schumpeter's reasons, not for Marx's!'[3]

What about socialism? Can it work? Schumpeter argued that it could. First, if a mature stage of industrial development has been reached, and second, that transitional problems can be successfully resolved. Schumpeter concluded, contrary to—for example—Hayek, that a socialist system is perfectly manageable. It should be borne in mind, warned Schumpeter, that a socialist economy requires a huge bureaucracy, or

---

[3] *The Worldly Philosophers*, 303.

at least social conditions favourable to its emergence and functioning. Schumpeter drove the argument even further: in a socialist system it is easier to handle uncertainties such as the ones that business leaders in capitalist economies encounter. There are no uncertainties, as the managers of socialised industries would know exactly what they are supposed to produce. The reader wonders whether all these rosy assumptions about a socialist society would be realistic, given the fact that Schumpeter was, at heart, a self-styled conservative.

The section dealing with the question whether socialism can work was written in an ironical, contradictory, typical Schumpeter style, and misunderstood by various commentators at the time. Schumpeter's biographer, Thomas McCraw, concluded in his *Prophet of Innovation* (2007) that careful reading of this section suggests that Schumpeter's purpose had been to praise capitalism and condemn socialism.

As for democracy, socialism poses more problems for democracy than capitalism does. Capitalism has an advantage because bourgeois life restricts the sphere of politics by limiting the sphere of public authority. Schumpeter points to the fact that modern democracy rose along with capitalism. The question is then, Can there be democratic socialism? Yes, says Schumpeter, but only with great difficulty. Socialist democracy can only function provided the vast majority of the people are resolved to abide by the rules of the democratic game.

Capitalism, Socialism and Democracy's third edition of 1950 includes the text of his speech 'The March into Socialism' delivered before the American Economic Association (AEA) in December 1949, of which he was the first non-American born president. In that speech Schumpeter talked about the tendencies in the American—and European—economies pointing to the possibility of stagnation of the capitalist process in favour of planned economies. Schumpeter said that he did not advocate socialism, nor did he have any intention of discussing its desirability. He did not want to 'prophesy' or to predict. What he did, he said, was to diagnose observable tendencies.

Although not a mathematician himself, Schumpeter was instrumental in establishing the Econometric Society, of which he held the presidency in 1940–1941. His interest in econometrics was a reflection of his quest for exact economics, as he called it. Schumpeter tried to make economics a science comparable to chemistry and physics. He didn't succeed as he realised that exceptional innovators and inventors, and their agent, the entrepreneur, change the course of economic events. Their innovations and inventions don't lend themselves to generalisations and, thus, limit economist's ability to forecast the future.

After Schumpeter died in 1950, his wife Elizabeth Boody prepared the publication of his *History of Economic Analysis* (1954). This book was truly a tour de force. Schumpeter wrote his publisher that the book would describe the development and the fortunes of scientific analysis in the field of economics from Greco-Roman times to the present. And that is what he accomplished.

His Legacy

Schumpeter provided the best guide to the rapid economic changes that the world witnessed after WWII. Schumpeter's term 'creative destruction' is probably the most widely used metaphor in contemporary economic writing.

As regards Schumpeter's theoretical legacy, his dynamic analysis of economic development could not be translated into mathematical models. After all, political, sociological and historical aspects play important parts in Schumpeter's analysis, which—by their nature—are unpredictable. It was therefore difficult to turn Schumpeter's insights into theoretical models capable of deriving testable implications.

Schumpeter does have intellectual heirs (i.e. the neo-Schumpeterian school). They have broadened the basis upon which innovations take place. While Schumpeter foresaw a diminishing role for individual innovators/entrepreneurs, his heirs introduced a national 'system of innovation' model, which studies the interaction between different actors, such as firms, universities, research institutes and government.

Scores of business schools are named after him. *The Economist* named a weekly column about entrepreneurship and innovation after him, and the European Union's innovation programme is inspired by Schumpeter's thinking, which—as some commentators said—was to economics what Freud was to the mind.

To memorialise Schumpeter, Harvard University put up a bronze tablet with the text, *Although he became one of the most cosmopolitan of men, the experience of those early years in Vienna never really left him. He remained to the end the cultivated Austrian gentleman of the old school.*

Capitalism, Socialism and Democracy

Schumpeter wrote *Capitalism, Socialism and Democracy* in the late 1930s and early 1940s when the Western world was trying to recover from the Great Depression, fascism was on the rise and WWII broke out.[4] In short, people were deeply apprehensive about the future: Would capitalism and democracy weather these storms or would communism be triumphant?

Schumpeter was of the opinion, inspired by Karl Marx, that capitalism would collapse under the weight of its own success and that socialism could very well replace it. He was wrong on both counts; that is, for now. The rules of the economic game in the world are, overwhelmingly, the ones of capitalism, and there are now more democracies than ever before. We only know two things about the future: (1) that in some ways history repeats itself and (2) the future is unpredictable.

Capitalism, Socialism and Democracy consists of five parts. Part I is a critical analysis of the Marxian doctrine. The second part deals with the question whether capitalism can survive. Part III asks whether socialism can work, while part IV compares socialism and democracy. Finally, part V provides a historical sketch of socialist parties in Europe and the United States from 1875 until WWII.

Schumpeter's writing style here and there shows a touch of irony. *Capitalism, Socialism and Democracy* is not an easy read; one really has to concentrate on what Schumpeter is telling the reader. The book contains a chapter on creative destruction; a term coined by Schumpeter that has become part of our vocabulary. He wrote in the preface to the second edition, 'And I hold that with increasing mechanisation of industrial

---

[4] Part V: A Historical Sketch of Socialist Parties has not been summarised. Schumpeter's speech 'The March into Socialism' before the American Economic Association in New York on 30 December 1949 is included.

'progress" (teamwork in research departments and so on) this element and with it the most important pillar of the capitalist class's economic position is bound to crumble in time.'[5]

The book is not defeatist, according to Schumpeter. It is addressed to sponsors of private-enterprise society and sponsors of democratic socialism. Both of them, says Schumpeter in the same preface, stand to gain from the book if they will see more clearly—than they usually do—the nature of the social situation in which it is their fate to act.

Part I: The Marxian Doctrine

Marx the Prophet

Writing about socialism without analysing what the great socialist thinker had to say about it would be inconceivable. Marxism enjoyed a revival when Schumpeter wrote his book. The Marxian doctrine was applied in the Soviet Union; however, there was a great gulf between what was practised there and the true meaning of Marx's message.

Karl Marx was a prophet and in order to appreciate his achievement one must visualise his work in his own time: roughly the middle of the nineteenth century when the bourgeois civilisation was at its zenith. The Marxist message relayed hope and a new meaning for life for the toiling masses. Marxism became a form of religion; it created fanatic 'believers' who blindly followed what the prophet had said, that is, that his followers would be victorious. Schumpeter admired Marx, because he was able to give hope to millions of people. He also recognised Marx's erudition; he found him a 'learned man'.

Marx the Sociologist

Marx had a passion for philosophy. The pure philosophy of the German variety was Marx's starting point. He was a neo-Hegelian. The economic interpretation of history does not mean that men are primarily inspired

---

[5] *Capitalism, Socialism and Democracy*, ix.

by economic motives. On the contrary, the explanation of the role and mechanism of non-economic motives and the analysis of the way in which social reality mirrors itself in the individual mind is an essential element of Marx's theory and one of its most significant contributions.

Marx tried to unveil the economic conditions that shape ethical ideas and political volitions that account for their rise and fall. Ideas and values were for Marx the transmission belts in the social engine. Marx's theory can be summarised in two propositions: (1) the conditions of production are the fundamental determinants of social structures which, in turn, breed attitudes, actions and civilisations; and (2) the forms of production themselves have a logic of their own; that is, they change according to necessities inherent in them so as to produce their successors by their own working.

Marx noted in an oft-quoted statement that the hand-mill creates feudal societies and the steam-mill capitalist societies. The rise and working of the steam-mill in turn creates new social functions and locations, new groups and views, which develop and interact in such a way as to outgrow their own frame. Here, then, we have the propeller which is responsible for economic and, in consequence, for social change. The history of society is the history of class struggle. But social structures and attitudes, Schumpeter argues, are 'coins that do not readily melt'; once they are formed, they persist.

What distinguished Marx from other economists is that he recognised the importance of the role of social classes. Others saw them as sets of individuals who display some common character like landlords, farmers or workmen. Marx saw two classes: the haves—the capitalists—and the have-nots who have to sell their labour; the labouring class, the proletariat. Marx recognised the existence of intermediate groups, such as clerks and professionals, but he saw them as anomalies that would disappear in the course of the capitalist process. Capitalists and the proletariat are antagonists in Marx's view and it is inherent in the design of capitalist society: the very nature of the relation between the capitalist class and the proletariat is strife. Capitalists will destroy each other and destroy the capitalist system as well.

The logic of the capitalist system is that it grew out of a feudal state of society, and not—as Schumpeter noted—as a result of very intelligent and hard-working people who made it capitalist. Marx turned a blind eye to this aspect. This is the weak part of his thinking; his thesis doesn't properly explain what really happened. The division between people who are supposed to be capitalists forever and those who are supposed to be proletarians forever is utterly unrealistic and misses the point about social classes: the rise and fall of families into and out of the upper strata.

For Marx the modes of production determine the social structure and, through it, all manifestations of civilisation and the whole march of cultural and political history. This explains why Marx was forced to make his two classes a purely economic phenomenon. It was in fact a smart stroke of analytical strategy which linked the fate of the class phenomenon with the fate of capitalism in such a way that socialism became by definition the only possible kind of classless society. This ingenious tautology could not well have been secured by any definitions of classes and of capitalism other than the ones chosen by Marx. What he deliberately overlooked was that there is not so much a relationship of antagonism between the two classes as there is typically one of cooperation. But he had no choice because of the requirements of his own analysis.

Marx the Economist

To talk about Marx the economist is to talk about his theories of surplus value. Marx was inspired by Ricardo and Quesnay. Both Marx and Ricardo say that the value of every commodity is proportional to the quantity of labour contained in it, measured in the hours of work. Neither have anything useful to say about monopolies or imperfect competition. We now know that the theory of value is unsatisfactory. Moreover, the theory of value doesn't work as a tool of analysis. First, it doesn't work outside the classic case of perfect competition and, second, it never works smoothly, except if labour were the only factor of production and if it were all of one kind. So reasoning along the lines of the labour theory is skating on very thin ice.

As regards Marx's theory of exploitation, it says that it did not arise from individual situations occasionally, but that it resulted from the very logic of the capitalist system, unavoidably and quite independently of any individual intention. The number of labour hours that enters into production, in a situation of a perfect equilibrium, is equal to the number of labour hours it takes to rear, feed and house a labourer.

However, the capitalist can exact more actual hours of labour than he paid for, thereby creating surplus value for the capitalist. So the capitalist exploits his worker. Marx doesn't deal with the phenomena of unfair pricing, restriction of production or cheating the markets; that would complicate his reasoning. Schumpeter rejects this theory also on the ground that it can never be applied to the commodity of labour as this would imply that workmen, like machines, are being produced according to rational calculations; and that is not the case in real life. Moreover, perfect competitive equilibrium cannot exist in a situation in which all capitalist employers make exploitation gains. This would trigger more production and wage increases and reduce the exploitation gains to zero.

Another aspect of Marx's theory is the inherent tendency of the rate of profit to fall. This follows from the increase in relative importance of the part of the total capital in the wage-goods industries: if the relative importance of plant and equipment increases in those industries, as it does in the course of capitalist evolution, and if the rate of surplus value remains the same, then the rate of return to total capital will decrease.

Marx's theory of accumulation boils down to the following: the main part of the profit, wrung out of exploited labour, is turned into capital. As already mentioned, exploitation gains induce the capitalist to expand production, which, in turn, leads to higher wages and lower prices.

Capitalist economies are not stationary; they are incessantly revolutionised from within by new enterprise. So, any existing structures and all the conditions involved in doing business are always in a process of change. New products, or old products being produced more cheaply, compete with the old ones, forcing their producers to invest by ploughing back part of their profits. The conclusion is that everyone accumulates. The aggregate rate of profit on total industrial production does not fall in the long run. However, the profit of every individual plant is incessantly being threatened by actual or potential competition from new commodities or methods of production.

Marx's theory of concentration says that there is a tendency of the capitalist process to increase the size both of industrial plants and of units of control. To predict the advent of big business was, considering the time Marx developed his theory, an achievement in itself.

Probably the best-known theory is Marx's theory of *Verelendung*, which Schumpeter translates as 'immiserisation'. In the course of capitalist evolution real-wage rates and the standard of living of the masses would fall in the better-paid strata of workers, and fail to improve in the worst-paid strata as a result of the logic of the capitalist process. However, economic development proved that this was not the case; in general the wages improved quite dramatically. Marx needed to introduce the phenomenon of an industrial reserve army of unemployed people to explain that wages would go down.

What Marx had to say about business cycles is difficult to appraise as he had no simple theory of the business cycle. Marx's mechanical process of accumulation as far as its logic is concerned, is essentially prosperity-less and depression-less. Marx used the term 'crisis'. Believing that capitalist evolution would someday disrupt the institutional framework of capitalist society, he thought that before the actual breakdown occurred capitalism would begin to work with increasing friction and would display the symptoms of a fatal illness. Marx showed a tendency to link recurrent crises with this unique crisis of the capitalist order. He even suggested that the former may in a sense be looked upon as previews of the ultimate breakdown.

Schumpeter suggests that capitalist evolution will eventually destroy the foundation of capitalist society. He uses other arguments for it than Marx. Schumpeter concludes,

> Thus, the author of so many misconceptions was also the first to visualise what even at the present time is still the economic theory of the future for which we are slowly and laboriously accumulating stone and mortar, statistical facts and functional equations.[6]

Marx the Teacher

The trait peculiar to the Marxian system is that it subjects historical events and social institutions themselves to the explanatory process of economic analysis. No longer is politics an independent factor that

---
[6] Ibid., 43.

may be abstracted from an investigation of fundamentals, but plays, in Schumpeter's words,

> either the role of a naughty boy who viciously tampers with a machine when the engineer's back is turned, or else the role of a *deus ex machina* by virtue of the mysterious wisdom of a doubtful species of mammals deferentially referred to as 'statesmen'.[7]

Schumpeter gives an example of Marxian synthesis as a problem-solving engine: the Marxian theory of imperialism. Colonial expansion is prompted by falling rates of profit in the capitalist countries. This occurs in the last stage of capitalism. Once the colonies start to produce their own manufactured products, exports from the mother countries decline, leading to frictions between the colonies and the imperial countries, and ensuing lack of outlets, bankruptcies and other disasters may be anticipated. History is as simple as that. But it isn't that simple. The theory doesn't reflect what really happened. For example: the time of colonial adventure was precisely the time of early and immature capitalism when accumulation was in its beginnings and any barrier to the exploitation of domestic labour was absent. All told, it was as much a movement towards higher wages as it was one towards higher profits, and in the long run it certainly benefitted the proletariat more than it benefitted the capitalist interest.

Finally, Schumpeter deals with the issue whether Marx's theory would fall under the term scientific socialism; scientific, implying—among other things—forecasting. Marx's theory suggests that the proletariat will 'take over', and, through its dictatorship, put a stop to the 'exploitation of man by man' and bring about a classless society. Obviously, Marx's forecast was wrong.

Part II: Can Capitalism Survive?

Can capitalism survive? Schumpeter answers, 'No. I do not think it can.'[8] What arguments does the author provide for his opinion? The main argument is that capitalism's very success undermines the social institutions in

---
[7] Ibid., 47.
[8] Ibid., 61.

which it will not be able to live and which strongly point to socialism as their heir apparent. Schumpeter notes that his final conclusion does not differ from that of most socialist writers; in particular that of all Marxists.

The Rate of Increase of Total Output

A first test of economic performance is total output, that is, the total of all the commodities and services produced in a unit of time: a year, a month, what have you. Schumpeter described the dramatic drop in the American output during the Great Depression and beyond. He said that the resumed slump after 1937 is easily accounted for by the difficulties in adapting to a newly introduced fiscal policy, new labour legislation and a general change in the attitude of government to private enterprise; all of which can be distinguished from the working of the productive apparatus as such. So extensive and rapid a change of the social scene affected productive performance. This accounted for the fact that the USA, which had the best chance of recovering quickly, was precisely the one to experience the most unsatisfactory recovery.

As for the evolution in the distribution of American incomes, there is, as long as the capitalist system is left to itself, no reason to believe that the distribution of incomes or the dispersion about America's average income would in 1978 be significantly different from what it was in 1928. Schumpeter concludes that if capitalism repeated its past growth performance of, on average, 2 % per year for another half century starting with 1928, this would do away with poverty, even in the lowest strata of the population. Measured in real terms, relative shares have substantially changed in favour of the lower-income groups. This follows from the fact that the capitalist engine has become an engine of mass production; whereas, climbing upwards in the scale of individual incomes, one finds that the increased proportion is being spent on personal services and on handmade commodities, the prices of which are largely a function of wage rates.

Appraisal of an economic order would be incomplete—and un-Marxian—if it stopped at the output which the corresponding 'economic conveyor' hands to the various groups of society and left out: (1) those things that the conveyor does *not* serve directly but for which it provides the means as well as the political volition, and (2) all those cultural achievements that are induced by the mentality it generates. As regards the former, Schumpeter touches upon unemployment. Supernormal unemployment is one of the features of the periods of adaptation that follow on the prosperity phase.

Unemployment has always been a scourge. Nevertheless, the real tragedy is not unemployment per se, but unemployment plus the impossibility of providing adequately for the unemployed. Unemployment would lose its terror if the private lives of the employed were not seriously affected by their becoming unemployed. Schumpeter ends the chapter by stating that the unemployment figure was increased by anti-capitalist policies beyond what it needed to have been in the 1930s, by the fact that public opinion immediately insisted on economically irrational methods of financing relief, and on lax and wasteful methods of administering it.

Plausible Capitalism

The commercial and industrial bourgeoisie rose by business success. It created a scheme of motives that is unsurpassed in simplicity and force. Spectacular prizes are thrown to a small minority of winners. However, maximum performance of an optimally selected group is geared to money-making and not to social service; it aims at maximising profits instead of welfare. In the classical theory every producer produces up to the point where the product earns as much as it gets without running into a loss.

The classics assumed a situation of perfect competition. But this doesn't exist in real life with the exception of the market of agricultural mass production. We live in the age of monopolistic competition. There is no longer the cherished situation of equilibrium. In the case of a monopoly or oligopoly there is in fact no determinate equilibrium at all, and the possibility presents itself that there may be an endless sequence of moves and countermoves, an indefinite state of warfare between firms. So the beneficial competition of the classics is replaced by cut-throat competition or simply by struggles of control in the financial sphere. There will be social waste, and many other types of waste, such as the costs of advertising campaigns, the suppression of new methods of production and so forth. Under these conditions there are no longer guarantees of full employment or maximum output in the sense of the theory of perfect competition. Equilibrium may exist *without* full employment; it is even bound to exist at a level of output below that maximum mark, because profit-conserving strategy, impossible in conditions of perfect competition, now imposes itself.

The Process of Creative Destruction

Perfect competition triggers maximum performance in production according to the classical theory. Once monopolies or oligopolies enter the scene, there is no perfect competition. However, nothing in the time series of total output suggests a break in the trend since the emergence of monopolistic competition. Moreover, the standard of living of the masses improved during the period of unfettered big business as shown by the fact that the workman was able to buy more than in the past based on the hours of work. It is big business that was responsible for the improvement in the standard of living.

Capitalism is by nature economic change; it can never be stationary. And this evolutionary character is not only due to the fact that economic life goes on in a social and natural environment which changes—and by its change—alters the data of economic action. These changes often condition industrial change; however, they are not its prime movers. The fundamental impulse that acts and keeps the capitalist engine in motion comes from the new consumer goods, the new methods of production and transportation, the new markets and the new forms of industrial organisation that capitalist enterprise causes.

The history of the productive apparatus is a history of revolutions. These revolutions occur in discrete rushes which are separated from each other by spans of comparative quiet. The process works continuously, however, in the sense that there always is either revolution or absorption of the results of revolution, both together forming business cycles. The economic structure creates and destroys from within old ways of producing goods and services. This process of creative destruction is the essential fact about capitalism.

Schumpeter notes that it doesn't make sense to appraise a process at a given point in time; one must judge it over a long period of time. Moreover, since we are dealing with an organic process, analysis of what happens in part of it (e.g. an individual concern) is inconclusive beyond that.

The problem that is usually visualised is how capitalism administers existing structures, whereas the relevant problem is how it creates and destroys them. Schumpeter underscores this point by saying that as long as a researcher doesn't recognise this, he or she does a meaningless job. In the past, price competition was most important in economic analysis. Now, quality competition and sales effort (i.e. advertising, marketing) are entering into the analysis. It is the competition from the new commodity, the new technology, the new type of organisation, that commands a decisive cost or quality advantage and that strikes not at the margin of the profits and the outputs of existing firms but at the foundations and their very lives. This type of competition is an ever-present threat.

Monopolistic Practices

The impact of new technologies considerably reduces the long-term scope of conserving established positions. It is through *restricting* practices that positions are temporarily maintained. Although there is no point in conserving obsolescent industries, there is a point in trying to avoid their coming down with a crash, and in attempting to turn a rout (which may become a centre of cumulative depressive effects) into an orderly retreat. Schumpeter warns that his argument for restraint doesn't cover all cases of restrictive or regulating strategy. It doesn't amount to a case against state regulation. Rational, as distinguished from vindictive, regulation by public authorities turns out to be an extremely delicate problem which not every government agency can be trusted to solve.

As regards the phenomenon of rigid prices this is typically a short-run one. There are no major instances of long-term rigidity of prices, as prices do not fail to adapt themselves to technological progress; frequently they fall spectacularly in response to it. Business strategy has it that it tries to avoid seasonal, random and cyclical fluctuations. This is why prices don't promptly fall in recessions.

The real question is how short-term rigidity may affect long-term development of total output. Rigidity of prices in an economic downturn may lead to depressive effects as buyers may be 'broke' by the amount to which the particular industry profits. If the buyers are the kind of people who spend all they can and if that particular industry doesn't spend the profit but keeps it idle, the total expenditure in the economy will be reduced. If this happens other industries may suffer and if they then restrict in turn, one may get an accumulation of depressive effects. In other words, rigidity may so influence the amount and distribution of national income as to decrease the balances and to increase idle balances (i.e. savings).

Price rigidity is motivated by low sensitiveness of demand to short-term price changes. The refusal of lowering prices strengthens the position of the industries which adopt that policy either by increasing their revenue or simply by avoiding chaos in their markets. Total output and employment may well keep on a higher level with the restrictions incident to that policy than they would if depression were allowed to play its part with the price structure. In other words, under the conditions created by capitalist evolution, perfect and universal flexibility of prices might in a depression further destabilise the system, instead of stabilising it.

Long-run monopolies are rare, as the power to exploit at pleasure a given demand can under the conditions of functioning capitalism hardly persist for a long period. Schumpeter adds that outside the field of public utilities, the position of a single seller can in general be conquered only on the condition that he or she does not behave like a monopolist.

Schumpeter presents quite a few examples which refute the classical doctrine of perfect competition and the related optimal allocation of resources with respect to a given distribution of income. That position is no longer tenable; not in the least since a new field of research arose: that of the dynamic theory developed by Hicks, Tinbergen and Frisch. Once equilibrium has been destroyed by some disturbance, the process of establishing a new one is not as sure, prompt and economical as the old theory of perfect competition made it out to be. There is the possibility that the very struggle for adjustment might lead such a system farther away from, instead of nearer to, a new equilibrium.

Closed Season

The main conclusion of the previous chapter was that the capitalist arrangement was favourable to producing more output. Yet, another challenge has to be faced. The achievements of the capitalist system could have been produced by exceptional circumstances; hence, the economic and political history of the period in question has to be examined. Schumpeter identified five of them.

The first is government action. The period of 1870–1914 was unique in that it would be difficult to find another equally free from either the stimuli or the depressants that may come from the political sector of the social process. The second is gold. Gold production was smaller than the increase in total output. So, gold production cannot have been a major factor in the productive performance of capitalism. The same holds true as regards monetary arrangements which at the time were adaptive rather than aggressive. The third is population increase, which partly explains the increase in output. The fourth exceptional circumstance concerns the opening up of new land. A wide expanse of land entered the Americo-European sphere during the period of 1870–1914. And the fifth circumstance, related to the fourth, concerns the huge mass of foodstuffs and raw materials that poured forth from it and fed the ever-growing cities; all were also exceptional factors explaining the rise in output.

Marx had predicted *Verelendung*. However, a contrary development happened during the period under discussion. The explanation given by Marxists was that the exploitation of virgin lands was responsible for the fact that there was no exploitation of labour; the proletariat was permitted to enjoy a closed season (so, no exploitation); hence the title of this chapter. Some would add technological progress as yet another factor explaining the consistent growth in total output by 2 %. That is not correct, says Schumpeter, as capitalist enterprise and technological progress are one and the same; the latter is an integral part of the former.

The question Schumpeter then poses is whether it is legitimate to assume that the capitalist engine will work on in the future as successfully as it did in the past.

The Vanishing Investment Opportunity

After the Great Depression there was a period of unsatisfactory recovery. However, Schumpeter noted that this is not necessarily a break in the trend of capitalist evolution. Other economists argue that given past experiences a fundamental change is facing the capitalist process, resulting from a permanent loss of *vitality*. Marx had predicted that capitalism, before breaking down altogether, would enter into a stage of permanent crisis. Since the capitalist system was geared to current investment, even partial elimination would suffice to make plausible the forecast that the process would flop. And that is what seemed to be happening in the 1930s.

Schumpeter drew attention to the fact that there wasn't a great difference of opinion between Marx and Keynes. Given the fact that the capitalist order is the framework of a *process* not only of economic but also of social change, the developments of the 1930s don't necessarily say that they will persist in the future. Yet, Schumpeter is pessimistic on three grounds. The capitalist process produces a distribution of political power and a socio-psychological attitude expressing itself in corresponding policies that are hostile to it and may be expected to gather force so that they will eventually prevent the capitalist engine from functioning. Reason number two relates to the capitalist engine itself. The theory of vanishing investment opportunity bears a relationship with the other theory that modern business represents a petrified form of capitalism in which restrictive practices, price rigidities and exclusive attention to the conservation of existing capital values are inherent. Schumpeter's third ground has to do with the 'material' the capitalist engine feeds on, that is, the opportunities open to new enterprise and investment. These are vanishing because of saturation, dropping population numbers, limited new lands and technological possibilities, plus the circumstance that investment opportunities now belong to the sphere of public rather than of private investment.

Schumpeter admitted that the new lands argument doesn't count much as much land is still unused and population is decreasing. As for technological progress, this is in fact not a limiting factor; it will promote further progress in output rather than limit it.

The development of new countries doesn't necessarily limit investment opportunities and they need not cause a void that would affect the rate of increase in total output. Most arguments lead to the conclusion that the possession of an extensive stock of capital goods that acquires economic immortality through continuous renewal should facilitate further increases in total output.

Some economists have discovered that new technological processes tend to require less fixed capital. So, spending on capital construction will henceforth decrease in relative importance. Since this will adversely affect those intermittent bursts of economic activity that evidently have much to do with the observed rate of increase in total output, it further follows that this rate is bound to decline, especially if saving goes on at the old rate. Schumpeter adds that it is not far from the truth that almost any new process that is economically workable economises both labour and capital. All this doesn't necessarily mean a decrease in the expansion of output. Moreover, it can be expected that national and municipal public investments will increase in a capitalist society.

The Civilisation of Capitalism

This chapter deals with the cultural component of capitalism: its socio-psychological superstructure. Pre-historians had things in common: a collective and affective nature, partly overlapping with the role magic played in those primitive societies. The rational attitude forced itself on the human mind from economic necessity; the economic pattern is the matrix of logic.

The profit motive and self-interest are also inspired by economic considerations. Capitalist practice turned the unit of money into a tool of rational cost–profit calculus, and double-entry bookkeeping. These in turn propelled the logic of enterprise. Mathematics in the fifteenth century was mainly concerned with commercial arithmetic. Individualism developed together with the rising capitalist class. Capitalism also created the space for the emergence of a new class that stood upon individual achievement in the economic domain.

It was only when capitalist enterprise—first commercial and financial, then mining, finally industrial, unfolded its possibilities that supernormal ability and ambition began to turn to business as a third avenue. Schumpeter concludes that capitalism has, after all, been the propelling force of the rationalisation of human behaviour. All the features of modern civilisation are, directly or indirectly, the products of the capitalist process. There is also the capitalist art and the capitalist style of life.

The capitalist process also provided for social legislation the means and the will; it was not simply something which has been forced upon capitalist society. Our inherited sense of duty becomes focused on utilitarian ideas about the betterment of humankind. Despite capitalism's impressive achievements, it doesn't follow that people are 'happier' or even 'better-off' now than, say, in the Middle Ages.

Schumpeter ends this chapter as follows: 'Most civilisations have disappeared before they had time to fill to the full the measure of their promise. Hence I am not going to argue, on the strength of that performance, that the capitalist intermezzo is likely to be prolonged.'[9] In fact he drew exactly the opposite conclusion in what follows.

Crumbling Walls

If we take account of the fact that as higher standards of living are attained, wants automatically expand and new wants emerge, satiety becomes a flying goal, particularly if one includes leisure among consumer goods. Schumpeter nonetheless assumes a state of perfection which does not admit further improvement. A more or less stationary state would emerge. Capitalism, being essentially an evolutionary process, would become atrophic; there would be nothing left for entrepreneurs to do. Profits and the rate of interest would converge to zero. The bourgeois strata of the population would disappear. The management of industry and trade would become a matter of administration, and staff would become bureaucrats. Socialism of a sober variety would almost automatically emerge. Human energy would turn away from business

---
[9] Ibid., 130.

and other than economic pursuits would attract the brains and provide the adventure. Such a development, maintains Schumpeter, is observable already.

It is now easier to innovate things, to getting things done than in the past. Schumpeter gives the example of innovation, which has become a matter of routine; technological progress is increasingly becoming the business of teams of trained specialists who turn out what is required and make it work. Economic progress tends to become depersonalised and automated. The old role of capitalist entrepreneurs is being undermined; their function in the social and economic process loses its importance. Economically and sociologically, the bourgeoisie depends on entrepreneurs and—as a class—live and die with them.

Since capitalist enterprise by its very achievement tends to automate progress, it will make itself superfluous. The perfectly bureaucratised giant industrial unit ousts the small and medium-sized firm and expropriates its owners. Schumpeter then concludes that it was not intellectuals or agitators who preached socialism, but in fact the Vanderbilts, Carnegies and Rockefellers!

Capitalist evolution first of all destroyed the institutional arrangements of the feudal world. Along with it came a change in the attitude of the legislative authority and of public opinion. Together with the old economic organisation vanished the economic and political privileges of the classes that used to play the leading role in it, particularly the tax exemptions and the political prerogatives of the landed nobility and the clergy.

In England, the aristocratic element continued to rule the roost right to the end of the period of intact and vital capitalism. The lords and knights metamorphosed themselves into administrators, diplomats, politicians and military officers of a type that had nothing to do with the medieval knight. However, as regards the industrialist and merchant, the opposite is true. The bourgeois is rationalist and unheroic. The bourgeoisie are ill-equipped to face problems that normally have to be faced by a country of any importance. But without the protection of some non-bourgeois groups, the bourgeoisie are politically helpless and unable to lead their nation or even to take care of their class interests.

Now, in breaking down the pre-capitalist framework of society, capitalism not only broke barriers that impeded its progress but also destroyed the flying buttresses that prevented its collapse. Having discovered this fact, it is quite correct to look upon capitalism as a social form or as anything else but the last stage of the decomposition of what we have called feudalism. So the capitalist process undermines its own institutional framework.

The capitalist process unavoidably attacks the economic position of the small producer and trader; the process will wipe them out. The political structure of a nation is profoundly affected by the elimination of a host of small and medium-sized firms, the owners-managers of which count quantitatively at the polls and have a hold on what we may term the foreman class that no management of a large unit can ever have. The very foundation of private property and free contracting wears away in a nation in which their most vital, most meaningful people disappear from the moral horizon of the people. The figure of the proprietor and with it the specifically proprietary interests have vanished from the picture. Instead there are now the salaried executives and sub-managers. And there are the stockholders.

The capitalist process, by substituting a mere parcel of shares for the walls of and the machines in a factory, takes the life out of the idea of property. It loses the grip that once was so strong; the grip of the legal right and the actual ability to do as one pleases with one's own property; the grip also in the sense that the holder of the title loses the will to fight, economically, physically, politically for 'his' factory and 'his' control over it. Eventually there will be no one left who really cares to stand for it; no one within and no one without the precincts of the big concern.

Growing Hostility

The previous two chapters sketched a dynamic picture of capitalism creating an almost universal hostility to its own social order. Marxism came to the same insight; however, in such an inadequate manner that, according to Schumpeter, it is desirable to develop the theory of it a little bit further.

The theory is verified by the high correlation that exists historically between bourgeois defencelessness and hostility to the capitalist order. Secular improvement that is taken for granted, coupled with individual insecurity that is actually resented, is the best recipe for breeding social unrest. For this unrest to develop, it is necessary that there be groups in whose interest it is to provoke and organise resentment. And capitalism by virtue of its civilisation creates, educates and subsidises a vested interest in social unrest.

Intellectuals play an important role in this realm. Intellectuals are not a special class as such (yet there is a close connection between them and professionals); they hail from all corners of the social world, and a great part of their activities consists of fighting each other, and in forming the spearheads of class interests not their own. Intellectuals are in fact people who wield the power of the spoken and written word. One of the aspects that distinguish them from other people who do the same is the absence of direct responsibility for practical affairs. Their value is, as Schumpeter puts it, their *nuisance value!*

Intellectuals could already be found in pre-capitalist times, but they were few in number; they were clergymen and monks, and their writings were only accessible to very few people. That changed with the introduction of the printing press. The humanists were the first who acquired a 'public'. The critical attitude of intellectuals grew stronger by the day. Towards the end of the eighteenth century freelance intellectuals started to apply the socio-psychological mechanism of public opinion. Schumpeter then notes that freedom of public discussion involved the freedom 'to nibble at the foundations of capitalist society'. On the other hand, the capitalist order was unable to control its intellectuals effectively. The intellectual group cannot help nibbling, because it lives on criticism and its whole position depends on criticism that stings and this will, in a situation in which nothing is sacrosanct, fatally criticise classes and institutions.

Then, there is the increase in the standard of living, and there is the ever-declining cost of books and newspapers, and there is the radio. But, above all, there is the vigorous expansion of education, in particular higher education. This may lead to sectional unemployment and it creates unsatisfactory conditions of employment—employment in substandard work or at wages below those of the better-paid manual workers. It may create unemployability of a particular disconcerting type.

Schumpeter noted (70 years ago!) that instances were reported of dozens of applications for a job, all formally qualified, but none of the candidates could fill the job satisfactorily. All those who are unemployed, or unsatisfactorily employed or unemployable drift into the vocations in which standards are least definite or in which aptitudes of a different order count. This breeds discontentment and creates resentment. It often rationalises itself into that social criticism which is, in any case, the intellectual spectator's typical attitude towards humankind. The ingredients are there for hostility towards the capitalist order. Moreover, this hostility increases with every achievement of capitalist evolution.

Intellectuals invaded labour politics, eventually imparting a revolutionary bias to the most bourgeois trade union practices. The social environment explains why public policy grows more and more hostile to capitalist interests, to the extent that it becomes a serious impediment to its functioning. The bureaucrat, never a true friend of the bourgeoisie, is now open to conversion by the modern intellectual with whom, through a similar education, he or she has much in common. Moreover, in times of rapid expansion of the sphere of public administration, much of the additional personnel required have to be taken directly from the intellectual group.

Decomposition

We have seen that the manager of a large corporation has become a salaried employee, and stockholders don't have the same identification with a company as the owner-manager would have. The modern corporation socialises the bourgeois mind; it relentlessly narrows the scope of capitalist motivation; worse, it will kill its roots.

There is another factor contributing to the decomposition of the system and that is the disintegration of the bourgeois family. As regards the style of life, capitalist evolution decreases the desirability of, and provides alternatives to, the bourgeois family home. The members of the bourgeoisie lose the capitalist ethic that enjoins working for the future irrespective of whether or not one is going to harvest the crop oneself. With the decline of the driving power supplied by the family motive, the businessman's time-horizon shrinks to his own life expectation. He drifts into an anti-saving frame of mind and accepts anti-saving theories, indicative of a short-run philosophy.

The bourgeoisie develops different values, influenced by enemies of the system, and seems to be willing to undergo a process of conversion to a creed hostile to its very existence. These developments lead not only to the *transformation* of the capitalist but also to the emergence of a socialist civilisation. Schumpeter concludes that Marx's vision was right. He also agrees with him in linking the particular social transformation that goes on under our eyes with an economic process as its prime mover. However, we don't know anything about the kind of socialism that may be looming in the future, notes Schumpeter. And he adds that, in fact, we don't know whether socialism will actually come to stay.

Yet, the middle class is still a political power. Competition is still a major factor and enterprise is still active, and the leadership of the bourgeois class remains a major factor in any business situation. The bourgeois family has not died yet. From the standpoint of immediate practice as well as for the purposes of short-run forecasting, this surface may be more important than the tendency towards another civilisation that slowly works deep down below. However, there are no purely economic reasons why capitalism should not have another successful run after the 1930s.

Part III: Can Socialism Work?

Clearing Decks

Can socialism work? Of course it can, says Schumpeter. That is, if a requisite stage of industrial development has been reached, and if transitional problems can be successfully resolved.

Schumpeter identifies two types of society: commercial and socialist. A commercial society is defined by an institutional pattern with two main elements: private property in means of production and regulation of the productive process by private contract. Such a type of society is not as a rule purely bourgeois. Nor is a commercial society identical with capitalist society. The latter, a special case of the former, is defined by the additional phenomenon of credit creation.

By socialist society is meant an institutional pattern in which the control of the means of production, and over production itself, is vested in a central authority. The economic affairs of society belong to the public and not to private spheres. Schumpeter applies the term centralist socialism to exclude the existence of a plurality of units of control. He furthermore introduces the term Central Board or Ministry of Production. Both aren't necessarily absolute in the sense that all the initiative that pertains to the executive proceeds from it alone. The Board or the Ministry may have to submit its plans to a congress or parliament. There may also be a supervising authority, such as an auditor general. Also some freedom of action must be left to the 'men on the spot', that is, managers of the individual industries.

The state will form part of the ashes from which the socialist phoenix is to rise. Schumpeter didn't use the term 'state' in his definition of socialism. Schumpeter maintains that there is no inconvenience in saying that the state dies in this act, as has been pointed out by Marx.

Regarding the idea that the economic pattern is the real driving force, Schumpeter noted that socialism aims at higher goals than full bellies, exactly as Christianity means more than the hedonistic values of heaven and hell. As for the cultural dimension of socialism, Schumpeter is at a loss to identify it satisfactorily. He refers to this aspect as: the cultural indeterminateness of socialism.

The Socialist Blueprint

There is nothing wrong with the pure logic of socialism. However, among others, Professor von Mises begged to differ. He stated that since there are no markets, which establish prices, there is, therefore, no basis for rational production. Consequently, the system will have to function in a haphazard manner, if at all. This view was countered by other economists. The production and distribution of the product are different aspects of the same process that affects both simultaneously. The most important difference between commercial and socialist economies is that in the latter this is no longer so.

Since there are no market values for the means of production, and since the principles of socialist society would not admit to making them the criteria of distribution, the distributive automatism of commercial society is lacking in a socialist one. This void has to be filled by a political act.

Distribution thus becomes a distinct operation and is completely severed from production. A rule for the distribution of goods will have to be established. An example: the assumption is an equalitarian distribution, but consumers are yet free to spend their 'vouchers' (provided by the Central Board or Ministry of Production) as they please. These vouchers can be called 'dollar incomes'. Given the tastes of the consumers, expressed in what they want to 'buy' with their vouchers, leaving alone products they don't want, the Ministry will have to accept those 'prices' if it wishes to clear the stores. This will accordingly be done and the principle of equal shares will thus be carried out in a very plausible way. This, of course, presupposes that a definite quantity of every good has already been produced.

It is assumed that the means of production are present in given quantities. An authority will be set up for each industry to manage it and to cooperate with the Central Board which controls and coordinates all the industrial managers. The Central Board does so by allocating productive resources to these industrial managers according to certain rules. There are three conditions to be fulfilled. First, they must produce as economically as possible. Second, they are required to transfer to the Central Board a stated number of consumer dollars which they have received from previous deliveries of consumer goods. Third, the managers will have to use such quantities to produce in the most economical manner without having to 'sell' any part of their product for fewer 'dollars' than they have to transfer to the Central Board for the corresponding amounts of the means of production.

What about 'progress'? Suppose a more efficient machine has been designed. This machine produces the same output with a smaller amount of inputs. Consequently, it would be in a position to transfer to the Ministry of Production an amount of consumer dollars smaller than the amount received from consumers. Call the difference 'profit'. The management would violate the condition set by condition number three if it realised that 'profit'. If it obeys that clause and immediately produces the greater amount now required in order to satisfy that condition, these profits will never emerge. The Central Board can offer premiums to prevent this from happening. The society can adopt the principle that 'incomes' should be proportional to the hours of standard work contributed by each worker. The result would be a system of labour notes. These 'incomes' would not be wages, as they exist only in the books of the

Central Board and consist of a mere index of significance associated with every type and grade of labour.

As regards rents, Schumpeter gives the example of land rents. Land must be used economically exactly like labour and capital. It therefore, must receive an index of economic significance with which any new use must be compared, and by means of which the land enters the social bookkeeping process.

The same principle would apply to profits, interest, prices and costs. Some economists have been anxious to recognise a comparison between a socialist economy and a commercial economy of perfect competition. They note that socialism offers the only method by which perfect competition can be attained in the modern world. However, in all that really matters—the principles governing the formation of incomes, the selection of industrial leaders, the allocation of initiative and responsibility, the definition of success and failure—in everything that constitutes the physiognomy of competitive capitalism, the blueprint is the very opposite of perfect competition.

There would have to be an authority to evaluate the indices of significance for all consumer goods. Given the system of values, that authority could do this in a perfectly determined manner. And the rest of the planning process could run its course. The vouchers, prices and the abstract units would still serve the purposes of control and cost calculation. So, all the concepts that derive from the general logic of economic action would turn up again!

Schumpeter maintains, contrary to Hayek, that a system as described is perfectly manageable. It should be borne in mind, however, that a socialist economy requires a huge bureaucracy or at least social conditions favourable to its emergence and functioning. Schumpeter goes even further: it is easier to handle uncertainties that business leaders in capitalist economies encounter. There are no uncertainties as the managers of socialised industries would know exactly what they are supposed to produce. Schumpeter concluded that

> This would immensely reduce the amount of work to be done in the workshops of managerial brains and much less intelligence would be necessary to run such a system than is required to steer a concern of any importance through the waves and breakers of the capitalist sea.[10]

---

[10] Ibid., 186.

Comparison of Blueprints

No socialist, Schumpeter warned, will accept the Russian experience as a full-weight realisation of socialism. It is often claimed that the socialist plan, by removing economic care from the shoulders of the individual, will release incalculable cultural energies that now go to waste in the struggle for daily bread.

There is a strong case for believing that the socialist scheme is superior to the capitalist one as regards economic efficiency. This superiority needs to be proved only with respect to big business or monopolistic competition. What productive apparatus would exist or would have existed had a socialist rather than a capitalist management presided over it? Schumpeter finds that system relatively more efficient which will in the long run produce the largest stream of consumer goods per equal unit of time.

An equalitarian system, as efficient as its commercial counterpart, will run at a higher level of welfare, since a given stock of consumer goods will in general produce the maximum of satisfaction if equally distributed. Any socialist society would realise an economy wherein the leisure class (the idle rich) would be eliminated. However, Schumpeter calculates that the gains made would result in a very small amount, if the American economy of 1929 would be the standard.

Uncertainty in a capitalist economy is done away within a socialist one, so efficiency will increase. Excess capacity can be avoided by socialist management. A case in point would be reserve capacity for the purpose of economic warfare.

Another aspect concerns business cycles. Planning of progress, in particular the systematic coordination and orderly distribution of new ventures, would incomparably be more effective in preventing bursts at some times and depressive reactions at others than any automatic or manipulative variations of interest or the supply of credit can be. In fact it would eliminate the cause of the cyclical ups and downs, whereas in the capitalist order it is only possible to mitigate them. Socialist management can steer a course approximating the long-run trend of output, thus developing a tendency which is not foreign to big-business policy. After all, Schumpeter admits that the above reflects the logic of blueprints, hence to 'objective' possibilities which socialism in practice may be quite unable to realise. Yet, it is undeniable that the socialist blueprint is drawn at a higher level of rationality.

Unemployment in a socialist society will be less a result of the nonexistence of depressions, and where it does occur, as a consequence of technological improvement, the Ministry of Production will be in a position to redirect workers to other employment.

There is one advantage of prime importance in a commercial society and that is the division between the private and public domains. They are staffed by different people, resulting in tension between the two domains. Think of the old bourgeois economist's phrase: government interference! A lot of energy and costs go into fighting government interference in a commercial society (think of the work done by lawyers). The Central Board can do a lot to prevent this unproductive employment of many of the best brains. Finally, there is the tax system in commercial societies. A huge bureaucracy has been established to collect them. The bourgeoisie have developed institutions to mitigate the onslaught of the tax authorities. No such conflict would exist in a socialist society.

The Human Element

This chapter opens with what opponents of socialism would say about the previous sections:

> Oh well, of course, if you had demigods to direct the socialist engine and archangels to man it, all that might well be so. But the point is that you have not and that, human nature being what it is, the capitalist alternative with its pattern of motivations and its distribution of responsibilities and rewards after all offers, though not the best conceivable, is yet the best practicable arrangement.[11]

Schumpeter retorts by noting that a given reality should not be compared with an *idea*. If one was to compare capitalist reality with socialist chances of success, it is best to choose capitalism of Schumpeter's own time: big-business capitalism in fetters.

---

[11] Ibid., 200.

Regarding the demigods, Schumpeter maintains that their tasks, once a transitional period is completed, are no more difficult than the ones of captains of industry in the modern world. As regards archangels, they stand for the well-known proposition that the socialist form of existence presupposes an ethical level that men, as they are, cannot be expected to reach.

What would have to change in a socialist society? Schumpeter is of the opinion that the agricultural sector can be left alone, in the sense that socialist management confines itself to a kind of agrarian planning that would only in degree differ from what is already developing. Then there is the world of the labourer and the clerk. Their work would substantially remain what it was.

The groups belonging to the upper, or leading, strata of society require a sensible approach. The representatives of these groups may be seen as the 'enemies' of socialism. Yet it is better to cooperate with them, as this can make all the difference between success and failure for the socialist order as this class is fulfilling vital functions that will have to be fulfilled also in a socialist society.

Thus the question is, on the one hand, can the bourgeois stock be harnessed into the service of socialist society and, on the other, can those functions be discharged by the bourgeoisie, which socialism takes away from it, be discharged by other agents or by other than bourgeois methods, or by both.

Rational exploitation of the bourgeois stock is the most difficult problem that a socialist regime will have. After all, the former are the exploiters of the proletariat. A successful solution of this problem requires that the bourgeois stock be allowed to do the work it is qualified to do and, hence, that a method of selection for managerial positions be adopted which is based upon fitness and does not discriminate against ex-bourgeois.

Bureaucracy is an inevitable component of modern economic development and it plays an important role in a socialist economy. In is not difficult, says Schumpeter, to insert the stock of bourgeois into the bureaucratic machine, and to reshape its habits of work. Some system of rewards in the form of social recognition and prestige will be advantageous. As regards real income, a combination of payments in kind with a provision in money for expenses of the proper discharging of functions would be appropriate.

As for saving, the central authority can do all that is now being done through private saving by directly allocating a part of the national resources to the production of new plant and equipment.

As to discipline—a socialist society will have more advantages to ensure discipline. First, it will have at its disposal many more tools of authoritarian discipline than any capitalist management can ever have. And there is more motive for the managing group to uphold authority than there is for government in capitalist democracy.

The Ministry of Production will be responsible for the functioning of the engine. Attempts at paralysing the operations will amount to attacking the government which will not be tolerated. In the Soviet Union labour unions were moulded into tools of discipline and performance, and later compounded by show trials and purge commissions. These sinister connotations do not imply that in other circumstances they would not be necessary.

Transition

The transition from a capitalist to a socialist order will always raise problems. Two sets of circumstances are being dealt with in this chapter regarding the way a transition can take place: the case of mature and premature socialisation. Previous chapters depicted a development which tends to socialise itself, including the human soul.

Different socialists will differ both in their opinions about that state which will be satisfactory to them and in their diagnosis of the degree of approximation which has been actually reached at any given time.

Socialisation in a mature state implies that resistance to change will be weak and that cooperation will be forthcoming from the greater part of *all* classes. The constitution will be amended in a peaceful manner as revolution is not likely. Moreover, there will be a group of experienced and responsible men ready to put their hands to the helm, both able and willing to keep up discipline and to use rational methods that will minimise the shock. They will be assisted by well-trained public and business bureaucrats who are in the habit of accepting orders from the legal authority, whatever it is, and who are not very partial to capitalist interests anyway.

The new order will leave the farmers alone so as to circumvent the very sensitive issue of property. Also the small craftsmen and small-shop owners will be able to continue supplying their goods and services, for a time at least. What about stockholders and those receiving an income from insurance schemes? They can be compensated by turning all their receivables into terminable annuities or else by an appropriate application of income and inheritance taxes that might render this their last service before disappearing forever.

Banks will be turned into branch offices of the central institution and in this form might still retain not only some of their mechanical function but possibly also some power over industrial arrangements that might take the form of the power of granting or refusing 'credits'. The central bank might be left independent of the Ministry of Production itself and become a sort of general supervisor. Transfer of lawyers into other functions will take place. It can be expected of socialism of this type that it would realise all the possibilities of superior performance inherent in its blueprint.

In case of a premature adoption, the picture is quite different. Schumpeter sketches the situation in America during the Great Depression. The majority of the firms were then still small to medium-sized; it would thus be very difficult indeed to take them over. Labour was not at all inclined to socialism; they would very likely resist it. Although the American bourgeoisie was losing its vitality at the time, it had not lost it completely: a very unfavourable environment for a transition to socialism.

If a takeover is to be done in such an adverse environment, a ruthless treatment of the population would be called for. Another thing to do is to bring about inflation. Lenin once said, 'In order to destroy bourgeois society, you must debauch its money.' The second thing to do is to socialise after a socialist regime has been set up by a political revolution. All large industries will have to be socialised. Yet again, the agrarian sector would remain untouched as well as small and medium-sized businesses. In most countries there is not yet a conducive environment to make a smooth transition. So, what to do in the meantime? Wait for another half century, or introduce socialisation policies before the act of takeover?

In England a policy of socialisation is conceivable. The banking sector and the insurance business are quite ripe for socialisation. Another sector is railroads and possibly trucking. Mining is yet another candidate for nationalisation. The same applies to the power supply. Nationalisation of the iron and steel industry would be more controversial, but it can be done. The building and building materials industries could successfully be run by a public body.

Part IV: Socialism and Democracy

The Setting of the Problem

Socialists in the past claimed to be the only true democrats. According to them, private control over the means of production is at the bottom, both in terms of the ability of the capitalist class to exploit labour and of its ability to impose the dictates of its class interest upon the management of the political affairs of the community. The political power of the capitalist class, therefore, appears to be but a particular form of its economic power. The practice of socialist parties in action is not particularly democratic, but this depends on the environment in which they operate. For example, socialist parties in Sweden or England conformed to the democratic rules of the game. The socialists in Germany called themselves social democrats.

Democracy is a political method, that is, a certain type of institutional arrangement for arriving at political, legislative, and administrative decisions and, therefore, incapable of being an end in itself.

The chapter provides a bird's-eye view of how the term democracy was interpreted by philosophers in the course of time and sheds more light on the classic doctrine of democracy, which will help to establish how democracy may be expected to fare in a socialist order of things.

The Classical Doctrine of Democracy

The democratic method is an institutional arrangement for arriving at political decisions which realises the common good by making the people itself decide issues through the election of individuals who are to assemble in order to carry out its will. This is in a nutshell the eighteenth-century philosophy of democracy. However, there is no uniquely determined 'common good' that all people agree on. And even if there was agreement on what the common good would be, there is still the possibility that people would want to see definite answers to individual issues. The philosophers of the democratic doctrine (utilitarians) did not see the importance of this simply because none of them seriously considered any substantial change in the economic framework and the habits of bourgeois society. As a consequence of the above, the particular concept of the will of the people, or the *volontée generale* that the utilitarians made their own, vanishes into thin air because that concept presupposes the existence of a uniquely determined common good discernible to all.

The will of the people is a difficult concept, as whenever individual wills are much divided, it is very likely that the political decisions produced will not conform to what people really want. The issue is even more difficult in qualitative matters such as entering into a war. The result attained may well be equally distasteful to all the people, whereas the decision imposed by a non-democratic ruler might prove much more acceptable.

Then, people do not necessarily think and act rationally. Think of the psychology of crowds. Second, people are also influenced by advertising and other methods of persuasion that producers often dictate to them instead of it being directed by them. An exception would be matters of local government. If a town is not too big, local patriotism may be a very important factor in making democracy work. Also, the problems of a town are in many ways similar to a manufacturing concern. So, the one who understands the latter also understands the former.

Third, there are many national issues that concern individuals and groups so directly that they evoke preferences that are genuine. However, when there is not a direct link to private concerns, the sense of reality is often lost. As Schumpeter notes,

> The reduced sense of responsibility and the absence of effective volition in turn explain the ordinary citizen's ignorance and lack of judgment in matters of domestic and foreign policy which are if anything more shocking in the case of educated people and of people who are successfully active in non-political walks of life than it is with uneducated people in humble stations.[12]

---

[12] Ibid., 261.

The citizen's thinking becomes associative and affective, which has two consequences. First, the citizen is prone to irrational prejudice and impulse. And second, all this opens the opportunities for groups with an axe to grind. Politicians are able to fashion and even to create within wide limits the will of the people. So, what we are confronted with is a *manufactured will.* The ways in which issues and popular will on any issue are being manufactured are exactly analogous to the ways of commercial advertising. There are, however, limits to all this. It is no doubt possible to argue that—given time—the collective psyche will evolve opinions that not infrequently strike us as highly reasonable.

The classical doctrine on democracy has survived all the rational arguments in contra. Why is that? First, because it is associated with religious belief, as the doctrine embodied features of Protestant Christianity; in fact it was derived from it. Second, the forms and phrases of classical democracy are for many nations associated with developments in their history which are approved by large majorities. Third, it must not be forgotten that there are social patterns in which the classical doctrine fit facts with a sufficient degree of approximation. This is the case with small and primitive societies which are not too different in their wishes and opinions. And fourth, politicians appreciate a phraseology that flatters the masses and offers an excellent opportunity not only for evading responsibility but also for crushing opponents in the name of the people.

Another Theory of Democracy

Given the unsatisfactory definition of democracy of the eighteenth-century utilitarians, Schumpeter proposes another one: 'The democratic method is that institutional arrangement for arriving at political decisions in which individuals acquire the power to decide by means of competitive struggle for people's vote.'[13] This definition distinguishes democratic governments from others. The classical definition meets with difficulties because both the will and the good of the people may be served as well, or better, by governments that are not democratic. The new definition also

---

[13] Ibid., 269.

takes into consideration leadership. Collectives act almost exclusively by accepting leadership. In politics there is always some competition. This definition clarifies the relation that subsists between democracy and individual freedom. The definition also implies—apart from the electorate to produce a government—the eviction of the same.

The social meaning of parliamentary activity is to turn out legislation and—in part—administrative measures. But in order to understand how democratic politics serve this social end, one must start from the competitive struggle for power and office, and realise that the social function is fulfilled, as it were, incidentally—in the same sense as production is incidental in making profits.

The wishes of the members of parliament are not the ultimate data of the process that produces government. A similar statement can be made as regards the electorate. Its choice does not flow from its initiative but is being shaped, and the shaping of it is an essential part of the democratic process. Voters do not decode issues. Neither do they pick their members of parliament from the eligible population with an open mind. In normal cases the initiative lies with the candidate who makes a bid for the office of Member of Parliament. Voters confine themselves to accepting this bid in preference to others. These candidates belong to political parties. And a party is a group whose members propose to act in concert in the competitive struggle for political power. If that were not so, it would be impossible for different parties to adopt exactly or almost exactly the same programme. Party slogans and march tunes are not accessories; they are the essence of politics, and so is the political boss.

The Inference

Socialists claim that democracy implies socialism and there cannot be true democracy except in socialism. Others claim that full-fledged socialism is completely incompatible with democracy. Schumpeter maintains that there is no necessary relation between socialism and democracy. However, there is also no incompatibility: in appropriate states of the social environment the socialist engine can be run on democratic principles. It all depends how the terms are being interpreted.

He argues that democracy does not mean, and cannot mean, that the people actually rule in any obvious sense of the terms 'people' and 'rule'. Democracy only means that the people have an opportunity of accepting or refusing the men who are to rule them. One aspect of this is that democracy is the rule of the politician. Politicians pursue a career. This in turn spells recognition of a distinct professional interest in the individual politician and of a distinct group interest in the political profession as such.

The efficiency of democratic government is impaired because of the tremendous loss of energy that the incessant battle in parliament and outside of it imposes upon the leaders. It is further impaired by the necessity of bending policies to the exigencies of political warfare. The democratic method produces legislation and administration as by-products of the struggle for political office.

Politicians take a short-term view, often at the detriment of long-term interests. The democratic method creates professional politicians whom it then turns into amateur administrators and 'statesmen'. Yet no system of selection, whatever the social sphere—with the possible exception of competitive capitalism—tests exclusively the ability to perform. One thing a politician knows well is the manipulation of people, as well as the ability to win a position of political leadership—the result of personal force.

Democracy thrives in social patterns that display certain characteristics and it might well be doubted whether there is any sense in asking how it would fare in others that lack them. For great industrial nations the characteristics are the following: (1) that politicians who make it to parliament or rise to cabinet office should be of sufficiently high quality; (2) that the effective range of political decisions should not be extended too far; (3) that government must be able to command the services of a well-trained bureaucracy of good standing and tradition endowed with a strong sense of duty and *esprit de corps*. Such a bureaucracy is the main answer to the argument about government by amateurs. The bureaucrats must also be strong enough to guide and, if need be, to instruct the politicians who head the ministries; (4) that parliamentarians must resist the temptation to embarrass the government at times. Above all parliaments must be on an intellectual and moral level high enough to be proof against the offerings of crooks; and (5) that effective competition for leadership requires a large measure of tolerance for differences of opinion.

Historically, modern democracy rose along with capitalism, and in causal connection with it. Schumpeter repeats that bourgeois society has lost its appeal. Bourgeois democracy is a very special historical case, based on acceptance of standards which are no longer ours. It should be remembered though that capitalist society qualified well for the task of making democracy a success. However, the democratic method never works at its best when nations are much divided on fundamental questions of social structure. The bourgeoisie did not create a successful stratum of its own. These considerations seem to suggest a pessimistic prognosis for this type of democracy. They also suggest an explanation of the apparent ease with which in some cases it surrendered to dictatorship.

The ideology of classical socialism is the offspring of bourgeois ideology. In particular, it fully shares the latter's rationalist and utilitarian background and many ideas and ideals that entered the classical doctrine of democracy. However, socialism didn't absorb the emphasis on the protection of private property.

The question is how well or badly socialism qualifies for the task of making the democratic method function. Socialist societies lack the automatic restrictions imposed upon the political sphere by the bourgeois scheme of things. Moreover, in a socialist society it will no longer be possible to find comfort in the thought that the inefficiencies of political procedure are, after all, a guarantee of freedom. Lack of efficient management will spell lack of bread in a socialist society. However, the agencies that are to operate the economic engine (such as the Central Board) may be so organised and manned as to be sufficiently exempt in the fulfilment of their duties from interference by politicians.

Democratic procedures don't have to disappear along with capitalism. General elections, parties, parliaments, cabinets, and prime ministers may still prove to be the most convenient instruments of dealing with the agenda for political decision-making. The agenda will be relieved by all those items that concern clashes of private interest and from the necessity of regulating them. But there will be others, such as how to decide what the volume of investment should be or how existing rules for the distribution of the social product should be amended.

It goes without saying that operating a socialist democracy would be hopeless except in the case of a society that fulfils all the requirements of 'maturity'; in particular the ability to establish the socialist order and the existence of a bureaucracy of adequate standing and experience. A society that does fulfil these requirements has an advantage of possibly decisive importance. At present there is no longer a vast majority who are resolved to abide by the rules of the democratic game, and this suggests frictions. This is not the case in a socialist society as sketched above. All remaining antagonisms may be further decreased in number and importance by the elimination of clashing capitalist interests. Political life would be purified. However, should there be tensions cropping up, the leadership may be tempted to apply a heavy hand. After all, effective management of the socialist economy means dictatorship not *of* but *over* the proletariat in the factories.

Schumpeter ends his book as follows:

> As a matter of practical necessity, socialist democracy may eventually turn out to be more of a sham than capitalist democracy ever was. In any case, that democracy will not mean increased personal freedom. And, once more, it will mean no closer approximation to the ideals enshrined in the classical doctrine.[14]

The 'March into Socialism'

Schumpeter delivered this speech on 30 December 1949 before the American Economic Association in New York.

Schumpeter defines (centralist) socialism as that organisation of society in which the means of production are controlled. The decisions on how and what to produce and on who is to get what, are made by a public authority instead of by privately owned and privately managed firms. The march into socialism is the migration of people's economic affairs from the private into the public sphere. It is hardly possible to visualise a socialist society in this sense without a huge bureaucratic apparatus that manages the productive and distributive process and in turn may or may not be controlled by organs of political democracy and a set of political officers who depend for their position upon the results of a competitive struggle for votes. Therefore, Schumpeter concludes that we may equate

---

[14] Ibid., 302.

the march into socialism to a conquest of private industry and trade by the state. Socialism does not exclude decentralised decision-making and neither does it necessarily exclude the use of competitive mechanisms. Freedom of consumers' choice of occupation may, but need not necessarily, be restricted in socialist societies.

Schumpeter underscores that he did not advocate socialism, nor did he have any intention of discussing its desirability. He did not want to 'prophesy' or to predict. What he did in his speech was to diagnose observable tendencies. No one could have predicted the rapid economic evolution taking place in the Soviet Union. The trade union practice in America suggests that a development towards some form of guild socialism may be in the cards.

Schumpeter then summarises the reasons he presented in *Capitalism, Socialism and Democracy* for the self-destruction of the capitalist order, and centralist socialism as the likely heir apparent. First, the success of the business class in developing the economy that has created a new standard of life for all classes has paradoxically undermined the social and political position of the same business class whose economic function tends to become obsolete and amenable to bureaucratisation. Second, capitalist activity tends to spread rational habits of mind and to destroy those loyalties and habits of subordination that are essential for the efficient working of the leadership of the production plant. Third, the concentration of the business class on the tasks of the factory and the office was instrumental in creating a political system and an intellectual class, the structure and interests of which developed an attitude of independence from, and hostility towards, the interests of the large-scale business. Fourth, in consequence of all this, the scheme of values of capitalist society is losing its hold not only on the public mind but also upon the capitalist stratum itself. Modern drives for security, equality and regulation can be explained as a result of these four self-destructive trends.

What one can observe in the process of disintegration are the various stabilisation policies to prevent recession, that is, a large amount of public management of business situations including the principle of full employment. Then there is the desirability of greater equality of incomes and, in connection with this, the principle of redistributive taxation. Added to this is a rich assortment of regulative measures as regards prices

3 Capitalism or Socialism? That's the Question   157

plus public control over the labour and money market. There is also an indefinite extension of wants that are to be satisfied by public enterprise and, of course, there are all types of security legislation. He then ironically refers to the Mont Perelin Society: 'I believe that there is a mountain in Switzerland on which congresses of economists have been held which express disapproval of all or most of these things.'[15]

Schumpeter warned that he did not disapprove or wish to criticise these policies. The only thing he wanted to demonstrate is the fact that

> … we have travelled far indeed from the principles of laissez-faire capitalism and the further fact that it is possible so to develop and regulate capitalist institutions as to condition the working of private enterprise in a manner that differs but little from genuinely socialist planning.[16]

What emerges are vast productive possibilities of the capitalist engine that promise indefinitely higher mass standards of living, supplemented by free services to the extent that capitalist interests can in fact be expropriated without bringing the economic engine to a standstill. This engine may be made to run in the interest of labour, in other words: the emergence of *labourist capitalism*. Some economists believe that this capitalism may survive indefinitely. Nevertheless, the civilisation of inequality and of family fortune will be vanishing. Past achievement was based on a more or less unfettered capitalism. It cannot be assumed that labourism will continue to perform in this manner.

Wars transform social orders rapidly. That happened in Europe after the Great War: the social framework caught fire, the latent tendency towards socialist reconstruction emerged. A return to pre-war policies proved impossible where it was attempted, such as in Britain where attempts to maintain the gold standard failed.

The Great Depression and WWII acted as additional accelerators. However, the most powerful accelerator of social change is inflation. It is difficult to stop or control inflation after a war. What happened after WWII was a process of controlled peacetime inflation along with

---

[15] Ibid., 418.
[16] Ibid., 418–19.

vigorous economic development. But the high level of employment will lead to wage demands which will increase production costs and lead to higher prices of consumer goods. So, Schumpeter noted, we are drifting into the Keynesian situation in which the money-wage rate no longer affects output and employment but only the value of the monetary unit.

Inflation will funnel the strengthening of subversive elements in a society. What would be the remedies in such a situation? First, put a cap on borrowing through higher interest rates or credit rationing. However, we don't live any longer in a world where everything is flexible. Credit restriction would lead to unemployment. This will not happen now, and even if it did, government would immediately neutralise it. Second, taxes could be increased to counter inflation. In an inflationary situation this would be good Keynesianism. But if the taxes concern corporate tax or the higher income bracket taxes, it will have little effect. A third measure would be price control and subsidies but this would be a surrender of private enterprise to public authority and it represents a big stride towards a planned economy.

Schumpeter concluded his address by stating that perennial inflationary pressure can play an important part in the eventual conquest of the private-enterprise system by the bureaucracy. It is a question of whether the American genius for mass production, on whose past performance all optimism for its way of life rests, is up to the test.

Biography: Karl Polanyi (1886–1964)

Károly Polányi was an economic historian, economic anthropologist, political economist, historical sociologist, and a social philosopher. Karl was born on 25 October 1886 in Budapest, Hungary, into a well-to-do Jewish family. His father was a railway tycoon who maintained rather outlandish pedagogical ideas about his children's education; they were educated in strict isolation. They saw only their four tutors: one British, one Swiss-French, one Swiss-German, and one Hungarian. Each tutor was teaching one child a week in turn. Polanyi senior was bringing them up according to French philosopher Jean-Jacques Rousseau's ideas, which demanded complete isolation from the hypocrisy and corruption of society. Management guru Peter Drucker commented (he knew the

Polanyis well), that none of the children turned into an idiot, yet they turned out different and unusual. Karl's brother Michael (Milály) became a well-known physical chemist and philosopher.

Young Karl's intellectual formation took place in Hungary's capital, Budapest. It was there that Polanyi developed socialist ideas. He founded the radical and influential Galilei Club while studying at the University of Budapest. He had intellectual encounters with philosophers such as Georgy Lukács and Karl Mannheim. In 1908 he earned a PhD in philosophy, and in 1914 he obtained a law degree. Loyal to his leftist ideas, he founded, together with Count Michael Karolyi, the Hungarian Radical Party in 1914, which he served as secretary. Polanyi was elected a member of the Hungarian Parliament when he was 25.

During the Great War Polanyi served as a cavalry officer in the Austro-Hungarian army. After the war, he returned to Budapest where he resumed his political activities. He supported Karolyi's social-democratic government. However, after the war ended in 1918 political turbulence ensued in Central Europe. Hungary formed no exception. In 1924 Béla Kun toppled the Karolyi government to create the Hungarian Soviet Republic.

Viennese Period

Polanyi left for Vienna where he took up the position of associate editor of the prestigious *Austrian Economist* (Der Österreichische Volkswirt). From 1924 to 1933 he lived and worked in Vienna, then still *the* cultural centre of Europe. Viennese intellectuals often met in *Kaffee Landtmann* (it still exists) to discuss the intricacies of psychoanalysis and Marxism. Sigmund Freud, Karl Popper, and Ludwig Wittgenstein lived in Vienna at the time, and so did economists like Ludwig von Mises, Friedrich Hayek and, briefly, Joseph Schumpeter. Also in Vienna at the time were painters like Egon Schiele, Gustav Klimt, and Oskar Kokoschka, as well as the authors Arthur Schnitzler and Stefan Zweig.

Peter Drucker wrote a lively portrait of the Polanyis in his *Adventures of a Bystander*.[17] He first met Karl Polanyi in 1927 during an editorial

---

[17] Drucker, P. (2007) *Adventures of a Bystander*. New Brunswick and London: Transaction Publishers.

meeting of the *Austrian Economist* to which he was invited as a guest. The meeting took place in the morning of Christmas day. The editors and Drucker had to wait for more than an hour before Karl bumped into the room with two large trunks under his arms full of books, papers, and magazines. He took out piles of them and proposed a host of possible stories which could be printed in the next issue of their newspaper. Polanyi invited Drucker to his house to share Christmas dinner with his family. As it turned out, the Polanyi family lived in a very poor Viennese neighbourhood and the food served was, according to Drucker, the worst meal of his life. This wasn't because Polanyi earned a meagre salary; it was because the Polanyis gave most of their income to Hungarian refugees who had fled to Vienna without any means. Drucker wrote that what made the Polanyi family so remarkable was that they shared the same cause: to overcome the nineteenth century and to find a new society that would be free and yet not 'bourgeois', or 'liberal'; prosperous and yet not dominated by economics; communal and yet not a Marxist collectivism. Each of the Polanyis went their separate ways, but each in search of the same goal.

Perhaps partly inspired by the stimulating intellectual Viennese environment, but certainly by the catastrophe of the Great War and its aftermath, Polanyi began to criticise the free-market philosophy of von Mises and Hayek; both prominent representatives of the Austrian School. Polanyi vehemently opposed the liberal free-market economics doctrine. He made the case for social and regulatory reform in his best-known book *The Great Transformation* (1944).

Great Britain, Canada and America

When Hitler came to power in Germany in 1933, Polanyi was asked to resign from his position at the *Austrian Economist*. He left Austria for London, where he worked as a journalist and as tutor at the Workers' Educational Association. He started to collect documentation for *The Great Transformation*, the book he began writing in 1940 and completed in 1944 when he was a visiting scholar at Bennington College, Vermont. The book, while receiving some criticism, is considered one of the most influential books on economic history.

Thanks to the attention that *The Great Transformation* received, Polanyi was offered a teaching position in economic history at Columbia University in New York City where he stayed from 1947 to 1953. His lectures at Columbia drew large audiences of interested students. His wife, Ilona Duczynska, who was a former communist, was refused a visa entry into the USA (Senator Joseph McCarthy led the anti-communist witch hunt at the time). The Polanyi's settled in Picketing, Ontario, Canada, from where Karl commuted to New York.

Polanyi received a large grant from the Ford Foundation to study the role of money, trade, and markets in pre-capitalist societies, as well as economic systems of ancient empires, with a view to put the present functioning of economic systems in historical perspective. In 1957 he published another acclaimed work: *Trade and Market in the Early Empires*. He died on 23 April 1964 in Picketing, Ontario.

Polanyi's Ideas

Polanyi's central theme is that instead of the historically normal pattern of subordinating the economy to society, the system of self-regulating markets required subordinating society to the market. It means no less than the running of society as an adjunct to the market, instead of the economy embedded in social relations, as in antique societies.

Embeddedness is central to Polanyi's thinking. Before the nineteenth century, when market liberalism took off, the human economy was always embedded in society. Polanyi described, for example, how the Trobriands in Melanesia went about their business in harmonious and balanced ways. Some anthropologists accused Polanyi of romanticising primitive cultures, as he seemed to suggest that non-modern, non-Western people were different and would not have been as economically rational in their dealings as Westerners.

Economic historian and economics Nobel Laureate Douglass North pointed out that it is easy to find fault with Polanyi's analytical framework. North noted that Polanyi selected a few historical examples which fitted into his thinking, while leaving out others that did not.[18] Nevertheless,

---

[18] North, D. (1977) Markets and Other Allocation Systems in History: The Challenge of Karl Polanyi. *Journal of European Economic History* 6 (Winter), 703–16.

Polanyi observed that price-making markets never completely dominated economic decision-making throughout history. Even in the nineteenth century—which was of special concern to Polanyi—a large percentage of allocative decisions did *not* occur in price-making markets; elements of reciprocity and redistribution played their part as well. North gave examples of allocation of resources beyond price-making markets, such as cooperatives, trade unions, guilds and so forth; all were—and are—institutions that allocate resources in place of markets. North concluded that further advance in economic history requires that economic historians succeed in defining and explaining the different allocative systems that have characterised economic organisation in the past. It was Polanyi's intuitive genius, according to North—and Peter Drucker—that he saw the issue of allocative systems at hand.

Market liberalism triggered a response by society, Polanyi noted, which in turn meant that market liberalism could not freely work as intended. The institutions that governed the global economy in the nineteenth century (such as the gold standard) created increasing *tensions* within and among nations. All this culminated in the catastrophe of the Great War and ensuing protectionism, followed by the Great Depression, which brought the preceding century of market liberalism to a definite end. Communism and fascism sprang up in some societies; in others social democracy developed.

Polanyi and Keynes

John Maynard Keynes and Karl Polanyi were contemporaries. Although Polanyi agreed with much of Keynes's critique of market liberalism, he cannot be considered a Keynesian. After all, Keynes was a liberal and Polanyi a socialist. Keynes, like Polanyi, criticised the neoclassical view on the functioning of economies. Keynes proposed—while accepting aspects of the neoclassical doctrine—a counterbalancing role through government intervention. Polanyi, however, rejected it as he argued that market liberalism had a disruptive effect on society; it was doomed. Marx also projected the collapse of market liberalism. But Polanyi wasn't a Marxist because he rejected Marx's economic determinism.

Polanyi did not agree with Keynes's analysis of the causes of the catastrophic developments after the end of the Great War. Keynes put the blame in his *The Economic Consequences of Peace* (1919) on the politically inspired greediness of the Allies (France, Great Brain, and the USA) over defeated Germany in demanding an impossible amount of war reparations as spelled out in the Treaty of Versailles. This was to prevent Germany from economically (and politically) getting back on its feet. The consequences of the Treaty would also destroy the economic system which had brought prosperity before the war, according to Keynes. Polanyi blamed the strain between the economic system and society for the ensuing catastrophic developments.

Polanyi the Moralist

Polanyi emphasised that it is wrong to treat nature and human beings as objects whose price is determined by market forces. Such a concept, he maintained, violates the principles that have governed societies for centuries: nature and human life have almost always been recognised as having a sacred dimension. Polanyi pointed to the fact that when the natural environment is turned into economic commodities, one can be sure of its destruction. Polanyi can thus be characterised as an environmentalist before it became fashionable.

When Polanyi published *The Great Transformation* towards the end of WWII, he hoped to see a situation emerging in which both national economies and the global economy would be subordinated to democratic politics. Polanyi argued that human beings should use the instruments of democratic governance to control and direct the economy to meet their needs.

As for the global economy, the Bretton Woods institutions have been established, and later broadened with the World Trade Organization. However, it can be doubted that they have so far been able to function as Polanyi wanted them to be, that is, that the logic of the market would be subordinate to society. As regards national economies, perhaps the Nordic countries, applying a Middle Way, come closest to functioning in a manner as wished for by Polanyi in maintaining a delicate balance between the exigencies of the market and societal considerations.

The Great Transformation: The Political and Economic Origins of Our Time

Karl Polanyi wrote *The Great Transformation* during WWII.[19] The book was well received and is now considered a twentieth-century classic. The book hasn't lost its relevance as *The Great Transformation* provides a strong critique of market liberalism, as again recently underscored by the financial crisis of 2008 and the ensuing Great Recession.

Polanyi analysed the political and economic origins of nineteenth-century civilisation, which was affected by the Industrial Revolution. The Great War and the Great Depression of the 1930s hastened the destruction of that civilisation. Among the institutions of the nineteenth century the gold standard was crucial and its fall was the proximate cause of the destruction of civilisation, according to Polanyi.

The Great Transformation's main theme is still relevant: self-regulating markets don't always work. Unchecked they lead to excesses, as confirmed by the endless—and sometimes extreme—ups and downs of markets and entire economies. Economics Nobel Laureate Joseph Stiglitz wrote in his foreword to Polanyi's book that the deficiencies of self-regulating markets—not only in their internal workings but also in their consequences (e.g. for the poor)—are so great that government intervention becomes necessary.

Composition of the Book

The Great Transformation consists of three parts. The first part, The International System, describes the 100 years' peace, roughly encompassing the nineteenth century and ending in 1914, at the beginning of WWI, followed by the conservative 1920s, the Great Depression, and the revolutionary 1930s. Part II is entitled Rise and Fall of Market Economy. Polanyi goes back to primitive and pre-nineteenth-century societies to demonstrate the balanced interplay between society and market.

---

[19] The edition I use here is the Beacon Press edition: (2001) *The Great Transformation: The Political and Economic Origins of Our Time*. Boston: Beacon Press.

3 Capitalism or Socialism? That's the Question

This part of the book also describes the political and economic developments in Britain from the fifteenth century to the 1795 Speenhamland Law (assuring a minimum income for the poor, irrespective of their earnings), followed by what the Industrial Revolution brought about in the realm of economic and social philosophies, and its social and economic consequences. Part III, Transformation in Progress, analyses the origins of the Great War, the Great Depression, the rise of fascism and communism in Europe, as well as the New Deal in America.

Part I: The International System

Polanyi distinguished four institutions which were crucial to the economic and political order that had characterised the Western world in the nineteenth century: (1) a balance of political power, (2) the gold standard, (3) a self-regulating market system and (4) the liberal state. In particular, the self-regulating market (SRM) was in Polanyi's own words: 'the fount and matrix of the system', and 'the innovation which gave rise to a specific civilization'.[20] Of these four institutions—the gold standard was crucial; its fall was the proximate cause of the destruction of nineteenth-century civilisation. The breakdown of the international gold standard was the invisible link between the disintegration of the world economy, which started at the turn of the century, and the transformation of an entire civilisation in the 1930s. By the time the gold standard failed in the early 1930s, most of the other nineteenth-century institutions had already been sacrificed in a vain effort to save it.

Market economy, free trade and the gold standard were English inventions. These institutions broke down everywhere in the 1920s. Polanyi concluded that

> ... in Germany, Italy, and Austria the event was merely more political and more dramatic. But whatever the scenery and the temperature of the final episode, the long-term factors which wrecked that civilization should be studied in the birthplace of the Industrial Revolution, England.[21]

---

[20] *The Great Transformation*, 3.
[21] Ibid., 32.

Part II: Rise and Fall of Market Economy

At the beginning of the nineteenth century the markets functioned nearly free. This inspired economic thinkers to emphasise the blessings of the self-regulating market system as originally conceived by Adam Smith in *The Wealth of Nations* (1776). John Stuart Mill and David Ricardo elaborated Smith's 'invisible hand' and the notion that economic actors' self-interest also serves society at large. After all, any producer makes a living from selling his produce, and these products, in turn, serve the demand of consumers. The market mechanism brings about equilibrium between supply and demand.

Given the economic progress made during the Industrial Revolution, the liberal economic philosophy gained the upper hand, and became the organising principle for the world economy at the time. It was as if market organisation of economic activity was the natural state of human affairs.

There was, nonetheless, nothing natural about laissez-faire; free markets could never have come into being merely by allowing things to take their course. Laissez-faire was enforced by the state, which was endowed with a large bureaucracy able to fulfil the tasks set by the adherents of liberalism. The downside was that the self-regulating market system disrupted society as it had existed hitherto. As Polanyi observed, 'the control of the economic system by the market is of overwhelming consequence to the whole organization of society: it means no less than the running of society as an adjunct to the market'.[22]

Instead of the economy being embedded in social relations, social relations are embedded in the economic system. Polanyi admitted that there was material improvement for the exploited workers. Nevertheless, he concluded that human society became subordinated to the self-regulating market.

The Great Transformation presents examples of economies that had been organised in ways other than through an SRM. Polanyi argued that the organisation of production and distribution in many societies, on scales as small as a band of Kung bushmen or as large as that of Hammurabi's empire, or even as large as the planned economy of the Soviet Union,

---

[22] Ibid., 60.

employed redistributive systems. In much of Western Europe a combination of redistributive and reciprocative systems dominated through the end of the feudal and manorial era. These systems came to be increasingly supplemented by market trading, the control and encouragement of which was a major focus of medieval municipal and mercantilist national governments.

> Polanyi emphasises the *reciprocity and redistributive* nature of the way societies went about the exchange of goods. One example concerns the Kula ring trade as practised in the Trobriand Islands:
>
> > The Kula ring in western Melanesia, based on the principle of reciprocity, is one of the most elaborate trading transactions known to man … [T]here are, as a rule, individual partners in Kula who reciprocate one another's Kula gifts with equally valuable armbands and necklaces, preferably such as have previously belonged to distinguished persons. Now, a systematic and organized give-and-take of valuable objects transported over long distances is justly described as trade. Yet this complex whole is exclusively run on the lines of reciprocity … Not the propensity to barter, but reciprocity in social behavior dominates.[23]

Towards the end of the eighteenth century, and with full force in the nineteenth century, two things happened. First, the rapidly expanding factor system altered the relationship between commerce and industry. Production now involved large-scale investment of funds with fixed obligations to pay for those funds. And second, it was the development of economic liberalism as a body of thought that provided justification of a new set of public policies that facilitated transformation of land, labour and capital into the 'fictitious commodities' of a self-regulating system; these three commodities were traded with complete freedom. These were fictitious, according to Polanyi, because land, labour and capital were *not* in fact produced for sale. Nor did the available quantity of these three disappear when prices were low.

---

[23] Ibid., 52–3.

> Peter Drucker wrote the following about the 'fictitious commodities' of land, labour and capital in his *Adventures of a Bystander*:
>
>> It was Karl's contention that a good society must use the market to exchange goods and allocate capital, but must not use it to allocate land or labor; for those either reciprocity or redistribution, that is, social and political rather than economic rationality, should apply. Indeed it was the contention of The Great Transformation that a good society must keep the market outside itself.[24]

> Regarding Polanyi's reciprocity, redistribution and market-exchange classification, Drucker concludes,
>
>> If ever we get to a structural theory of economics ... it will avail itself of Polanyi's identification of the social principles of economic integration: redistribution, reciprocity and market exchange. Yet, this classification, which is the most important contribution of The Great Transformation, was noted at the time only by a few.[25]

Polanyi describes how, in spite of the threat to social order, the laissez-faire philosophy evolved into a true faith in humanity's secular salvation through a self-regulating market. Polanyi referred to Thomas Malthus who accepted poverty as part of a natural order. Malthus projected a mismatch between population growth and the capacity of a society to feed its people. Because he failed to see that technological improvement could boost agricultural production, he concluded that once the population had outgrown the available agricultural potential, famine would ensue, after which equilibrium would be restored between people and the food supply.

Market liberalism also produced an inevitable response; a concerted effort to protect society from the market. Polanyi called the continuing tension and conflict between the efforts to establish, maintain and spread the SRM, and the efforts to protect people and society from SRM's consequences, the 'double movement'. This was clearly illustrated by developments in Britain. On one side was a concerted philosophical and

---

[24] *Adventures of a Bystander*, 136
[25] Ibid., 137.

legislative programme there to establish the SRM from the enclosures of the 1790s through the Poor Law Reform of 1834 to the Ricardian Bank Charter Act of 1844 and the repeal of the Corn Laws in 1846. The other side was a widely varying, unorganised set of movements, legislative reforms and administrative actions to limit the effects of self-regulation, from the Chartists through early legislation to limit the hours of work of women and children, through the growth of labour unions, and to the reimposition of tariffs on foodstuffs, to the first legislation presaging the welfare state.

What are the double movement's implicit tensions? SRM's can't function freely, precisely because of the correcting influence of the other movement. In this context Polanyi's definition of socialism is interesting. He defines socialism as the tendency inherent in an industrial civilisation to transcend the self-regulating market by consciously subordinating it to a democratic society. This definition allows for a continuing role for markets *within* socialist societies. Polanyi noted that socialist working-class parties were, on the whole, committed to the reform of capitalism, not to its revolutionary overthrow.

The SRM was impaired in operation, and it meant that justifications for international cooperation and the liberal state were weakened. In fact, increasing protectionism so impaired the SRM that it led to political intervention. When foreign debtors refused to pay, Polanyi suggested that governments should respond to the resulting strain. In an emergency, the unity of society asserted itself through the medium of intervention. More disruptive strains cropped up. Under the gold standard, any measure that caused a budgetary deficit might start a depreciation of the currency. If on the other hand, unemployment was being fought by the expansion of bank credit, rising domestic prices would hit exports and affect the balance of payments. In either case, exchanges would slump and the country concerned would feel the pressure on its currency; in other words a catch-22 situation.

Protectionism blocked free international trade; within a few years, free trade was a matter of the past. Whether protection was justified or not, a weakness of the world market system was brought to light. The import tariffs of one country hampered the exports of another and forced it to seek markets in unprotected regions. Economic imperialism was mainly a struggle among the industrialised powers for the privilege of extending their trade into politically unprotected markets. Yet, maintenance of the gold standard was imperative. At the heart of the transformation was the failure of the market utopia.

When the last of the nineteenth-century's surviving institutions—the gold standard—collapsed in the 1930s, the stress within nations was diminished. Their responses were adjustments to the disappearance of the traditional world economy. Polanyi concluded part II as follows: 'when it disintegrated, market civilisation itself was engulfed. This explains the almost unbelievable fact that a civilisation was being disrupted by the blind action of soulless institutions the only purpose of which was the automatic increase of material welfare.'[26]

Part III: Transformation in Progress

When in the 1920s the international system failed, the almost forgotten issues of early capitalism reappeared. Popular government was one of them. The struggle to restore the nineteenth-century system by re-establishing the gold standard subsequently destroyed the international financial system.

In Europe the charge of inflationism became an effective argument against democratic legislatures in the 1920s, with far-reaching and devastating consequences. The consequences of not cutting wages or social services were inescapably set by the mechanism of the market. Invariably the danger was to the currency. And with equal regularity the responsibility was fixed on inflated wages and unbalanced budgets. The New Deal never had a chance if the USA wouldn't have gone off gold.

In other countries, going off gold meant dropping out of the world economy. Perhaps the only exception was Great Britain, whose share in world trade was so large that it had been able to lay down the modalities under which the international monetary system should work, thus shifting the burden of the gold standard to other shoulders. War reparations after WWI had a highly destabilising effect on the currencies of the

---

[26] Ibid., 228.

3 Capitalism or Socialism? That's the Question   171

defeated countries; Germany and Austria in particular. The burden of the international credit mechanism was shifted first to the European victors and from there to America. The collapse of the American economy in October 1929 drew the rest of the industrialised world into the Great Depression. Fear gripped the people and leadership was thrust upon those who offered an easy way out at whatever price. The time was ripe for radical solutions, concluded Polanyi.

Fascism and communism sprang up as a response to the collapse of the SRM. Fascism has as little to do with the Great War as with the Versailles Treaty. After all, the movement also appeared in defeated countries like Bulgaria and in victorious ones like Finland and Norway, and those of southern temperament like Italy and Spain. Polanyi concluded that the part played by fascism was determined by one factor: the condition of the market system. The Disarmament Conference stopped meeting; Germany left the League of Nations in 1933. The political and economic system of the world disintegrated together. The Nazis were banking on the final dissolution of the nineteenth-century economy.

Russia's rise was also linked to its role in the transformation. The collectivisation of the farms meant the supersession of the market economy by cooperative methods in regard to the decisive factor of land. Russia emerged as the representative of a new system which could replace the market economy. The failure of the international system let loose the energies of history—the tracks were laid down by the tendencies inherent in the market society. The conflict between the market and the elementary requirements of an organised society provided the century with the dynamics and produced the typical strains and stresses which ultimately destroyed that society. External wars only hastened its destruction.

Economic history reveals that the emergence of a national market was in no way the result of the gradual and spontaneous emancipation of the economic sphere from governmental control. On the contrary, the market has been the outcome of a conscious and often violent intervention on the part of government which imposed the market organisation on society for non-economic ends. Polanyi concluded that the congenital weakness of nineteenth-century society was not that it was industrial but that it was a market society.

Polanyi was optimistic about the longer-term results of the reaction to the nineteenth-century economic system. He hoped to see a situation emerging in which both national economies and the global economy would be subordinated to democratic politics and individual freedom. There are three facts in the consciousness of the Westerner: knowledge of death, knowledge of freedom, and knowledge of society. The discovery of society is either the end or the rebirth of freedom. Polanyi ends his book as follows:

> As long as he [man] is true to his task of creating more abundant freedom for all, he need not fear that either power or planning will turn against him and destroy the freedom he is building by their instrumentality. This is the meaning of freedom in a complex society; it gives us all the certainty that we need.[27]

---

[27] Ibid., 268.

4

Affluence

Introduction

In the history of humankind, poverty has been the rule, affluence the exception. Glimmers of future affluence, to be shared by many more than the 'happy few', became visible in the 1930s. Keynes, who normally didn't take much interest in the long run, wrote an essay entitled *Economic Possibilities for our Grandchildren*.[1] Therein, he predicted that humankind will solve the economic problem, as by 2030 the standard of life in advanced capitalist societies would improve between four and eight times. This would give us time to devote to other things than fulfilling our needs. Freed from the daily struggle for survival, Keynes saw another problem looming: How to use this freedom 'to live wisely and agreeably and well'? He concluded that we haven't mastered the art of life yet; how to enjoy the abundance. This is the challenge which Tibor Scitovsky analysed in *The Joyless Economy* (1976).

---

[1] Keynes, J.M. (1931) Economic Possibilities for our Grandchildren. In *Essays in Persuasion*. London, MacMillan, 349–57.

In 1938 the Carnegie Corporation approached the Swedish economist Gunnar Myrdal to study the race problem in America. The results of his wide-ranging investigations were published in *The American Dilemma* (1944). One of Myrdal's insights was that the American economy performed worse as a result of discrimination against blacks. A recommendation was his principle of cumulative causation, meaning that the provision of employment opportunities for blacks would increase income, which—in turn—will help improve health, education and mould law-abiding citizens.

Apparently the phenomenon of poverty was still a priority of American philanthropic foundations in the 1950s. The Guggenheim Foundation requested John Kenneth Galbraith to study poverty in the USA. Meanwhile, however, affluence had spread widely throughout America, thanks to the postwar economic boom. This prompted Galbraith not to write about poverty, but about affluence. Yet, he included a chapter about poverty, as he wrote in the introduction of *The Affluent Society*, 'There is no blight on American life so great as the enduring poverty in our great cities and of the still unseen poor in rural and mountain regions.'

Biography: John Kenneth Galbraith (1908–2006)

When trying to capture Galbraith's very long life one is at a loss. John Kenneth Galbraith ('Ken' for friends) was not only one of the best-known economists of the past century, he was also a formidable liberal political activist, Harvard professor, art historian, novelist, editor at *Fortune* magazine, photographer, BBC TV presenter and diplomat.

Galbraith, born on 15 October 1908 on a farm in Ontario, Canada, as the son of a family with Scottish roots, was larger than life. Indeed, he was tall (6'8"), he was articulate, a prolific author (he wrote more than 40 books and approximately 1000 articles) and he was not hindered by modesty. In his memoirs *A Life in Our Times* (1983) he wrote that he suffered from a problem in personal relations. His own analysis: the damage arose from the fear that his superiority would not be recognised! Above one of the oak bookcases in his elegant sitting room in Cambridge, MA, Galbraith's 'First Law' was displayed: *Modesty is a vastly overrated virtue.*

Galbraith's Education

Having been trained at Ontario Agricultural College, Galbraith moved on to the liberal-oriented University of California. He acquired there his PhD in agricultural economics in 1934, after which he moved east to tutor initially at Harvard and later at Princeton.

Galbraith came under the spell of Alfred Marshall's *Principles of Economics* (1890), and of the eccentric economist Thorstein Veblen, the author of *The Theory of the Leisure Class* (1899) in which the rich were ridiculed. Galbraith confessed in his memoirs that Veblen was dangerously attractive to someone of Galbraith's background. Veblen's writings were, according to Galbraith, an eruption against all who, in consequence of wealth, occupation, ethnic origin, or elegance of manner, made invidious claims to a superior worldly position. Galbraith admitted in his memoirs that Veblen's influence on him lasted long.[2]

Keynes was to make a lifelong impression on him. Galbraith was a Keynesian all his life. He had the opportunity to visit King's College in Cambridge (UK) as a postdoctoral student in 1937, 1 year after the publication of Keynes's *The General Theory of Employment, Interest, and Money*. As Keynes was recovering from a massive heart attack, Galbraith could not meet the master in person.

Washington D.C.

Galbraith came to Washington D.C. in 1934 to work for the Department of Agriculture during the time of President Franklin Delano Roosevelt's (FDR) New Deal, which intended to pull the American economy out

---

[2] In *Economics in Perspective* (1987) Galbraith recounts the following anecdote about Veblen, who was known to be a womaniser: 'A Harvard legend tells of Veblen's being invited to the university by President A. Lawrence Lowell to be considered for an appointment as a member of the department of economics. After being entertained by fellow economists, he had a last-night dinner with Lowell, who used the occasion to bring up, in a suitable careful way, Veblen's most noted academic drawback, which was then much discussed. "You know, Dr. Veblen, if you come here, some of our professors will be a little nervous about their wives." To which Veblen is said to have replied: "They need not worry, I have seen their wives"' (171).

of the Great Depression. It was during his early Washington days that Galbraith decided to become a US citizen.

In 1941 he became deputy administrator of the American Office of Price Administration; he was in charge of price control. A lot of raw materials and foodstuffs had to be devoted to military equipment. Moreover, the funding of colossal wartime production triggered large budget deficits, which in turn could have led to inflation. Rationing and putting caps on prices became necessary. Inflation was kept under control. However, Galbraith turned out to be too strict in discharging his responsibilities, according to his many critics. He was removed from his position in 1943, much to his chagrin.

Galbraith suffered from the blow to the extent that he sought the help of a psychiatrist, an experience he described movingly in his memoirs. He contacted old friends at the *Time-Life Corporation* and was appointed editor of *Fortune* magazine, where he stayed until 1948. In his memoirs Galbraith said that his time at *Fortune* taught him to write. In 1949 he was appointed professor of economics at Harvard, where he was to stay for the rest of his academic career.

Galbraith returned temporarily to Washington in charge of the economic assessment of the US Strategic Bombing Survey. In that position he visited Germany shortly after the war, where he interrogated top Nazis such as Albert Speer, Herman Goering, Field Marshall Keitel, and Julius Streicher.

Galbraith the Democrat

Galbraith was a prominent member of the Democratic Party and a personal advisor, speech writer and campaigner for all Democratic presidents and presidential candidates from Adlai Stevenson up to George McGovern. In 1947 he founded, together with Eleanor Roosevelt and Hubert Humphrey, Americans for Democratic Action, to support the cause of economic and social justice. Galbraith was in favour of *détente* with the Soviet Union and he became a strong opponent of the Vietnam War.

Galbraith had a special relationship with President Kennedy, who fulfilled Galbraith's long-time wish of becoming America's Ambassador to India from 1961 to 1963. Reflective of his special relationship with the president, and rather atypical for an ambassador, he often reported directly to Kennedy. The reason Galbraith gave was that sending reports through the State Department was 'like fornicating through a mattress'.

His ambassadorship in India was probably the most cherished period of his life. He had direct access to then-Indian Prime Minister Jawaharlal Nehru, whom he—among others—advised on bringing India's brief border war with China to an acceptable end. He thoroughly enjoyed cruising the Indian subcontinent and fell in love with sixteenth- to eighteenth-century Indian paintings. He co-authored *Indian Painting: The Scenes, Themes and Legends* (1968).

Radio and TV

After his stint in India, Galbraith returned to Harvard. While lecturing and writing there, the BBC asked him to present the series *The World at War*, in which he described his experiences during the Roosevelt Administration during WWII. The BBC invited him again to deliver the Reith lectures (named after then-omnipotent BBC Director General John Reith). In these lectures Galbraith dealt with the contents of his next book, *The New Industrial State* (1967). His next series of lectures for the BBC on the history of economics, entitled *The Age of Uncertainty*, was hugely popular. Galbraith reworked the script into a book with the same title, which came out in 1977.

> Galbraith explained in his memoirs how he was able to write such an impressive number of books and articles. For years he reserved 3–4 h each morning to write the book on hand, or to read the related reading and fact-finding, and the rest of the day for supporting reading or thought. He developed the talent of shutting himself off from his environment, such as noises in the house, airports, fellow passengers who wanted to start a conversation and so forth. He regularly was given permission by Harvard to take leave for a couple of months to complete a book, either on his estate in Vermont or in Gstaad, Switzerland. Most manuscripts were revised four to five times by Galbraith before they were sent to Andrea Williams who was his personal editor for more than 20 years.

Galbraith the Economist

What was Galbraith's relevance as an economist? This is a difficult question, as on the one hand Galbraith was the world's best-known economist in the 1950s and 1960s, but on the other, he never was awarded the Nobel Prize for economics.

Some scholars accused Galbraith of not having produced a robust economic theory. Others, like Keynes's biographer, Robert Skidelsky, thought that Galbraith lacked the theoretical brilliance, or perhaps merely interest in pure theory. Economics Nobel laureate Paul Krugman was unforgiving: he called Galbraith a 'policy entrepreneur', being an economist who writes solely for the public, as opposed to one who writes for other academics, and consequently offers over-simplistic answers to complex economic problems.

Friedman was his opposite in various ways: ideologically, in appearance (Friedman was slight), and in mathematical prowess. He was equally unforgiving in his analysis of Galbraith's contributions to economics, reflected in the textbox, Friedman on Galbraith, below. However, what Galbraith sharply exposed was that the principles of neoclassical economics were no longer valid for economies which had rapidly evolved since the nineteenth century when the theory was formulated. The neoclassics were blind to the role of power and of political interests. Galbraith has also been characterised as an institutionalist. He interpreted reality as a constantly changing institutional structure; the role played by institutions was crucial in the analysis of economic problems.

In *A Theory of Price Control* (1952), a book clearly inspired by his experience at the Office of Price Administration, Galbraith defended the need for price controls to prevent inflation spiralling out of control. His view was that markets do not balance out prices; no, it is oligopolistic firms that set prices. Price control is made easier by the fact that oligopolies only control a limited sector of the market.

In *American Capitalism: The Concept of Countervailing Power* (1952), Galbraith introduced the phenomenon of countervailing power: large firms were being balanced by labour unions, which—in turn—are being supported by the federal government. In the introduction to the ninth edition (1993), Galbraith recognised that the role of exploitative market power, that of monopoly or trust with which countervailing power contends, had diminished due to the globalisation of markets. And regarding the power of large firms, he wrote in that same introduction that we have now less to fear from corporate power than from corporate incompetence.

Bestsellers were *The Great Crash* 1929 (1954) about the Great Depression, followed by *The Affluent Society* (1958), whose main message is that a lot of produced goods and services are superfluous. Consumer demand is stimulated through advertising to the detriment of public goods such as education, roads, and the environment. And without adequate investments in the public sector future economic development will be impaired.

The New Industrial State (1967) portrayed a society, reflective of the American variety, in which large producers held all the economic power and competition was irrelevant. These firms are no longer managed by entrepreneurs; they are replaced by 'management'. It is the larger group of professionals who bring specialised knowledge to the decision-making in the organisation. Galbraith called this organisation the *technostructure*. Stockholders play a passive role in approving whatever actions management takes. The objective of these large firms is to control the market (i.e. to make it more predictable) rather than to be controlled by it. Vertical integration and advertising are some of the means applied to neutralise competition and to control consumer tastes.

Friedman on Galbraith

Friedman stripped Galbraith's views bare in a speech in 1976 entitled *The Conventional Wisdom of J.K. Galbraith* at the Institute of Economic Affairs.[3] And this he did with venom. Friedman immediately lands the first punch by noting that the puzzle he found on reading Galbraith was how to reconcile Galbraith's conviction in the validity of his view of the world with the almost complete failure of any economist to document its validity.

On Galbraith's *The Affluent Society*, Friedman was of the opinion that the book was not really about the affluence of society. Rather it was devoted to

---

[3] Friedman, M. (1978) From Galbraith to Economic Freedom. London: *Occasional Paper 49, the Institute of Economic Affairs*.

> other themes: to denigrating the tastes of ordinary people, the tastes of those who prefer pushpin to poetry, who prefer large tailfins to nice compact, expensive little cars. It was directed to developing the advantages of extending the power of government. A major theme was the alleged contrast between private affluence and public squalor.
>
> Friedman pointed out that the American and British governments' budgets had grown enormously over the past decades. In the USA it had grown from about 10 % of the national income in 1929 to something over 40 % in the late 1970s. So it was very hard to maintain the claim that it is private spendthrift and not public spendthrift that is impoverishing the nation.
>
> Friedman challenged Galbraith's opinion about advertising, referring to many economic analyses that demonstrated that most advertising was informative, rather than persuasive.
>
> As for the term 'countervailing power', Friedman pointed out that some of the largest concentrations of union power were in industries in which employers have little concentration of power. At the time, the coal miners' union was a large concentrated union, able to gain advantages for its members precisely because the industry itself was so dispersed. The same applied then to the teamsters' union.
>
> Friedman wondered how such an intelligent, thoughtful and independent mind as Kenneth Galbraith would hold such an apparently indefensible view of reality. Friedman regarded Galbraith not as a scientist, but as a missionary seeking converts. In doing so, one would see that Galbraith's view of the world derives from his ideological position, and not the other way around, concluded Friedman.
>
> He concluded his attack on Galbraith by stating that for those who believe in the dignity of the individual human being, the only way in which we have any right to try to affect the values of others is by *persuasion*. And that includes commercial advertising, which is a form of free speech.

Had Galbraith still been alive in 2014, he could have analysed Friedman's belief in the free market and in the autonomy of people to choose what they want, in equally sour terms as Friedman did of his. After all, it is after the financial crisis of 2008 and ensuing Great Recession, and clearer than ever that the free market needs to be regulated to prevent it from spinning out of control.

Regarding their differences of opinion, Galbraith once quipped that he would much rather have history on his side than professor Friedman.[4]

---

[4] Sint, M., Verbruggen, H. (1982) *Economen over Crisis*. Amsterdam, Brussel: Uitgeverij Intermediair, 193.

What about the role of large firms and labour unions? Moises Naim's *The End of Power*,[5] presents the following picture. Surely, there still are large firms today but their position is more fragile. In 1980 a corporation in the top fifth of its industry had only 10 % chance of falling out of that tier in 5 years. Now that chance has risen to 25 %. Schumpeter's 'creative destruction' is much faster than in the past. Internet giants can no longer rely on the economies of scale that kept General Motors on top for decades. As for the countervailing power of American labour unions, their power is waning faster than that of big business. Unionisation in the private sector has fallen from 40 % in 1950 to less than 7 % today.

What does this tell us? First of all, it tells us that Galbraith may not have been entirely wrong and Friedman wasn't entirely right. Economic philosophies flourish best when the real economy confirms what a particular philosophy says. The unfortunate overall conclusion, however, is that the predictive capacity of economics is poor indeed.

All told, Galbraith very well captured the way societies evolved from scarcity to affluence, and he wrote about them in a critical, here and there ironic, but always in an entertaining manner. His bestseller *The Affluent Society* is a masterful example of his style of writing. He introduced new terms, such as 'countervailing power', 'conventional wisdom', 'the bland leading the bland' and 'private opulence and public squalor', with which he enriched day-to-day language.

The Affluent Society

John Kenneth Galbraith published *The Affluent Society* in 1958, at the time the American economy was booming. His book analyses something which by 1958 should have been obvious: namely that the American economy—that 'empire of energy', according to Alfred Marshall—had produced opulence.[6] Galbraith described the signs of the times brilliantly.

---

[5] Naim, M. (2013) *The End of Power.* New York: Basic Books, Fortieth Anniversary Edition (1999). London: Penguin Group.

[6] Galbraith initially had the title *Why People are Poor* in mind. However, that title was not entirely to his liking. The working title became *The Opulent Society*. But he found that 'opulent' had an unattractive sound. He looked opulent up in Webster's Collegiate and the first synonym was affluent!

Hardly anybody before him had done so. Thorstein Veblen (1857–1929) was one who did it more than half a century earlier in *The Theory of the Leisure Class* (1899). *The Affluent Society* is also a book full of bold, often controversial, observations on the conventional wisdom of mainstream economics and of die-hard political convictions.

Galbraith didn't like mathematical approaches. He made economics accessible to a larger public. This was probably inspired by the experience with the publication of *A Theory of Price Control* (1952), a scholarly piece of work. He told a *New York Times Book Review* reporter that most people who had read it said that it was the best book he had ever written. Galbraith then told the reporter, 'The only difficulty is that five people had read it, may be ten ... I set out to involve a larger community.' Supported by his experience as an editor of *Fortune* magazine, he achieved what he had in mind. *The Affluent Society* was on the *New York Times* bestsellers list for some 30 weeks.

The idea for *The Affluent Society* was born in the early 1950s when Galbraith studied poverty in America. It was the contrast between rich and poor which triggered the idea. Galbraith told the story of America's wealth and what it meant for American society. The book's purpose was to describe the way economic attitudes are rooted in the poverty, inequality and economic peril of the past, after which the partial and implicit accommodation to affluence was examined.

In the introduction to the fortieth anniversary edition of 1998, Galbraith looked back at the book's original text to establish in which aspects he was right, and in which he was wrong. From a theoretical point of view, he concluded that, sadly, economic writing and teaching instil attitudes and beliefs that resist accommodation to a changing world. In hindsight, Galbraith said that he would have more strongly emphasised the inequality in income, as it was getting worse. He was confirmed in his belief that the productive process incorporates the means by which wants are created, and these are further sustained by fashion, social aspiration and simple imitation: the most important and most evident source of consumer demand is the advertising and salesmanship of those providing the product. In earlier editions Galbraith expressed concern about the dangers of inflation caused by the then-raging wage–price spiral. When writing the new introduction, there was low inflation combined with low unemployment; a much celebrated circumstance, Galbraith added. Hence, the original chapter on inflation was adjusted.

The author claims that his original emphasis on the compelling difference between public and private living standards still holds. Galbraith noted in this realm that we are now more than affluent in our private consumption; the inadequacy of our schools, libraries, health care and law enforcement are matters of regular comment. His emphasis on the deterioration of the environment was justified as there is now more attention paid to the subject.

The Affluent Society

'Wealth is not without its advantages and the case to the contrary, although it has often been made, has never proved widely persuasive.' With this memorable sentence the book begins. And the author continues in his near baroque style: As we escape from the preoccupations associated with the assumption of poverty, we are able to see for the first time the new tasks and opportunities that are before us. The shortcomings of economics are not original error but uncorrected obsolescence. These are days when men of all social disciplines and all political faiths seek the comfortable and the accepted; when the man of controversy (as Galbraith portrayed himself) is looked upon as a disturbing influence; when originality is taken to be a mark of instability; and when the bland lead the bland. The problems of an affluent world that doesn't understand itself can needlessly threaten the affluence itself. But they are not likely to be as serious as those of a poor world where the simple exigencies of poverty preclude the luxury of misunderstanding but where no solutions are to be had.

The Concept of the Conventional Wisdom

'Conventional wisdom' is a term coined by Galbraith. He described it as follows: it is convenient to have a name for the ideas which are esteemed at any time for their acceptability, and these ideas represent the conventional wisdom. In economics necessary adjustments are slow, and 'old', often aesthetically attractive, interpretations persist because they are acceptable to large groups of people, since they understand and like them. Moreover, the individual has the satisfaction of knowing that other, and more famous, people share his own conclusions. Conventional wisdom is not the property of any political group. On many social and economic issues there is a remarkable consensus. The enemy of conventional wisdom is not ideas but events. Once events happen, the irrelevance of conventional wisdom will be exposed by someone.

Ever since the nineteenth century, liberalism embodied the conventional wisdom. However, in the course of time the desire for protection and security, and some sense of equality in bargaining power, became stronger. It became a fact with which the conventional wisdom could not deal. Galbraith mentions Roosevelt, Lloyd George and the Fabians Sydney and Beatrice Webb, who helped to accept this new fact. The result was what became known as the welfare state. But there have never ceased to be warnings that the break with nineteenth-century classical liberalism was fatal.

Another conventional wisdom was that of the balanced budget in times of depression. Even President Roosevelt initially believed in it. But then the Great Depression broke out. It was Keynes who demonstrated in *The General Theory of Employment, Interest, and Money* (1936) the irrelevance of the conventional wisdom of the balanced budget. The Keynesian Revolution embodied the new conventional wisdom.

Economics and the Tradition of Despair

This chapter describes the development of the economic science since Adam Smith (1723–1790). *The Inquiry into the Nature and Causes of the Wealth of Nations* (1776) portrays a liberal society in which regulation was by competition and the market, and not by the state, and in which each man, thrown on his own resources, laboured effectively for the enrichment of society. David Ricardo (1772–1823) and Thomas Malthus (1766–1834) introduced the notion of massive deprivation and great inequality as a basic premise. Malthus predicted misery and famine as the population growth would outstrip agricultural potential. Ricardo analysed the distribution of wealth. He concluded that the laws which determined this distribution worked with ferocious *inequality*. Smith, Ricardo and Malthus represented the *central tradition* of economics.

Mid-nineteenth-century ideas about economics split. The central classical ideas continued more or less in the same vein. But Karl Marx (1818–1883) branched off to the left. Marx also predicted misery and deprivation, but he also predicted the collapse of the liberal society.

The Uncertain Reassurance

Contrary to what Malthus and Ricardo predicted, real wages stared to rise. But inequality rose as well. The likes of Rockefeller and Carnegie made tens of millions of dollars. As for wages, Alfred Marshall (1842–1924), author of the *Principles of Economics*, maintained that eventually there was a cap on wages equal to cover the costs of rearing children and other necessary costs. So, the tendency was still minimalistic. It was believed that if men were poor, not much could be done about it.

However, the economy's behaviour became more at odds with the central tradition. Where the latter called for many firms in a market, in real life there were actually fewer. Instead of perfect competition, monopolistic or imperfect competition emerged. Control over economic life seemed to be passing into fewer hands. The rich became very much richer. The Great Depression changed things. Ups and downs of the business cycle used to be 'normal'; the system would itself restore equilibrium. But the Great Depression was so devastating that the system could not correct itself. Something had to be done. It was John Maynard Keynes who provided the response.

The American Mood

British economists had called the shots so far. But weren't there American economists offering some optimism, Galbraith wondered? Not really, but there was one who made a lasting—but not optimistic—impression: Thorstein Veblen. Galbraith described Veblen's observations as follows:

> The rich and successful were divorced from any serious economic function and denied the dignity of even a serious or indignant attack. They became,

instead, a subject for detached, bemused, and even contemptuous observation ... Work, by contrast was merely a caste mark of inferiority ... It is, therefore, a mark of inferiority, and, therefore comes to be accounted unworthy of man in his best estate.[7]

In the central tradition inequality was inevitable and permanent. However, how did inequality evolve in economically advanced countries? Natural selection was at work, in line with Herbert Spencer's social Darwinism. However, the conviction in America grew that, at a minimum, any properly energetic Anglo-Saxon and Protestant American could by his own efforts become comfortably opulent.

The Marxian Pall

The iron law of wages continued in Marx but in a modified form. The worker is kept on the margin of destitution, less because he breeds up to this point than because of his weakness in dealing with his employer. In the end the system—after a prolonged depression—will collapse; after the unavoidable revolution a new order will be ushered in.

Productivity, inequality, and insecurity were the ancient preoccupations of economics. They were never more its preoccupations than in the 1930s as the subjects stood, as Galbraith formulated it, in a great valley facing a mountainous rise in well-being. We have now had that mountainous rise. However, this was an occasion when one would expect the conventional wisdom to lose touch with reality. This is not to say that the change has had no effect on conventional attitudes. Especially on inequality and insecurity there have been important modifications.

Inequality

In the nineteenth century the social radicals were pleading for the redistribution of wealth. Opponents argued that were income widely distributed, it would all be spent. But if it flowed in a concentrated stream

---

[7] *The Affluent Society*, 45–6.

to the rich, a part would certainly be saved and invested. However, few things are more evident in modern social history than the decline of interest in the issue of inequality as an economic issue. Yet, inequality is great and is getting greater. In 1972, only about 7 % of all family units had incomes before taxes of more than $25,000. They received, nonetheless, 21 % of total income. At the other extreme, 17 % had before-tax incomes of less than $5000 and received only 4 % of the income. In the years since, the share going to the very rich has much increased.

The first reason inequality as an issue has faded is that while it has continued and increased, it hasn't promoted violent reaction. The second reason is that wealth is not any longer identified with tycoons such as J.P. Morgan, Rockefeller, Harriman, and the like. And as the rich have become more numerous, they have become a 'debased currency'.

The fruits of progress are now also shared with the low-income earners thanks to increased production, which was an attractive alternative to redistribution. It has been the great reliever of tensions involved in inequality. Galbraith underscored that the goal of an expanding economy became embedded in the conventional wisdom of conservatives and the American left alike. The disputants have concentrated their attention on the goal of increased productivity. Yet, there is a self-perpetuating margin of poverty at the bottom of the income pyramid.

Economic Security

Insecurity was seen, in the model of the competitive society, as useful because it drove businessmen, workers and the self-employed to render their best and most efficient service, since severe punishment was visited on those who did not.

Large businesses engaged themselves in an effort to reduce risk (by controlling prices and limiting competition) rather than to maximise profit. Consumers' taste was brought under control through advertising. Investment in research and technological change ensured large corporations to stay abreast of the latest developments in these fields. They funded their own capital investments. This insulation from risks was achieved without government help. In contract, workers, farmers and other citizens had to call in government's help in the form of minimum prices, subsidies, unemployment insurance and the like, to ensure economic security. Labour unions also helped to promote the security of their members by protecting them against firing, or demotion, and ensuring pension arrangements.

Since the Great Depression the mitigation of the business cycle became a principal goal of public policy. By the end of the 1930s, thanks to Keynes and the New Deal, the belief emerged that depressions could be controlled. Since then, economic stabilisation became an end in itself.

It was not in poor economies where the concern for economic security emerged; no, the years of increasing concerns for economic security were the ones of unparalleled growth. The most impressive increases in output in the history of the United States and other Western countries occurred since people began to concern themselves with reducing the risks of the competitive system. The conflict between security and progress—once billed as the social conflict of the century—doesn't exist.

Since the Great Depression, increased output was not so much sought for the goods involved but to strengthen economic security. To falter on production was to expose some people to loss of employment. Nothing was more detrimental to a government than to allow unnecessary unemployment. The remedy was more employment and higher production. The effort to enhance economic security became the driving force behind production. Production has become the solvent for the discomforts associated with economic insecurity.

The Paramount Position of Production

Production was paramount. The question, however, is, Which production? What type of goods? The emphasis is on abundant consumer goods at the detriment of public goods. The production of frivolous goods is looked upon with pride whilst the production of public goods is a necessary evil at best. The production of public goods is seldom a source of pride.

Now, why is this? There are some explanatory factors, such as governments being perceived as unreliable and expensive providers of these goods. Public services are necessary but they are perceived as a burden which must be carried by the private producers. Another perception is that the political structure may also be at stake. In one branch of the conventional wisdom, the American economy is never far from socialism, and the movement toward socialism may be measured by the rise in public spending.

Galbraith pointed at the potential negative consequences of the imbalance between private and public goods:

> Clearly the competition between public and private services, apart from any question of the satisfactions they render, is an unequal one. The social consequences of this discrimination—this tendency to accord superior prestige to private goods and an inferior role to public production—are considerable and even grave.[8]

The Imperatives of Consumer Demand

Production needs to be absorbed by demand. Now, once the basic needs such as shelter, food, clothing, and the like are satisfied, psychologically grounded desires will have to be satisfied. Economic theory applauds increases in production as it increases welfare. Some economists have wondered about the urgency of various (frivolous) products brought to the market, given the diminishing utility, which found customers only after the help of massive advertising.

Galbraith wondered whether society itself had lost its sense of the urgency of the economic problem. He expected that the reaction will be a denial, as people will say that here is still poverty; so, more production helps to limit poverty. However, it is human nature to want more, and wants have a sustained urgency; without production there will be stagnation.

The Dependence Effect

The urge to consume is fathered by the value system which emphasises the ability of the society to produce. Having surpassed the situation of satisfaction of basic needs, the link between production and wants beyond

---
[8] Ibid., 112.

that point is established, as noted, through advertising and salesmanship. They create the desires; they bring to the surface wants that did not exist in the past. Investments in the development of a new product are now equally important as enlarging the advertising budget. In a variation to Say's Law it can be stated that each supply is meeting its own demand created by advertising. Economic theory at the time may have been uneasy about this new phenomenon; it did not take it into account. This being so, production remained the prime urgency. Nonetheless, wants thus came to depend on output.

Galbraith introduced the term 'dependence effect': the higher level of production has a higher level of want-creation necessitating a higher level of want-satisfaction. The cost of want-formation is formidable. In 1987, total advertising expenditure amounted to approximately $110 billion. Nonetheless, economists have closed their eyes to the most obtrusive of all economic phenomena: modern advertising. This is why the notion of independently determined wants still survives. This means that since the demand for this want-creation wouldn't exist, were it not contrived, its utility is zero. If we regard this production as marginal, the marginal utility of present aggregate output, minus advertising and salesmanship, is also zero.

The Vested Interest in Output

No one questions the superior position of the businessman in American society. But no one should doubt that it depends on the continuing preoccupation with production. Modern government is a threat to the businessman's prestige. The American liberal was the businessman's bedfellow. The liberal agenda of progressive income tax, greater economic security and the protection of liberties, the aid to farmers, social security; none of these measures was thought much to affect total output of the economy.

All this changed a great deal during the 1930s. The attention shifted from production to fighting unemployment. Now, expanded production began to acquire a growing significance to political liberalism in its American sense. Then John Maynard Keynes appeared with his notion of aggregate demand which determined production. To increase production was to ameliorate unemployment, agricultural insecurity and so forth.

And a few years after Keynes, the level of production became the critical factor in war mobilisation.

To manipulate production, the role of government had to become bigger. High production meant low unemployment, and was thus an attractive political proposition. Liberals accepted the rationalisation by which we persuade ourselves of the continued urgency of additions to our stock of consumer's goods. Keynesian attitudes became the new conventional wisdom.

But cracks were appearing in the façade. For businessmen, production no longer means secure prestige. For liberal politicians it is no longer a certain formula for public office. Environmental issues play their part. Meanwhile, the intellectual has gained prestige as well. Finally, the modern liberal no longer identifies production with all political success. It is no longer unusual to inquire about the quality of life as opposed to the quantity of production. Yet, in doubting the supreme power of production, we are still challenging a myth of heroic power.

The Bill Collector

A recession in demand and production remains a major uncovered risk of the modern large corporation. It is for reasons of economic security that production must be at capacity, because of the importance of production for its bearing on the economic security of individuals. But this is also the source of dangers.

One of them is buying on credit. Consumers bade farewell to the Puritan canon that required people to save first and enjoy later. The effect of the rapid expansion of consumer credit was to add uncertainty to the hitherto more reliable consumer spending. Nonetheless, consumer credit obviously greased the wheels of more demand to ensure continuity of production. Hence, measures to control the potential damage of liquidation were not popular. There is easy borrowing for consumer goods; no such thing exists for public goods.

As we expand debt in the process of want-creation, we come necessarily to depend on this expansion. An interruption in the increase in debt means an actual reduction in demand for goods. But debt cannot be indefinitely expanded. Surely, periods for payment can be lengthened, but eventually there comes a point when they exceed the life of the asset which serves as the collateral. An increase in unemployment could induce a general effort to avoid new debt and reduce the old. The further effect on consumer spending, thereafter on employment, and thence once again in reducing borrowing and magnifying efforts to meet debts, could be considerable. However, measures (i.e. regulation) to prevent the competitive liberalisation of consumer credit will encounter the heaviest resistance. Though such regulation is a commonplace in the UK, and has been used in the past in America in wartime, it is unlikely to be authorised in the future, except in the aftermath of disaster.

The encouragement to indebtedness which the society accords to the man who wants to buy an automobile is matched by the stern mistrust with which it views the local government that might want to borrow for a school.

Inflation

Inflation, the scourge of any stable economy, persisted in the 1950s and spiralled out of control in the mid-1970s. It was thought that peacetime inflation might correct itself. There was also the fear that if inflation was to be addressed, it might trigger an economic downturn, and that had to be prevented at all cost. Yet, prices and wages showed an upward spiral. Those with fixed incomes, such as pensioners, are the victims of inflation. The same applies to producers of inelastic goods, such as farmers. Their products won't be sold more, yet their production costs will rise.

Wants do not have an origin that is independent of production. They are nurtured by the same process by which production is increased. Accordingly, the effect of increased production from existing plant capacity is to increase also the purchasing power to buy that production and the desires which ensure that the purchasing power will be used.

If production is nearing capacity, an increased output will require an increase in capacity. The increased investment that this implies will—in the form of wages, payments for materials, returns to capital and profits—add to the purchasing power and the current demand for goods. The ingredients for a wage–price spiral are thus created. Note that only in industries characterised by oligopoly does the relation between demand, capacity and price have a degree of play. Prices are not restricted immediately when demand is curbed or excess capacity appears.

Now, what could be done about it? First, inflation can peter out when there is a slack in the economy. Second, inflation can be lowered by a reduction in the level of demand or by price and wage control. However, these measures were in conflict with the conviction that resources must be allocated efficiently. And lowering demand was in conflict with the importance accorded to production. Can the conflict be avoided by use of monetary policy?

> In the early days of WWII, a grateful citizenry rewarded its soldiers, sailors, and airmen with a substantial increase in pay. In the teeming city of Honolulu, in prompt response to this advance in wage income, the prostitutes raised the prices of their services. This was at a time when increased volume was causing a reduction in their average unit cost. However, the high military authorities ordered a return to the previous scale. This was done under the authority of the Office of Price Administration, under Galbraith's responsibility.

The Monetary Illusion

Keynes was already of the opinion that monetary policy was of small practical utility. Yet, after WWII monetary policy became prominent. Price controls, and the like, were not acceptable. Monetary policy seemed the right policy to curb inflation. However, it could not solve the problem as this policy makes no direct contact with the price–wage interaction. So it must work through reducing aggregate demand by increasing the interest rate and by a diminished supply of loan funds. By reducing the demand for goods the pressure on capacity and on the labour force is lessened, so prices could be kept stable; that was the idea.

The money supply decreases or increases as a result of decreases or increases of bank lending. When one restricts the money supply, one restricts the spending associated with the lending and borrowing of funds. Galbraith argues that limiting consumer borrowing would immediately be opposed by the machinery of consumer-demand creation. And an increase in the interest rate of consumer loans translates to a very small increase in monthly repayments. All told, the effect on consumer lending will be negligible. The large corporations rely less and less on borrowed funds for their investments; they finance their own. However, smaller firms, contractors, and farmers do rely on bank lending. Now, if the interest rate increases, these firms must refrain from investing thus leading to less production and more unemployment. They won't like the prospect and will exert political pressure to prevent damage being done.

In concluding, monetary policy is a blunt, unreliable, discriminatory and somewhat dangerous instrument of economic control. Yet, it survives, because an active monetary policy means that interest rates will be high—a circumstance that is far from disagreeable for those with money to lend.

Production and Price Stability

Monetary measures are the instrument of conservatives. Fiscal policy is the weapon of liberals. Yet, since WWII fiscal policy has revealed itself as a very poor defence against inflation, as it was not applied vigorously. Moreover, a policy which holds production below capacity in the interest of price stability sacrifices economic growth. So long as the use of fiscal policy is in unresolved conflict with other prior economic goals, it will not be used with effective vigour, at least in peacetime.

One last possibility remains and that is price control in combination with fiscal policy. They reconcile capacity output—and also the related growth—with price stability. Price controls prevent a wage–price spiral should the economy run at capacity. Neoclassical economists object to price controls, which would have to be applied across the board, as they interrupt the functioning of the free market and affect the efficient allocation of resources. Galbraith pointed at the combined work of price controls and increased output during the war. These controls do not have to be universal; a limited restraint will do.

Galbraith added to the text of the fortieth anniversary edition that in 1998 the USA had seen some years of relatively low unemployment and very limited inflation. This new situation reflected the declining power of the unions and the growing importance of industries—consumer services, entertainment, the arts and professions—where the unions were absent or unimportant.

The Theory of Social Balance

The disparity between the opulent supply of some things and a meagre yield of others creates social discomfort and social ills. This is an unsolved problem of the affluent society. Galbraith formulated the basic dilemma as follows:

> The line which divides our area of wealth from our area of poverty is roughly that which divides privately produced and marketed goods and services from publicly rendered services. Our wealth in the first is not only in startling contrast with the meagreness of the latter, but our wealth in privately produced goods is, to a marked degree, the cause of crisis in the supply of public services. For we have failed to see the importance, indeed the urgent need, of maintaining a balance between the two.[9]

Obviously an increase in the production of private goods triggers the need for an increase in the production of public goods. More cars require more roads, more traffic light, control of air pollution, you name it. So it goes with many other private goods and services. But the production of public goods dramatically lagged behind that of private goods. Why is this? Galbraith argued that all private wants are inherently superior to all public desires which must be paid for by taxation and with an inevitable component of compulsion which impairs civil liberties. Given this imbalance, people live in an environment of private opulence and public squalor. The box that follows, containing the most-quoted section of *The Affluent Society*, illustrates this imbalance.

> The family which takes its mauve and cerise, air-conditioned, power-steered, and power-braked car out for a tour passes through cities that are badly paved, made hideous by litter, blighted buildings, billboards, and posts for wires that should long since have been put underground. They pass on into a countryside that has been rendered largely invisible by commercial art. (The goods which the latter advertise have an absolute priority in our

---

[9] Ibid., 186.

> value system. Such aesthetic consideration as a view of the countryside accordingly comes second. On such matters we are consistent.) They picnic on exquisitely packaged food from a portable icebox by a polluted stream and go on to spend the night at a park which is a menace to public health and morals. Just before dozing off on an air mattress, beneath a nylon tent, and the stench of decaying refuse, they may reflect vaguely on the curious unevenness of their blessings. Is this indeed, the American genius?[10]

It is convenient to have a term which suggests a satisfactory relationship between supply of privately produced goods and services and those of the state: social balance. The tendency will always be for public services to fall behind private production. In an atmosphere of private opulence and public squalor, the private goods have full sway. The social imbalance triggers social disorder and it impairs economic performance.

Social balance is also the victim of two further features of our society—the truce on inequality and the tendency to inflation. The position of the federal government for improving the social balance has also been weakened since WWII by the strong conviction that its taxes are at artificial levels and that a tacit commitment exists to reduce taxes at the earliest opportunity. Finally, social imbalance is the natural offspring of inflation. The tax revenues of states and localities are relatively inelastic. While the wages of their public servants rise, the funds available for public services decline.

As mentioned before, all private wants where the individual can choose are inherently superior to all public desires which must be paid for by taxation and with an inevitable component of compulsion. With time, the disorder associated with social imbalance has become visible, even if the need for balance between private and public services is still imperfectly appreciated.

The Investment Balance

Modern economic activity requires many trained and qualified people. Investment in human capital is as important as investment in material capital; the one depends on the other. Technological advance, intimately related to economic progress, is almost wholly dependent on investment

---
[10] Ibid., 187–8.

in education and scientific research. So, public investment in education and research has become a prerequisite for continued growth and prosperity. Nearly all investments in individuals are in the public domain. It is the state which makes the largest investment in individuals.

Unfortunately there is no machinery for automatically allocating resources between material and human investment. The process by which wants are synthesised is a potential source of economic instability. However great or small these dangers, they will be lessened if consumption is widely distributed—if productive energies serve uniformly the whole range of human wants—public and private.

Galbraith believed that a balance between private and public wants can be restored by investing in education. Education is not only essential given the technical and scientific requirements of a modern economy. It also provides the potential to widen tastes of a more esoteric nature and promotes independent critical attitudes.

The Transition

An affluent society—as opposed to a poor society—requires a transition in conventional wisdom; in economic thinking, in its political implications and in morality. The main task of the book is to demonstrate that the production of goods, by its overpowering importance, was the central problem. Happiness was more or less identified with productivity. This is still the official test. What can or should replace this profound preoccupation with production? There is a psychological problem: many who will find it possible to believe that production has lost its urgency will *still* find the changes in behaviour difficult to accept.

However, there is an emerging understanding of the declining importance of goods and the axiomatic rule of production. Yet, even in its deteriorated form, people cling to the criterion of production. Happiness was more or less implicitly identified with productivity. This is so much simpler than to substitute the other tests—compassion, happiness and well-being, the minimisation of community or other social tensions—which now become relevant.

More than decisions on economic policy are involved; a system of morality is at stake. In the past, the person that did not work was penalised for not having an income. That penalty still exists, even though it now enforces the production of relatively unimportant goods. Obviously the rewards of affluence will not be reaped until this problem is solved.

The Divorce of Production from Security

Income and employment have become the basic economic concerns, rather than production. Good times are identified with high employment, and not with production. But to provide employment to all creates pressure on production, which may trigger inflation. To take away the pressure on employing everybody, Galbraith proposes unemployment compensation at a level close to the weekly wage. Galbraith noted that beyond a certain point, and given the shortage of qualified workers that exists, it is not realistic to pull the uneducated, the inexperienced, the mentally or physically ill, and the black workers into jobs. Hence, to ease the pressure on more production (and on inflation) a reasonable amount of unemployment compensation would be useful.

The Redress of Balance

The next thing to do is to redress the balance between the affluence in private goods and the poverty in public goods so as to eliminate social disorder. Sales taxes can restore the balance (as an increase in the income tax would be politically unacceptable). After all, the relation of sales tax to the problem of social balance is direct. The community is affluent in privately produced goods and poor in public services. So the solution is to tax the former to fund the latter by making private goods more expensive. Production will then be based on the whole range of human wants, and not only on part of it.

The Position of Poverty

Alfred Marshall said that the study of the causes of poverty is the study of the causes of the degradation of a large part of humankind. Since Marshall's time, poverty diminished sharply in America (and thus its political relevance); yet the poor, now a minority, are there and they need support. There were 13.4 million poor Americans at the time *The Affluent Society* was first published in 1958. Galbraith proposed financial support to poor families, and for their children good education, better health services, special provisions for nutrition and recreation. All this would create the possibility for the children of the poor to escape poverty. Hence, to a large extent the remedy for poverty leads by and large to the same requirements as those to restore the social balance.

Labour, Leisure and the New Class

An affluent society can make work more palatable; that is, less toil and more time for leisure. Fewer people are needed to produce goods and services. Those who cannot be employed may receive unemployment compensation. The old and the young can be spared from work. More and more women have joined the workforce in the course of time. The young can go to school longer than in the past. Education is the vehicle for social and economic progress.

In this vein Galbraith pointed to the emergence of a so-called New Class (a successor to Veblen's Leisure Class), composed of people with a good education. This growing class finds fulfilment in their work; they contribute their best regardless of financial compensation. Membership of this class ensures exemption from manual work; escape from boredom, the chance to spend one's working life in a clean and intellectually stimulating environment.

Galbraith warns that technical advances such as automation, an already realised dividend of the expansion of the New Class, may proceed so rapidly as to leave a surplus of those who still merely work. This is probably the greater danger. Although the *conventional wisdom* still doesn't recognise investment in education as the central goal of society, it is in fact already widely accepted. Hence, conventional wisdom cannot resist it indefinitely.

On Security and Survival

Released from the compulsion of producing goods, people are now free to learn what other opportunities there are that may promote happiness. The Soviet Union's space accomplishments resulted in the fact that over half of America's public expenditures went into military spending. America is involved in winning a race from the Soviets in technological innovation. The past arms race had a deep organic relation with economic performance. Military research and development have positive spill-over effects on the private sector, in particular air transport and computer technology. This research has done more to save America from the technological stagnation that is inherent in a consumer goods economy. But it is an inefficient way of subsidising general scientific and technical development. It has the additional effect of associating technological advances with an atmosphere of fear. There are the millions of poor the world over. Without helping them disorder would be inevitable.

Even when the arms race ends, the scientific frontier will remain, either as an aspect of international competition or in the pursuit of the esteem and satisfaction that go with discovery. Whatever the future may bring, such as the depletion of natural resources or overpopulation, the basic demand on America will be on its ability, intelligence and education, which is subject to the impediments to resource allocation between private and public use. To have failed to solve the problem of producing goods would have kept humanity in its oldest and most grievous misfortune. But to fail to see that we have solved it, and fail to proceed thence, would be fully tragic.

Afterword

Born in a world of poverty, economics as a subject matter has been slow to recognise the difference that is made by wealth. Increasing and more general affluence has changed political and social attitudes and behaviour. Two effects of affluence need to be emphasised. The first is the danger that we will settle into comfortable disregard for those excluded from its benefits and its culture. There is the likelihood that we will develop a doctrine to justify the neglect. The second effect is that out of great well-being come the resources for the production of weapons of ever-increasing danger. Our well-being is an object of envy by the less fortunate and—above all—by those whose economic system denies possession of property and resulting income. So we arm ourselves out of our affluence to protect our good fortune which we so greatly enjoy.

Galbraith ended with two pleas: let us put elimination of poverty in the affluent society strongly on the social and political agenda. And let us protect our affluence from those who would leave the planet only with its ashes. The affluent society is not without its flaws. But it is well worth saving it from its own adverse or destructive tendencies.

Biography: Tibor Scitovsky (1910–2002)

Tibor de Scitovsky, better known as Tibor Scitovsky, was born on 3 June 1910 in Budapest, Hungary. He died in Stanford, California, USA, on 1 June 2002. He wrote scores of articles on various aspects of the economic science and beyond, and published close to ten books, of which *The Joyless Economy: The Psychology of Human Satisfaction* is his best known.

Scitovsky was born into a noble family. His father, Tibor de Scitovsky Sr, was a banker and for a short period Foreign Minister in one of Hungary's governments. Young Tibor received his academic education at Pazmany Peter University in Budapest from which he held an undergraduate degree in law. In 1930 he went to Trinity College, Cambridge to study economics. When he came back to Budapest he started working at his father's bank in a low position so as to learn the trade from the bottom up. He didn't like the banking business and he became more and more concerned about the rise of Nazism in Germany. He decided to return to England in 1935 to study at the London School of Economics. In 1939 he came to the USA on a scholarship, studying at Columbia, Harvard and at the University of Chicago.

When America started the war against Germany and Japan he enlisted in the United States Army, initially as an army truck driver and later as a counter-intelligence officer. While enlisting, he realised that he still had family in German-allied Hungary, so he changed his name to Thomas Dennis. Tibor thought that this new name was easier to spell than Scitovsky. However, his commanding officer asked him 'Is Dennis spelled with one n or two?'

As Lieutenant Dennis he served with the United States Strategic Bombing Survey, under the leadership of John Kenneth Galbraith.

Word has it that the memoranda of Thomas Dennis were considered impressive by those who read them. And that was quite an accomplishment, as Galbraith wrote about the contributors to the Survey report in his memoirs *A Life in Our Times*:

> My subordinates, in a manner of speaking, for in the long history of human conflict few in any military formation were so little given to any form of obedience, were a roster of the famous of the next economic generation. Nicholas Kaldor, later Lord Kaldor, E.F. Schumacher of Small is Beautiful; my old partner Griffith Johnson; Paul A. Baran, with Paul Sweezy to become the most distinguished and by far the most entertaining of American Marxists; Tibor Scitovsky, another noted economist; Edward Dennison, later to become one of the leaders in modern statistics; and many more.[11]

Scitovsky enjoyed a good play, a nice concert, a challenging talk and—not in the least—academic research. He gave a misleading impression of his diffidence and delicacy, as Kenneth Arrow remembered in his obituary of Scitovsky; in fact, Scitovsky was very fit, swimming his daily half-mile until a few years before his death, and displaying remarkable mechanical ability. Scitovsky believed that having a good life didn't hinge on having a lot of money. This belief may well have been implanted in young Tibor's mind by his parents' driver, a staunch Marxist with whom Tibor spent a lot of time. Scitovsky wrote in his memoirs that in his younger days he was favourably impressed by the ideas of Communism, but this sympathy was quickly dissipated by the Spanish Civil War and Stalin's extreme brutality.

His father's pleasant attitude towards people, rich or poor, also had its influence. Despite his affluence, Tibor Sr remained polite, generous and compassionate; virtues that set him apart from the 'insolent swagger' of much of the ruling gentry. Scitovsky wrote in his memoirs that his resentment of their uncivil behaviour may have been the origin of his lifelong leftist sympathies.

---

[11] Galbraith, J.K. (1983), *A Life in Our Times*, 212.

His Academic Career

Scitovsky's career as an economist took off in 1946 when he was appointed lecturer in economics at Stanford University. Right from the beginning of his tenure, Scitovsky was instrumental in raising the quality of Stanford's Economics Department. He had a good eye for intellectual talent and was able to attract promising young economists, among them Kenneth Arrow who later was awarded the Nobel Prize for Economics.

In 1958 he left Stanford for Berkeley where he would stay for a decade. While at Berkeley he was visiting professor at Harvard. During the last 2 years at Berkeley he was on leave to do research at the Organisation for Economic Cooperation and Development (OECD) in Paris, France. From 1968 to 1970 Scitovsky was Heinz Professor of Economics at Yale where he wasn't very happy. His former Stanford colleagues successfully lobbied to bring him back to Stanford in 1970. He was Eberle Professor of Economics until his retirement in 1976. As if all of this was not enough, after 1976 he taught at the London School of Economics, again at Stanford, and at the University of California-Santa Cruz. He also kept on publishing articles on economics through the 1990s.

His Academic Work

Tibor Scitovsky had a major influence on different areas of economics, such as the basic concepts of welfare economics (he developed the Scitovsky Reversal Paradox), economic development, foreign trade and notions on externality. His Reversal Paradox lives on. The paradox occurs when the gainer from the change of allocation A to allocation B can compensate the loser for making the change; however, the loser could also then compensate the gainer for going back to the original position.

The Joyless Economy is a psychological analysis of the nature of human satisfaction and happiness in an affluent society. It is the work of a behavioural economist *avant la lettre*.[12]

---

[12] Cassidy devotes an entire section on behavioural economics, entitled 'Psychology Returns to Economics', in *How Markets Fail* (see Chap. 7, p. X).

Scitovsky confessed that he learned to think at Cambridge, where the great economist and Keynes pupil, Joan Robinson, was his stern tutor.

> Scitovsky explains in his memoirs how Joan Robinson taught him to think. Mrs Robinson had asked young Tibor to write an essay on the theory of money:
>
> > I had just started economics a month earlier and did not even know there was a theory about money. But I worked hard to prepare myself for what was to be my first English composition ... And so I read everything I could find on the subject, trying to present it all as an integrated whole. Joan read it while I watched her and waited with abated breath for her to deliver her verdict. There was no harm, she said, in listing what other people had to say about money but she looked in vain for my theory of it. So she suggested that I write the paper again, this time presenting my own ideas on the subject. I felt humiliated and went home devastated. My one year's study of law in Hungary had not prepared me for independent thinking and contributions of my own. I spent an agonizing fortnight chewing my pencil, walking up and down like a caged animal, trying not to read, just to think, and to think of nothing but what I thought about the theory of money. Somehow, I managed to produce a paper Joan found acceptable; and while it probably was not much good, since I have no recollection of what it said, I have been grateful to Joan ever since for having taught me to think.[13]

His earliest research was about the foundations of John Maynard Keynes's analysis of unemployment. Scitovsky related the presence of unemployment to rigidities in product prices and in the capital markets. He wrote a book about it: *Capital Accumulation, Employment and Price Rigidity* (1941). He simultaneously studied the nature of welfare judgments, showing that then current criteria for welfare improvements could lead to a paradox—the Scitovsky Reversal Paradox.

In *A Reconsideration of the Theory of Tariffs* (1942) Scitovsky presented a scenario where attempts by nations acting independently to promote their own welfare could lead the world into a downward spiral of protectionism and impoverishment. This work contributed to the foundations

---

[13] Quote from András Nagy's review of *The Memoirs of a 'Proud Hungarian'*, in *The Hungarian Quarterly*, Vol. 40, autumn 1999, 109–10.

for tariff reductions after WWII. He then concentrated his attention on economic aspects of the nature of external economies and applied his work to the evaluation of alternative forms of competition. His book *Welfare and Competition: The Economics of a Fully Employed Economy* (1951) became a classic on the subject matter.

Scitovsky remained interested in problems of international trade and finance. In particular he focused his attention on the institutional development of trade liberalisation in Europe in his book *Economic Theory and Western European Integration* (1958) in which he wrote about customs unions. He analysed the consequences of protection among developing countries in *Industry and Trade in Some Developing Countries*, which he published in 1970 together with I.M.D. Little and M.F.G. Scott. This book focused on the adverse consequences of excessive protection of domestic industries applied by some developing countries; a doctrine which was popular among—especially—Latin American developing countries and international institutions, such as UNCTAD.

Perhaps Scitovsky's lifelong interest was human happiness. Economics did not provide a theory which explained human behaviour in the pursuit of happiness; it took too narrow a view, Scitovsky felt. He studied physiological psychology to better understand human behaviour, the results of which he put in *The Joyless Economy*. This book gave him the greatest joy in writing it, as he himself confessed in the preface to the revised edition of 1991:

> Let me just add that despite the word 'joyless' in the title, this was by far the most enjoyable of my books to write, and I very much hope that some of the joy its writing gave me will also be found in its reading.[14]

The Joyless Economy (1976) tries to explain why economic growth is not necessarily accompanied by a comparable growth in welfare, happiness and joy. Striving after welfare is a process which is more complex than most economists—with their narrow focus on incomes and consumer satisfaction—imagined. *The Joyless Economy*, written by an author with a European soul in an American setting, deals with, on the one hand,

---

[14] *The Joyless Economy*, xii.

pleasure in life triggered by a good conversation, the arts, a sense of belonging, of being useful and, on the other, with concern about the difficulties of American Puritan society, as opposed to European societies, to enjoy life: America is an affluent society striving after comfort at the detriment of joy.

Development economist Irma Adelman once said about Scitovsky's writings that they were brilliant, original and full of subtlety. They always enlighten the reader and move the debate forward. This certainly applies to *The Joyless Economy*.

Honours

Scitovsky was elected Distinguished Fellow of the American Economic Association, Fellow of the Royal Economic Society, Member of the American Academy of Arts and Sciences and Corresponding Fellow of the British Academy.

The Joyless Economy: The Psychology of Human Satisfaction

The Joyless Economy (1976) is one of the first books by an accomplished economist that looks at human behaviour and contrasts it with the neoclassical view of it.[15] John Kenneth Galbraith's *The Affluent Society* confronted the classic economic premise of scarcity with the abundance of affluent societies, including its lopsided attention to consumption triggered by advertising and the neglect of public services. *The Joyless Economy* zoomed in on consumers of affluent societies who spend their money unwisely: they buy comfort at the detriment of joy in life.

Scitovsky summarised what physiological psychologists had to say about human behaviour. The highly entertaining and original way in which he treated the subject made him into a behavioural economist *avant la lettre*.

---

[15] Edition used is the 1992 revised edition published by Oxford University Press.

A central theme in *The Joyless Economy* is that Puritan tradition, the work ethic and the educational system all contribute to depriving people of many of the skills and tastes necessary for the enjoyment of stimulating and creative leisure activities. The book challenges economists' unquestionable acceptance of the consumers' judgment of what is best for themselves, their tastes and their market behaviour as a reflection of their tastes. Scitovsky points out that it does not correspond with what psychologists have discovered about human economic behaviour. His book offers, in his own words,

> ... the groundwork for something humbler and better. The scientific approach, to my mind, is to observe behavior—different people's behavior in similar situations and the same people's behavior in different situations—in order to find, contained in those observations, the regularities, the common elements, the seeming contradictions which then become the foundations of a theory to explain behavior.[16]

The Joyless Economy consists of two parts, each subdivided in chapters. Part I is entitled The Psychology and Economics of Motivation. Part II is The American Way of Life.

In part I Scitovsky summarises what physiological psychologists have to say about behaviour, as that body of psychology is most relevant to extend and correct the economist's theory of economic behaviour. Chapter 5 brings the psychologist's and economist's approaches together. Needless to say, psychologists take a much wider view of human behaviour than economists do. Drives to relieve discomfort, stimulation to relieve boredom and the pleasures that can accompany and reinforce both—these are the three motive forces of behaviour distinguished by psychologists. Economists, on the other hand, view consumer satisfaction as the goal of all economic activity. They measure economic efficiency by the economy's success in satisfying the consumer's desires, and economic progress by the higher and higher levels of consumers' satisfaction. But is this measurement an adequate reflection of consumer satisfaction? The author zooms in on the phenomena of comfort and pleasure in his analysis of an affluent

---

[16] *The Joyless Economy*, xii–xiii.

society. The remainder of the *The Joyless Economy* integrates elements of the insights of psychologists and economists into a more general theory of human striving for satisfaction, and projecting it on the American way of life. After all, the most important motive force of behaviour, including consumption behaviour, is human yearning for novelty, the desire to know the unknown. In Scitovsky's own words, 'The yearning for new things and ideas is the source of all progress, all civilization; to ignore it as a source of satisfaction is surely wrong.'[17]

Part I: The Psychology and Economics of Motivation

While economists banked on the rationality of behaviour, psychologists took instinct (later replaced by 'drive') as the point of departure for their study of the motivation of behaviour. Since biologically inspired drives cannot explain all behaviour, a more general framework was needed to supplement or supplant the drive theory. The insights of neurophysiology tell us that nerve cells can and do fire spontaneously; hence, independent of biologically inspired drives. The brain's activity—arousal—is continuous, whether we are awake or asleep. And the brain's activity can be monitored with the help of an electroencephalograph. The faster the electric discharges of neurons, the higher the arousal level. Different brain waves (alpha, beta, gamma etc.) correspond to different levels of agitation. The best known are the slow and fairly regular alpha waves when we are at rest and completely relaxed.

The arousal level depends on the stimulation which the central nervous system receives from different sources: the senses, from the muscles and internal organs, and also from the brain itself. The arousal level never drops to zero as long as the organism is alive. We can not only measure arousal, we can also feel it; we experience pain or pleasure. Moreover, because we seek pleasure and try to avoid pain, the concept of arousal is central to the explanation of behaviour. A high arousal is associated with vigilance and quick reaction. It makes one feel excited, emotional, anxious and tense. On the other hand, when one feels slow, less vigilant, drowsy, these are expressions of low arousal.

---

[17] Ibid., 11.

The effects of various stimuli on the arousal level seem to be addictive, however different their nature and sources might be, so that total arousal is the sum of the arousing effect of each stimulus taken separately. There is a relationship between behavioural efficiency and arousal level. For example, people are better able to memorise poetry and to solve arithmetic problems when they raise their arousal level. Since we are aware of the need to attain and maintain the proper activation level for efficient action, we will deliberately try to raise or lower it. The use of pep pills and coffee to keep us alert for intellectual activity, singing to keep awake while driving or counting sheep to fall asleep and so forth, are all examples of raising or lowering our arousal levels. More importantly, the arousal level has much to do with our general feeling of well-being, and thus with influencing our behaviour. Extreme arousal levels are unpleasant; the most pleasant level of total stimulation is intermediate between too much and too little. Scitovsky assumed in his further elaboration that arousal always increases with stimulation, so that the optimum is an intermediate level both of stimulation and arousal.

Personality

As regards personality traits, Scitovsky referred to Jung's extroversion–introversion scale. When we measure the average arousal levels of people classified on this scale, there is a significant difference between introverts and extroverts, suggesting that personality has a lot to do with average arousal. Now, personality measurement is useful in predicting behaviour. For example, it is a well-established fact that introverts do many tasks better in the morning, while extroverts perform better in the afternoon. Extroverts seek excitement, outside stimulation, contact with people to boost their low arousal level while introverts, who have high arousal levels, prefer a quieter life. *The Joyless Economy* tries to unearth the ways in which people seek satisfaction, and the ways in which they are successful in it, influenced by their personality.

We tend to think of people having different tastes, but in fact they have different personalities. Scitovsky concluded that the economist registers differences in what people consume and views these as evidence of their revealed preference. However, the psychologist doesn't stop there; no, he or she tries to delve deeper to find the causes of and explanations for the differences. Arousal reduction (or drive reduction) is important in the economist's point of view as almost all economic activities (i.e. consumption and production) fall into this category. But different—and quite alien—to economics thinking is the other half of the psychologist's theory of motivation of behaviour, dealing with raising a too low arousal.

The Pursuit of Novelty

The chapter on the pursuit of novelty sets the stage up-front. Perfect comfort and lack of stimulation are restful at first, but they soon become boring. At that stage we seek stimulation. Fighting boredom is the opposite of relieving discomfort: the one raises too low, the other lowers too high arousal levels. Boredom is general, while discomfort can be attributed to a particular cause. Boredom, therefore, is more difficult to analyse, because we must take into account the whole gamut of activities capable of fighting boredom, while trying at the same time to find their *common* element that explains their ability to stimulate. There are various types of activities which heighten the arousal level. Probably the most familiar one is physical stimulation.

Then there is mental stimulation; the satisfaction of scientific or idle curiosity also increases one's arousal level. But here again, the extremes don't work. New and surprising sensations are sometimes frightening. An intermediate degree of newness seems most pleasing. The ancient Greeks already understood this; they called it the Golden Mean.

Some information we receive and process is familiar, other is new. The familiar information, which has no need of processing, is called redundant information, and its ratio to the total inflow of objective information is called relative redundancy. The other, the new part of information, is subjective information or subjective novelty; its ratio to the objective information is called relative information. For example: any piece of music loses subjective information content and gains relative redundancy through repeated hearing.

What makes the stimulus of novelty pleasant? Novelty creates a problem, but its enjoyment comes from overcoming that problem. In so doing, the subjective novelty is eliminated by incorporating into what is already familiar to us. The more difficult that is, the more enjoyable it becomes provided it remains within the realm of the possible.

Novelty is a major source of satisfaction. All things first in ones' life, like first love, first exposure to alcohol, first taste of special food, are exciting and are cherished in our memory. However, in the course of time they wear thin. This phenomenon is especially great in affluent economies in which identical consumer durables are produced by the millions.

Another problem regarding novelty is the fact that for maximum enjoyment it must come combined with the already familiar, and it implies that to enjoy it a person must first acquire related knowledge. In other words, the enjoyment of novelty requires learning; the consumption of novelty is *skilled* consumption.

Comfort Versus Pleasure

A crucial juxtaposition in *The Joyless Economy* is comfort versus pleasure. There is behaviour that aims at securing comfort, including (1) the satisfaction of bodily and (2) mental needs to combating boredom. This type of behaviour raises low arousal levels. Although somewhat different and of opposite sign, these two kinds of behaviour are alike, in that both aim at securing a negative good: freedom from pain, unpleasantness or discomfort. The *positive* good is pleasure, and—as Scitovsky underscored—it is very different from comfort. Feelings of comfort or discomfort have to do with arousal levels and depend on whether arousal is not at its optimum level, especially when these changes bring arousal either up from too low or down from too high a level towards its optimum. Comfort and discomfort have to do with the level of one's emotions, and pleasure with the acceleration and deceleration of those emotions. Pleasure accompanies the relief of discomfort. In other words, discomfort precedes pleasure. Psychiatrists call it the hedonic contrast. Continuing in this line of thought implies that too much comfort precludes pleasure. This proposition, Scitovsky claimed, explains the widespread dissatisfaction in America in spite of the high standard of living.

Men and animals demonstrate the tendency to over-satisfy a need, namely because satisfying a need is pleasurable in itself and strengthens the force of whatever activity one is currently engaged in, causing the organism to continue whatever it is doing, often to—and beyond—the point of satiation. This is contradicting the economist's theory of rational consumer behaviour. They expect that market sales at market prices correctly reflect what consumers want and provide the standard to which the structure of production must conform.

Here we have a conflict between the psychologist and the economist, it seems. Not necessarily so, argued Scitovsky. Psychologists are interested in behaviour directly related to the satisfaction of needs, such as eating, while the economists are concerned with budgeting and shopping, events *preceding* that behaviour. Consumers who have to economise on food can decide to space their meals more than before or to eat less at each meal, and by doing the first they can often resolve this problem.

So far, pleasure associated with *reduction* in arousal has been dealt with, but what about a *rise* in arousal? Well, the pleasure that accompanies mounting arousal reinforces and sustains the stimulating, yet taxing, activity once begun, causing it to raise arousal even further. For example, without the mounting excitement of grappling with a problem and the ultimate triumph of resolving it, we would hardly be willing to accept the anguish and the difficulties which accompany all major achievements in the arts and sciences.

The more we are able to satisfy our needs—and that applies especially to affluent societies—the effect is obviously more comfort. However, it appears that this is accompanied by less pleasure. Comfort hinges on the level of arousal being at or close to its optimum, while pleasure accompanies *changes* in the arousal level towards the optimum. The continuous maintenance of comfort eliminates pleasure, precisely because arousal being continuously at its optimum level, there is thus no change in arousal: comfort gained, pleasure lost.

So, choices have to be made. Economists assume that the consumer is weighing the merits—and demerits—of available alternatives. Sometimes they do, but sometimes they don't. There is not just one source of pleasure resulting from satisfying a need; there is another one: the pleasure from escaping boredom. The satisfaction of wants eliminates a discomfort whose initial presence is a necessary condition of pleasure. By contrast, stimulation eliminates the discomfort of boredom, but the condition of deriving pleasure from stimulation is the discomfort not of the boredom it relieves, but of the temporary strain it creates.

Drives to relieve discomfort, stimulation to relieve boredom and the pleasures that can accompany and reinforce both—these are the three motive forces of behaviour distinguished by psychologists. Scottish philosopher David Hume (1711–1776) had more or less the same three motivations in mind. Economists have thrown overboard two of them and only maintain one: the desire for satisfaction.

Scitovsky chose two of the psychologists' classifications applied to affluent societies: comfort and pleasure; where the main scope for choosing between pleasure and comfort lies in the area of stimulation, because affluence crowds out the pleasure of want-satisfaction. In such societies want-satisfaction can be more or less equated with comfort. Hence, in such a society, most pleasure for people comes from stimulation in such a society.

Enter Economics

After covering the psychological ground, economics comes in. Economic activity is only one of many sources of satisfaction. Scitovsky wondered why it is that some satisfactions depend on economic activity while others do not, and are kept out of the market altogether. What is needed is an understanding of economy's place in the total scheme of human satisfaction. On top of this we need to reclassify satisfactions according to some principle which will separate the economic from the non-economic, which can help identify the factors that distinguish them.

One distinguishing criterion is whether a satisfaction goes through the market and thus acquires a market value in the process. Quantifiability is another distinguishing characteristic of economic satisfactions. After all, the market price is the only index of the value people place on the satisfactions they receive and the services they render.

What satisfactions do we get beyond the economic realm? Scitovsky accords value to mutual stimulation. One of the main forms of human satisfaction is stimulus and—as such—is usually outside the economic domain. However, those involved should ideally speaking be of a more or less equal match. If this is not the case, the mutuality of satisfaction will suffer. In such cases, where people have nothing to offer but something to gain, they may provide a monetary inducement which—if sufficient—will turn the activity into an economic one. In those cases, concluded Scitovsky, tennis pros, masters of ceremony, prostitutes, and gigolos represent professions.

In addition to market goods and services, there are many other products and services that don't go through the market, but are rendered free, their reciprocity being assured by, for example, custom, tradition, social pressure and the like. For example the products of one's own kitchen garden, household chores, advice parents give to their children and so forth, fall into this category. All these products and services, which add so much to human satisfaction, are nonetheless left out of the national product.

Work can be a source of satisfaction and in many instances it really is. The national product also doesn't include the satisfaction resulting from labour. The reason is simple—the satisfaction the worker gets out of a job well done doesn't go through the market and, thus, its value cannot be measured. Economists have nothing to say on whether work is pleasant or unpleasant, whereas psychologists find work a source of stimulation, and hence is potentially pleasant.

Empirical evidence shows that there are great variations in different people's evaluation of their work. People who do not have to work according to rules and discipline imposed by others and who are free to vary their tasks sufficiently to avoid boredom and keep up their interest, appear to get more personally involved in their work and find it more challenging and enjoyable. Nevertheless, they are as likely to experience periods of tension and strain as anyone else, but their way of relieving such strain is not to stop working but to keep at it until their sense of accomplishment brings relief. Volunteer work is also proof of the fact that work can be satisfying.

Another example is philanthropy. Philanthropists very likely enjoy their work for itself, as well as making money, and it is the satisfaction of their work which keeps them going long after all their needs for money are fully satisfied.

Those working with gusto tend to bring the same spirit to their leisure; while those who are disgruntled in their work are usually just as disgruntled after work. Scitovsky concluded that if such differences in attitude are due to the nature of the work and correlated with income, then inequalities of income clearly have a deeper meaning than the mere differences in money expenditure they lead to.

The author not only studied the way psychologists looked at human satisfaction but also at how economists' notions on the same would fit; he also considered the economists' classification of economic goods and services as the point of reference and related them to the psychologists' categories.

Economists view consumer satisfaction as the goal of all economic activity. They measure economic efficiency by the economy's success in satisfying the consumers' desires, and economic progress by the higher and higher levels of consumers' satisfaction. But is this measurement an adequate reflection of the consumer's satisfactions? Goods and services can be classified; the simplest being necessities and luxuries. However, the dividing line between them is not an objective one: what for one person is a luxury may be a necessity for another (think of people addicted to nicotine or alcohol), so that is not a useful distinction. Another one, proposed by Sir Ralph Hawtrey, is the distinction between defensive (e.g. to remedy pain) and creative (e.g. giving positive gratification) products. Scitovsky finds his own distinction between comfort and stimulus better, as most products are not just defensive or just creative; they often yield both comfort and pleasure.

Economic progress has created a new situation. The distinction between pain and pleasure has become interesting and relevant only now, as the satisfaction of one of them (i.e. pain) may be within reach. The avoidance of pain is now a satiable desire. By contrast, the desire for pleasure seems insatiable as confirmed by laboratory tests. The difference between satiable and insatiable desires acquires practical relevance as technical, chemical, medical and economic progress brings complete pain avoidance ever closer. Comforts are like necessities (defensive products) or potential necessities, things that will become necessities as increasing affluence renders them more accessible. And this results in an overuse of defensive products. In turn, defensive products have the tendency to contribute to pollution and so inflict a burden on the general public. Creative products are more valuable and defensive products less valuable for society than they appear to the individual.

Scitovsky asked whether this is really true: Is the need for comforts limited and the demand for goods that provide them satiable? To save time and energy in all uses (work, routine living and enjoyment in life) but one is rational and adds to one's satisfaction if, and only if, the time and energy so saved can be put to better purpose than that one use. If one's ability to do that is limited, one's need for the comfort derived from saving time and energy in all the other uses is equally limited. Scitovsky then concluded, 'That can create a quandary, and it almost certainly does in modern America, where the average person's not getting enough exercise and not knowing what to do with his leisure time are becoming universally recognized as increasing serious social problems.'[18]

But what does provide satisfaction according to psychologists? Defensive products turn out to be both the source of comfort and a second cousin to necessities. Since the demand for necessities is satiable, the question arose whether the demand for the sources of it is also satiable. To answer this question, status and addiction have to be considered. The first is a source of comfort, the second a psychological process which can turn almost anything into a comfort, and both exceptions to the rule that demand for defensive products is satiable. Such exceptions disrupt the obvious relation between money expenditure and satisfaction.

Income and Happiness

Are consumers more satisfied the more they can spend? That is, at least, the economist's assumption. But is this correct? It isn't, argued Scitovsky. Despite the fact that over the period 1946–1970 of solid economic growth, resulting in a real per capita rise of more than 60 % in the USA, the proportion of Americans who considered themselves very happy, fairly happy, and not too happy, had hardly changed at all. The explanation is that one's happiness depends on where one stands in relation to

---

[18] Ibid., 113.

'the Joneses' and not at all on one's absolute standard of living; status and rank play their part.

Scitovsky argued that there are other sources of happiness besides income. Work is another important source of happiness. Work satisfaction is positively correlated with one's ranking in the social and economic hierarchy. In addition, people get addicted to their rank and status. Novelty, as a source of stimulus satisfaction, comes in as a result of a rise in income which, in turn, adds to our comfort. In other words, there is novelty in the *change* from a lower to a higher level of living. Our economic sources of satisfaction are just *some* among very many. Hence, the economist's valuation of national income is inappropriate as an index of human welfare.

Having reached this stage of understanding, *The Joyless Economy* subsequently addresses the question why affluence leaves so many people unsatisfied. Scitovsky introduced the metaphor of the menu of a Chinese restaurant with hundreds of dishes. We don't know what to order. Only when an expert does the ordering, do we realise how badly we do our own and what good things we are missing. In other words, we don't seem to have the right *skills* to order and we lack the right consumption skills. The traditional theory of consumer behaviour fails to recognise the need for novelty and variety.

Part II: The American Way of Life

We need comfort as well as stimulus. The American consumer seems reluctant to recognise the need for stimulus, which is reflected in his consumption pattern: lots of comfort, but little stimulation. One explanation is the American Puritan ethic. Comparison with Western European behaviour does show where the challenges are. The difference between American and Western European consumption patterns is that the former have a lot more to do with comfort and a lot less with pleasure. Americans economise on effort when they are more affluent.

Now, what about time? Time and effort are often considered as two of a pair. In the course of time, the workweek has shortened, leaving more time for consumers to do with it as they please. However, there is a paradox in that the elite, the professionals, independents and executives continue to put in long hours of work. The others watch more and more TV, without getting much pleasure from it hence—a rather irrational way to spend one's time.

Time and effort are not the only inputs into our daily existence on which we tend to economise too much. Care and bother fall into the same category. People don't bother to turn the TV off when they leave the room, food not eaten is thrown away, and in shopping the Americans are also careless, according to Scitovsky. In contrast, Europeans seem to take more time and effort when they shop. The result is that this puts more pressure on producers to satisfy European consumer tastes and it also increases the correlation of price with quality. European products are typically of better quality than American ones.

'Is it Too Dull?'

Are Europeans pleasure-loving, frivolous and sophisticated and are Americans sober, hard-working, and frugal? In the chapter 'Is it Too Dull?', the author compares Western Europeans with Americans in how they take time and enjoy food, take vacations and enjoy the company of friends. Europeans pay more attention and devote more time to all these activities.

Differences in behaviour can be explained by the difference in personality. And personalities, as already noted, can be ordered according to average arousal levels. Studies have been done to capture these personality differences between countries. It appears that there is a positive relationship between populations with—on average—low arousal levels and the high intake of stimulants and low intake of depressants.

America, together with Great Britain, New Zealand, Australia and Norway, is at the low end of the scale. Japan, Germany, Austria, Italy and France are at the opposite end of the scale. On average, high arousal populations are low consumers of stimulants but high on depressants. However, the American peculiarities happen to be out of character: the pressure of extroverts for novelty, for change for alteration, is not very manifest in Americans' acceptance of dull food, drab surroundings, their tendency to sit at home, instead of being with friends and less enterprising in leisure.

Scitovsky concluded as follows: 'our predisposition to do one thing and the outside pressures that make us do the opposite thing may well create a feeling of frustration and dissatisfaction with our own behaviour'.[19]

'Our Puritan Ghost'

The chapter 'Our Puritan Ghost' concerns the strong influences at work that make Americans go against rationality and temperament. Scitovsky pointed to cultural, educational and economic forces whose cumulative effect might account for the conflict between what Americans want and what they get, which explains *some* of their frustrations. He downplayed the influence of advertising; true, producers have a strong influence on consumer tastes; however, empirical evidence at the time demonstrated that advertising wasn't an important channel of influence.

The most important influence is the Puritan heritage and its effect on American consumers. The Puritan ethic is ideally suited to sway people's preferences against stimulation and in favour of comfort, as they are against pleasure but will allow the legitimacy of consumption necessary for a healthy and productive life. However, Puritan disapproval of pleasure is not against *all* enjoyment, but only against activity and expenditure *specifically and exclusively* aimed at providing or enhancing enjoyment. Production, the creation of market value, and one's contribution to production, including the earning of an income from it, are highly respected by the Puritans, contrary to consumption, hence people's concern with maximising money income rather than with getting satisfaction from the goods and services bought with that income. Another important cultural force which influences Americans' way of life is caused by a bias in their education which—again—is swaying their consumption pattern in favour of comfort and against stimulus enjoyment. What is education preparing Americans for? The ability to enjoy culture, music and literature is best acquired by training. All this requires a lot of practice; its careful sequencing from the easy toward the more difficult. In short, all stimulus enjoyment is *skilled* consumption.

---

[19] Ibid., 202.

However, the Puritan attitude towards culture exerts its influence here as well. In the nineteenth and early twentieth centuries, education in the USA shifted more and more towards training in production skills and less and less towards preparation for the enjoyment of life. The curriculum was greatly influenced by the needs of industry and business. Paradoxically, while professional and vocational training increasingly crowded consumption skills out of the curriculum, the need for such skills was growing with the rise in the standard of living. The lack of interest in culture expresses a bias in favour of comfort and against stimulation.

Our Disdain for Culture

Scitovsky defines culture as knowledge. Culture is the preliminary information we must have to enjoy the processing of further information. Consumption skills are, therefore, part of culture; production skills are not. And since the enjoyment of stimulation is skilled consumption, while the enjoyment of comfort requires no skill, only stimulus enjoyment is a cultural activity. All stimulus enjoyment requires a certain degree of skill. It is, therefore, useful to define culture a bit more narrowly, that is, as the training and skill to enjoy stimulus satisfactions, whose enjoyment requires training. The three favourite pastimes in the USA are watching TV, driving a car for pleasure and shopping. When leisure increases, these three ways of enjoyment are inadequate to satisfy the demand for stimulation; moreover, their respective novelty wears out quickly.

Scitovsky's remedy, as noted, is culture. Americans must acquire the consumption skills that will give them access to society's accumulated stock of past novelty and enable them to supplement the currently available flow of novelty as a source of stimulation. Music, painting and literature are the obvious examples. But why didn't it work out like that? The anti-cultural bias of America's Puritan tradition may well have been the most important reason.

The author also underscored the value of conversation: talk between people is mutually stimulating. It is pleasant when the partners are well matched. This requires knowledge on the part of the conversationalists. A major part of information is—of course—obtained through education. However, given the emphasis on production skills, courses on literature, art, music and history are less popular. Hence, the skills to engage in a stimulating conversation are being neglected. One of the consequences is that Americans by and large are lonelier than for example, Europeans. More emphasis on liberal arts education and subsidies to the arts will help to revive the pleasures of conversation and add to stimulation and satisfaction; in short the pleasure of life.

Mass production was introduced in nineteenth-century America in response to a shortage of skilled labour. It enhanced productivity. The downside was that the monotony of mass production was fully matched by the monotony of its product. The drawback was the transformation of much interesting, demanding, challenging work into effortless, but dull, monotony for all but a small portion of the labour force. What was also not taken into account was the concomitant change in the nature of products which has gradually changed the environment. In the mass-production economy, stimulus satisfaction also depends on novelty, which in goods produced in the millions is used up much sooner than the comfort they yield.

Then there is scarcity of imagination. The economy hasn't been able to increase the effectiveness of human imagination in producing novelty to stimulate our pleasure in life. Thus the rising cost of access to imagination (such as opera's, plays, concerts, ballet etc.) raises the price of novelty. The rising cost of ordinary labour is offset by its increasing productivity and, therefore, doesn't raise the price of comfort. The rise in the relative price of novelty squeezes its supply and confronts its suppliers—artists, entertainers, musicians—with the uncomfortable choice between a reduction in their incomes or a decimation of their numbers.

However, technological innovations have made novelty more accessible and wider spread than in the past. This has led to—as Scitovsky called it—the *banalisation of art*. The great frequency with which we are exposed to poor reproductions of paintings and of music wears their novelty thin.

What's Wrong with Specialisation?

Specialisation is the key to the high efficiency of production which explains the specialist's high prestige in the American production-oriented society. If specialisation is the necessary condition for efficient production, efficiency in consumption demands the very opposite. People's welfare depends on the *balanced satisfaction* of their needs. And one of their needs is enjoyable stimulation, which has a great variety of sources. Therefore, a full and interesting life demands the ability to enjoy at least a good selection of these sources. Specialisation also has a bearing on the division of labour between specialists and generalists. Consumers are generalists and Americans are poor generalists. The reader is reminded of the metaphor of the Chinese restaurant with its extensive menu. As long as the consumer doesn't know what to order, he can't enjoy the richness of Chinese cuisine.

Why is the American consumer a poor generalist? The generalist has less prestige than the specialist, while the former's task is getting more and more complex given the ever more complex environment he or she is supposed to understand and act in. Generalists being looked down upon, combined with the ever-increasing difficulty to perform generalist tasks, has dangerous implications as the generalist's tasks are being neglected. Another consequence is that generalist professions, such as handyman, are on the decline; their tasks are being taken over by specialists.

Scitovsky considered the steep increase in do-it-yourself activities, such as house repairs, renovation, home decoration and gardening, a noticeable demonstration of a revolt against the increase in specialisation and the division of labour, leading to ever-increasing dissatisfaction with work. The importance of such work is an outcome of the conflict between the American tendency to seek rather more stimulation than people in other countries, in sex, in stimulants, in frequent job and domicile changes, and the willingness to accept less stimulation than others enjoy in most areas of consumption. The first stems, as we have seen, from the American national character, its extrovert nature; the second was explained in terms of the cultural and economic influences that result in the impoverished consumption patterns of Americans, which deprive them of so much of the stimulation that for other nations is an important ingredient of a satisfying life.

What is the main message of *The Joyless Economy*? It is the *notion of novelty* as an object of desire and as a source of satisfaction, of fulfilment in life. Scitovsky noted, before concluding, that the American lifestyle can't be maintained when duplicated by other nations, as it is simply too expensive in terms of air, water and soil pollution, ecological degradation, and energy consumption. It is very doubtful that the planet could sustain many more people with an American-type lifestyle. So it is high time to re-examine it.

Scitovsky feared that it is hard to accept the idea that one way of making the high-cost lifestyle less costly is to make it less austere and more frivolous. He ended the book as follows: 'Such a remarkable notion goes very much against our ingrained habits of thought, yet the findings of this book clearly point in that direction.'[20]

---

[20] Ibid., 290.

5

The Return of Neoclassical Economics

Introduction

Keynesianism wasn't equipped to solve stagflation in the 1970s, while neoclassical recipes only deepened the Great Depression of the 1930s. This suggests that the popularity of economic schools of thought depends on what is happening in the real world; one of the two main schools—Keynesianism or neoclassical economics—flourished when the time was ripe. For the neoclassical school the time was getting ripe towards the end of the 1970s. Daniel Stedman Jones wrote in *Masters of the Universe*,

> By the 1970s, however, the political climate was different. Neoliberalism was on the verge of a breakthrough. Still very much in the minority at the start of the decade, by 1980 neoliberal policies were at the core of the manifestos for government of both Ronald Reagan and Margaret Thatcher. The economic crises of these years—the collapse of the Bretton Woods international monetary system, stagflation across the western world, the virtual collapse of labour relations in Britain, two oil crises, and the failures of prices and incomes policies—transformed the prospects of transatlantic neoliberal policies.[1]

---
[1] Stedman Jones, D. (2012) *Masters of the Universe: Hayek, Friedman, and the British Neoliberal Politics*. Princeton: Princeton University Press, 179.

However, the neoclassics' Achilles heel is their assumptions, such as rational expectations and markets achieving an optimal state of the economy; they were stripped bare by the Great Recession, well argued by, among others, John Cassidy in *How Markets Fail* (2009),[2] the summary of which is included in Chap. 7. Well before the outbreak of the crisis, these assumptions were already challenged by economists who didn't believe that they were reflective of the real world.

New Institutional economist Douglass North argues that when applied to economic history and development, the neoclassical theory focused on technological development and, more recently, on human capital development. He concluded that the neoclassical analysis of economic performance through time contained two erroneous assumptions: (1) that institutions wouldn't matter and (2) nor would time. North demonstrated that it is institutions that constitute the underlying determinant of sustained economic growth of societies.

Another economist who refuted the unchanging level of rationality of economic actors was Albert Hirschman in his book *Exit, Voice and Loyalty* (1970), a thought-provoking antidote to the neoclassical doctrine.

Friedrich Hayek and Milton Friedman spearheaded the counter-revolution, as some commentators argued, of the return of neoclassical economics. They influenced political and economic thinking, particularly in the Anglo-Saxon world, with their philosophies of small government, free functioning of the market and individual liberties. The biographies of Hayek, Friedman and—by way of some 'antidote'—Hirschman are included in this chapter, as well as summaries of their books mentioned Chapter 1.

Biography: Friedrich August Hayek (1899–1992)

Friedrich August von Hayek was born in Vienna, Austria, on 8 May 1899. Friedrich, who was to live a long and productive life, was the son of August von Hayek, a medical doctor in Vienna's health department.

---
[2] Cassidy, J. (2009) *How Markets Fail: The Logic of Economic Calamities*. London: Allen Lane.

Young Friedrich hailed from noble families both from his father's and mother's side. After the Great War noble titles were banned by law in Austria; consequently; von Hayek became Hayek. His mother was related to the Wittgensteins and Friedrich was a cousin of philosopher Ludwig Wittgenstein.

Hayek was one of the leading economists of the twentieth century, and in many ways he was the opposite of John Maynard Keynes. There is even a rap on *YouTube* about their opposite views (see Keynes's biography in Chap. 2 on his relationship with Hayek). A representative of the Austrian School, he advanced its classical philosophy, after having bid farewell to his earlier socialist ideas.

Like Ludwig Wittgenstein, Hayek was enlisted in 1917 and fought in an artillery regiment of the Austrian-Hungarian army in Italy. He was a spotter in an air force plane. During the war he had time to read scholarly books in the trenches. After the war, Hayek decided to pursue an academic career. He studied law at the University of Vienna.

Through his cosmopolitan friend Herbert Furth he was introduced to a sophisticated young crowd who regularly gathered and discussed contemporary themes, such as Marxism and psychoanalysis, in Café Landtmann, close to the university. Through them he got to know English philosophers and authors such as Bertrand Russell and the 'Fabians' Sydney and Beatrice Webb. Hayek was also influenced by Friedrich von Wieser's democratic socialism. Furth and Hayek established the Democratic Students Association. Later on they organised the Geist-Krcis, where subjects ranging from logical positivism to plays were discussed. Amongst the Geist-Kreis members were economists Oskar Morgenstern, Gottfried Haberler and Fritz Machlup.

His Academic Career and Publications

Hayek obtained his law PhD title in 1921, after which he took a job at the War Claims Settlement Bureau. This position allowed him sufficient time to get a second doctorate in the combined field of political science and economics. Hyperinflation, under which the Austrian population had to suffer (including the Hayek family, who lost almost all their property), became a lifelong preoccupation.

Hayek had started attending Friedrich von Wieser's lectures during his student days. Von Wieser contended that prices were the key to understanding how the market works and that entrepreneurs play a key part in ensuring progress through developing new markets. Von Wieser introduced Hayek to the economist Ludwig von Mises, who got him the job at the War Claims Settlement Bureau. Von Mises was the founding father of the Austrian School of economics, emphasising the self-regulating role of markets.[3]

Meanwhile the Bolsheviks had been victorious in Russia. The Renner government threatened to nationalise Austria's key industries. At the time there was a wave of socialist philosophy and sympathies moving through Europe which was contrary to the heart of the Austrian School's thinking. Von Mises published a provocative book in 1922: *Socialism: An Economic and Sociological Analysis*, which made a deep impression on the politically left-leaning Hayek. Von Mises's book made Hayek doubt socialism. He remembered, 'Socialism promised to fulfil our hopes for a more rational, more just society. And then came [Mises's socialism] … Our hopes were dashed. Socialism told us that we had been looking for improvement in the wrong direction.'[4]

Mises wrote in *Economic Calculation in the Socialist Commonwealth* (1920) that a centrally planned economy lacked the necessary data to calculate prices that bring supply and demand into balance. Substituting planners for markets, there are no longer market prices which planners would need for making accurate calculations of the prices of scarce resources, and for ensuring an efficient distribution of these resources. In a centrally planned society, consumers are deprived of expressing their preference for a particular good by paying the price for it. Central planning deprives individuals of a fundamental freedom.

---

[3] Ha-Joon Chang noted in *Economics: The User's Guide* that there are differences between the Austrian school and neoclassical economics: 'Not all Neoclassical economists are free-market economists … The adherents of the Austrian school are even more ardent supporters of the free market than most followers of the Neoclassical school … While emphasizing the importance of individuals, the Austrian school does *not* believe that individuals are atomistic rational beings, as assumed in Neoclassical economics … "custom and tradition stand *between* instinct and reason", Hayek intoned' (138–9).

[4] Wapshott, N. (2011) *Keynes–Hayek: The Clash That Defined Modern Economics*. New York: Norton & Company, 29.

As noted, von Mises's arguments impressed Hayek, which inspired him to write a paper on house rent control, that the Austrian government had introduced after the end of WWI. The rent control policy turned out to be disastrous. Hayek devoted a chapter in *The Constitution of Liberty* (1960) on housing and town planning.

The United States, Booms and Depressions

With von Mises's help, Hayek got the chance to visit the United States in 1923–1924 where he worked as a research assistant at New York University (NYU) under professor Jeremiah Whipple Jenks, a currency expert on the Allied Reparation Commission.[5] Hayek's main motive for coming to New York was to find out what the American thinking was on booms and depressions.

Von Mises had been talking to Hayek about the idea of starting a programme of business-cycle research and producing forecasts for the Vienna Chamber of Commerce. His attempts to land Hayek a job at the Chamber of Commerce failed. Von Mises then raised enough money to create an independent forecasting institute: the Austrian Institute of Business Cycle Research. Hayek led the institute. He was then only 30 years old. In the institute's February 1929 newsletter, Hayek rightly predicted that the American stock market boom would collapse: 'The boom will collapse within the next few months.'[6]

In 1931 Hayek published *Prices and Production*. Two years later *Monetary Theory and the Trade Cycle* (1933) was published, which he had begun while in New York. Hayek's view on recessions was that their cause was the preceding booms during which growth had become unbalanced.

Recessions were a way of restoring the balance between savings and investment. Hayek observed that production in advanced economies is more and more sophisticated, more 'roundabout'. This meant that it took

---

[5] When Hayek reported at NYU, Jenks was at Cornell where he had a second professorship. Hayek took a temporary job as a dishwasher because he ran out of money. To Hayek's relief, Jenks came back from Cornell just in time, and so he ended his short-lived dishwasher career. He would have loved to stay another year in the USA, but he received word of a Rockefeller scholarship too late; he was already on his way back to Austria.

[6] Nasar, S. (2011) *Grand Pursuit: The Story of Economic Genius*. London: Fourth Estate, 280.

more and more time to supply goods for the market, as more sophisticated equipment and machinery had to be developed first. Hayek pointed to the role of money as another factor explaining business cycles. In a situation where banks issue more loans and when there is no more saving taking place, this will trigger an increase in the demand for consumer goods. The price of these goods will go up; inflation will be the result. Producers will meanwhile try to satisfy the increase in consumer demand by quickly applying fewer sophisticated and time-consuming production processes. However, the increase in prices pushes interest rates up as well to compensate the inflated price level. This increase, in turn, will have a dampening effect on consumer demand, leading to lower production of these goods and to workforce lay-offs. The past emphasis on fast production of consumer goods resulted in less investment and fewer employment opportunities within firms producing investment goods, adding to the unemployment problem.

While Keynes explained unemployment as a result of a drop in aggregate demand, Hayek explained it as a result of the change in the *composition* of demand; that is, more consumer goods and fewer investment goods. Hayek's remedy was thus to cut down on consumer goods, so that extra savings are being freed up to finance additional, more sophisticated 'roundabout' investment goods. Hayek argued that Keynes's recipe for depressions, that is, stimulating aggregate demand, would only distort the recovery process; it would worsen the situation instead of improving it.

From Vienna to London and Cambridge

These insights drew the attention of Lionel Robbins, a young professor at the London School of Economics (LSE). He invited Hayek to come to London, and in 1931 Hayek took up the position of Tooke Professor of Economic Science and Statistics at LSE. Hayek adopted British citizenship at the time of the Austrian *Anschluss* in 1938.

By the time Hayek settled in London, Keynes had just published *A Treatise on Money* (1930), which Hayek attacked brutally in LSE's journal *Economica* (see Keynes's biography in Chap. 2 for more information). Keynes was concentrating on finalising what would become the most influential book on economics of the twentieth century: *The General Theory of Employment, Interest, and Money* (1936).

Whatever the differences between Hayek and Keynes, more and more of Hayek's LSE students deserted him in favour of Keynes's ideas. Hayek's ideas were dismissed by most economists, not in the least as his business-cycle theory failed to provide solutions to end the Great Depression, while Keynes's ideas did. Hayek's mood of gloom was compounded by the fact that after Austria's *Anschluss* into the Third Reich, many of his Geist-Kreis friends fled Austria, including von Mises.

The Road to Serfdom

Hayek had hoped to assist the British during the war by broadcasting propaganda in German to help undermine the morale of the German population. It was not to be. Hayek continued to run LSE's dramatically shrunken economics department. Despite these setbacks he found inspiration to write *The Road to Serfdom* (1944), which was supposed to turn out like Keynes's *The Economic Consequences of Peace* (1919), which was published right after the end of WWI and was addressed to a general readership. Hayek had meanwhile become more and more convinced that government's role in the economy, and in the society at large as promoted by socialist parties, was detrimental to economic development as well as to individual liberties.

Not surprisingly, *The Road to Serfdom* was a defence of capitalism and free markets. What he said about the role of government was accompanied by a warning: government policy limits individual liberties which eventually take the society down on the slippery *Road to Serfdom*. Hayek foresaw a period of gloom, as later echoed by George Orwell's novel *Nineteen Eighty-Four*. Apart from limiting individual liberties, government's income redistribution policies would put a break on economic growth, as the rich will have less incentive to invest; the fruits of their efforts will be taken away by high taxes. Equal opportunities are also damaging, Hayek said, because if all the children would have the same starting point, that would imply that all the parents would have to have the same level of income. Such a situation can only emerge under totalitarian rule.

His friend, Fritz Machlup, sent *The Road of Serfdom*'s manuscript to several publishers, who rejected it. Harper's, for example, dismissed it as 'labored' and 'overwritten'. Routledge accepted it finally in 1943. The first edition was published in March 1944. Early the following year Hayek heard that the University of Chicago Press had accepted it as well. *The Road to Serfdom* was reviewed by the well-known commentator Henry Hazlitt on the front page of the *New York Times*. Hayek, like Keynes before him, became instantly famous in America with his anti-big government tradition. The Book-of-the-Month Club edition sold 600,000 copies. The timing of the book's publication was superb, as WWII was drawing to a close and the American public was preoccupied with future US–Soviet relations. The sales in Europe were much more modest; Europe had meanwhile embraced the welfare state philosophy.

Keynes and Hayek never came to terms on their long-running debate over how much and what kind of government intervention in the economy was compatible with a free society. Keynes firmly believed that a prosperous society, in which everyone is employed, was the surest way of maintaining the independence of thought and action which was the guarantor of true democracy. Nonetheless, Keynes endorsed *The Road to Serfdom* (Keynes was not at all impressed by what he had seen in the Soviet Union in 1925) and nominated Hayek, rather than his pupil Joan Robinson, for membership of the British Academy in 1944. When Keynes died of a heart attack on 21 April 1946, Hayek wrote to Keynes's wife that Keynes was 'the one really great man I ever knew, and for whom I had unbounded admiration. The world will be a much poorer place without him.'[7]

The Mont Perelin Society

After the war Hayek didn't return to Vienna, since most of his friends had left Austria or were dead. He had hoped to re-create the Geist-Kreis as a way of demonstrating that the ideas of the European Enlightenment were still alive. In 1945 Hayek's article 'The Use of Knowledge in Society' was published in the *American Economic Review*. This article was selected as

---

[7] Skidelsky, R. (2003) *John Maynard Keynes 1883–1946; Economist, Philosopher, Statesman*, 833.

5 The Return of Neoclassical Economics   233

one of the twenty top articles published in the *Review* during its first 100 years. Hayek argued that the market system provides the information necessary to take economic decisions. The great advantage of organising production in a market system is that firms don't need to go out and ask consumers what things to produce and what quantities to make as prices are guiding them. Hayek compared the price system with a *system of telecommunications*. Distortions of this system, for example caused by inflation or wage and price controls, give the wrong signals. Prices will no longer reflect the most efficient modes of production. Chances are then great that resources will be employed in areas that are neither the most optimal for the firms involved, nor for the economy as a whole. This reduces efficiency and a society's standard of living.

Hayek neglected to account for serious failures of the market system. Joseph Stiglitz, just to cite one critic, demonstrated that information is key to different types of market failure. Information is not fully revealed by market prices, according to Stiglitz. He argued that information is more like air: Its adequate provision is a precondition for other things to take place. When this information is lacking, or is only partly available, Hayek's telecommunications system can't work.

In 1947 the conservative Volker Fund, established by a banker of the Schweitzerishe Kreditanstalt and a few other funders, offered to sponsor a conference to found a community of like-minded liberals. Hayek organised the first meeting of what came to be known as the Mont Perelin Society, named after the hill overlooking Lake Geneva where Hotel du Parc was located; the venue for the first conference.

Most attendees were European émigrés. They included the philosopher Karl Popper, the economists Ludwig von Mises and Fritz Machlup, as well as young Milton Friedman and his brother-in-law Aaron Director. Journalists Henry Hazlitt of *Newsweek* and *Fortune*'s John Davenport attended as well. After 3 days of sometimes heated debates, LSE's Lionel Robbins drafted the final communiqué. Sylvia Nasar presented a few notable quotes in her *Grand Pursuit*:

> '… freedom of thought and expression, is threatened by the spread of creeds which, claiming the privilege of tolerance when in the position of a minority, seek only to establish a position of power in which they can

suppress and obliterate all views but their own', the statement emphasised free enterprise, opposition to historical fatalism, and the obligation of nations as well as individuals to be bound by moral codes and, above all, support for complete intellectual freedom.[8]

The Constitution of Liberty

Much of what the communiqué said is to be found in more depth in Hayek's *The Constitution of Liberty* (1960), which was published 13 years after the first Mont Perelin conference. *The Constitution of Liberty* is more a work on political philosophy rather than an economic treatise. Hayek published the book at the height of Keynesianism. Initially, his book was not favourably reviewed and sold badly. Hayek was at the time seen as a 'preacher of an obscure sect', as John Cassidy wrote.[9] Even his friend Lionel Robbins was not appreciative; he found Hayek's book unreasonably extreme in its treatment of liberalism. It would take two decades after the book's publication before Hayek's opinions gained appreciation by none other than Prime Minister Margaret Thatcher and President Ronald Reagan.

The Constitution of Liberty depicts an ideal society in which citizens enjoy freedom, shows how it can be achieved and explains what its realisation would mean in practice. This ideal has to do with liberty, with individual freedom. The coercive power of government should be limited as much as possible. Yet, Hayek acknowledges that government has to play a role in particular, well-identified fields. Markets should be allowed to function as freely as possible, thereby providing the right price signals for consumers and producers alike.

Hayek has been characterised by his critics as a political conservative. He objected to this qualification as he explained in the book's postscript, entitled 'Why I am Not a Conservative'. Hayek considered himself to be a liberal in the British connotation of the term.

---

[8] Nasar, *Grand Pursuit*, 404.
[9] Cassidy, *How Markets Fail*, 38.

Austria and Germany

Hayek visited his home town Vienna after the Mont Perelin conference. The once radiant and cosmopolitan city was in bad shape and so were its inhabitants. The Allies, who were still in charge of the city, managed it with an iron fist, banning any economic activity. Hayek observed that the Austrians were barred from helping themselves out of their desperate situation. After his visit to Vienna, he went on a speaking tour in Germany organised by the British Council. He wrote to his friend Fritz Machlup about his experience in Darmstadt:

> I didn't have any idea the Germans knew anything about me at the time; and I gave a lecture to an audience so crowded that the students couldn't get in, in an enormous lecture hall. And I discovered then that people were circulating hand-typed copies of *The Road to Serfdom* in German, although it hadn't been published in German yet.[10]

Upon his return to London, Hayek organised a drive to collect books published since 1938 that censorship and WWII had kept out of the hands of Austrian and German scholars. Before long he had collected 2500 volumes which were sent to Vienna.

In 1948 the Marshall Plan was adopted and Germany—which was industrially speaking on its knees—revived, thanks to: (1) a slice of the Marshall Plan pie, (2) currency reform and (3) the lifting of price controls. Promoter of the *Wirtschaftswunder*, Ludwig Erhard, commented that the liberalisation of the economy awakened entrepreneurial impulses. The worker became ready to work, the trader to sell and the economy to produce. Hayek was happy about Germany's recovery as it was proof of his faith in free markets, free trade and sound monetary policies. It was also a hopeful sign that the liberal European civilisation wasn't doomed.

---

[10] Nasar, *Grand Pursuit*, 405.

University of Chicago

After having returned to London, he received an invitation in 1950 to teach at the University of Chicago. He accepted and resigned from the LSE. His lectures at the University of Chicago about the liberal tradition were attended by, among others, Milton Friedman on whom Hayek would have a big influence. Yet, Friedman was also appreciative of Keynes for the latter's originality of mind and for his invention of macroeconomics. Hayek's return to the USA was initially welcomed by American conservatives. However, they were in for a disappointment. Hayek despised most Republican politicians and he didn't like the American materialistic way of life.

The Final Years

Hayek came back to Europe in 1962 to teach at the Albert-Ludwigs University of Freiburg, West Germany, where he started writing his *Law, Legislation and Liberty* which would appear in three volumes in 1973, 1976 and 1979, respectively. After his retirement there, he was invited back to the United States. He spent a year as visiting professor of philosophy at the University of California, Los Angeles. From 1968 to 1977 he taught at the University of Saltzburg. Upon completion his term there, Hayek returned to Freiburg.

The collapse of the Soviet Union and the spread of free-market reforms in Eastern Europe confirmed what he had professed in his last book *The Fatal Conceit: The Errors of Socialism*, which he published in 1988, 1 year before the fall of the Berlin Wall.

Hayek died on 23 March 1992 in Freiburg, Germany. He was buried in Neustift am Wald cemetery in the northern outskirts of Vienna.

Honours

To his own surprise—and immense pleasure, as he had lost international recognition—in 1974 he was awarded the Nobel Prize in Economics, together with the Swedish economist Gunnar Myrdal. However, Hayek did not like that he was awarded the prize together with Myrdal, a staunch social democrat. According to Nicholas Wapshott, Hayek delivered a critical Nobel Address probably inspired by his indignation. Wapshott gave the following account:

> 'The theory which has been guiding monetary and financial policy during the last thirty years', he explained, was 'fundamentally false' ... He described stagflation as a self-inflicted wound that 'has been brought about by policies which the majority of economists recommend and even urged governments to pursue'. Curing stagflation would require painful readjustments, such as even higher unemployment and widespread bankruptcies, but exactly how 'an equilibrium will establish itself' was beyond the knowledge of all economists, including himself. The Keynesian belief that there was a solution to every economic problem had only conspired to make inflation and unemployment worse.[11]

Hayek's comeback was not complete yet. That happened when Ronald Reagan and Margaret Thatcher came to power. Both publicly praised Hayek's works. One anecdote has it that the only book, besides the one on astrology, on Reagan's bedside table was *The Road to Serfdom*. As for Margaret Thatcher, when visiting the Conservative Research Department in April 1975, where a speaker gave a talk about the Middle Way (i.e. avoiding the extremes of the political spectrum), before the speaker had finished, Thatcher reached into her handbag and took out Hayek's *The Constitution of Liberty*. She held the book up and said in her characteristic voice, 'This is what we believe', and banged the book on the table.

In 1984 Hayek was appointed member of the Order of the Companions of Honour by Queen Elizabeth II. President George H.W. Bush awarded Hayek the Presidential Medal of Freedom in 1991.

The Constitution of Liberty

The Constitution of Liberty is as much a work on political philosophy as an economic treatise.[12] Hayek published the book in 1960 at the height of the Cold War, when Keynesian thinking and the welfare state were in full

---

[11] Wapshott, *Keynes–Hayek*, 257.
[12] Edition used: the Routledge Classics edition of 2006.

bloom. It would take two more decades for Hayek's libertarian philosophy to gain appreciation, from none other than British Prime Minister Margaret Thatcher and President Ronald Reagan.

The Constitution of Liberty consists of three parts: (1) The Value of Freedom, (2) Freedom and the Law, and, (3) Freedom in the Welfare State. The Routledge Classics edition of 2006, which formed the basis for this summary, also features Hayek's postscript entitled, 'Why I am Not a Conservative'. *The Constitution of Liberty*, together with Hayek's *The Road to Serfdom*, is a classic.

The Constitution of Liberty depicts an ideal society, shows how it can be achieved and explains what its realisation would mean in practice. This ideal has to do with liberty, with individual freedom. Hayek has often been identified with the politically conservative. He felt that this qualification was incorrect, as he explained in the postscript.

Introduction

The introduction sets the stage. The author points out that a large segment of the people of the world borrowed from Western civilisation and adopted Western ideals at a time when the West had become unsure of itself and had largely lost faith in the traditions that made it what it is. This was a time when intellectuals in the West had almost abandoned the very belief in freedom that had made its unprecedented fast economic growth possible. Future leaders of developing countries learned during their Western training how the West did not enjoy the moral support of the people of the world, the lack of firm beliefs putting the West at a great disadvantage.

Hayek's original concern was with problems of economic policy. However, he was led to the broader task of approaching the social questions of his time through a restatement of the basic principles of the philosophy of freedom. But this philosophy was being undermined by intellectual trends under various names and disguises. The civilisations based on the philosophy of freedom are in decline, according to Hayek, and if they are not to sink deeper, the philosophy on which they are based ought to be revived, and that is what Hayek set out to do.

Part I: The Value of Freedom

A state of liberty or freedom is achieved when the coercion of some by others is reduced as much as possible in society. Individual or personal freedom is the state in which a person is not subject to coercion by the arbitrary will of another. Freedom presupposes that the individual has some assured private sphere, that there is some set of circumstances in his or her environment with which others cannot interfere. Hayek's interpretation of freedom should be distinguished from political freedom, that is, the participation of people in the choice of their government. Free people in this sense are not necessarily a people of free individuals. A different meaning of freedom is that of inner or metaphysical freedom. It refers to the situation in which people are guided in their actions by their own will.

There is yet another confusion of individual liberty with different concepts denoted by the same word: the use of 'liberty' to describe the physical ability to do what one wants. This kind of freedom appears in dreams, such as the ability to fly. Until recently few people confused this *freedom from* obstacle with the individual freedom that any kind of social order can secure. Hayek warned that only since this confusion was deliberately fostered as part of the socialist argument, has it become dangerous. Once the identification of freedom with power is admitted, there is no limit to the misuse of the word 'liberty' to support measures which destroy individual liberty.

The erroneous identification of liberty with power leads to the former's identification with wealth. Hayek warns the reader that we may be free and yet miserable. Liberty does not automatically mean the absence of all evil. In a negative sense liberty means the absence of a particular obstacle—coercion by other men. The term becomes positive only through what we *do* with liberty.

Obviously the meaning of liberty also depends on the meaning of the concept of coercion. This means such control of the circumstances of a person by another that, in order to avoid greater evil, one is forced to act, not according to a coherent plan of one's own, but to serve the ends of another. Coercion is evil, says Hayek, precisely because it eliminates an individual as a thinking and valuing person and makes him or her a tool in the achievement of the ends of another. However, coercion cannot be altogether avoided. A free society has solved this challenge by conferring the monopoly of coercion on the state and by limiting its power to instances where it is required to prevent coercion by private persons.

The Creative Powers of a Free Civilisation

Civilisation begins when the individual—in the pursuit of her ends—can make use of more knowledge than she herself acquired, and when she can transcend the boundaries of her ignorance by profiting from knowledge she does not herself possess. It is wrong to believe that to achieve a higher civilisation we have merely to put into effect the ideas now guiding us. If we are to advance, we must leave room for a continuous revision of our present conceptions and ideals which will be required by further experience. The conception of humanity deliberately building its civilisation stems from an erroneous intellectualism that regards human resources as something possessed of knowledge and reasoning capacity *independent* of experience. Growth of the human mind is part of the growth of civilisation, and the mind can never foresee its own advance. Unfortunately, the popular effect of scientific advance has been a belief that the range of our ignorance is diminishing and that we can, therefore, aim at more comprehensive and deliberate control of all human activities.

Ways of doing things and traditions and institutions are the products of cumulative growth of civilisations without ever having been designed by any one mind. The examples that prevail spring from the many humble steps taken by persons in doing familiar things in changed circumstances. They are as important as intellectual innovations which are explicitly recognised and communicated as such. Essential to the functioning of the process is that each individual be able to act on his practical knowledge, always unique, and that he be able to use his individual skills and opportunities within the limits known to him and for his own individual purpose.

Hayek then concludes that the case for individual freedom rests chiefly on the recognition of the inevitable *ignorance* of all of us concerning a great many of the factors on which the achievement of our ends and welfare depend. So, liberty is essential to leave room for the unforeseeable and unpredictable. Freedom means renunciation of direct control of individual efforts so that a free society can make use of so much more knowledge than the mind of the wisest ruler could comprehend by itself. The benefits that a particular person derives from freedom are largely the result of uses of freedom by others, and mostly of those uses of freedom that the particular person could never have availed of herself.

In the voyage into the unknown, which is what research is, we are dependent on the vagaries of individual genius and of circumstances. Scientific advance, like a new idea that will spring up in a single mind, will be the result of a combination of conceptions, habits and circumstances brought to society by one person, the result being of lucky accidents as much as of systematic effort.

One of the characteristics of a free society is that people's goals are open, that new ends of conscious effort can spring up, first with a few individuals, to become in time the ends of most. However, it is not only in knowledge, but also in aims and values, that people are the creatures of civilisation. All that we know is that the ultimate decision about what is good or bad will be made not by individual human wisdom but by the decline of the groups that have adhered to the 'wrong' beliefs. The ends of the successful group will tend to become the ends of all members of the society.

The argument for liberty is not an argument against organisation, which is one of the most powerful means that human reason can employ. It is an argument *against* all exclusive, privileged, monopolistic organisation, against the use of coercion to prevent others from trying to do things better. To turn the whole society into one organisation directed according to a single plan would be to extinguish the very forces that shaped the individual human minds that planned it. That society would come to a standstill, not because the possibilities of further growth had been exhausted, but because humanity had succeeded in subjecting all its actions to its existing state of knowledge so that there would be no possibility for new knowledge to appear.

The process of the advance of reason rests on freedom and the unpredictability of human action. However, Hayek warns the reader that 'We are not far from the point where the deliberately organised forces of society may destroy those spontaneous forces which have made advance possible.'[13]

---

[13] *The Constitution of Liberty*, 35.

Of progress Hayek says that it represents a process of adaptation and learning in which not only the possibilities known to us, but also our values and desires continually change. As progress consists of the discovery of the unknown, its consequences must be unpredictable. The most one can expect is to gain an understanding of the kind of forces that bring it about. It is not by the fruits of past success but by living for the future that human intelligence proves itself.

New knowledge has to pass through a long course of adaptation and improvement before full use can be made of it. This means that there will always be people who already benefit from new achievements that have not yet reached others. The rapid economic progress is to a large extent the result of this inequality and was impossible without it. Knowledge, once achieved, becomes available for the benefit of *all*. But before the great majority can benefit, it is the ones with more resources and imagination who promote the introduction and adaptation of new products. In a progressive society it is thus the comparatively wealthy who are somewhat ahead of the rest in the material advantages which they enjoy. So, the existence of groups ahead of the rest is an advantage to those who are behind.

As regards inequality between rich and poor countries, Hayek notes that it is in part the consequence of a greater accumulation of capital, the result of the former's more effective utilisation of knowledge. Yet, there is little doubt that the prospect of poor countries reaching the present level of the West is very much better than it would have been had some world authority, in the course of the rise of modern civilisation, seen to it that no part pulled too far ahead of the rest.

Now, what about inequality within a nation? A society in which only the political privileged are allowed to rise, where those who rise first gain political power and use it to keep the others down, would not be better than an egalitarian society. Obstacles to the rise of some are in the long run obstacles to the rise of all.

The accomplishments of Western civilisation, especially material progress, have become the desire and envy of the rest of the world. The aspirations of the great mass of the world's population can only be satisfied by rapid material progress. Hence, the West is not only the creature but also the captive of progress, in that it has to satisfy the desires of the masses deprived of the material well-being the West enjoys.

The development of a theory of liberty took place in England and France in the eighteenth century. The British theory was empirical and unsystematic; the one developed in France was rationalistic. The first was based on an interpretation of traditions and institutions which had spontaneously grown up; the French one aimed at creating a utopia. However, they merged in the nineteenth century.

Hayek favours the British philosophers as they have given us an interpretation of the growth of civilisation that is still the indispensable foundation of the argument for liberty. An example: the British philosophers find the origin of institutions not in contrivance or design, but in the survival of the successful. This enabled philosophers and economists like Smith, Hume and Ferguson to understand how institutions and moral language and law evolved by a process of cumulative growth and that it was only within this framework. The emergence of order is the result of trial and error, of adaptive evolution.

The British argument was never a complete laissez-faire. They knew that it was not some sort of magic but the evolution of well-constructed institutions where the rules and principles of contending interests and compromised advantages would be reconciled.

As regards traditions, a successful free society will always be a tradition-bound society. The argument for liberty is an argument for principles and against expediency in collective action. Liberty is a system under which all government action is guided by principles. It is also an ideal that will not be preserved unless it is itself accepted as an overriding principle governing all particular acts of legislation.

Now, what is the role to be played by reason in the ordering of social affairs? Hayek says the following:

> What we have attempted is a defence of reason against its abuse by those who do not understand the conditions of its effective functioning and continuous growth. It is an appeal to men to see that we must use our reason intelligently and that, in order to do so, we must preserve that indispensable matrix of the uncontrolled and non-rational which is the only environment wherein reason can grow and operate effectively.[14]

---

[14] Ibid., 61.

All efforts to improve things must operate within a working whole which we cannot entirely control, and the operation of whose forces we can hope merely to facilitate and assist so far as we understand them. Hayek is not against the use of reason as such, but only against such uses as require any exclusive and coercive power of government, and against the consequent preclusion of solutions which are better than the ones to which those in power have committed themselves.

The other side of the liberty coin is responsibility. People must bear the consequences of their actions and will receive praise or blame for them. However, Hayek notes that this belief in individual responsibility has declined together with the esteem for freedom. This is caused by the popularity of determinism, which dominated nineteenth-century science, saying that all natural phenomena are determined by external circumstances. The human mind, so it was believed, must obey uniform laws which appeared to eliminate the role of an individual personality that is essential to the conception of freedom *and* responsibility.

Responsibility has become a legal concept, but it is also a moral concept. The significance of the concept extends beyond the sphere of coercion. Its greatest importance lies in its role in guiding human free decision: when people are allowed to act as they see fit, they must also be held responsible for the results of their efforts.

A person does not necessarily pursue his own aims; one of the main aims is to promote the welfare of other people. It is of the essence of a free society that a man's value and remuneration depend not on capacity in the abstract but on success in turning it into concrete service which is useful to others who can reciprocate.

As for skills, in a free society we are not remunerated for our skills but for using them rightly. True, it is almost never possible to determine which part of a successful career has been due to superior knowledge, ability or effort and which part to fortunate accidents. All that a free society offers is an *opportunity* of searching for a suitable position; no one is 'entitled' to a job or a particular position in the social scale. In a free society there cannot be a collective responsibility of members of a group. The development of large cities has destroyed much of the feeling of responsibility for local concerns.

The great aim of liberty has been equality before the law. Equality of the general rules of law and conduct is the only kind of equality conducive to liberty that can be secured without destroying liberty. Not only has liberty nothing to do with any other sort of equality, but it is even bound to produce inequality in many respects:

> … many of those who demand an extension of equality do not really demand equality but a distribution that conforms more closely to human conceptions of individual merit and that their desires are as irreconcilable with freedom as the more strictly egalitarian demands.[15]

There is a growing tendency to secure equality of conditions in access to education. When looking into the justification of these tendencies/demands, one finds that they rest on the discontent that the success of some people often produces in those that are less successful, or—more bluntly—on *envy*, which, according to John Stuart Mill, is the most anti-social and evil of all passions.

Any attempt to base the case for freedom on the argument of proportionality of reward to moral merit is very damaging to it, since it concedes that material rewards ought to be made to correspond to recognisable merit. The proper answer is that in a free system it is neither desirable nor practicable that material rewards should be made generally to correspond to what is recognised as merit. It is furthermore an essential characteristic of a free society that an individual's position should not necessarily depend on the views that her fellows hold about the merit she has acquired.

What is true of the remuneration for the same services rendered by different people is even more true of the relative remuneration for different services requiring different gifts and capacities; they will have little relation to merit. The market will generally offer for services of any kind the value they will have for those who benefit from them.

Then justice; it requires that those conditions of people's lives that are determined by government be provided equally for all. But equality of those conditions must lead to inequality of results. There is another argument

---

[15] Ibid., 77.

often used in the context of demands for a more equal distribution of wealth and that is the contention that membership of a particular nation entitles the individual to a particular material standard that is determined by the general wealth of that nation. Although there are good reasons to make provisions for the weak, the sick or the victims of disaster, this is no justification for anyone claiming, as a right, a share in *all* the benefits.

Majority Rule

Liberalism is concerned mainly with limiting the coercive powers of governments, whether democratic or not, whereas the dogmatic democrat knows only one limit to government: majority opinion. Liberalism is a doctrine about what the law ought to be, while democracy is a doctrine about what the law will be. Liberalism accepts majority rule as a method of deciding, but *not* as an authority for what the decision ought to be.

To the doctrinaire democrat the fact that the majority wants something is sufficient ground for regarding it as good; for him the will of the majority determines not only what is the law but what is good law. The liberal believes that the powers of any temporary majority be limited by long-term principles, while the crucial conception of the doctrinaire democrat is that of popular sovereignty. It is the acceptance of these principles that makes a collection of people a community. And this common acceptance is the indispensable condition for a free society. If the rights of minorities are recognised, this implies then that the power of the majority ultimately derives from the principles which the minorities also accept. A minority opinion may become a majority one.

Democracy is not necessarily unlimited government. Nor is a democratic government any less in need of built-in safeguards of individual liberty than any other. There are three chief arguments by which democracy can be justified: (1) democracy is the only method of peaceful change that humanity has yet discovered; (2) democracy is an important safeguard of individual liberty and (3) democracy is the only effective method of educating the majority.

Democracy is above all a process of forming opinions independent of government. Freedom of speech and discussion and democracy are inseparable.

It is only because majority opinion will always be opposed by some that our knowledge and understanding progress. Democracy in its dynamic aspects proves itself. Advance occurs when the few convince the many, as new views must appear somewhere before they can become majority views.

The successful politician owes her power to the fact that she moves *within* the accepted framework of thought; that she thinks and talks conventionally. Her task is to discover what the opinions of the majority of voters are. Political and moral views are slowly developed by those who professionally handle abstract ideas. As the great economist John Maynard Keynes noted, in the long run it is ideas that govern evolution. New ideas begin to exercise their influence on political action typically a generation or more after they have been formulated.

Hayek advises caution for the handing over of power by democratic assemblies to the administrators charged with the achievement of particular goals that constitute the danger to individual freedom today. Having agreed that the majority should prescribe rules we will obey in pursuit of our individual aims, we find ourselves more and more subjected to the orders and the arbitrary will of its agents.

If democracy is to survive, it must recognise that it is not the fountainhead of justice and that it needs to acknowledge a conception of justice which does not necessarily manifest itself in the popular view on every particular issue.

Employment and Independence

In the past, most people were self-employed; now more and more are employees of large organisations. If independents now constitute a much smaller and less influential portion of society, are their contributions for this reason less important, or are they still essential to the well-being of a free society? The employed should recognise that it is in their interest to ensure the preservation of a substantial number of independents.

It is in the support of aims, which the market mechanism cannot take care of, that the man of independent means has this indispensable role to play in any civil society. Though the market mechanism is the most effective method for securing those services that can be priced, there are others of great importance that the market will not provide because they cannot be sold to the individual beneficiary. The recognition that there are needs that the market cannot provide does not mean that government ought to be the only agency able to do things that do not pay, that there should be no monopoly, but as many independent centres as possible, able to satisfy such needs.

The leadership of individuals or groups that can back their beliefs financially is particularly essential in the fields of cultural affairs, fine arts, education and research, preservation of natural beauty, historic treasures and—above all—in the propagation of new ideas in politics.

There is something seriously lacking in a society in which *all* the intellectual, moral and artistic leaders belong to the employed class, especially if most of them are employed by government. But we are moving in that direction. The gentleman scholar, such as Darwin, de Tocqueville, Schliemann and even Marx, has disappeared. Even successful leisure needs pioneering and we owe many of the now common forms of living to people who devoted all their time to the art of living. Many of the toys and tools of sport that later became the instruments of recreation for the masses were invented by playboys. Hayek concludes that

> It is one of the tragedies of our time that the masses have come to believe that they have reached their high standard of welfare as a result of having pulled down the wealthy, and to fear that the preservation or emergence of such a class would deprive them of something they would otherwise get and which they regard as their due. If through envy we make certain exceptional kinds of life impossible, we shall all in the end suffer material and spiritual impoverishment.[16]

Part II: Freedom and the Law

Coercion and the State

Coercion occurs when one man's actions are made to serve another man's will, not for his own but for the other's purpose. Coercion implies both the threat of inflicting harm and the intention to bring about certain

---

[16] Ibid., 113.

conduct. Coercion is bad because it prevents a person from using his mental powers to the full, and—consequently—from making the greatest contribution that he is capable of to the community.

A complete monopoly of employment, such as would exist in a fully socialist state, in which the government was the only employer and the owner of all instruments of production, would possess unlimited power of coercion. The recognition of private property is an essential condition of the prevention of coercion. The decisive condition for mutually advantageous collaboration between people is that there be many people who can serve one's needs, so that no one has to be dependent on specific persons for the essential conditions of life or the possibility of development in some direction. Deception and fraud are forms of coercion. For example, deception is a form of manipulation that makes a person do things that the deceiver wants him to do.

Law, Commands and Order

The rule whereby an indivisible border line is fixed within which the being and activity of each individual obtain a secure and free sphere is the law. This nineteenth-century conception of the law has since largely been lost. A transition from specificity and concreteness to increasing generality and abstractness can be found in the evolution from the rules of custom to law in the modern sense. It was with the growth of individual intelligence, and the tendency to break away from the habitual manner of action, that it became necessary to state explicitly the rules and gradually to reduce the positive prescriptions to the negative confinement to a range of actions that will not interfere with the similarly recognised spheres of others.

The conception of freedom under the law rests on the contention that when we obey laws we are not subject to another person's will and are therefore free. This is true only if by law we mean the general rules that apply equally to everybody.

The 'law' that is a specific command, an order that is called a 'law' merely because it emanates from the legislative authority, is the chief instrument of oppression. The confusion of these two conceptions of law (i.e. the general rules and the specific command) is among the chief causes of liberty's decline. Hayek's concern is not the particular content but certain general attributes which the rules ought to possess in a free society. An example: that the legislator confines herself to general rules, rather than particular commands, is the consequence of her necessary ignorance of the special circumstances under which they apply. Yet few beliefs have been more destructive of the respect for rules of law and of morals than the idea that a rule is binding only if the beneficial effect of observing it in the particular instance can be recognised.

The enemies of liberty have always based their arguments on the contention that order in human affairs requires that some should give orders and others should obey. Hayek quotes with appreciation philosopher Michael Polanyi who observed, 'When order is achieved among human beings by allowing them to interact with each other on their own initiative—subject only to the laws which uniformly apply to all of them—we have a spontaneous order in society.'[17]

So, the task of the lawgiver is not to set up a particular order but merely to create the conditions in which an orderly arrangement can be established and renewed. In societies where free individuals cooperate under conditions of division of labour, and do provide the essential condition of individual freedom (and to secure it), then, the main function of law is fulfilled.

The Origins of the Rule of Law

The new power of the highly organised national state which arose in the fifteenth and sixteenth centuries used legislation for the first time as an instrument of deliberate policy. The conception of limited government which emerged in seventeenth-century Britain was a departure, driven by the need of dealing with new problems. During the eighteenth and nineteenth centuries the preservation and perfection of individual liberty became the guiding ideal in England; its institutions and traditions became the model for the civilised world.

---

[17] Ibid., 140.

Hayek looked closer at the classical inheritance as it has relevance for our time. The Greeks had *isonomia*, which meant equality of all citizens before the law, which came to England in the sixteenth century. It continued in use during the next century until 'equality before the law', 'government of law' or 'rule of law' gradually replaced it. There is a difference between isonomia and democracy, as democratic government came to disregard that very equality before the law from which it had derived its justification. Plato and Aristotle both made this clear distinction.

In the seventeenth century the influence of Latin writers eclipsed the Greeks. The *Laws of Twelve Tables* form the foundation of its liberty. The first public law in them provides that no privileges or statutes shall be enacted in favour of private persons, to the injury of others contrary to the law common to all citizens, and which individuals, no matter of what rank, have a right to make use of.

Cicero became the main authority for modern liberalism. We owe to him many of the most effective formulations of freedom under the law. However, after the second century AD the conception that legislation should serve to protect the freedom of the individual was lost. When the art of legislation was rediscovered, it was the Code of Justinian, with its conception of a prince who stood above the law, that served as a model on the European Continent.

In England, however, the developments went into a different direction. Soon after Elizabeth's death in 1603, a struggle began between king and parliament from which emerged, as a by-product, the liberty of the individual. John Locke's *Second Treatise on Civil Government* had a profound influence on further developments in England, America and on the Continent. It was his codification of the victorious political doctrine of the Glorious Revolution which was to control the powers of government. One of his main concerns was how power can be prevented from becoming arbitrary. Locke was loath of sovereign power. The main safeguard against the abuse of authority is the separation of powers.

The process was reversed 200 years later. The new liberalism came more and more under the influence of rationalist tendencies of French philosophers. The likes of Jeremy Bentham and his Utilitarians introduced the desire to remake British law and its institutions on rational principles.

American Constitutionalism

The early colonisers of America were devoted to liberty according to English principles, while the British Parliament meanwhile became committed to the principle of parliamentary sovereignty, very much against the colonists' opinion. The British colonisers discovered that the British constitution had little substance and could not be applied against the claims of parliament, so they concluded that the missing foundation had to be supplied.

They felt that a *constitution* was essential to any free government and that that constitution would mean limited government. The American Constitution was thus conceived as a protection of the people against all arbitrary action by the legislative as well as by other branches of government. It laid down general principles involving the idea of hierarchy of authority, including a hierarchy of rules or laws. The Constitution takes a long-term view, meaning that a majority will abide by the general principles as laid down in the Constitution. Constitutionalism means that all power rests on the understanding that it will be exercised according to commonly accepted principles. Persons on whom power is conferred are selected because it is thought that they are most likely to do what is right.

A commitment to long-term principles gives the people more control over the general nature of the political order than they would possess if its character were to be determined solely by successive decisions of particular issues. The constitution which the new American nation was to give itself was definitely meant not merely as a regulation of the derivation of power but as a constitution of liberty, a constitution that would protect the individual against all arbitrary coercion. In the early nineteenth century the liberal movement in Europe became inspired by the American example.

Liberalism and Administration: The 'Rechtsstaat'

In most countries in continental Europe, 200 years of absolute government had by the middle of the eighteenth century destroyed the traditions of liberty. The main revival came from England. But as the new movement grew it encountered a situation different from that which existed in America at the time, or which had existed in England 100 years earlier. This new factor was the powerful administrative machinery which absolutism had built; a body of professional administrators who had become the main rulers of people. This bureaucracy concerned itself much more with the welfare and the needs of the people than the limited government of the Anglo-Saxon world. So, the Continental liberals had to face problems which in England and the USA appeared much later.

However, the French Revolution was inspired by the ideal of the rule of law. It is doubtful, as Hayek observes, whether it really enhanced its progress. The fact that the ideal of popular sovereignty gained a victory at the same time as the ideal of the rule of law made the latter soon recede into the background. Though the French Revolution was inspired by the American Revolution, it never achieved what had been the chief result of the latter: a constitution which puts limits to the powers of legislation. The Revolution did not touch the power of the administrative authorities, and thus it strengthened the power of the state. The Napoleonic regime only enhanced this. True, the Conseil d'Etat, established in 1799, gave the citizen more protection against discretionary action by administrative authorities.

It was, however, developments in Germany that gained the upper hand in the further development of law. The continuance of monarchic institutions there never allowed confidence in the efficacy of democratic control. The new German legal theories undermined the rule of law.

Immanuel Kant influenced the thinking in that his chief contribution was a general theory of morals which made the principle of the rule of law appear as a special application of a more general principle of the categorical imperative. Codification of all the laws was done in Prussia in the eighteenth century (and taken over by Napoleon). Prussia also developed the rule that all disputes between the administrative authorities and private citizens were referred to the jurisdiction of the ordinary courts. As Hayek noted, this was one of the chief prototypes in the ensuing discussion on the Rechtsstaat.

The development of the Rechtsstaat, together with the ideal of constitutionalism, became the main goal of the new liberal movement. The limitation of all government by a constitution, and the limitation of all administrative activity by law enforceable by courts, became its central aim. Nonetheless, despite these liberal intentions, the police state continued; so, who was to be the guardian of public law? Hayek responded: none other than that very administration against whose drive for expansion and activity those fundamental laws had been meant to protect.

Later on, administrative courts were created that were meant to be completely independent, and deal exclusively with questions of law. It was hoped that in the course of time they would assume a strictly judicial control over all administrative action. However, soon after the rise of state socialism and the welfare state, conceptions of liberalism were abandoned. There was thus little willingness to implement the conception of limited government. The newly created system exempted from judicial review the discretionary powers required by the new tasks of government.

Although the German achievement proved to be more considerable in theory than in practice, still it systematically drew lessons from liberalism for the problems confronting the modern administrative state. The Rechtsstaat concept which they developed was the direct result of the old ideal of the rule of law, where an elaborate administrative apparatus, rather than a monarch or a legislature, was the chief agency to be restrained. Hence, the Germans are better adapted to present-day problems than many of the older institutions. The advance of the welfare state, which began earlier in Continental Europe than in England or in America, soon introduced new features which could hardly be reconciled with the ideal of government under the law.

The Safeguards of Individual Liberty

What are the essential conditions of liberty under the law? Number one is the limitation on the powers of all government, including the powers of the legislature. The rule of law is more than constitutionalism; it requires that all laws conform to certain principles. The rule of law is, therefore, not a rule of the law, but a rule concerning what law ought to be, a meta-legal doctrine or political ideal. It is also important to remember that the rule of law restricts government only in its *coercive* activities.

Another important attribute which must be required of the laws is that they be known and certain. Hayek underscores that there is probably no single factor which has contributed more to the prosperity of the West than the relative certainty of the law which has prevailed there.

The third chief requirement of true law is equality. And the law must also be just. The rule of law requires that the executive in its coercive action be bound by rules that prescribe not only when and where it may use coercion but also in what manner it may do so. The only way in which this can be ensured is to make all actions of this kind subject to judicial review.

The crucial issue in modern times is the legal limits of administrative discretion. Disputes must be settled by an appeal to the rules and not by a simple act of will. Hayek ended the chapter as follows:

> I do not question, but rather wish to emphasize, that the belief in the rule of law and the reverence for the forms of justice belong together and that neither will be effective without the other. But it is the first which is chiefly threatened today; and it is the illusion that it will be preserved by scrupulous observation of the forms of justice that is one of the chief causes of this threat.[18]

Economic Policy and the Rule of Law

To Adam Smith and his successors the enforcement of the ordinary rules of common law would certainly not have appeared as government interference; nor would they ordinarily have applied this term to an alteration of these rules or the passing of new rules by the legislature so long as it was intended to apply equally to all people for an indefinite period of time.

A functioning market economy presupposes certain activities on the part of the state, and it can tolerate more, provided that they are of the kind that is compatible with the market. However, there are others which run counter to the very principle on which a free system rests and which, therefore, must be excluded if such a system is to work.

---

[18] Ibid., 192.

The rule of law provides the criterion which enables us to distinguish between those measures which are and those which are *not* compatible with a free system. The observation of the rule of law may be necessary, sufficient it is not. The vital point, however, is that all coercive action of government must be unambiguously determined by a *permanent* legal framework which enables the individual to plan with a degree of confidence and which reduces human uncertainty as much as possible. Government provides services, such as the provision of a monetary system, or the setting of standards of weights and measures, statistics and some kind of education, which facilitate the acquiring of reliable information. All these activities are part of government's effort to provide a favourable condition for individual decisions; they supply means which individuals can use for their own purpose.

There are also services that are desirable but that will not be provided by the private sector because it would be either impossible or difficult to charge the individual beneficiary for them. Think of sanitary and health services, construction and maintenance of roads and so forth. And there may be yet other services which the government may wish to provide, such as the encouragement of the advancement of science. In any event, it is by no means necessary that government engage in the actual management of these services. In many cases it is more efficient to leave the management to competent agencies, while the financial responsibility would remain in government hands. However, when government subsidises its own enterprises, the same subsidies should be given to competing private enterprises, to maintain a level playing field.

There are also government measures that the rule of law excludes. One such measure is decisions as to who is allowed to provide different commodities at what prices or in what quantities. Regarding the latter, Hayek's principle doesn't necessarily exclude the possible advisability in some instances of permitting it only for those who possess specific qualifications. The restriction of coercion of the enforcement of general rules requires, however, that any one possessing these qualifications has an enforceable claim to such permission and that the grant of permission depends only on satisfying the conditions obtaining.

Price controls cannot be exercised according to rule but must in their very nature be discretionary and arbitrary. To grant such powers to authority means in effect to give it power arbitrarily to determine what is to be produced, by whom and for whom. That is why price and quantity controls must be excluded in a free system. They are incompatible with a free system for two reasons: (1) all such controls are arbitrary and (2) it is impossible to exercise them in such a manner to allow the market to function adequately.

Hayek feels that a range of government actions can be reconciled with a free system. But while there is thus scope for improvement within the rule of law, the reformers have constantly weakened and undermined it. A government which cannot use coercion, except in the enforcement of general rules, has no power to achieve particular aims that require means other than those explicitly entrusted to its care and cannot determine the material position of particular people or enforce distributive or social justice.

In order to achieve these aims it would have to pursue a policy which is best described by the term *dirigisme*, which means a policy which determines for what specific purposes particular aims are to be used. This is precisely what a government bound by the rule of law cannot do. Hayek calls this determination of which particular people should be rewarded 'distributive justice'. And this type of justice requires an allocation of all resources by a central authority. However, the conflict between the ideal of freedom and the desire to 'correct' the distribution of incomes so as to make it more 'just' is not clearly recognised. What happens is not a modification of the existing order but a complete abandonment, and its replacement by an altogether different system: the command economy.

The Decline of the Law

The legal theories which undermined the rule of law originated, as described, in Germany and spread from there across the world. The fact that Germany's unification was achieved by the artifice of statesmanship, rather than by gradual evolution, strengthened the belief that deliberate design could remodel society according to a preconceived pattern. The demand that government should enforce distributive justice had been present since the French Revolution. A leading doctrine at the time was that there is no greater injustice than to treat as equal what is in fact unequal. And there was Anatole France who scoffed: 'the majesty equality of the law that forbids the rich as well as the poor to sleep under bridges, to beg in the streets and to steal bread'.[19] Statements like these were to undermine the foundations of all impartial justice, Hayek noted.

There was a sense of a common dislike of any limitation of authority by rules of law and there was a shared desire to give the organised forces of government greater power to shape social relations along the lines of social justice. Movements like legal positivism, historicism, the free law school and the school of jurisprudence, all arose. While lightly touching on the latter three, Hayek deals with legal positivism in some detail. The doctrines of legal positivism have been developed in direct opposition to a tradition that has to do with the conception of a law of nature. The different schools belonging to this movement have one thing in common: the existence of rules which are not of the deliberate making by any lawgiver. The legal positivists deny this. For them law, by definition, consists exclusively of deliberate commands of a human will. For this reason legal positivism has no use for those meta-legal principles that underlie the ideal of the rule of law.

This legal positivism gained popularity especially in Germany. Hayek noted that it was there that the ideal of the rule of law was first deprived of real content. In Germany, after WWI, there was a definite eclipse of all traditions of limited government. As one law scholar noted, there was an emancipation of democratisation from liberalism. There were no possible limits to the power of the legislator, and there were no fundamental liberties. These developments opened the doors to the victory of fascism and bolshevism. As one non-Communist Russian scholar observed that what

> ... distinguishes the Soviet system from all other despotic government is that ... it represents an attempt to found the state on principles which are the opposite of those of the rule of law ... and it has evolved a theory which exempts the rules from every obligation or limitation.[20]

---

[19] Ibid., 206.
[20] Ibid., 210.

In England developments away from the rule of law had started early but for a long time remained confined to the sphere of practice and received little attention. Under the influence of positivist thinkers, however, there has been a rapid growth of very imperfectly checked powers of administrative agencies over the private life and property of the citizen.

Developments like these have gone equally far in the United States. European thought became crystallised into the public administration movement, which played a role there similar to the Fabians in Britain. The movement's members were populisers of the idea that liberty for liberty's sake is clearly a meaningless notion; it must be liberty to do and enjoy something. If more people are buying automobiles and taking vacations, there is more liberty. One US commentator warned that the majority are moving into the line of administrative absolutism, which is a phase of the rising absolutism throughout the world.

Fortunately, Hayek noted, there are clear signs in many countries of a reaction against these developments. They are perhaps the most conspicuous in the countries that have gone through the experience of totalitarian regimes and who have learned the dangers of relaxing the limits on the powers of the state. The advance of the principle of judicial review since the war and the revival of the interest in the theories of natural law in Germany are other symptoms of the same tendencies. And in France another law scholar captured the changing mood by observing that it was jurists who undermined the conception of individual rights without being aware that they, thereby, delivered these rights to the omnipotence of the political state.

Part III: Freedom in the Welfare State

The Decline of Socialism and the Rise of the Welfare State

Efforts towards social reform have been mainly inspired by the ideals of socialism. This development reached its peak after WWII when Britain plunged into its socialist experiment. The common aim of all socialist movements was the nationalisation of the means of production, distribution and exchange, so that all economic activity might be directed in accordance with a comprehensive plan towards some ideal of social justice.

When Hayek published his book in 1960, he already observed that socialism, in this strict sense of a particular method of achieving social justice, had collapsed. So, what happened? What happened in the Soviet Union was the necessary outcome of the systematic application of the traditional socialist programme. But the experience there had only discredited the Marxist brand of socialism. The widespread disillusionment with the basic methods of socialism is due to more direct experiences.

Production on socialist principles meant less instead of more productivity. And instead of more freedom, it led to despotism. Perhaps the most important disillusionment factor was the growing apprehension among socialist intellectuals of the extinction of individual liberty. Left-leaning British intellectuals, such as R. Crossman, began to doubt socialism. One of them noted that the task of socialists now was to convince the nation that its liberties were threatened by this new feudalism. The most important outcome of the socialist epoch has been the destruction of the traditional limitations upon the powers of the state.

Unlike socialism, the conception of the welfare state has no precise meaning. The term is sometimes used to describe the state that concerns itself with problems other than those of the maintenance of law and order. All modern governments have made provisions for the indigent, unfortunate and disabled and have concerned themselves with questions of health and the dissemination of knowledge. There is nothing wrong with these provisions; the problem is with the *methods* of government action.

The programme of the welfare state comprises a great deal more than is represented as equally legitimate and unobjectionable. The reason why many of the new welfare activities of government are a threat to freedom is that, though they are represented as mere service activities, they really constitute an exercise of the coercive powers of government and rest on its claiming exclusive rights in certain fields.

The current situation has greatly altered the task of the defender of liberty and made it much more difficult. The arguments against socialism were clear and convincing; those against the welfare state are more blurred. After all, some of the aims of the welfare state can be attained without affecting individual liberty, but there are others, and they are those particularly dear to the hearts of the socialists, which cannot be realised in a society that wants to preserve personal freedom. One example is when government uses its coercive power to insure that particular people get particular things. In that case it requires a kind of discrimination between different people which is irreconcilable with a free society. This is the kind of welfare state that aims at social justice and becomes primarily a redistributor of income. It is bound to lead back to socialism and its coercive methods. Impatience and haste to redress societal shortcomings (such as poverty, lack of old age care) may be barring better and more lasting solutions. As Hayek concluded,

> The controlled single-channel development toward which impatience and administrative convenience have frequently inclined the reformer and which, especially in the field of social insurance, has become characteristic of the modern welfare state, may well become the chief obstacle to future improvement.[21]

On subsidies Hayek supported the only acceptable form and that is as a means of using the market to provide services that cannot be confined to those who individually pay for them.

As for enterprise monopoly, Hayek is of the opinion that it may be good to treat the monopolist as a sort of 'whipping boy' of economic policy. He adds that current policy fails to recognise that it is not monopoly as such, or bigness, but only obstacles to entry into an industry or trade and certain other monopolistic activities that are harmful.

Labour Unions and Employment

The basic principles of the rule of law have nowhere in recent times been so violated, and with such serious consequences, as in the case of labour unions. The stage has been reached where they have become uniquely privileged institutions to which the general rules of law don't apply. More and more labour unions came to be viewed, not as a group which was pursuing a legitimate selfish aim and which must be kept in check by competing interests possessed of equal rights, but as a group whose

---

[21] Ibid., 227.

aim—the comprehensive organisation of all labour—must be supported for the good of the public.

In the case where a labour union controls the workers of a firm or industry, they are in a position to have the wages raised above the level that would prevail in a free market. The decisive point is that this can never be in the interest of all workers, except in the unlikely case where the total gain from such action is equally shared among them, irrespective of whether they are employed or not. However, the union can achieve this only by coercing some workers against their interest to support such a concerted move. The interest of those who will get employment at the higher wage will, therefore, always be opposed to the interests of those who will find employment only in the less highly paid jobs or who will not be employed at all.

Conventional wisdom has it that unions have been instrumental in negotiating better and ever higher wages for their members. Hayek referred to a study by Milton Friedman that showed that real-wages have not risen much faster when unions were weak than when they were strong. Even the rise in particular trades or industries where labour was not organised has frequently been much faster than in highly organised and equally prosperous industries.

Unions exert an upward pressure on the level of money wages, with its inevitable effect on inflation. The effect on relative wages is usually greater uniformity and rigidity of wages within any one union-controlled group and greater and non-functional differences in wages between different groups. This is accompanied by a restriction of the mobility of labour, of which the former is either an effect or a cause. Hayek fired another shot at unions: because unions are most powerful where capital investments are heaviest, they tend to become a deterrent to investment, probably second only to taxation. And it is often union monopoly in collusion with enterprise that becomes one of the chief foundations of monopolistic control of the industry concerned.

Hayek had also positive things to say about the role of labour unions. Stripped from their coercive power, unions can play a useful role in collective negotiations with employers on, for example, the alternative between wage increases and more leisure time, and the establishment of differentials in wages between different jobs. Nonetheless, he pointed to the danger of unions contributing to inflation. The chief reason is that the dominant 'full employment' doctrines explicitly relieve unions of the responsibility for any unemployment and place the duty of preserving full employment on the monetary and fiscal authorities. The only way in which the latter can prevent union policy from producing unemployment is to counter it through the inflation that excessive rises in real-wages unions tend to cause. The consequence is the so-called wage–price spiral which has prevailed since WWII, that is since Keynesian full-employment policies became generally accepted.

Hayek corrected the possible misunderstanding that wage increases directly produce inflation. What really happens is that if the supply of money and credit were not expanded, the wage increases would rapidly lead to unemployment. But under the influence of a doctrine that represents it as a duty of the monetary authorities to provide enough money to secure full employment at any given wage level, it is politically inevitable that each round of wage increases would lead to further inflation. His conclusion was that the present position of the unions cannot last, for they can function only in a market economy that they are doing their best to destroy.

Social Security

In the Western world some provision for those threatened by the extremes of indigence or starvation, due to circumstances beyond their control, has long been accepted as a duty of the community. In modern societies people should be compelled to insure themselves against sickness, the needs of old age and unemployment. The justification is not that people should be coerced to do what is in their own interest but that, by neglecting to make these provisions, they would become a charge on the public. Once this is agreed by the society, then the state should assist in the development of the appropriate institutions. Some should be allowed to 'experiment' with regards to which institutions would be the most appropriate to play a role. Up to this point, agued Hayek, the justification for the whole apparatus of social security can be accepted. However, the proponents of social security went a step further, that is, individuals were required to obtain their social protection through organisations run by government.

Social security, from the beginning, meant not merely compulsory insurance but compulsory membership in a state organisation. The argument at the time was that running social insurance by one organisation would be more efficient and thus cheaper. It was also claimed that there would be sufficient funds for all those in need. That sounded reasonable, but the principle that all sheltered monopolies become inefficient in the course of time applies in this case as much as in any other. The system in place could prevent the evolution of other organisations that might function better.

There are two distinct aims that a government organisation with coercive powers can achieve, that are beyond the reach of private organisations. One is that it can give individuals what they 'ought' to get, or make them do whatever they 'ought' to do. The second aim is to redistribute income among persons or groups as it sees fit. This redistribution of income is now the chief purpose of social insurance, according to Hayek. In other words, what was started as a means to relieve poverty has been turned into a tool of egalitarian redistribution. Hayek concluded that in this sense the welfare state has become the substitute of old-fashioned socialism. Freedom is critically threatened when the government is given exclusive powers to provide certain services—powers that, in order for government to achieve its purpose, it must use for the discretionary coercion of individuals.

A third system has emerged almost everywhere under which people in certain circumstances, such as sickness or old age, are provided for, irrespective of whether or not they have made provisions for themselves. Hayek felt that this is all part of the endeavour to persuade public opinion to accept a new method of income distribution, which the managers of the new machine seem to have regarded as a mere transitional half-measure which must be developed into an apparatus expressly aimed at redistribution. He also wondered whether people fully understand what was really involved in social security. Would Germans, for example, where about 20 % of their national income is placed in the hands of the social security administration, not feel that this percentage is much higher than they would expressly wish?

The chief branches of social security are: the provision for old age, for permanent disablement and for loss of the breadwinner of the family, for medical and hospital care, and for the protection against loss of income through unemployment. The provision for old age will probably create the most serious problems. Inflation will rob a part of what people have put aside for their old age. In addition, future generations will be burdened with the duty to pay into a pension fund which is facing an increasingly diminishing capacity to cover all entitlements.

The growth of health insurance is a good development. Even making it compulsory is, to some extent, understandable. But there are strong arguments against a single scheme of state insurance, and there is an overwhelming case against a free health service for all. Once such a scheme is introduced, it is politically inconceivable that it can be stopped, even if it proves to be a mistake. The case for free health service is usually based on two fundamental misconceptions. The first one is the belief that medical needs are of an objectively ascertainable character and that they should be attended to, irrespective of the costs involved. Second, that this is economically possible because an improved medical service can be expected to result in a restoration of economic effectiveness or earning power and, therefore, pays for itself. Apart from the fact that there is no objective standard to ascertain what and how much should be done in medical terms, the real issue is whether the individual concerned has a say and is able to get more attention or whether this decision is to be made for him or her by somebody else.

Surely, it may seem harsh, but it is probably in the interest of all that under a free system those with full earning capacity should be rapidly cured of a temporary disablement at the expense of some neglect of the aged and mortally ill. Where systems of state medicine operate, one generally finds that those who could be promptly restored to full activity have to wait for long periods because all the hospital facilities are taken up by people who will never again contribute to the needs of the rest. Then, there is the transformation of doctors who have been members of a free profession primarily responsible to their patients into paid servants of the state; officials who are necessarily subject to instruction by authority and who could be released from the duty of doctor–patient confidentiality so far as authority is concerned.

As regards the provision against unemployment, the problem raised by the unemployed is that of how and by whom any further (than the basic) assistance based on their normal earnings should be provided for them, and whether this need justifies a coercive redistribution of income according to some principle of justice. One has to look at the development of wages as well. If wages have been pushed too high by unions, curing unemployment requires flexibility of wages and mobility of workers to prevent unemployment. However, a system that assures all unemployed a certain percentage of their wages takes away the pressure to restore employment opportunities.

The chief significance of the comprehensive system of unemployment compensation is that it operates in a labour market dominated by the coercive action of unions and that it has been designed under strong union influence. Such a system, which—as noted—relieves the unions of the responsibility for the unemployment that their policies have created, and which places on the state the burden not merely of maintaining those who are kept out of jobs, can in the long run only make the employment problem more acute. The reasonable solution of these problems in a free society is that beyond the provision of a minimum by the state, any further provision should be left to competitive and voluntary efforts.

True, the provision of a uniform minimum for all those who cannot provide for themselves involves some redistribution of income. But there is a great deal of difference between the provision of a minimum for those who cannot maintain themselves on their earnings in a normally functioning market, and a redistribution aiming at a 'just' remuneration in all the more important occupations—between a redistribution wherein the great majority earning their living agree to give to those unable to do so, and a redistribution wherein a majority takes from a minority because the latter has more. The former preserves the impersonal method of adjustment under which people can choose their occupation; the latter brings us nearer to a system under which people will have to be told by authority what to do.

Given the dangers involved in social security systems as they evolved, Hayek proposed a gradual transformation of the sickness and unemployment allowance systems into systems of true insurance under which the individuals pay for benefits offered by competing institutions. While in former times social evils were gradually disappearing with the growth of wealth, the remedies we have introduced are beginning to threaten the continuance of that growth of wealth on which all future improvement depends.

Taxation and Redistribution

Hayek started the chapter on this subject as follows:

> In many ways I wish I could omit this chapter. Its argument is directed against beliefs so widely held that it is bound to offend many. Even those who have followed me so far and have perhaps regarded my position as on the whole reasonable are likely to think my views on taxation doctrinaire, extremist, and impractical.[22]

Redistribution by progressive taxation has come to be almost universally accepted as just, although John Stuart Mill called it a mild form of robbery. Income tax may be graduated to compensate for the tendency of many indirect taxes to place a proportionally heavier burden on the smaller incomes. This is the only valid argument in favour of progression. It is possible to bring about considerable redistribution under a system of proportional taxation. In Germany resistance to progressive taxation was overcome in 1891 when Prussia introduced a progressive income tax rising from 0.67 % to 4 %. It was almost two decades later that Great Britain and the United States adopted graduated income taxes. The justification moved in time from the capacity to pay to bringing about a more just distribution of income.

Higher income taxes were defended by the need to finance the ever-increasing outlays for social security. However, the revenue derived from the high taxation rates, particularly in the highest brackets, is so small compared with the total revenue (between 2.5 % and 8.5 % of the total) as to make hardly any difference to the burden borne by the rest. That a majority, merely because it is a majority, should be entitled to apply to a minority a rule which it does not apply to itself, is an infringement of a principle much more fundamental than democracy itself.

---

[22] Ibid., 266.

It is the great merit of proportional taxation that it provides a rule which is likely to be agreed upon by those who will pay absolutely more and those who will pay absolutely less and which—once accepted—raises no problem of a separate rule applying only to a minority. Progression provides no criterion whatsoever of what is and what is not to be regarded as just. Apart from applying a uniform percentage to all taxpayers, proportional taxation has also the advantage of leaving the net remuneration for particular services unchanged.

One of the chief reasons why progressive taxation has come to be so widely accepted is that the great majority of people have come to think of an appropriate income as the only legitimate and socially desirable form of reward. They think of income not as related to the value of the services rendered but as conferring what is regarded as an appropriate status in society. Hayek added that a society which will recognise no reward rather than what appears to its majority as an appropriate income can in the long run preserve a system of private enterprise. Progressive taxation, furthermore, discourages individual capital formation which would have a negative impact on further growth and prosperity. Hayek then wondered whether there is much doubt that poor countries, by preventing individuals from getting rich, will also slow down the general growth of wealth.

There can be no objection that an economically weak minority gets some relief in the form of proportionally lower taxation. The maximum rate of taxation should have a relation to the total burden of taxation. The most reasonable kind would be one that fixed the maximum admissible rate of direct taxation at a percentage of the total national income that the government takes in taxation. This would still leave taxation somewhat progressive, since those paying the maximum percentage would also pay indirect taxes which would bring their total contribution above the national average. To further this argument, the lower-income earners would be reduced in proportion to what they were taxed indirectly.

The Monetary Framework

The experience of the last 50 years has taught us the importance of a stable monetary system. Compared with the preceding century this period has been one of great monetary turbulence. Governments have assumed a much more active part in controlling money, and this has been as much a cause as a consequence of instability. It is, however, inevitable that this system would be largely executed by government. There are three reasons for this: (1) changes in the relative supply of money are so much more disturbing than changes in any other circumstances that affect prices; (2) the supply of money is closely related to credit; and (3) the present volume of government expenditure is a circumstance that must be accepted in all decisions about monetary policy.

Spontaneous fluctuations in the supply of money can be prevented only if somebody has the power to change deliberately the supply of money in the opposite direction. This is a function generally entrusted to a single national institution: the central bank. This central agency is able to provide cash and so can influence the total supply of credit. Given the large share of government expenditures in a national economy, an effective monetary policy can only be conducted in coordination with the financial policy of government. Hence, the independent monetary authority has in fact to adjust its policy to that of the government. The latter becomes the determining factor.

The chief threat is inflation. Governments everywhere and at all times have been the chief cause of the depreciation of the currency. We have seen how the welfare state tends to encourage inflation. We have seen also how wage pressures from labour unions, combined with full-employment policies, work towards that end. And we have seen how the heavy financial burden of old-age pensions, which governments are assuming, are likely to lead them to repeat their attempts to lighten these burdens by reducing the value of money. Because of progressive taxation, inflation tends to increase tax revenue proportionally more than incomes, therefore, the temptation to resort to inflation becomes very great.

On balance, probably some mechanical rule could be introduced which aims at what is desirable in the long run and ties the hands of the authority in its short-term decisions. However, how far is it practically possible to tie down the monetary authority by appropriate rules? The old arguments in favour of independent central banks still have great merit. But monetary policy is tightly connected to government's financial policy. This strengthens the case against allowing much discretion and for making decisions on monetary policy as predictable as possible.

The issue nowadays is whether to keep a stable level of employment or some level of prices. These two aims are not necessarily in conflict, provided that the requirement for monetary stability is given first place and the rest of economic policy is adapted to them. However, a conflict arises when full employment is the chief objective—and this is interpreted as that maximum of employment that can be produced by monetary means in the short run, as it triggers inflation.

Hayek stressed two points: first, it seems certain that state control will increase, unless inflation is stopped. Second, any continued rise in prices is dangerous because once we start to rely on its stimulating effect we shall be committed to a course that will leave us no choice but that between more inflation on the one hand and paying for our mistake with a recession on the other.

Inflation makes it more and more difficult for people of moderate means to provide for their old age themselves. It discourages saving and encourages running a debt. And by destroying the middle class, it creates that dangerous gap between those completely without property and the wealthy that is so characteristic of societies that have gone through long periods of inflation, and which is the source of so much tension in them.

Housing and Town Planning

Economists have given little attention to the problems of coordinating all the different aspects of city development. One of them is housing. Rent restriction has probably done more to restrict freedom and prosperity than any other measure, except inflation. Now, what are the side-effects? First, any fixing of rents below the market price perpetuates the housing shortage. Second, mobility is greatly reduced and, in the course of time, the distribution of people between districts and types of dwellings ceases to correspond to needs and desires. Third, houseowners lose interest in maintaining their property, not in the least since inflation reduces the value of fixed rents even more. What has done much to undermine the respect for property and for the law and the courts is the fact that the authority is constantly called upon to decide on the relative merits of needs, to allocate essential services and to dispose of what is still nominal private property.

Affordable housing for the poor has become an integral part of the welfare state. Provision of only part of the supply of dwellings by the authority will in effect be not an addition to, but merely a replacement of, what has been provided by private building activity. Second, cheaper housing provided by government will have to be strictly limited to the class it is intended to help, and to satisfy the demand at the lower rents, government will have to supply considerably more housing than that class would otherwise occupy. And government should not provide more and better housing for the poor than what they had before; otherwise the people thus assisted would be better housed than those immediately above them on the economic ladder.

Hayek was critical of town planning if planners do not take into account the market and market prices. The chapter ends with the statement that it is doubtful whether a planner could guide developments as successfully as the market does. It is remarkable how much the market does accomplish by making individuals take into account those facts which they do not know directly but which are merely reflected in the prices.

Agriculture and Natural Resources

The increase in productivity combined with an inelastic demand means that if those engaged in agriculture are to maintain their average income, their number will have to decrease. Spontaneous movements out of agriculture will be induced if incomes from agriculture go down relative to those in urban occupations. However, there are policies that keep people in agriculture for electoral and strategic self-sufficiency reasons. This implied that government has to ensure an 'adequate' income for the farmers. Elimination of marginal land and farms will help to redress the situation. Equally important are the changes in the internal structure which will be generated by the changes in the relative prices of different products.

Hayek used the price of cereals as an example. Once the general income level increases, the demand for cereals will decline, as the population can now afford food with higher protein contents. The price of cereals drops until it becomes profitable to use them as fodder for cattle. Such development would prevent the total consumption of grain from shrinking as much as it would otherwise and, at the same time, decrease the cost of meat.

Government intervention, such as ensuring an adequate income for the farmers and other subsidies, prevented agriculture from adapting itself to the changed conditions. So, in the long run price controls serve no desirable purpose and, even for a limited period, can be made effective only if combined with direct controls of production. These policies not only lead to a heavily subsidised agricultural sector but also to enormous surplus stocks. As a result, farmers become more and more dependent on government for their livelihood.

It does not mean that government doesn't have a useful role to play in agriculture. Its tasks would include the gradual improvement of institutions that will make the market function more effectively and to provide services in the area of access to information, for example, advances in appropriate knowledge.

In underdeveloped countries a movement to the contrary is ongoing. Quite a few of the newly independent, young countries rushed into industrialisation, with the assumption that this would bring about a more rapid rate of growth. What they forgot is that this can only happen if and when there is an agricultural surplus available so that the industrial population can be fed. Moreover, given the shortage of available capital, if there were to be any investment in industry, it should certainly not be sunk into capital-intensive industries, which often require a sophisticated technological know-how to operate.

As regards the exploitation of natural resources, the prevalent opinion is that the peculiar situation in place requires governments to undertake far-reaching controls. The argument for government control was the assumed wastefulness of competition and the desirability of a central direction of important economic activities. Another argument was that the community has a greater interest in, and a greater foreknowledge of, the future than the individuals. Moreover, the preservation of particular resources raises problems different from those of the provision for the future in general.

All resource conservation constitutes investment and should be judged by precisely the same criteria as all other investments. There is nothing in the preservation of natural resources that makes it a more desirable object of investment than man-made equipment or human capacities. So long as society anticipates the exhaustion of particular resources and channels its investment in such a manner that its aggregate income is made as great as the funds available for investment can make it, there is no further economic case for preserving any one kind of resource.

There is a role for government in the provision of amenities or of opportunities for recreation, the preservation of natural beauty or of historical sites; all of which enable the individual beneficiary to derive advantages for which she cannot be charged a price, and the size of the tracts of land usually required make this an appropriate field for collective effort. Now, if the taxpayer knows the full extent of the bill she will have to foot, and has the last word in the decision, there is nothing to prevent government from exploiting these amenities.

Education and Research

In contemporary society there are strong cases for compulsory education up to a certain minimum standard. The first is that all of us will be exposed to fewer risks and will receive more benefits from our fellow citizens if all share the same basic knowledge and beliefs. And in a country with democratic institutions there is the further important consideration that democracy is not likely to work, except on the smallest local level, with a partly illiterate people.

If we accept compulsory education, then the question arises, How is it going to be provided? And, how much of it is to be provided for all? Prussia was the first country where compulsory education was introduced at the beginning of the eighteenth century. If government is footing the bill of compulsory education, this would not necessarily require government to run the schools. The more highly one rates the power that education can have over people's minds, the more convinced one should be of the danger of placing this power in the hands of a single authority. Indeed, we may soon find that the solution has to lie in government ceasing to be the chief dispenser of education and becoming the impartial protector of the individual against all uses of such newly found powers.

As Milton Friedman proposed, it is now practicable to defray the costs of general education out of the public purse without maintaining government schools, by giving the parents vouchers covering the costs of education of each child which they could hand over to schools of their choice. Another advantage is that parents don't have to accept whatever education the government provides, or paying the entire cost of a different—and slightly more expensive—education themselves. If they should choose a school out of the common run, they would be required to pay only the additional costs.

The case for subsidised higher education must rest not on the benefit it confers on the recipient but on the resulting advantages for the *community* at large. There is, therefore, little case for subsidising any kind of vocational training, where the greater proficiency acquired will be reflected in the greater earning power of the individual. However, the benefits which a society receives from its scientists and scholars cannot be measured by the price at which these persons can sell particular services, since much of their contribution becomes freely available to all. There is, therefore, a strong case for assisting at least some of those who show promise and inclination for the result of such studies. There is the problem of having more intellectuals than can profitably be employed. There are few greater dangers to political stability than the existence of an intellectual proletariat, as Schumpeter observed before, who find no outlet for their learning.

If no more can be spent on any child than on every child (because of the equality principle), then this would constitute a strong case against government's concerning itself with education beyond the elementary level, which can indeed be given to all, and for leaving all advanced education in private hands.

It may be in the interest of the community that some who show exceptional capacities for scholarly or scientific pursuits should be given an opportunity to follow them irrespective of family means. But this does not confer a right on anyone to such opportunity. Nonetheless, there is much to be said for some members of different groups of the population being given a chance for higher education, even if the best from some groups seem less qualified than members of other groups who do not get it. For this reason, different local, religious, occupational or ethnic groups should be able to assist some of their young members, so that those who receive higher education will represent their respective group somewhat in proportion to the esteem in which the latter hold education.

However, all human differences, whether they are differences in natural gifts or in opportunities, create unfair advantages. But since the chief contribution of an individual is to make the best use of the accidents he encounters, success must to a great extent be a matter of chance.

On research Hayek noted that the decisive and unforeseeable steps in the general advance usually occur not in the pursuit of specific ends but in the exploration of those opportunities which the accidental combination of particular knowledge, and gifts and special circumstances and contacts, have placed in the way of some individual. This is best promoted by academic freedom. This term means, according to Michael Polanyi, that there should be as many independent centres of work as possible, on which at least those who have proved their capacity to advance knowledge and their evolution to their task can themselves determine problems that they are to spend their energies on and where they can expound the conclusions they have reached, whether or not these conclusions are palatable to their employer or the public at large.

There is perhaps no more important application of Hayek's main theses than that the advance of knowledge is likely to be fastest where scientific pursuits are not determined by some unified conception of their social utility, and where each proved person can devote himself to the tasks in which he sees the best chance to making a contribution.

Hayek concluded *The Constitution of Liberty* as follows:

> Nowhere is freedom more important than where our ignorance is greatest—at the boundaries of knowledge, in other words, where nobody can predict what lies a step ahead … But the ultimate aim of freedom is the enlargement of these capacities in which man surpasses his ancestors and to which each generation must endeavor to add its share—its share in the growth of knowledge and the gradual advance of moral and aesthetic beliefs, where no superior must be allowed to enforce one set of views of what is right or good and where only further experience can decide what should prevail. It is wherever man reaches beyond his present self, where the new emerges and assessment lies in the future, that liberty ultimately shows its value.[23]

---

[23] Ibid., 340.

Postscript: Why I Am Not a Conservative

Hayek is often associated with conservatives. They quote him often and believe that they and Hayek are soulmates. That is wrong. He sets the record straight in this postscript.

The small essay starts with noting that in matters of current politics, liberals generally have little choice but to support conservative parties. Conservatism proper is a legitimate, probably necessary, and certainly widespread attitude of opposition to drastic change. Until the rise of socialism its opposite was liberalism. Hayek's major objection to conservatism is that it cannot offer an alternative to the direction in which we are moving. Conservatives, liberals and socialists can be depicted in a triangle, with the conservatives taking up one corner, with the socialists pulling towards the second, and the liberals towards the third. But, as the socialists have been able to pull harder, the conservatives have tended to follow them rather than the liberal direction and have adopted at appropriate intervals of time those ideas made respectable by radical propaganda. It has regularly been the conservatives who have compromised with socialism.

The main differences between the conservatives and liberals are as follows. One of the fundamental traits of the conservative is a fear of change, while the liberal position is based on courage and confidence, on a readiness to let change run its course. The conservative is inclined to use the forces of government to prevent change. He is a man of very strong moral convictions. Conservatives are fond of authority and its lack of understanding of economic forces. A conservative does not object to coercion or arbitrary power so long as it is used for what he regards as the right purposes, and—like the socialist—he regards himself as entitled to force the values he holds on other people.

For the liberal neither moral nor religious ideals are proper objects of coercion. Both the conservative and the socialist recognise no such limits. This may explain why it seems to be easier for the repentant socialist to find a new spiritual home in the conservative fold than in the liberal.

Regarding superiority and the role of elites, the liberal—though fully aware of the important role that cultural and intellectual elites have played in the evolution of civilisation—believes that these elites have to prove themselves by their capacity to maintain their position under the same rules that apply to all others.

Conservatives usually oppose collectivist measures in the industrial field. At the same time, however, they are also usually protectionist and have frequently supported socialist measures in agriculture.

Conservatives feel instinctively that it is new ideas more than anything else that causes change. Though the liberal certainly does not regard all change as progress, he does regard the advance of knowledge as one of the chief aims of human effort and expects from it the general solution of such problems and difficulties which need to be solved. Hayek finds the most objectionable feature of the conservative attitude is its propensity to reject well-substantiated new knowledge because it dislikes some of the consequences which seem to follow from it. Connected with the distrust of the new is its hostility to internationalism and its proneness to strident nationalism.

There is one respect in which there is justification for saying that the liberal occupies a position midway between the socialist and the conservative and that is that she is far from the crude rationalism of the socialist, who wants to reconstruct all social institutions according to a pattern prescribed by her individual reason, as from the mysticism to which the conservative so frequently has to resort.

What Hayek calls 'liberalism' has little to do with any political movement that goes under that name today. What he wants is a word which describes the party of life, the party that favours free growth and spontaneous evolution. Whiggism is historically the correct name for the ideas in which Hayek believed. Conservatism may sometimes be a useful practical maxim, but it doesn't provide any guiding principles which can influence long-range developments.

Biography: Milton Friedman (1912–2006)

Milton Friedman's 'finest hour' must have been when President Ronald Reagan and Prime Minister Margaret Thatcher applied his economic philosophy while in office. He had to wait quite a while to get the recognition he thought he deserved after the publication of *Capitalism and*

Freedom, way back in 1962. Friedman complained about the fact that his book hadn't been reviewed by leading American newspapers: *The New York Times*, *The Herald Tribune*, *Time* and *Newsweek* did not review the book. He attributed this neglect to the anti-welfare state and anti-socialist contents of the book, which didn't go down well at the time. Now, who was Milton Friedman, and what exactly brought him to fame?

At the beginning of his professional career, Friedman belonged to the first Keynesians in America. After distancing himself from Keynesianism, he was to become the major protagonist of the efficacy of the free market and of monetarist policies. When Keynesianism was on the defence in the 1970s Friedman's fame started to rise and he became the most influential economist of the Western world. However, since the outbreak of the Great Recession in 2008, Keynes made a comeback while Friedman was not even mentioned in the list of the most influential economists of the past decade published in the British newspaper *The Economist* in February 2011.

His Life

Milton Friedman was born on 31 July 1912 in Brooklyn, New York City. He died in San Francisco on 16 November 2006 at the age of 94, having concluded a highly productive and successful life. His parents were Ukrainian Jewish immigrants, who were trying their luck in a variety of unsuccessful businesses (amongst them an ice cream parlour) in Rahway, New Jersey, and later in Brooklyn, New York. His father died when Milton was 15 years old. Amory Blaine, the protagonist of Scott Fitzgerald's coming-of-age novel *This Side of Paradise*, made a big impression on young Milton. What attracted him in Blaine were not so much his looks (Milton was rather slight and wearing glasses) as Blaine's complete, unquestioned superiority. That was what Friedman certainly achieved later in life.

After high school, he went to Rutgers University to study accounting. One of his teachers, Arthur Burns (who was later to become Fed chairman), convinced Milton to give up accounting and study mathematics and economics instead. To pay for his studies, Milton sold firecrackers, helped other students prepare for their exams and sold textbooks. He obtained his BA in 1932 and, after a trip around the country, enrolled at the University of Chicago, where he would return in 1946 and stay for most of his professional life. He was accepted by the University of Chicago as it was not barring Jews, unlike quite a few Ivy League universities at the time. Through Aaron Director, one of his professors there, he met Rose Director, Aaron's younger sister. He married Rose in 1938. Milton and Rose Friedman led a very happy and academically very productive life which they vividly described in their memoirs, *Two Lucky People* (1998).

His Career in a Nutshell

Friedman worked at the National Resource Committee (NRC) from 1935 to 1937, where he was involved in calculating a cost-of-living index. After the NRC he was a researcher at the National Bureau of Economic Research (NBER) from 1937 to 1940. He worked there under Simon Kuznets, who developed national income and wealth data. Friedman had hoped to get a lectureship somewhere, but the positions were in short supply, and his Jewish background also didn't help. Nevertheless, in 1940 Friedman was offered a visiting professorship at the University of Wisconsin, where he became the victim of campus politics; he resigned at the end of the academic year.

At the beginning of WWII, Friedman joined the Treasury Department in Washington D.C., which he left in 1943 for the Statistical Research Group (SRG). At the SRG he developed techniques for improving the effectiveness of war materiel. After the war had ended he was offered a position at the University of Minnesota. At the end of the academic year he applied for a position at the University of Chicago, which he obtained and where he taught price theory and monetary economics for some 30 years. Together with his colleague and friend George Stigler he created the Chicago School of Economics. After his retirement from Chicago he became a senior scholar at the Hoover Institution in California.

Friedman was a prolific writer. He wrote a large number of academic articles and books, but also newspaper articles. He was a Newsweek columnist for many years. His one-liners live on. Apart from his oft-quoted line, 'There's no such thing as a free lunch', he quipped about government, 'If you put the federal government in charge of the Sahara, in 5 years there'd be a shortage of sand', and 'Nothing is so permanent as a temporary government program.' Of civil servants he observed, 'When you stand before a civil servant, is there any real doubt who is the servant and who is the master?'

Milton and Rose Friedman together wrote *Free to Choose* which was based on the ten-part series of television programmes of the same title. The book came out in 1980 which was perfect timing as Ronald Reagan had just then announced that he would run for president of the United States. Friedman served as economic adviser to Reagan's campaign. After Reagan won the presidential election, he appointed Friedman as a member of the President's Council of Economic Advisors.

Friedman's influence was not confined to the USA and the United Kingdom. He paid a controversial visit to Chile in April 1975. Friedman attributed the Chilean inflation (500 % per annum) to the 40-year trend towards collectivism, socialism and the welfare state. Upon his return from Chile, Friedman wrote Pinochet a long letter (included in an appendix to *Two Lucky People*), strongly advising him to apply a cold-turkey approach to Chile's ailing economy, which was to include controlling the money supply, slashing government spending and removing as many obstacles as possible that hindered the private sector. Pinochet took the advice and things turned out fine for quite a while. However, the Chilean economy took a nosedive in 1982 caused by financial scandals. In 1985 a new team of economic reformers took office and they continued Friedman's economic philosophy. To date, Chile is still among the best-performing Latin American economies.

Friedman defended his controversial visit to Chile in his memoirs by pointing out that he went there at the invitation of a private foundation to speak on the principles of economic freedom, and that he never served as adviser to the Chilean government. He pointed out that since his visit, Chile's income per capita increased 2.5 times, that infant mortality fell from 66 per 1000 to only 13, and life expectancy at birth rose from 64 to 73 years. And political freedom had been restored with the turnover of power by the *junta* to freely elected governments.

Friedman's Academic Work

It would take an entire volume to describe the contents and relevance of Milton Friedman's academic achievements. The most notable ones are mentioned here.

After having obtained his MA degree in economics from the University of Chicago in 1935, where he was taught by Jacob Viner and Frank Knight, Friedman was offered—as mentioned above—a position at the NRC, a New Deal institution.[24] He could now start to play an influential role in policymaking. At the NRC he was charged with assembling nationwide data on consumers and their purchases. This information was required to calculate an index of the cost of living.

In 1937 Friedman joined the NBER at the invitation of Simon Kuznets, who was engaged in putting together America's first-ever complete set of National Accounts, as proposed by Keynes in his *General Theory* (1936). After all, if a country doesn't know how much it produces, what income it generates, how much it consumes, saves and invests from that income, and what its employment rate is, it is very hard indeed to fine tune the economy so that imbalances can be redressed, slumps prevented and full employment ensured. Friedman was assigned the task of completing the work Kuznets had started on incomes of independent professionals, such as doctors, lawyers and accountants.

In that study Friedman made a distinction between permanent and transitory incomes. He concluded that people do not decide how much to spend on consumption each day, week or year by how much they receive as their current income, but on a longer-term expectation of the amount that they will have available to spend. Friedman and Kuznets together published the results in *Incomes from Independent Professional Practice* (1945), which at the same time formed the basis of Friedman's PhD thesis for Columbia University.

---

[24] Ironically, Milton Friedman commented in *Two Lucky People: Memoirs* (1998) that in later years he and Rose, who was an accomplished economist herself, came to be among the best-known critics of the growth in centralized government that the New Deal initiated. Yet, they admitted that the New Deal was a lifesaver for them. Friedman, M. and Friedman, R. (1998) *Two Lucky People: Memoirs*. Chicago: University of Chicago Press.

> It was at the NBER that Friedman discovered that despite the large numbers of Jewish physicians immigrating into the USA from Europe before WWII, the number of medical licenses had not increased simultaneously. This finding prompted Friedman to write a critical section in *Capitalism and Freedom* on the abusive power of the American Medical Association. It was also inspired by the fact that his findings were made public only 3 years after his research work was completed. This delay was caused by an NBER board member who had links with the pharmaceutical industry, as the Friedmans remembered in their memoirs.

His research at the NRC, and later at the NBER, resulted in the classic, *A Theory of the Consumption Function* (1957). In this book he presented the 'permanent income hypothesis', meaning that whenever the expectation is that one's future income will rise, one will save less.[25] Friedman himself long regarded this book as his best purely scientific contribution, though not the most influential.

The book was a reaction to what Keynes had said about consumption in *The General Theory*. A centrepiece of Keynes's theory is the relation between consumption expenditures and income, or, equivalently, between savings and income. Keynes called that the consumption function. The marginal propensity to consume was an important aspect in Keynes's thinking, that is, the fraction of an additional dollar spent on consumption rather than saved. According to Keynes this was less than one, since—as a rule—the average propensity to consume declines when one's income increases. As a result, an economy is condemned to stagnation unless government undertook higher spending financed by deficits.

What did Friedman mean by the term 'purely scientific'? The answer is to be found in his essay 'The Methodology of Positive Economics' (1953). He had come under the influence of Karl Popper's philosophy when the two of them had long discussions at the first Mont Perelin Society gathering in 1947. A proposition or hypothesis should be presented that is falsifiable (some scholars consider Friedman a Popperian falsificationist). Friedman strongly felt that economics as a science should be free of value judgements for it to be objective. And an economic theory should be judged by its simplicity and usefulness as an instrument of prediction.

---

[25] At the NBER Simon Kuznets had found that the percentage of income saved in the USA since 1899 had not changed much. And the savings ratio after WWII had been even lower. This showed the inadequacy of Keynes's consumption function.

5 The Return of Neoclassical Economics

In *The Methodology of Positive Economics*, Friedman referred to an article written by John Neville Keynes (indeed, John Maynard's father). Keynes Sr made a distinction between a positive science, being a body of systematised knowledge concerning *what is*, and a normative or regulative science, being a body of systematised knowledge discussing criteria of *what ought to be*. The challenge concerning positive science is, according to Keynes Sr, and supported by Friedman, how to decide whether a suggested hypothesis or theory should be tentatively accepted as part of the body of systematised knowledge concerning what is.

Friedman says about hypotheses that a hypothesis is important if it 'explains' much by little; that is, if it abstracts the common and crucial elements from the mass of complex and detailed circumstances surrounding the phenomena to be explained and permits valid predictions on the basis of them alone. As regards assumptions, theories should be evaluated not on the basis of the realism of their assumptions but exclusively on the basis of the accuracy of their predictions. A hypothesis must be descriptively false in its assumptions; it takes account of none of the many other attendant circumstances, since its very success shows these assumptions to be irrelevant for the phenomena to be explained. (Samuelson objected to Friedman's claim about the irrelevance of assumptions. He argued that on the basis of the principles of logic, true assumptions can only produce true conclusions. But false assumptions can produce both true and false conclusions, and economics, underscored Samuelson, needed true conclusions.)

The evidence for a hypothesis—and this is clearly inspired by Popper's falsification dictum—always consists of its repeated failure to be contradicted, and continues to accumulate so long as the hypothesis is used. Friedman noted that the construction of hypotheses is a creative act of inspiration, intuition and invention; its essence is the vision of something new in familiar material.

Friedman characterised economics as a positive science to be a body of tentatively accepted generalisations about economic phenomena that can be used to predict the consequences of changes in circumstances.[26] He noted that the necessity of relying on uncontrolled experience, rather than on controlled experiment, makes it difficult to produce dramatic and clear-cut evidence to justify the acceptance of tentative hypotheses. Reliance on uncontrolled experience does not affect the fundamental methodological principle that a hypothesis can be tested only by the conformity of its implications or predictions with observable phenomena. Yet, it renders the task of testing hypotheses more difficult and gives greater scope for confusion about the methodological principles involved. Friedman then warned social scientists, in that they—more than other scientists—needed to be self-conscious about their methodology.

---

[26] Alfred Marshall had this to say on the subject matter: economics cannot be compared with the exact physical sciences for it deals with the ever-changing and subtle forces of human nature.

Friedman developed an interest in statistics after joining the SRG in 1943, which—as already noted—worked for the American Armed Forces to contribute to their combat effectiveness. While at the SRG, he was instrumental in developing sequential analysis, a new statistical sampling device which proved to be more powerful than the classical sample test.

Before his work for the SRG, Friedman had joined the NRC, a research team that produced the study *Taxing to Prevent Inflation*. As America was preparing for war, the economy heated up and inflation started to rise. Friedman's contribution to this study prompted the Treasury Department to offer him a position in their Tax Research Division. He was to find out by how much taxes had to be raised to contain inflation. He advised a Congressional Committee to introduce an additional tax burden that would be most effective in containing inflation. Surprisingly, he did not then propose to control the money supply, the cornerstone of his monetary policy which he developed later in life. He attributed this oversight to the 'Keynesian temper of the times'. At any event, Friedman's wartime advice of raising taxes, which was put into practice, resulted in an enormously powerful revenue-raising machine with tax revenues rising faster than GDP for decades after WWII, thanks to the interaction between robust economic growth and progressive tax rates.

> In *Two Lucky People* Friedman recounts two anecdotes from his time at the Treasury. Once he was testifying before the Senate Finance Committee. Senator Tom Connally of Texas asked Friedman why the Treasury had made a change in a particular tax proposal. Friedman proceeded to answer, saying, 'There are three reasons, first ... second.' Before Friedman could mention the third reason, the senator stopped him and said, 'Young man, one good reason is enough.'
>
> At the Treasury, Friedman had a great deal of contact with Secretary of the Treasury, Henry Morgenthau, Jr.[27] To his surprise he found the Secretary quite limited in his intellectual capacity. Morgenthau had the habit of saying during meetings, 'We're going to have to make that clear to

---

[27] Apart from being Roosevelt's Duchess County neighbour, before becoming Secretary of the Treasury, Morgenthau was a gentleman farmer specializing in growing Christmas trees.

> the ordinary citizen. Take, for example, my daughter Joan, she's in high school. I want you to say that so Joan could understand it.' At one such session, a couple of years later, Morgenthau began to say something like that, and then stopped, saying, 'I guess I can't use Joan as my example any more. She's in college now.'

Friedman, his brother-in-law Aaron Director and his University of Chicago colleague George Stigler were invited by the conservative Volker Fund to attend a seminar held in April 1947 in Geneva, Switzerland. Its purpose was to establish a community of like-minded conservative and libertarian academics. Friedrich Hayek organised the seminar. The location was a hotel on a mountain (Mont Perelin) overlooking Lake Geneva. Other invitees were, among others, the philosopher Karl Popper, and liberal economists Ludwig von Mises and Lionel Robbins. The seminar ended with agreement on the notion 'that freedom of thought and expression is threatened by the spread of creeds which, claiming the privilege of tolerance when in the position of a minority, seek only to establish a position of power in which they can suppress and obliterate all views but their own', as written in the Statement of Aims of the Mont Perelin Society. His involvement in this society, his research work and his appointment to the University of Chicago led Friedman to gradually give up his Keynesian beliefs.[28] Yet, he admitted that he continued to use a Keynesian language and apparatus while rejecting its conclusions.

Friedman was again invited to a series of the Volker Fund's conferences at which he lectured. These lectures, dealing as much with economic as

---

[28] The following lyrics (to the tune of Gilbert and Sullivan's 'When I was a Lad') were written by University of Chicago (U. of C.) graduate students and performed at an economics department party in 1949: When I was a lad I served a term/Under the tutelage of A.F. Burns/I read my Marshall completely through/From beginning to end and backwards too/I read my Marshall so carefully/That now I am Professor at the U. of C./(chorus) He read his Marshall so carefully/That now he is Professor at the U. of C./Of Keynesians I make mincemeat/Their battered arguments now line the street/I get them in their weakest assumption:/'What do you mean by consumption function?'/They never gave an answer that satisfied me/So now I am Professor at the U. of C./(chorus) They never gave me an answer that satisfied me/So now he is Professor at the U. of C. Source: Ebenstein, L. (2007) *Milton Friedman: A Biography*. New York: Palgrave MacMillan, 59.

with political and philosophical issues, formed the basis of *Capitalism and Freedom* (1962), to which his wife Rose contributed. But that wasn't all. Friedman also provided a, then politically incorrect, monetarist explanation of the cause of the prolonged Great Depression.

Capitalism and Freedom formed in fact Friedman's public policies agenda, which he elaborated in his *Newsweek* columns, in his advice to Senator Goldwater (who unsuccessfully campaigned for the American presidency), President Nixon and—above all—President Reagan and British Prime Minister Thatcher. Some commentators said that this book was in fact an American version of Hayek's *The Constitution of Liberty*, which had appeared 2 years earlier, although Hayek's approach was more philosophical. The main thrust of Friedman's book is not only that economic freedom is an end in itself; but also that it is an indispensable means towards achieving political freedom. The book revived the laissez-faire view of the economy as a self-regulating mechanism.

> John Maynard Keynes wrote in his essay 'The End of Laissez-Faire' (1926), It is *not* true that individuals possess a prescriptive 'natural liberty' in their economic activities. There is *no* 'compact' conferring perpetual rights on those who Have or on those who Acquire. The world is *not* so governed from above that private and social interests always coincide. It is *not* so managed here below that in practice they coincide. It is *not* a correct deduction from the *Principles of Economics* that enlightened self-interest always operates in the public interest. Nor is it true that self-interest generally *is* enlightened; more often individuals acting separately to promote their own ends are too ignorant or too weak to attain even these. Experience does *not* show that individuals, when they make up a social unit, are always less clear-sighted than when they act separately. We cannot, therefore, settle on abstract grounds, but must handle on its merits in detail, what Burke termed 'one of the finest problems in legislation, namely, to determine what the State ought to take upon itself to direct by the public wisdom, and what it ought to leave, with as little interference as possible, to individual exertion'.[29]

---

[29] Keynes, J.M. (1931) The End of Laissez Faire. In: *Essays in Persuasion*. London: MacMillan & Co., 312.

5 The Return of Neoclassical Economics 287

Friedman also argued that government had to be kept as small as possible and that taxes should be brought down to an across-the-board flat rate. Friedman was a 'supply-sider'. He said that a supply-side fiscal policy consists of cutting high marginal tax rates in order to stimulate entrepreneurship and innovation. Furthermore, he defended the abolition of medical licenses, ending the military draft system, free exchange rates, education vouchers and a negative income tax. Fellow economist Kenneth Arrow didn't agree with Friedman's proposal to abolish medical licenses. He argued that for any patient it is crucial to find a good doctor and not an incompetent one. And government licenses ensure that medical doctors have the necessary professional qualifications.

Friedman maintained that the private sector is basically a stable factor in the economy; as long as there are no major shocks in the economy, production and employment will develop gradually. But once a shock occurs, for example when government restricts credit or lowers taxes, this will have repercussions in the economy and recovery from these positive or negative shocks will take some time. This view is contrary to the Keynesian analysis in which government intervention is required to redress shocks, while in Friedman's opinion the private sector is the stable actor and government is creating the shocks.

The main cause of the Great Depression, Friedman said, was that the Fed should have pumped money into the economy in the early 1930s to prevent more bank failures and to counter the ever-declining quantity of money in the economy.[30] In *Two Lucky People* he wrote,

> Instead of using its powers to offset the depression, it presided over a decline in the quantity of money by one-third from 1929 to 1933. If it had operated as its founders intended, it would have prevented that decline and, indeed, converted it into the rise that was called for to accommodate the normal growth in the economy. Far from the depression being a failure of the free-enterprise system, it was a tragic failure of government.[31]

---

[30] In *Free to Choose* (1990), the Friedman's devote an entire chapter, 'The Anatomy of Crisis', to the Great Depression and the Fed's role in it .

[31] Friedman and Friedman, *Two Lucky People*, 233.

Friedman based his opinion on research he had undertaken together with Anna Jacobson Schwartz at the NBER, in which they analysed the role of money in business cycles. They published the results of their analysis in 1963 in *A Monetary History of the United States, 1867–1960*. This book initiated a counter-revolution in monetary thought. The Keynesian conventional wisdom was that money didn't matter much. What did matter was autonomous spending, that is, primarily government spending plus private investment; fiscal policy was crucial, monetary policy was of minor interest. Friedman and Schwartz argued quite the contrary. Their book presented extensive evidence spanning almost a century on the consistent relation between monetary changes and subsequent economic change. Their argument goes back to the quantity theory of money ($MV = PQ$), which says that the amount of money in an economy (M) multiplied by the number of times each dollar or euro is used in a year to buy goods or services (V) must be equal to the value of the economic output sold during that particular year ($PQ = Price \times Quantity$). So, changes in M or in V must be related to changes in economic activity.

Friedman and Schwartz found in their empirical study that V had been rather stable during the period investigated, which implied that M, the money supply, affected the level of economic activity positively or negatively.[32]

Regarding *A Monetary History of the United States* and *A Theory of the Consumption Function*, Friedman's biographer Lanny Ebenstein concluded,

> *A Theory of the Consumption Function* and *A Monetary History of the United States* constitute Friedman's twin critique of Keynes and Keynesianism. The former work explains what did *not* happen in the Great Depression; the depression was not caused by excess saving and a declining marginal

---

[32] Joseph Stiglitz challenged this reasoning. He wrote in *The Price of Inequality*, 'Monetarism was based on the assumption that the velocity of circulation—the number of times a dollar bill turns over in a year—was constant. And while in some countries and in some places that had been true, in the rapidly changing global economy of the end of the twentieth century, it was not. The theory became deeply discredited just years after it was the rage among all the central bankers. As they quickly abandoned monetarism, they looked for a new religion consistent with their faith in minimal intervention in the markets.' *The Price of Inequality: How Today's Divided Society Endangers Our Future*. New York: W.W. Norton & Company, 258–9.

propensity to consume as economies develop. The latter work explains what *did* happen; the depression was primarily the result of inappropriate monetary policy that allowed the money supply to contract.[33]

Gradually, a consensus developed about the notion that money does matter, and that what happens to the quantity of money has important effects on economic activity in the short run and on the price level in the long run. Too much money in circulation triggers too much demand for goods, leading to inflation. To do something about inflation is to limit the supply of money. Friedman advised that any growth in the money supply should be at a steady but limited rate somewhere between 3 % and 5 %. Monetary policies do have the tendency to be applied too late after an economic problem has cropped up. Once a monetary policy decision has been taken, it takes time to have an impact. It may very well be that these lags result in the chosen policy to be inappropriate.

> John Kenneth Galbraith, didn't think that monetary policy helped. In the fortieth anniversary edition of *The Affluent Society* he wrote that monetary policy is a blunt, unreliable, discriminatory and somewhat dangerous instrument of economic control. In a footnote on page 176 of his book Galbraith elaborated his opinion:
> The Vietnam War, and the delay in raising taxes to offset the increased spending occasioned by the eccentric enterprise, forced an unparalleled reliance on monetary policy. As this inflationary influence receded, the wage–price spiral took over as a strong inflationary force with abetting effect from fiscal policy and materials shortages. Interest rates were raised to levels unknown for 40 years. This was with punishing effect on those who had to pay them. This punishment extended to states and localities which are heavily dependent on borrowed funds … While General Motors was not inhibited in its investment, the municipality contemplating a school-bond issue most certainly was. So was the home-builder. And withal, prices continued to rise—inflation was doubtless tempered, but it was not controlled. The lessons of this dismal experience were not lost, at least on the less passionate friends of monetary policy. Yet in economics, as in love, hope dies hard. No other course of action in economics has ever rivalled monetary policy in its capacity to survive failure.

---

[33] Ebenstein, *Milton Friedman*, 113.

Most economists now agree that Friedman and Schwartz were right. As former Fed chairman Ben Bernanke admitted during a conference in honour of Milton's 90th birthday,

> Let me end my talk by abusing slightly my status as an official representative of the Federal Reserve. I would like to say to Milton and Anna: Regarding the Great Depression: You're right, we did it. We're very sorry. But thanks to you, we won't do it again.[34]

During the 1960s and early 1970s many Keynesians believed that there was an inverse relationship between inflation and unemployment; that is, inflation would help bring unemployment down. This belief was based on the so-called *Phillips Curve*, named after the London School of Economics researcher Bill Phillips who had studied the relationship between wage increases and unemployment in England. Paul Samuelson and Robert Solow were the ones to develop the Phillips Curve, based on US data from 1933 to 1958. They found that inflation and unemployment were indeed inversely related. Imagine Keynesians' unpleasant surprise when at the end of the 1970s inflation went up and up into double digits, but so did unemployment combined with negligible growth! Keynesians couldn't explain this stagflation phenomenon. Friedman, with the help of Columbia University economist Edmund Phelps, had in fact already presented an explanation in his American Economic Association address of 1967. In that address Friedman introduced the 'natural rate of unemployment' phenomenon, which represents the percentage of the workforce out of work. This can be for various reasons, such as people looking for better-paid work or people who move from one place to another. The natural rate of unemployment is always there in any economy; it can't be avoided. Now, if government brought unemployment down to below its natural rate, thereby promoting inflation, workers would claim higher wages and businesses would increase prices, triggering a wage–price spiral. In preventing inflation spinning out of control, government will have to allow unemployment to rise back to its natural rate. Friedman concluded that there is no permanent

---

[34] Cassidy, *How Markets Fail*, 77.

trade-off between inflation and unemployment. Keynesians didn't have a response.[35]

Through Friedman neoclassical economics regained its central position. His basic philosophy is compelling as it is based on the equally simple and aesthetically attractive neoclassical theory of the free functioning of the market, in which each individual is free to promote his or her own interest. The market establishes the right prices for goods and services; this would also apply to currency markets. Government should interfere as little as possible. The money supply should be managed in parallel with the normal expectation of economic growth. This—in a nutshell—is Friedman's neoclassical and monetarist philosophy, typically associated with the Chicago School economics. However, well before Friedman, Chicago economics professors, such as Jacob Viner and Frank Knight, did not reject government action in the areas of providing infrastructure, education and even funding of cultural activities; their views resembled those of British liberalist economists such as John Stuart Mill. And on the subject of redistribution, Henry Simons, another Chicago economist, argued that redistribution was advisable so as to spread economic power in a society. Given the Chicago School's history, both Hayek and Friedman take up rather extreme libertarian positions.

It seemed as if Friedman would have the ideological last word during the long period of the Great Moderation. However, there isn't such a thing as uninterrupted steady economic growth. Economies expand and shrink all the time, caused by, among others, Keynes's animal spirits and Robert Shiller's irrational exuberance. The financial crisis of 2008 and the ensuing Great Recession underscored that Friedman only explained part of the story. True, he influenced the Fed's response to the financial crisis. But it was also Keynes whose thinking revived, and was widely applied in response to, the Great Recession.

---

[35] Later, New Keynesian Joseph Stiglitz provided one. He wrote in *The Price of Inequality*: 'These ideas provided intellectual comfort to central bankers who didn't want to do anything about unemployment. But there were strong grounds for skepticism about these ideas: some countries, like Ghana and Israel, have managed to bring down their inflation rates very quickly at little cost. The underlying hypothesis that there is a stable relationship between the unemployment level and the rate of *acceleration* of inflation has not withstood the test of time' (262–3).

Honours

Apart from many honorary doctorates, Milton Friedman was awarded the John Bates Clark Medal by the American Economic Association in 1951. This medal is awarded every other year to the American economist under the age of 40 who is adjudged to have made the most significant contribution to economic thought and knowledge. Friedman was elected president of the American Economic Association in 1967. Nine years later he was awarded the Nobel Prize for Economics. In 1988 he received the Presidential Medal of Freedom as well as the National Medal of Science.

The Cato Institute established the Milton Friedman Prize for Advancing Liberty. The first laureate was Peter Bauer in 2002. Other early prize-winners were the Peruvian advocate of libertarian ideas, Hernando de Soto and former Estonian Prime Minister Mart Laar. In 2014, Leszek Balcerowicz, former Deputy Prime Minister and Finance Minister of Poland, was awarded the prize.

Capitalism and Freedom

Capitalism and Freedom is one the most influential political and economic works of the twentieth century as it dealt the economic conventional wisdom a blow.[36] Friedman published the book in 1962 when it went totally unnoticed. Friedman wrote in the preface to the 1982 edition,

> when this book was first published, its views were so far out of the mainstream that it was not reviewed by any major national publication—not by *The New York Times* or the *Herald Tribune* (then still being published in New York) or the *Chicago Tribune*, or by *Time* or *Newsweek* or even *the Saturday Review*—though it was reviewed by the London *Economist* and by the major professional journals.

Friedman went on lamenting in that same preface, 'And that for a book directed at the general public written by a professor at a major

---

[36] Edition used: fortieth anniversary edition (2002). Chicago: University of Chicago Press.

U.S. University and destined to sell more than 400,000 copies in the next eighteen years.' The author explained this oversight as follows: 'It would have been inconceivable that such a publication by an economist of comparable professional standing but favourable to the welfare state or socialism or communism would have received a similar silent treatment.' However, Friedman got his revenge as his economic philosophy was highly rated by Ronald Reagan and Margaret Thatcher, who—once in power—applied much of what he proposed in *Capitalism and Freedom*.

Now, what did Milton Friedman propose way back in 1962 when Keynesianism and the welfare state were riding high? Friedman's economic philosophy is based upon liberal philosophers John Locke and Jeremy Bentham, who argued that humans were essentially good despite their self-interest, and that governments were formed for mutual benefits, not to sacrifice natural liberties. Another inspiring figure was—of course—the 'father of economics', Adam Smith.

Capitalism and Freedom echoes in many ways what Friedrich Hayek wrote in *The Constitution of Liberty*, which came out 2 years earlier. Friedman's book emphasises the economic aspects of his argument, while Hayek's book is best characterised as a work on political philosophy. Both Hayek and Friedman belong to the libertarian school of thought.

According to Friedman, the heart of liberal philosophy focuses on a belief in the equality of people in one sense; but in their inequality in another, as each person has different talents. Therefore a free society distinguishes sharply between equality of rights and equality of opportunity on the one hand, and material inequality on the other. The role of government should be as minimal as possible; in fact, it should not be much more than Adam Smith's 'duties of the Sovereign'. Friedman argues that governments in the Western world have expanded far too much and have, with a few exceptions, failed to achieve their objectives.

Let's take a closer look at what *Capitalism and Freedom* offers. In its introduction it is acknowledged that government is necessary to preserve individuals' freedom. But—and then comes Friedman's counter-argument—by concentrating power in political hands, government is a threat to freedom. It is voluntary cooperation and private enterprise that put checks on the powers of government, and protect freedom of speech, of religion and of thought. Friedman underscored the importance of freedom by writing that the great advances of civilisation, whether in architecture or painting, in science or literature, in industry or agriculture, have never come from centralised government, as the latter can never duplicate the variety and diversity of individual action.

The Relation Between Economic Freedoms and Political Freedom

There is a relationship between economic and political freedom; after all, a socialist society cannot also be democratic. Economic freedom is an indispensable means toward the achievement of political freedom. Now, how does this come about? Well, economic arrangements, such as the imposition of tariffs or price controls are important precisely because of their effect on the concentration or dispersion of power. The kind of economic organisation that provides economic freedom (i.e. competitive capitalism) also promotes political freedom because it separates economic power from political power and in this way enables the one to offset the other. History confirms this relationship. The typical state of humankind was tyranny, servitude and misery. It is only since the nineteenth and early twentieth centuries that the Western world began to stand out as a striking exception to the general trend of historical development. Since then political freedom came along with the free market and the development of capitalist institutions. However, there is not a mutual relationship, in that in some countries (e.g. China) there can be a fair degree of economic freedom while political arrangements are not free.[37]

The nineteenth century, the Age of Liberalism, was followed by a reaction toward increasing intervention by government in the economy. This tendency of collectivism was greatly accelerated by the two world wars. The welfare state seemed to eclipse the liberal state of affairs. Recognising the implicit threat to individualism, liberal thinkers such as the Austrians von Mises and Hayek feared that a continued movement towards

---

[37] Friedman admitted that, in hindsight, the one major defect in his book was the inadequate treatment of the role of political freedom, which under some circumstances promotes economic and civic freedom, and under others inhibits both.

centralised control of economic activity would go down *The Road to Serfdom*, to quote the title of Hayek's famous book of 1944.

From a sociological point of view, the organisation of economic activities can be done in only two ways. One is central direction, involving the use of coercion as applied in the modern totalitarian state. The other is voluntary cooperation, applying the rules of the marketplace, by which both parties stand to benefit, provided the transaction is bilaterally voluntary. If a buyer doesn't want a product of one supplier, she is free to go to another seller. There is also the non-discriminatory aspect, in that no one who buys, for example bread, knows whether the wheat from which it is made was grown by a communist, by an African American or by a white person. The impersonal market thus separates economic activities from political views and protects people from being discriminated against in their economic activities.

The Role of Government in a Free Society

The million-dollar question is, What should the government's role be in a free society? Where does it start and where does it end? With respect to clearly indivisible matters, such as national defence, these cannot be organised through the market. So, that is one clear case for government to play its part.

Now, what are the other areas that cannot be handled through the market, or can be handled only at so great a cost that the use of political channels may be preferable? Government establishes the rules of the game and it makes sure that we respect them; it plays the role of referee. Society's acceptance of the definition of property rights would be another one. And there is wide acceptance of government's responsibility for the monetary system.

Does government have a role to play in breaking monopolies? Noting that monopolies constitute a relatively small part of all economic activities, while recognising that monopolies limit the freedom of choice for consumers, Friedman would accept what he calls 'technical monopolies', because it is technically efficient to have a single producer or enterprise to supply a particular service, such as telephone services. Friedman concluded that, if tolerable, private monopoly for that particular service may be the least of evils. He predicted that dynamic changes are likely to undermine this type of monopoly.

Another example in which strictly voluntary exchange is impossible, arises when actions of individuals affect other individuals for which it is not feasible to charge or recompense them. Friedman calls this 'neighbourhood effects'. These effects apply in circumstances under which the action of one individual imposes significant costs on other individuals, for which it is not feasible to make him compensate them, or yields significant gains to other individuals for which it is not feasible to make them compensate him. An example would be the pollution of a river. The one who pollutes the river is in fact forcing others to exchange good water for bad.

Then there is government's action on the grounds of paternalism. It is assumed that freedom is a tenable objective only for responsible individuals. As not all individuals are responsible persons (like children and the mentally impaired) there is some ambiguity in the ultimate objective of freedom. The question, however, is where to draw the line, as there is no formula that tells us where to stop. Each case should be judged on its merits, while a consensus is reached on the decisions to be taken.

Now, if all these roles have been established, government has an important and justified role to play. After all, a consistent liberal is not an anarchist. However, US federal and state governments, and their counterparts in other Western countries, play a much broader role. The book mentions 14 functions performed by the US government for which there is no justification according to liberal principles. They range from price support for agricultural products, via conscription, to publicly owned and operated toll roads.

The Control of Money

The reader of the 1960s might conclude: so far, so good. But then, Friedman puts forward a bombshell of a proposition:

> The fact is that the Great Depression, like most other periods of severe unemployment, was produced by government mismanagement rather than

by any inherent instability of the private economy. A governmentally established agency—the Federal Reserve System—had been assigned responsibility for monetary policy. In 1930 and 1931, it exercised this responsibility so ineptly as to convert what otherwise would have been a moderate contraction into a major catastrophe.[38]

The author mentioned the catastrophic crash on Wall Street in October 1929. Conventional wisdom had it that the crash and other factors, such as the Smoot–Hawley Tariff Act of 1930 and the budget-balancing orthodoxies of President Herbert Hoover, all contributed to the Great Depression, which was not due to government's mismanagement. Friedman refuted this opinion. The Federal Reserve System (Fed) should not have allowed the money stock to decline (which it dramatically did). Liquidity shortages led to bank failures and panics. The Fed should have provided cash to the banks. Had this been done, the many bank closures would have been cut short and the monetary debacle averted.

Regarding economic stability, government policy concerns monetary policy and fiscal or budgetary policy. The extremes of the continuum in this realm are on one end the automatic functioning of the gold standard and, on the other, the assignment of large discretionary powers to a group of technicians of an 'independent' central bank. A liberal is fundamentally fearful of concentrated power. Yet, there is widespread agreement that government should have some responsibility for monetary matters. The challenge for the liberal is thus to limit government's power and to prevent this power from being used in ways that will tend to weaken a free society. Friedman compares the situation before WWI when America was on the gold standard, and after 1914. Monetary turbulences, including the panic of 1907, turned the feeling of dissatisfaction with the financial system into an urgent demand for governmental action. In 1913 the Federal Reserve Act was passed. While admitting that the period thereafter was a very difficult one caused by two world wars and the Great Depression, Friedman concluded that the second period was clearly more unstable. The reason being the different monetary institutions in the period before and after 1914:

---

[38] *Capitalism and Freedom*, 38.

This evidence persuades me that at least a third of the price rise during and just after World War I is attributed to the establishment of the Federal Reserve System and would not have occurred if the earlier banking system had been retained; that the severity of each of the major contractions—1920–21, 1929–33, and 1937–38—is directly attributable to acts of commission and omission by the Reserve authorities and would not have occurred under earlier monetary and banking arrangements.[39]

From July 1929 to March 1933, the money stock in the US fell by one-third, and over two-thirds of the decline came after Britain's departure from the gold standard. Had the money stock been kept from declining, the contraction would have been both shorter and far milder. The Great Depression, concluded Friedman, is a testament to how much harm can be done by mistakes on the part of a few 'technicians' when they wield vast power over the monetary system of a country. Such a system is a bad system, argued Friedman. Clemenceau, the former French President once said, 'Money is much too serious a matter to be left to Central Bankers.'

Friedman proposes to enact a rule instructing the monetary authority to achieve a specified rate of growth in the stock of money. More specifically,

the Reserve System shall see to it that the total stock of money so defined rises month by month, and indeed, so far as possible, day by day, at an annual rate of X per cent, where X is some number between 3 and 5.[40]

Further reforms would be needed to curtail undesirable interventions of the Fed and Treasury authorities. These further reforms are far less basic than the adoption of a rule to limit the discretion of the monetary authorities with respect to the stock of money.

---

[39] Ibid., 45.

[40] Ibid., 54. Friedman's ideas of the 1960s have been revitalized by market monetarists. *The Economist* of 31 December 2011 writes in its article entitled 'Marginal Revolutionaries', 'The market monetarists point out that their 5 % target is consistent with inflation of about 2 %, provided the economy grows at about 3 % a year, its rough average for the pre-crisis years. If growth slowed to 1 %, inflation would have to be permanently higher, i.e. 4 %. If output suffered a one-time drop, inflation might have to surge temporarily above 5 %. But as growth returned to normal, inflation would recede.'

International Financial and Trade Arrangements

Loyal to his liberal convictions, Friedman warns that the most effective way to convert a market economy into an authoritarian economic society is to start imposing direct controls on foreign exchange. The best way to achieve a balance of payments is freely floating exchange rates determined in the market by private transactions without governmental intervention. This enables free-market forces to provide an effective and automatic response to changes in conditions affecting international trade. This proposal is not favoured by many as free-floating exchange rates have often been associated with financial and economic instability (think of hyperinflation in Germany and Austria before WWII and—later—in some Latin American countries). Friedman, however, argued that we want a system in which prices are free to fluctuate, but in which the forces determining them are sufficiently stable so that prices move within moderate ranges.

He proposed a radically different approach towards foreign aid. Instead of making grants to poor countries—and thereby promoting socialism—it would be far better to offer full cooperation on equal terms to all.

As regards fiscal policy, since the introduction of the New Deal in 1933 there has been a supposed necessity for government spending to eliminate unemployment. Later on, other reasons were used to justify a permanently high level of government spending. Take the so-called 'pump priming' argument to get an economy out of a recession. This has no validity, according to Friedman, as many of the programmes concerned didn't come into effect until after the recession was over.

All told, the most unstable component of America's national income is federal expenditure. The federal budget is, therefore, itself a major source of instability. The author proposed to plan expenditure programmes entirely in terms of what the community wants to do through government rather than privately, and without any regard to problems of year-to-year economic stability. And to plan tax rates so as to provide sufficient revenues to cover planned expenditures on the average of 1 year with another, again without regard to year-to-year changes in economic stability.

Fiscal Policy

Friedman refutes the idea that an increase in government spending relative to tax receipts is *necessarily* expansionary and a decrease contractionary. There is no empirical evidence to support this erroneous idea. Fiscal policies typically take effect when the recessions are already over. Instead of offsetting recessions, fiscal policies introduce an inflationary bias into governmental policy. Keynes's widely acclaimed multiplier is not safe in Friedman's hands. He demonstrated that the more stubborn moneyholders are with respect to the ratio they wish to maintain between their cash balance and their income, the closer the result will be to no change in income.

The Role of Government and Education

The chapter on government's role in education is especially interesting as the attentive reader's insight into Friedman's mind and liberal philosophy would at first sight expect a refutation of government's role. But that is not the case, as Friedman finds that government's intervention can be defended on two grounds. The first one concerns the above-mentioned 'neighbourhood effects'. The second is the paternalistic concern for children. Each ground has different implications for government's intervention.

A stable and democratic society is impossible without a minimum degree of literacy and knowledge on the part of most citizens and without widespread acceptance of some common set of values. Education contributes to both. Education to a child does not only accrue to him or her but also to other members of the society. Therefore, there is a significant neighbourhood effect. Government carries the financial burden of this 'general' education. However, vocational training is another matter. This type of education directly benefits the student and should, in principle, not be subsidised by government.

Then who should run the schools? Government or private institutions? Friedman proposes the introduction of a voucher system which allows parents to send their children to 'approved schools'—nationalised ones or private—of their own choice. The role of government is then limited to financing the vouchers and to make sure that the approved school meets minimum pedagogical standards. A nationalised schooling system also implies uniform salary systems, blocking payment of incentives or top-ups for very talented teachers. This isn't to Friedman's liking: 'We are threatened with an excess of conformity. Our problem is to foster diversity, and the alternative would do this far more effectively than a nationalised school system.'[41]

What about university and college education? At this level of education, neighbourhood effects lose their relevance. However, public expenditures on higher schooling can be justified as a means of training youngsters for citizenship and for community leadership. But restricting the government subsidy to schooling obtained as a state-administered institution cannot be justified. The subsidy should be granted to individuals to be spent at institutions of their own choice. Any government schools that are retained should charge fees covering educational costs and so compete on an equal level with private schools.

Capitalism and Discrimination

The rise of capitalism has been accompanied by a reduction in the extent to how particular religious, racial or social groups have been discriminated against. The impersonal market separates economic activities from political views and protects people from being discriminated against in their economic activities. From a market perspective, those of us who regard colour of skin or religion as irrelevant can buy some things more cheaply as a result. Needless to say that applying positive discrimination in employing staff doesn't go down well with Friedman. After all, the American Civil Liberties Union would fight to the death to protect the right of a racist to preach on a street corner the doctrine of racial segregation. But it will favour putting him in jail if he acts on his principles by refusing to hire an African American for a particular job.

---

[41] *Capitalism and Freedom*, 97.

Monopoly and Social Responsibility

Monopoly exists when a specific individual or enterprise has sufficient control over a particular product or service to determine the terms on which other individuals shall have access to it. Monopoly raises two problems for a free society: (1) a limitation on voluntary exchange and (2) it raises the issue of social responsibility of the monopolist as he is visible and has power. One would be inclined to think that he then furthers his own interest by taking on his social responsibility.

As regards monopolies, there are three types: one in industry, another in labour and a third in government. Industrial monopolies are fairly unimportant from the point of view of the US economy as a whole. On the basis of available evidence at the time, Friedman concluded that private sector monopolies account for 15 % of the economy, far less than one would have expected. Moreover, this percentage may well decrease, he added.

The same applies to monopoly in labour; also as regards unions, there is a tendency to overestimate their importance. Labour unions represent roughly one-quarter of the workforce. Friedman added that many unions are utterly ineffective. In addition, since unions have generally been strongest among groups that would have been highly paid anyway, their effect has been to make high-paid workers higher paid at the expense of lower-paid workers. So, labour unions crowd out employment opportunities and contribute to a wider income distribution among workers by reducing the opportunities available to the most disadvantaged workers.

Government, or government-sponsored, monopolies are not very extensive in America. The post office, power supply and highways are examples of government monopolies. Added to these, the federal government has become essentially the only purchaser of many enterprises and whole industries in the realm of defence, space and research. Government can break monopolies by eliminating measures which directly support monopoly. Beyond this, an extensive reform of the tax laws would also help. Friedman proposes the abolition of the corporate tax.

Price controls, tariffs and other restrictions imposed by government constitute sources of monopoly. Take tariffs: they are imposed to protect domestic industries, meaning to handicap potential competitors. And they interfere with the freedom of individuals to engage in voluntary exchange. After all, the liberal takes the individual, and not the nation, as her unit.

Regarding social responsibility of business and labour, Friedman stated that anybody who thinks that business CEOs and labour leaders would have a social responsibility beyond their core task shows a fundamental misconception of the character and nature of a free economy. In such an economy there is only one social responsibility of business and that is to increase its profits while complying with the rules of the game. The social responsibility of labour leaders is to serve the interests of the membership. It is the responsibility of the rest of us to establish a framework of law such that an individual in pursuit of her own interests is led by Adam Smith's invisible hand to achieve a social end which was not part of her intention. Smith himself noted in his *Wealth of Nations* that he had never known much good done by those who affected to trade for the public good. Friedman ended the section on social responsibility as follows:

> Permitting corporations to make contributions for charitable purposes and allowing deductions for income tax, is a step in the direction of creating a divorce between ownership and control, and undermines the basic nature and character of our society. It is a step away from an individualistic society and toward the corporate state.[42]

Occupational Licensure in Medicine

On occupational licensure, the book provides an analysis of the pros and cons of licensure in medicine, which is widely accepted and practised. Friedman's general principle on licensure is that it is difficult to justify, for it goes against the rights of individuals to enter into voluntary contracts. Nonetheless, there are some justifications given for licensure that the liberal will have to accept. Take the case of an incompetent physician who produces an epidemic. In this case it is conceivable that everybody will be willing to submit to the restriction of the practice of medicine to competent people only. But who is to determine what a competent physician

---

[42] Ibid., 136.

would be? That is typically decided by physicians. The result is control over entry by members of the occupation itself, hence the establishment of a monopoly position.

In the USA the American Medical Association (AMA) is in fact a trade union and arguably the strongest in the land. It can limit the number of people to enter the profession. They do that at the stage of admission to medical schools. AMA's Council on Medical Education and Hospitals approves medical schools. The power of the Council has been demonstrated at various times when there has been pressure to reduce numbers. Their argument in countering a rise in the number of qualified doctors is to maintain ethical practices which can only be maintained at a standard of income which is adequate to the merits and needs of the medical profession. Friedman commented that leaders of the medical profession should proclaim publicly that colleagues must be paid to be ethical.

The result of all this is that medical licensure has reduced both the quantity and quality of medical practice. Indeed, it has reduced the opportunities available to people who would like to be physicians and has forced the public to pay more for less satisfactory medical services. Friedman proposed instead that anyone should be free to practice medicine without restriction except for legal and financial responsibility for any harm done to others through fraud or negligence. The market would be opened up to many more entrants. Group practices would spring up, in which there would be an efficient division of labour between doctors and specialists, as well as between doctors and medical technicians. They would have a great interest in establishing a reputation for reliability and quality. For the same reason consumers would get to know their reputation. These medical teams would also have the specialised skill to judge the quality of physicians; indeed, they would be the agent, or the consumer, in doing so.

The Distribution of Income

Concerning belief in the equality of income developed in Western countries in the twentieth century, two questions must be answered: (1) What is the justification for state intervention to promote equality? (2) And what has been the effect of the measures taken? An accepted core belief in society is that payment in accordance with product is ethically fair.

This can imply that there would be considerable inequality of income and wealth. But when one looks at the historical development of capitalism, its achievement has been to offer opportunities to men and women to improve their earning capacities. So, over time capitalism has led to less inequality than any alternative system. The advances in technology have made available to the masses luxuries that in the past were available only to the wealthy. A contributing factor to limiting the gap between rich and poor has been the shrinking of family size. As capitalist societies progress, there is a trend towards smaller families. Hence the family income divided by the number of family members led to an appreciable increase in income per head.

As regards the second question whether government's measures brought about more equality, Friedman's impression was that tax measures have had a relatively minor, though not negligible effect in the direction of narrowing the difference between the average position of groups of families. He also pointed to the fact that the progressive income tax rates triggered ingenious tax evasions which resulted in the actual rates being much lower than the nominal ones.

He proposed a flat income tax rate, while stating that a progressive income tax system with redistributive objectives would be unacceptable, as it constitutes a case of coercion to take from some in order to give to others, which conflicts head-on with individual freedom. The book provides a calculation on page 175 of the total amount of actual individual and income tax returns divided by the number of tax payers, resulting in a flat rate of 23.5 %.

The author pointed out that a number of the actual inequalities can be attributed to market imperfections. Many have been created by government action or could be removed by government. For example, special monopoly privileges, tariffs and other measures benefitting particular groups are all sources of inequality. Another measure would be to extend educational opportunities in order to reduce inequalities.

Social Welfare Measures

The egalitarian sentiment which formed the inspiration for progressive tax systems, also led to a host of social welfare measures which are analysed by Friedman in their positive and negative effects. Take public housing: this has resulted in more people having to live in a smaller number of houses. Another measure is the minimum wage law. The objective, of course, is to alleviate poverty of low-income earners. What actually happens is that firms will lay off workers to keep their labour costs under control. The net result is that it leads to more unemployment; so, the effect is an increase in poverty.

Farm price supports do not help farmers who need help, if that was the intention of the subsidy. This measure is ineffective for poor farmers as they consume part of their own harvest and thus bring relatively little produce to the market. These price supports trigger larger production, and do not raise the income per poor farmer. The consumer has to pay more for farm products, and a protected local farm market triggers import quota for farm products.

Friedman referred to the controversy that surrounded old-age and survivor's insurance inception. Yet it is now taken for granted, so much so, that its desirability is no longer questioned. Nevertheless, there is the ethical question of what the justification is for the young to subsidise the old regardless of their economic status. Then there is also the consideration that the system is not likely to be self-financing; so, there will be a need for continued subsidising. The liberal will ask whether this is justified. The answer is no. Friedman stated that we may wish to help the poor. But is there any justification for helping people whether they are poor or not, just because they happen to be of retirement age?

The author is also against the compulsory purchase of annuities to provide for the elderly. Compelling people to buy an annuity is only justified if, say, 90 % of the population would become a burden on the public at age 65, in the absence of compulsory purchase of such annuities. However, if only 1 % would impose on the community, would that then justify it? Worse, these annuities have to be bought from government, thereby inhibiting competition.

The Alleviation of Poverty

Poverty is declining in Western countries that have seen a spectacular rise in income and wealth. Still poverty has not been eradicated. The best way to alleviate it is by means of private charity. However, the extension of government welfare activities triggered a decline in private charity. Some measures taken by government with the intention to help the poor were not effective. Minimum wage, price control and tariffs often had detrimental effects on the poor.

A negative income tax would be more effective, argues Friedman. It would set a floor below which no one's net income could fall. Furthermore, such a negative income tax system would be more than two times cheaper than the existing system.

A liberal may approve state action towards ameliorating poverty as a more effective way in which the great bulk of the community can achieve a common objective. He will do so with regret, however, at having to substitute compulsory for voluntary action. Friedman added that

> The egalitarian will go this far, too. But he will want to go further. He will defend taking from some to give to others, not as a more effective means whereby the 'some' can achieve an objective they want to achieve, but on grounds of 'justice'. At this point, equality comes sharply into conflict with freedom; one must choose. One cannot be both an egalitarian, in this sense, and a liberal.[43]

The final chapter concludes by comparing the functioning of the market and what it brought about with government and what it intended to achieve. Friedman admitted that, as for the market, there is a difference between its actual and ideal operation. However, this is nothing compared to the difference between the actual effects of government interventions and their intended effects.

Positive measures of government were the construction of highways criss-crossing the nation, the building of magnificent dams, orbiting satellites into space, the school system which opened up opportunities for the youth, public health as well as law and order were provided; all of them are tributes to the capacity of government to command great resources. Yet, on balance government's record is dismal, as the greater part of government efforts have failed to achieve their very objectives as elaborated in the book. Government has rather hampered than helped

---

[43] Ibid., 195.

America's tremendous progress. The invisible hand has been more potent for progress than the visible hand for retrogression.

Friedman expressed a hope for the future in the book's final paragraph:

> I believe that we shall be able to preserve and extend freedom despite the size of the military programmes and despite the economic powers already concentrated in Washington. But we shall be able to do so only if we awake to the threat that we face, only if we persuade our fellow men that free institutions offer a surer, if perhaps at times a slower, route to the ends they seek than the coercive power of the state. The glimmerings of change that are already apparent in the intellectual climate are a hopeful augur.[44]

Biography: Albert Otto Hirschman (1915–2012)

Otto Albert Hirschmann was born on 7 April 1915 in Berlin; he was the son of Carl and Hedwig Marcuse Hirschmann. He changed his name to Albert Otto Hirschman upon arrival in New York in 1943, adapting himself to and learning from new environments while never losing sight of his heritage, as his biographer noted.[45] Hirschman died on 10 December 2012 at the age of 97 in Ewing Township, New Jersey.

Young Otto Albert attended the Französisches Gymnasium in Berlin, at the time an intellectual hothouse, from which he graduated in 1932. His final thesis was based on a quotation from Spinoza: 'One should neither laugh nor cry at the world, but understand it.' He then went to Berlin's Friedrich-Wilhelm Universität to study law. However, after the rise of the Nazis in 1933 he left Germany and continued his studies at the Sorbonne in Paris, the London School of Economics and the University of Trieste, where in 1938 he received a PhD in economics, something his parents didn't like because they considered economics a 'breadless art'.

Soon after, he joined those who fought on the side of the Spanish Republic in the Spanish Civil War (1936–1939), an episode about which

---

[44] bid., 202.
[45] Adelman, J. (2013) *Worldly Philosopher: The Odyssey of Albert O. Hirschman*. Princeton: Princeton University Press, 2.

he remained silent for the rest of his life.⁴⁶ After the Nazis occupied France, he helped many artists and intellectuals escape to the United States. Together with Harvard-educated classicist Varian Fry, who worked for the American Emergency Rescue Committee, Albert, who was fluent in French, managed to get the necessary visas and smuggled the refugees across the border to Spain and on to Portugal. Some of them became famous, such as Hannah Arendt, André Breton, Marc Chagall, Max Ernst, Marcel Duchamp, Heinrich Mann and Alma Mahler.

Hirschman left Europe for the United States via the same route, carrying Michel de Montaigne's *Essais* (his favourite book) in his rucksack. He had obtained a Rockefeller Fellowship at the University of California at Berkeley where he wrote his first book, *National Power and the Structure of Foreign Trade* (1945). The book was inspired by Machiavelli's ideas about the relationship between power and trade.

After the Japanese bombing of Pearl Harbor on 7 December 1941, Hirschman enlisted in the US army. Originally assigned to a combat unit, Hirschman was shifted to the Office of Strategic Services, where he worked as an interpreter. After the war ended, he continued for some time to be an interpreter for the first Allied war crimes trial in which Nazi general Dostler was tried.

After the war Hirschman started job-hunting in Washington D.C. where—after a long search—he landed a job at the Commerce Department. The work there didn't inspire him. He was recruited to join the Federal Reserve Board by Alexander Gerschenkron, an old Berkeley colleague, who was head of its research staff. In 1948 he was appointed Chief of the Western European and British Commonwealth Section of the Fed's Division of Research and Statistics, and, later, of the Economic Cooperation Administration (ECA), the Marshall Plan's executing agency. At the ECA Hirschman underlined the need for multilateral trading and helped to develop the Marshall Plan. Some say that he provided 'the thinking behind the thinking'. He was—as his biographer Jerry Adelman wrote—'one of the invisible men behind the Marshall Plan'.⁴⁷

---

⁴⁶ 'On the whole, he was reluctant to discuss the Spanish Civil War after he left Catalonia. His wife, Sarah—who met him years later—found him silent on the topic, and sensing his unease, she didn't press him for details.' *Worldly Philosopher*, 134.

⁴⁷ *Worldly Philosopher*, 261.

The ECA requested that Hirschman elaborate on the idea of a common monetary authority for Europe. Adelman wrote about it in *Worldly Philosopher*:

> The issue for Hirschman was not whether Europe should have a common currency, but rather how 'to think of a monetary and financial organization for Europe that does not ask for the impossible, yet which would result in a closely knit European monetary and financial structure'. He did not discount the idea of a common currency but made it clear that it was a goal rather than a means for creating a larger, integrated market. He likened the arrangement to a return to the principles of the nineteenth-century open markets, but without the gold standard whose inflexibility gave way to nationalism and bilateralism.[48]

Hirschman was one of the victims of McCarthyism. His dossier was already opened in 1943. His loyalty towards the USA was questioned; the investigators wrongly concluded that Hirschman was somewhat sympathetic to communism. As a result, he was dismissed from the federal government in 1951. Meanwhile the Wold Bank was looking for someone to fill the position of economic advisor to the Board of Colombia's National Planning Council (NPC). Hirschman got the job.

In 1952 he started working for the NPC in Bogotá, Colombia in 1952. After his contract ended in 1954, he remained in Bogotá for the next 2 years and worked as a private economic advisor. He and his wife, Sarah Chapiro, were very happy in Colombia. They made friends with European émigrés and, gradually, also with Colombians. They developed a lifelong love for Latin America.

Hirschman's Colombian experience focused his attention on economic development. However, his point of view was at odds with mainstream thinking. Hirschman published *The Strategy of Economic Development* (1958) while at Yale, where Hirschman had been offered a visiting research professorship. After Yale, Hirschman held a succession of academic positions in economics at Columbia University (1958–1964), Harvard (1964–1974) and, finally, the Institute for Advanced Study at Princeton (1974–2012).

---

[48] Ibid., 272–3.

Hirschman's Philosophy

Some of his intellectual loves, among many others, were Machiavelli (who showed how things *really* happen in politics) and Michel de Montaigne (whose advice was to 'observe, observe perpetually'). Hirschman liked to say that he had a propensity for self-subversion; he qualified and questioned, and hedged as a matter of habit. He highlighted another aspect of his way of looking at the world in one of his paradoxes: 'The only way in which we can bring our creative resources fully into play is by misjudging the nature of the task, by presenting it to ourselves as more routine, simple, undemanding of genuine creativity, than it will turn out to be.' He was fond of the *petite idée*, which was, he said, 'The attempt to come to an understanding of reality in portions, admitting that the angle may be subjective.'

Contributions to the Social Sciences

Although educated as an economist, Hirschman did cast his analytical net much wider. He made inroads into political science, psychology and sociology and touched upon moral issues.

While at Berkeley, Hirschman studied the effects of international trade on national economies. As noted, he wrote *National Power and the Structure of Foreign Trade* at Berkeley. The book contains statistical indices designed to measure market concentration and market power. O.C. Herfindahl used Hirschman's indices in his 1950 study of the American steel industry. They became known as the Herfindahl–Hirschman Index, which measures the level of concentration in industries and helps show how competitive they are.

Hirschman attacked the prevailing wisdom of 'balanced growth' and 'top-down planning' in *The Strategy of Economic Development* (1958). Instead, he argued for providing economic support to industries with strong 'linkages'. If one sector is closely linked to others, its own development, however *unbalanced*, can spur additional development and promote growth. He also said that development depends 'on calling forth and enlisting for development purposes, resources and abilities that are hidden, scattered, or badly utilized'. Developing countries need more than capital. They need practice in making difficult economic decisions. Economic progress was the product, Hirschman noted, of successful habits. And there is no better teacher than a little adversity.

He would rather encourage settlers and entrepreneurs at the grass-roots level to cope with impediments themselves (i.e. the ability to make development decisions) than run the risk that aid, as prescribed by 'economic missionaries' might infantilise its recipients. Hirschman did not warm to overarching development models, such as Rostow's stages of economic growth. He was more interested in the disequilibria in development processes. Hirschman saw that the messy nature of development required specific strategies and not overarching development models. Needless to say the book didn't only receive praise, it also received critical reviews. For example, Adelman summarised Holllis Chenery's review: 'While he praised Hirschman for addressing "motivational factors" in economic theory, he charged him with "overstating his case", replacing simplifying notions of capital scarcity with new, no-less reductive assumptions about the centrality of decision making as key.'[49] Hirschman's development philosophy didn't trigger a particular Hirschman school in development economics, as his ideas were not reflected in an encompassing model.

The term for which he is probably best remembered is the 'hiding hand', elaborated in his essay 'The Principle of the Hiding Hand' (1967). Hirschman wrote that people are apt to take on and plunge into new tasks because of the erroneously presumed absence of a challenge (i.e. the hiding hand), as the task looks easier and more manageable than it will turn out to be.

His most influential book is *Exit, Voice and Loyalty: Responses to the Decline in Firms, Organisations and States* (1970). Hirschman got the idea for this book after having taken an awful train ride with Nigerian Railways. He wondered how it was possible that the passengers accepted such appalling service. In *Exit, Voice and Loyalty* Hirschman argued that people have three different ways of responding to bad goods and services and to disappointments. He explored these responses to unjust or inefficient organisations. You can either leave (exit) or complain (voice). And if you remain loyal, you will not exit, and you may—or may not—speak out.

---

[49] Ibid., 351.

He introduced the role of quality in the analysis. He noted that traditional demand analysis is mainly in terms of price and quantity, categories which have the great advantage of being recorded, and which are measurable. The consumer who is insensitive to price increases is often highly sensitive to quality declines. Therefore, they are the ones who are most likely to make a fuss in case of the deterioration of a product's quality until they exit.

A prominent message of the book is that 'exit' sometimes fails to send a strong message to underperforming firms or organisations; it can entrench the status quo. Hirschman asked rhetorically, 'Weren't there cases where monopolists were relieved when their critics left?' 'Exit' may also reinforce the cycle of decline. And, in countering Milton Friedman's proposed school vouchers, Hirschman wrote that the worst thing that ever happened to incompetent public schools was the growth of private schools: they siphoned off the kind of parents who would otherwise have agitated more strongly for reform at those public schools. *Exit, Voice and Loyalty*'s main point is that exit and voice work best together.

The book is not only looking at the subject matter from an economist's point of view, but includes insights into psychology, sociology and political science, as well as politics at large. Hirschman took a critical stance against the way the Johnson Administration dealt with the Vietnam War.

> Attempts to apply the book's perspective were made over many areas of social life. Hirschman even suggested that his *exit–voice* theorem would also apply to family life, in particular to marriage and divorce. When a marriage is in difficulty, the partners can either make an attempt, usually through a great deal of *voicing*, to reconstruct their relationship or they can divorce (*exit*).

Exit, Voice and Loyalty was very well received, but there were dissenting opinions, in particular from public-choice economists.[50] Their criticism

---

[50] Public-choice economists study the links between economics and politics. They apply economic analysis to study political decision-making as well as the behaviour of politicians.

boiled down to Hirschman's treatment of exit in the case of a monopoly. Adelman summarises Gordon Tullock's critique as follows:

> Hirschman's argument in chapter 5 was that a level of competition might induce exit from the monopolist, and thus diffuse angry, vocal customers. Competition, in this scenario, 'comforts and bolsters' the flaccid monopolist by ridding it of 'its most troublesome customers'. So, we get a hybrid world of lazy giants and welcome competition—just the kind of complex, mixed systems made of apparent contradictions.[51]

As mentioned, Montaigne was one of Hirschman's inspirations. This is clearly shining through in *Exit, Voice and Loyalty*, in which he makes the reader change how he or she observes the world. For example, economic textbooks portray the dynamics between supply and demand by putting price on the X-axis and quantity on the Y-axis. Hirschman brings in the dimension of quality. What happens if a product's quality deteriorates or an organisation's performance, including the performance of a political party, becomes less effective? Do we quit (exit), speak out (voice) or—sometimes against better judgment—stay put out of a sense of loyalty? The book also attempts to demonstrate that economics cannot be done in isolation. Hirschman observed the following:

> A central place is held in economics and social science in general by principles and forces making for order or equilibrium in economic and social systems. Disorder and disequilibrium are then understood as resulting from some malfunction of these principles or forces. Explanations of order–disorder or equilibrium–disequilibrium have typically been discipline-bound, dealing with either the political or the economic world. Since the two are interrelated it would be useful to have a construct that bridges them. Such is the claim of the exit–voice perspective.[52]

Latin America's development sputtered in the 1970s, resulting in dictatorships, increasing poverty and violation of human rights. Hirschman

---

[51] *Worldly Philosopher*, 447.
[52] Hirschman, A.O. (1998). Lemma on Hirschman. In: *The New Palgrave: A Dictionary of Economics*. Vol. 2. London: MacMillan, 219.

saw a parallel with developments in early modern European history. He studied the historical development of capitalism and wrote about it in *The Passions and the Interests: Political Arguments for Capitalism before Its Triumph* (1977). In this book he rejects the notion of a supposedly lost world of republican virtue, free of commercial avarice. He also rejects the suggestion (still prominent in economics) that markets simply take human beings as they are, with their inevitable self-interest, as professed by the father of modern economics, Adam Smith. Instead, Hirschman observed that other early theorists of free markets thought that commerce would transform people by cooling their passions and making them gentler. At the same time, Hirschman worried that efforts to focus people on economic gain could have the side-effect of killing the civic spirit and thereby opening the door to tyranny. Adelman provides a nice explanation of the relevance of *The Passions and the Interests* at the time when neo-classical economics was gaining ground:

> For those yearning for an expanded view of economics, one that saw through the Milton Friedmans of the world and their iron law of money, Hirschman's appeal to a more social and political *homonidae* gave some intellectual muscle to challenge the growing 'neoclassical' orthodoxy and its influential battery of foundations and think tanks.[53]

Hirschman wrote *The Rhetoric of Reaction: Perversity, Futility, Jeopardy* (1991) while in his mid-seventies. The book's target is conservative rhetoric. Yet, the book ends with a demonstration that the Left also has its own rhetoric. Where conservatives argue that further reforms jeopardise precious accomplishments, the Left disregards the concept of the unintended consequences of human action. Hirschman concluded that 'progressives are forever ready to mold and remold society at will and have no doubt about their ability to control events'.

The Rhetoric of Reaction was intended to challenge intransigence on the part of both the Right and the Left, and to get people to listen to one another in a spirit of humility, rather than making their standard, rhetorical moves. He wrote that purveyors of 'timid ignorance' rely on three

---

[53] Ibid., 519.

types of argument: jeopardy (i.e. reforms cost a lot and endanger previous gains), perversity (reforms will harm the people they are intended to help) and futility (problems are so huge that nothing can be done about them).

Hirschman's own favourite book was *The Passions and the Interests*. He said that writing it was the fruit of free creation. That book gave him pleasure to write, feeling free to discover things without having to prove someone wrong.

> Hirschman was fond of *paradoxes*. One of them concerns his description of the Karnaphuli Paper Mills in East Pakistan (now Bangladesh). The mill was built to exploit the vast bamboo forests of the Chittagong Hill Tracts. Not long after the mill came online the bamboo unexpectedly flowered and then died, a phenomenon now known to recur every 50 years or so. Dead bamboo was useless for pulping; it fell apart as it was floated down the river. Because of ignorance and bad planning, a new multi-million dollar plant was suddenly without the raw material it needed to function. What impressed Hirschman was the response to the crisis. The mill's operators quickly found ways to bring in bamboo from villages throughout East Pakistan, building a new supply chain using the country's many waterways. They started a research programme to find faster-growing bamboo to replace the dead forests, and planted an experimental tract. They found other kinds of lumber that worked just as well. The result was that the plant was blessed with a far more diversified base of raw materials than had ever been imagined. If bad planning hadn't led to the crisis at the plant, the mills' operators would never have been forced to be creative. And the plant would not have been nearly as valuable as it became. Success grew from original failure.

Honours

Hirschman was not awarded the economics Nobel Prize. Why was that? Adelman concluded that Hirschman's increasing breadth and originality coincided with his decreasing interest in speaking only to economics, his discipline.[54]

---

[54] Ibid., 614–15.

He received strings of honorary doctorates, amongst others from Harvard, Amherst College, Rutgers, the University of Southern California and from many European universities.

In 2003 Hirschman won the Benjamin E. Lippincott Award from the American Political Science Association for his book *The Passions and the Interests*. And in 2007, the Social Science Research Council established an annual prize in honour of Albert Hirschman. Development economist Dani Rodrik was its first laureate.

The Economist wrote in its obituary on Hirschman that his 'exit' will not silence his 'voice'.

Exit, Voice and Loyalty: Response to the Decline in Firms, Organizations and States

This book is a small volume of 155 pages, including appendices.[55] It's more an elaborate essay than a full-blown treatise. Yet, it is touching upon a wide variety of economic, social, political and moral phenomena, thereby stripping bare the conceptual limitations of the economic science; in particular of neoclassical economics. Hirschman wrote in the book's introduction,

> Under any economic, social, or political system, individuals, business firms, and organisations in general are subject to lapses from efficient, rational, law-abiding, virtuous, or otherwise functional behavior. No matter how well a society's basic institutions are devised, failures of some actors to live up to the behavior which is expected of them are bound to occur, if only for all kinds of accidental reasons.

True, Hirschman was not the only economist to point out the weaknesses of the assumption of the economically rational behaviour of people. After all, the study of economics has been broadened by the inclusion of insights of other social sciences, such as psychology and political science.

---

[55] Edition used: Harvard University Press, 1970.

This book must be seen as the application of a new field of argument which maintains that non-market forces are not necessarily less 'automatic' than market forces in the classical sense of the term. Hirschman proposes the view that when the market fails to achieve an optimal state, society will recognise the gap, and non-market social institutions will arise and attempt to bridge it.

Introduction and Doctrinal Background

Economists have paid little attention to repairable lapses of economic actors. There are two reasons for this neglect. First, in economics one assumes an unchanging level of rationality on the part of economic actors. For example, economists have typically assumed that a firm that falls behind (or gets ahead) does so for a good reason; the concept of a random and more or less easily 'repairable lapse' has been alien to their reasoning. Second, in the traditional model of the competitive economy, recovery from any lapse is not really essential. As one firm loses out in the competitive struggle, its market share is taken up by others; in the upshot, total resources may well be better allocated. The economist can afford to watch lapses of any one of his business firms with far greater equanimity than either the moralist who is convinced of the intrinsic worth of every one of his firms, or the political scientist whose firm (the state in his case) is unique and irreplaceable.

Hirschman then concludes that the image of the economy as a fully competitive system, where changes in the fortunes of individual firms are exclusively caused by basic shifts of comparative advantage, is a defective representation of the real world. There are well-known large realms of monopoly, oligopoly and monopolistic competition: deterioration in performance of firms operating in that part of the economy could result in more or less permanent pockets of inefficiency and neglect. It must be viewed with an alarm approaching that of the political scientist who sees his polity's integrity threatened by strife, corruption or boredom.

Even where vigorous competition prevails, unconcern with the possibility of restoring temporarily lagging firms to vigour is hardly justified. In these circumstances, mechanisms of recuperation would play a very useful role in avoiding social losses and human hardship. Such a mechanism of recuperation is readily available through competition itself. After all, isn't competition supposed to keep a firm 'on its toes'? Indeed, it is one major mechanism of recuperation. Hirschman argued, however, that (1) the implications of this particular function of competition have not been adequately spelled out and (2) a major alternative mechanism can come into play either when unavailable or as a complement to it.

Enter 'Exit' and 'Voice'

What applies to firms can also apply to organisations, such as voluntary associations, trade unions or political parties that provide services to their members without direct monetary counterpart. The assumption is that the performance of a firm (or organisation) is subject to deterioration for unspecified, random causes which are neither so compelling nor so durable as to prevent a return to previous performance levels, provided managers direct their attention to that task.

Deterioration is typically reflected in an absolute or comparative deterioration of the quality of the product or service provided. Management finds out its failings via two alternative routes: (1) some customers stop buying the firm's products (this is the exit option) and (2) the firm's customers or the organisation's members express their dissatisfaction directly to management or to some other authority to which management is subordinate, or through general protest addressed to anyone who cares to listen (this is the voice option).

As a result, management once again engages in a search for the causes and possible cures of customers' and members' dissatisfaction. The remainder of the book is largely devoted to the comparative analysis of these two options and to their interplay. One of the questions asked is, What institutions could serve to perfect each of the two options as mechanisms of recuperation?

Latitude for Deterioration and Slack in Economic Thought

How is the subject of this book related to economic and social science? The reason why humans have failed to develop (unlike baboons, for example) a finely built social process assuring continuity and steady quality in leadership is probably because they didn't have to. Most human societies are marked by the existence of a surplus above subsistence which allows society to take considerable deterioration in its stride. A lower level of performance, which would mean disaster for baboons, merely causes discomfort for humans.

The wide latitude human societies have for deterioration is the inevitable counterpart of increasing human productivity and control over the environment. Occasional decline, and prolonged mediocrity, are among the many penalties for progress. Because of the surplus and the resulting latitude, any homeostatic controls with which human societies might be equipped are bound to be rough. Recognition of this unpleasant truth has been impeded by a utopian dream: that economic progress, while increasing the surplus above subsistence, will also bring with it disciplines and sanctions of such severity as to rule out any backsliding that may be due, for example, to political processes.

It is a fallacy to expect that economic growth and technical progress would erect secure barriers against 'despotism', 'anarchy' and irresponsible behaviour in general. The common assumption of these constructs is simply stated: while technical progress increases society's surplus above subsistence, it also introduces a mechanism of the utmost complexity and delicacy, so that certain types of social misbehaviour, which previously had unfortunate consequences, would now be so clearly disastrous that they will be more securely barred than before. As a result society is, and then it is not, in a surplus situation: it is producing a surplus, but it is not at liberty *not* to produce it or to produce less of it than is possible; in effect social behaviour is as simply and as rigidly prescribed and constrained as it is in a no-surplus, but bare subsistence, situation. This is similar to the situation of perfect competition. For this model contains the same paradox: society as a whole produces a comfortable and perhaps steadily increasing surplus, but every individual firm considered in isolation is barely getting by, so that a single false step will be its undoing. So, everyone is constantly made to perform at the top of one's form and society as a whole is operating at its forever-expanding 'production frontier'.

This image, Hirschman notes, of a relentlessly taut economy, has held a privileged place in economic analysis, even when perfect competition was recognised as a purely theoretical construct with little reality content. People like surplus but are fearful of paying its price. While unwilling to give up progress, we hanker after the simple rigid constraints on behaviour that governed us when we were totally absorbed by the need to satisfy our most basic needs. Who knows, wondered Hirschman, whether this hankering is at the root of the paradise myth?

The fact that people can produce a surplus implies that they can also produce less than the maximum producible surplus. That is one aspect of the slack economy, as opposed to the taut economy. The author is not referring to results of malfunctions at the macroeconomic level; no, he is referring to what H.A. Simon observed about firms, in that they are normally aiming at no more than a 'satisfactory' rather than the highest possible rate of profits. Other authors referred to 'organisational slack'. Gary Becker showed that some of the basic microeconomic theorems are consistent with a wide range of irrational and inefficient behaviour on the part of consumers and producers, even though these theorems had originally been derived on the assumption of undeviating rationality. Professor Postan had contended that Britain's ailments are better understood by focusing on microeconomic slack than on any mistaken macroeconomic policies.

Slack can be squeezed out by additional investment, hours of work, productivity and decision-making through pressure mechanism. What causes slack? Hirschman suggested the existence of obstacles to entrepreneurial and cooperative behaviour needed for making development decisions. The first thing people do to counter slack is a determined search for ways and means to take up the slack, to retrieve the ideal of that taut economy.

Hirschman's own research in this realm concentrated on pressure mechanisms such as inter-sectoral or intra-sectoral imbalances and on production processes that exact high penalties for poor performance or don't tolerate it at all. The advocates of social revolution have contributed to this line of thought: one of their most seductive arguments has long been that only revolutionary changes can tap and liberate people's abundant but dormant, repressed or alienated energies.

The idea that slack fulfils some important—if unintended or latent— functions was put forward by authors who point out that it permits firms to ride out adverse markets or other developments. Slack helps to cut excess costs, introduce innovations and apply more aggressive sales techniques. In the political domain slack appears in the form of apathy, which is compensated by contributing to the stability and flexibility of a political system and provides for 'reserves' of political resources that can be thrown into the battle in crisis situations.

The above reactions to slack take it as a gap of a given magnitude between actual and potential performance of individuals, firms and organisations. Hirschman took it further, in that he recognised the pervasiveness of slack. It is continuously being generated as a result of some sort of entropy characteristic of human surplus-producing societies. Firms and other organisations are conceived to be permanently and randomly subjected to decline and decay. This radical pessimism, which views decay as an ever-present force constantly on the attack, generates its own cure; for as long as decay is hardly in undisputed command at all times, it is likely that the very process of decline activates certain counter-forces.

Exit and Voice as Impersonations of Economics and Politics

Exit belongs to economics, while voice belongs to politics. A dissatisfied customer buys from another producer. The affected firm learns its lesson, and eventually regains its competitive position. Recovery of the declining firm comes by courtesy of the 'invisible hand'. This is the sort of mechanism economics thrives on.

Voice is just the opposite of exit. Yet, it is messier; it can range from grumbling to violent protest. Voice is political action par excellence. And in the whole gamut of human institutions, from the state to the family, voice is the only tactic the members normally have to work with. In the political realm, exit has fared much worse than has voice in the realm of economics. Exit has often been branded as criminal, for it has been labelled as desertion, defection and treason.

A close look at the interplay between market and non-market forces will reveal the usefulness of certain tools of economic analysis for the understanding of political analysis in isolation, and vice versa. The analysis of this interplay will lead to a more complete understanding of social processes than can be afforded by economic or political analysis in isolation.

This book can be viewed as the application to a new field of argument which maintains that non-market forces are not necessarily less 'automatic' than market forces in the classical sense of the term. Hirschman proposed the view that when the market fails to achieve an optimal state, society will, to some extent at least, recognise the gap and non-market social institutions will arise and attempt to bridge it.

This doesn't imply that any disequilibrium will be eliminated by some combination of market and non-market forces, nor do they necessarily work at cross-purposes. But they leave room for a conjunction of the two forces, whereas both laissez-faire and interventionist doctrines have looked at market and non-market forces in a dualistic way; it being understood that the laissez-faire advocate's forces of good are the interventionist's forces of evil and vice versa. Hirschman hoped to demonstrate to political scientists the usefulness of economic concepts and to economists the usefulness of political concepts. Economists have succeeded so far in occupying large portions of the political science discipline, while political scientists—whose inferiority complex vis-à-vis the tool-rich economist is equalled only by that of the economist vis-à-vis the physicist—have shown themselves quite eager to be colonised and have often actively joined invaders.

Exit

Competition helps to cure the temporary and remediable lapses. One non-static aspect of competition has been amply scrutinised, namely its aptitude to generate innovation and growth. But no study has been made of the related topic of competition's ability to lead firms back to 'normal' efficiency, performance and growth standards.

How the Exit Option Works

The first conceptual element is a variant of the familiar demand function, with the difference that quantity bought is made to depend on changes in quality rather than on price. It is now convenient to assume that price doesn't change when quality drops. Costs also remain constant, because, by definition, the quality decline is the result of a decline in efficiency rather than from a firm's attempt to reduce costs by lowering quality.

First, any exit in response to quality decline will result in revenue losses. A price increase can result in an increase in the firm's total revenue in spite of some customer exit, and revenue can at best remain unchanged, but it will decline steadily as quality drops. Second, there exists a management reaction function which relates quality improvement to the loss in sales—upon finding out about customer desertion management undertakes to repair its failings, that is, if the damage done is repairable.

The interaction between the exit function and the reaction function can now be described. If there is a drop in quality it is desirable that it be of a size which leads to recuperation. If demand is highly inelastic with respect to quality change, revenue losses will be quite small and the firm will not get the message that something is wrong. But if demand is very elastic, the recuperation process will not take place either, because the firm will be wiped out before it will have had time to find out what hit it. This is a case of too much, too soon. It is therefore desirable that quality elasticity of demand be neither very large nor very small.

For competition (exit) to work as a mechanism of recuperation from performance lapses, it is generally best for a firm to have a mixture of alert and inert customers. The alert customers provide the firm with a feedback mechanism which starts the effort at recuperation while the inert customers provide it with the time and dollar cushion needed for this effort to come to fruition. If all customers would be alert, disastrous instability might result and firms would miss out on chances to recover from their occasional lapses.

Assume a small departure from the perfectly competitive model so that the firm has some latitude in varying quality. Then performance deterioration *can* (and is perhaps likely to) take the form of quality decline. If the market in which the firm sells is highly competitive, that is, full of highly knowledgeable buyers, the firm will be competed out of existence in very short order. In other words, the world of quasi-perfect competition doesn't avail of an effective recuperation mechanism. If one gives up the concept of a firm with no latitude whatsoever as to quality, then the optimal arrangement is not one close to that of perfect competition, but one far removed from it; and incremental moves in the direction of perfect competition are not necessarily improvements—the argument of the second best applies here in full force.

Competition as Collusive Behaviour

No matter what the quality elasticity of demand is, exit could fail to cause any revenue loss to the individual firm if the firm acquires new customers as it loses the old ones. A decline in quality could fall upon all firms. In these circumstances the exit option is ineffective in alerting management to its failings, and a merger of all firms would appear to be socially desirable—that is, monopoly would replace competition to advantage, for customer dissatisfaction would then be vented directly and perhaps to some effect in attempts at improving the monopoly's management, whereas under competition dissatisfaction takes the form of an ineffective flitting back and forth of groups of consumers from one deteriorating firm to another without any firm acquisition of a signal that something has gone awry.

The argument presented so far maintained the premise that the unsatisfactory features of the product turned out by the various competing firms could be eliminated as a result of pressures and a resultant search for solutions. But even if this premise is dropped, the competitive solution may again be inferior to one in which a single firm is the sole producer.

It will be evident that competitive political systems have frequently been portrayed in just these terms. The radical critique is correct in pointing out that competitive political systems have a considerable capacity to divert what might otherwise be a revolutionary ground swell into tame discontent with the governing party.

A less speculative illustration of the issue at hand can be drawn from the history of the trade union movement in America. A study revealed that most petitions to the National Labor Relations Board were unsuccessful and that those that were granted were equally divided between Congress of Industrial Organizations (CIO) petitions to displace an American Federation of Labor (AFL) union, and AFL petitions to displace a CIO union. These results led to the conclusion that raids between AFL and CIO unions were destructive to the interests of the unions involved, as well as the entire trade union movement.

Voice

The idea that voice is another recuperation mechanism which can come into play alongside, or in lieu of, the exit option is likely to be met with raised eyebrows. Let's examine the conditions under which the voice option is likely to make an effective appearance, either as a complement to exit or as its substitute.

Voice is defined as any attempt to effect change, rather than to escape from an objectionable state of affairs, whether through: (1) individual or collective petitions directly to the management in charge, (2) appeal to a higher authority with the intention of forcing a change in management or (3) various types of actions and protests, including those that are meant to mobilise public opinion. Voice is a succinct term for interest articulation. The choice is often between articulation and 'desertion'—voice and exit, in the neutral terminology.

The initial assumption, like in exit, is a decline in performance of a firm or organisation that is remediable, provided the attention of management is sufficiently focused on the task. If conditions are such that the decline leads to voice rather than exit, then the effectiveness of voice will increase, up to a certain point, with its volume. But voice is like exit in that it can be overdone: the discontented customers or members could become so harassing that their protests would at some point hinder rather than help whatever efforts at recovery are undertaken.

It has long been an article of faith of political theory that the proper functioning of democracy requires a maximally alert, active and vocal public. In the United States, this belief was shaken by empirical studies of voting and political behaviour which demonstrated the existence of considerable political apathy on the part of large sections of the public. As in the case of exit, a mixture of alert and inert citizens, or even an alternation of involvement and withdrawal, can actually serve democracy better than either total, permanent, activism or total apathy. According to another line of reasoning, the democratic political system requires a 'blending of apparent contradictions': on the one hand, the citizen must express her point of view so that the political elites know and can be responsive to what she wants; on the other, these elites must be allowed to make decisions. The citizen, therefore, must be influential and deferential.

Voice has the function of alerting a firm or organisation to its failings. But it must then give management, old or new, some time to respond to the pressures. The relation between voice and improvement in an organisation's efficiency is considerably similar to the modus operandi of exit. In the case of any one particular firm or organisation and its deterioration, either exit or voice will ordinarily have the role of the dominant reaction mode. In the case of normally competitive business firms, for example, exit is clearly the dominant reaction to deterioration. Voice is a badly underdeveloped mechanism.

Voice as a Residual of Exit

The voice option is the only way in which dissatisfied customers or members can react whenever the exit option is unavailable. This is usually the situation in the family, the state or the church. In the economic sphere, the theoretical construct of a pure monopoly would spell a no-exit situation, but the mixture of monopolistic and competitive elements, characteristic of most real markets, should make it possible to observe the voice option in its interaction with the exit option.

Let's look at a situation of deterioration of a product and declining sales where customers don't desert. They are likely to experience different degrees of unhappiness about the quality decline. These non-exiting customers are the source of the voice option. The other determinant of voice is the degree of discontent of the non-exiting customer.

Voice can be viewed as a residual: whoever decides not to exit is a candidate for voice, and voice depends, like exit, on the quality elasticity of demand. But the direction of the relationship is turned around: with a given potential for articulation, the actual level of voice feeds on *in*elastic demand, or on the lack of opportunity for exit. In this view, the role of voice would increase as the opportunities for exit decline, up to the point where, with exit wholly unavailable, voice must carry the entire burden of alerting management to its failings.

That such a see-saw relationship between exit and voice exists to some extent was at the time illustrated by the many complaints about quality and service that were published for years in the Soviet press. While exit completion played a much smaller role in the Soviet economy than in the market economies of the West, it was found necessary to give voice a more prominent role. Similarly, voice is a much more commanding position in less developed countries where one simply cannot choose between as many commodities as in an advanced economy. Therefore, the atmosphere in the former countries is more suffused with loud, often politically coloured, protest against poor quality of goods and services than it is in the advanced countries, where dissatisfaction is more likely to take the form of silent exit.

It is now assumed that exit is the dominant reaction mode. The possibility of voice having a destructive rather than constructive effect may therefore be excluded. Both the propensity to protest and the effectiveness of complaints vary widely from one firm–customer complex to another. Three general statements can be made: (1) voice functions as a *complement* to exit, not as a substitute, leading to a net gain from the point of view of the recuperation mechanism; (2) the more effective voice is (the effectiveness of exit being given), the more quality-inelastic can demand be without the chances for recuperation stemming from exit and voice *combined* being impaired; and (3) considering that beyond a certain point, exit has a destructive rather than a constructive effect, the optimal pattern from the point of view of maximising the combined effectiveness of exit and voice over the whole process of deterioration may be an elastic response of demand to the first stages of deterioration and an inelastic one for the later stages.

Voice as an Alternative to Exit

Only if a customer does not shift to another product or service is it evident that the decision whether to exit will often be taken in view of the prospects for the effective use of voice. If customers are sufficiently convinced that voice will be effective, then they may well *postpone* exit. If deterioration is a process unfolding in stages over a period of time, the voice option is more likely to be taken at an early stage. Once you have exited, you have lost the opportunity to use voice, but not vice versa; in some situations, exit will therefore be a reaction of last resort after voice has failed.

It appears, therefore, that voice can be a substitute for exit, as well as a complement to it. What are the conditions under which voice will be preferred to exit? One condition would be when the customer feels that he is able to do something about quality improvement of the product which has deteriorated in quality. Another possibility is that customers expect other customers to open the eyes of management, together with their own faithfulness. Yet other customers will not desert out of 'loyalty', which is a less rational, though far from wholly irrational, action. Many of these loyalists will actively participate in actions designed to change a producer's policies and practices, but some may simply refuse to exit and suffer in silence, confident that things will soon get better. Thus the voice option includes vastly different degrees of activity and leadership in the attempt to achieve change from within. But it always involves the decision to 'stick' with the deteriorating firm or organisation, and this decision is in turn based on: (1) an evaluation of the chances of getting the firm or organisation which produces the product or service back on track, through one's own action or through that of others, and (2) a judgment that it is worthwhile, for a variety of reasons, to trade the certainty of a competing product or service which is available against these chances.

It is necessary to introduce cost, which so far has been identified only as the entry into the exit option. In addition to this opportunity cost, account must be taken of the direct cost of voice, which is incurred as buyers of a product or members of an organisation spend time and money in the attempt to achieve changes in the policies and practices of the firm from which they buy or of the organisation to which they belong. In comparison to the exit option, voice is costly and conditioned on the influence and bargaining power customers and members of an organisation can bring to bear.

As voice tends to be costly in comparison to exit, the customer will become less able to afford voice as the number of goods and services over which she spreads her purchases increases; the cost of devoting even a modicum of her time to correcting the faults of any one of the entities she is involved in is likely to exceed her estimate of the expected benefits for a large number of them. This is also one of the reasons for which voice plays a more important role with respect to organisations of which an individual is a member than with respect to firms whose products she buys; the former are far less numerous than the latter.

Voice is likely to be an active mechanism primarily with respect to the more substantial purchases and organisations in which buyers and members are involved. Voice is also likely to function as an important mechanism in markets with few buyers or where few buyers account for an important proportion of total sales, both because it is easier for a few buyers than for many to combine for collective action, and simply because each one may have much at stake and wield considerable power, even in isolation. It is more common to encounter influential members of an organisation than influential buyers of a product; the voice option will therefore be observed more frequently among organisations than among business firms.

The upshot of the above discussion for the comparative roles of voice and exit is double-edged: the sheer number of available goods and varieties in an advanced economy favours exit over voice, but the increasing importance in such an economy of standardised durable goods requiring large outlays works in the opposite direction.

Once voice is recognised as a mechanism with considerable usefulness for maintaining performance, institutions can be designed in such a way that the cost of individual and collective action would be decreased. Or, in some situations, the rewards for successful action might be increased for those who initiated it.

There is a militant 'consumer revolution' in the USA as part of the general 'participation explosion'. Consumer voice will be institutionalised at three levels: (1) through independent entrepreneurship à la Ralph Nader, (2) through revitalisation of official regulatory agencies and (3) through stepped-up preventive activities on the part of the more important firms selling to the public. The propensity to resort to the voice option depends also on the general readiness of a population to complain and on the invention of such institutions and mechanisms that can communicate complaints cheaply and effectively. While exit requires nothing but a clear-cut 'either/or' decision, voice is essentially an art constantly evolving in new directions. The presence of the exit alternative can therefore tend to atrophy the development of the art of voice.

A Special Difficulty in Combining Exit and Voice

Hirschman drew inspiration for his book from analysing the incapacity of the Nigerian Railways to act in spite of fierce competition from truckers. Exit didn't have its usual attention-focusing effect because the loss of revenue was not a matter of the utmost gravity for management, while voice did not work as long as the most aroused and, therefore, the potentially most vocal customers were the first ones to abandon the railroads for the trucks. If this last aspect would have generality, then the chances that voice will ever act in conjunction with exit would be poor and voice would be an effective recuperation mechanism only in conditions of full monopoly when the customers are securely locked in.

Insensitivity to exit is exhibited by public agencies, such as the Nigerian Railways, that can draw on a variety of financial resources outside and independent of sales revenue. Those customers who care most about the quality of the product and who, therefore, are those who would be the most active, reliable and creative agents of voice are for that very reason also those who are apparently likely to exit first in case of deterioration.

In terms of the economic language, we all know that when the price of a commodity goes up, it is the marginal customer, the one who cares least, who drops out first. How is it that with a decline in quality the opposite seems quite plausible? Is it possible that the customers who drop out first as price increases are not the same as those who exit first when quality declines? The basic reason for this paradox lies in the still insufficiently explored role of quality (as contrasted with price) in economic life. Traditional demand analysis is cast overwhelmingly in terms of price and quantity, categories which have the immense advantage of being recorded, measurable and finely divisible.

Quality changes have usually been dealt with by economists and statisticians through the concept of the equivalent price or quantity change.

If a quality decline can be fully expressed as an equivalent rise in price that is uniform for all buyers of the article, the effects on customer exit of the quality decline and of the equivalent rise in price would be identical. The crucial point can now be made.

For any one individual, a quality change can be translated into equivalent price change. But this equivalence is frequently different for different customers of the article because appreciation of quality differs widely among them. This implies that a given deterioration in quality will inflict very different losses (i.e. different equivalent price increases) on different customers; someone who had a very high consumer surplus before deterioration may drop out as a customer as soon as quality deteriorates, provided a non-deteriorated competing product is available, be it at a much higher price. So, in the case of 'connoisseur' goods the customers who drop out when quality declines are not necessarily the marginal consumers who would drop out if price increased, but may be intra-marginal consumers with considerable consumer surplus; the consumer who is insensitive to price increases is often highly sensitive to quality declines. Therefore, they are the ones who are most likely to make a fuss in case of deterioration of a product's quality until they exit.

Consumer surplus measures the gain to the consumer of being able to buy a product at its market price: the larger that gain the more likely is it that the consumer will be motivated to 'do something' to have that gain safeguarded or restored. The nature of an available substitute has something to do with the question whether or not connoisseur goods will be rapidly forsaken, in case of deterioration, by the more quality-conscious customers. The rapid exit of the highly quality-conscious customers—a situation which paralyzes voice by depriving it of its principal agents—is tied to the availability of better-quality substitutes at higher prices.

The proposition that voice is likely to play a more important role in opposing deterioration of high-quality products than of lower-quality products can be maintained for the case of a good with many varieties, if these varieties can be assumed not to be spread with equal density over the whole quality range. If only because of economies of scale, it is plausible that density is lower in the upper ranges of quality than in the lower and middle range. If this is so then deterioration of a product in the upper-quality ranges has to be fairly substantial before the quality-conscious will exit and switch to the next-better variety. Hence, the scope for the voice option will be greatest in these ranges; it will be comparatively slight in the medium- and low-quality ranges.

This finding permits two inferences: (1) since in the case of essential services (such as education), resistance to deterioration requires voice, and since voice will be forthcoming more readily at the upper- than at the lower-quality ranges, the cleavage between the quality of life at the top end and at the middle or lower levels will tend to become more marked. This would be especially the case in societies with upward social mobility. In societies which inhibit passage from one social stratum to another, resort to the voice option is automatically strengthened: everyone has a strong motivation to defend the quality of life at his own station; (2) a rather different inference results if the assumption of a progressive thinning out of varieties at the upper end of the quality scale is brought into contact with the plausible notion that a combination of exit and voice is needed for best results. If this notion is accepted, then the recuperation mechanism may rely too much on exit at the lower end of the quality scale, but suffer from a deficiency of exit at the upper end.

How Monopoly Can Be Comforted by Competition

A no-exit situation will be superior to a situation with some limited exit on two conditions: (1) if exit is ineffective as a recuperation mechanism, but does succeed in draining from the firm or organisation its more quality-conscious, alert and potentially activist customers or members; and (2) if voice could be made into an effective mechanism once these customers or members are securely locked in.

What if we have to worry, not only about the profit-maximising exertions and exactions of the monopolist, but also about his proneness to inefficiency, decay and flabbiness? This may be the more frequent danger: the monopolist sets a high price for his products not to amass super-profits, but because he is unable to keep his costs down; or, more typically, he allows the quality of the product or service he sells to deteriorate without gaining any pecuniary advantage in the process.

Political power is very much like market power in that it permits the power holder to indulge either her brutality or her flaccidity. But here again the dangers of abuse of power, of invasion of individual's rights, have stood at the centre of attention, rather than those of maladministration and bureaucratic ineptitude. Accordingly, the original purpose of the ombudsman was to help redress citizens' grievances against officials who had exceeded the constitutional limits of their power. Later, however, the institution experienced a shift in its main purpose, which today has become the promotion of better administration, the correction of malpractices and the like. This implies that the institution is now also used to correct and reprimand official indolence.

The presence of competition could do more harm than good when the main concern is to counteract the monopolist's tendency toward flaccidity and mediocrity. For, in that case, exit-competition could fatally weaken voice along the lines of the example of the Nigerian Railways, without creating a serious threat to the organisation's survival. But there are many other cases where competition does not restrain monopoly as it is supposed to, but comforts and bolsters it by unburdening it of its more troublesome customers. As a result, one can define an important and too-little-noticed type of monopoly-tyranny: a limited type, an oppression of the weak by the incompetent and the exploitation of the poor by the lazy, which is the more durable and stifling as it is both not ambitious and escapable.

In the economic sphere such 'lazy' monopolies which 'welcome competition' as a release from effort and criticism are frequently encountered when monopoly power rests on location and when mobility differs strongly from one group of local customers to another. If the mobile customers are those who are most sensitive to quality, their exit permits the monopolist to persist in his comfortable mediocrity. An example would be the 'ghetto' store, or sluggish electric power utilities in developing countries whose more demanding customers will decide at some point that they can no longer afford the periodic breakdowns and will move out or install their own independent power supply.

Those who hold power in the lazy monopoly may actually have an interest in creating some limited opportunity for exit on the part of those whose voice might be uncomfortable. The lazy monopolist would much rather price the most avid customers out of the market so as to be able to give up the strenuous and tiresome quest for excellence. For the most avid customers are not only willing to pay the highest price, but are also likely to be most demanding in the case of lowering standards.

Latin American power holders have long encouraged their political enemies and potential critics to remove themselves from the scene through voluntary exile. The right of asylum, so generously practised by all Latin American republics, could almost be considered a 'conspiracy in restraint of voice'.

On Spatial Duopoly and the Dynamics of Two-Party Systems

In the previous chapters consumers were portrayed as being more or less sensitive to a change in quality, but they all experienced the change as either positive or negative. This assumption will now be dropped. In this respect, quality and price are once again revealed as totally different phenomena: a decline in the price of a commodity is good news for all customers, just as a rise in price means a loss in real income for all. But one and the same change in quality may make the commodity more appreciated by some consumers while others find it less to their taste than before.

This is also the case for shifts in the positions of political parties and other organisations. What quality change will be done? The economist will select that point on the quality scale which will maximise its profits. However, the criterion of profit maximisation may not yield a unique solution at all. It is plausible to introduce another criterion: in addition to maximising profits, the firm will tend to minimise discontent of its customers, for the rational purpose of earning goodwill or reducing hostility in the community of which it is a part. With this criterion in operation, the firm is in general likely to select a point in the middle of the quality range along which its profits are maximised.

The concept of voice has it that in selecting the middle of the quality range the firm is simply responding to voice—or, rather, to customers' voices which have been assumed to be pulling the firm in opposite directions. The concern with voice can be expected to qualify the concern with maximum profits. Should profit maximisation conflict with discontent-minimisation, there will be some compromise or trade-off between these two objectives. Therefore, customers who can't go elsewhere have the maximum incentive to threaten and otherwise induce the firm to pay attention to their needs and tastes.

Harold Hotelling published an article in the *Economic Journal* which pioneered a number of fields: duopoly, location theory and the dynamics of two-party systems. In essence, Hotelling maintained that customers or, in the political variant of his model, voters are assumed to be evenly distributed along a finite linear scale from A to B or from Left to Right. Suppose that initially two firms (or two parties) have divided up this linear territory among themselves by locating at the midpoints of the left and right halves. Now, assume that one of the two firms or parties, say, the one on the left-hand side, is allowed to shift its location without cost, while the other is tied down. A profit-maximising firm, or a vote-maximising party is, under these conditions, likely to move toward the right. The reason is that as long as it makes a point of staying to the left of the tied-down firm it retains a firm hold on its far-left customers or voters, while it can snatch new customers and voters away from the right-wing firm or party by advancing into its territory.

Two conclusions follow: (1) under the assumed conditions of duopoly there will be a tendency for the two firms to move toward the middle of the scale, and (2) profit- or vote-maximising behaviour leads in this fashion to socially undesirable results since goods will be made available to consumers at higher total costs than would obtain if the firms had remained anchored at the quartiles. In a similar way it can be argued that it is probable, but socially undesirable, for parties in a two-party system to move ever closer together. Hirschman then ironically commented that the success this elegant model had is matched only by its failure to predict correctly the actual course of events.

Hotelling assumed zero elasticity of demand throughout the linear market. However, if demand is elastic, a firm or party would lose customers or voters at its own end of the market as it moved towards the centre, and this loss would at least restrain the socially undesirable clustering tendency of the original model. The concept of voice permits a more fundamental revision of the Hotelling model than was achieved in the 1930s by introducing elastic demand.

It was not Hotelling's inelastic demand assumption that was wrong, but the inference that the 'captive' consumer (or voter) who has 'nowhere else to go' is the epitome of powerlessness. That customer, or voter, will bring all sorts of potential influence into play so as to keep the firm or party from doing things he doesn't like. Hotelling's clustering tendency can therefore be countered and restrained not by substituting elastic for inelastic demand in his model, but by realising that inelastic demand at the extremes of the linear market can spell considerable influence via voice. In other words, a party that is beleaguered by protests from disgruntled members, because they disliked proposed 'wishy-washy' platforms or policies, will often be tempted to give in to these voices because they are in the very real here and now, while the benefits that are to accrue from wishy-washiness are highly conjectural.

There can be no guarantee that the voice mechanism will bring the party exactly back to the somewhat problematical 'social optimum'. The influence of those who have nowhere to go may well force the party to overshoot that point, with disastrous consequences for its vote-gathering objectives.

It is possible to predict the quality path of the firm or organisation. Suppose small quality changes in the organisation's performance occur constantly as a result of random events. If the organisation responds more to voice than to exit, it is much more likely to correct deviations from normal quality that are obnoxious to its 'captive' consumers; whereas deviations from quality that lead to exit of its non-captive, exit-prone consumers would tend to go uncorrected for a considerable time. The whole matter is complicated by the phenomenon of organisational *loyalty*.

A Theory of Loyalty

The Activation of Voice as a Function of Loyalty

Two principal determinants of the readiness to resort to voice when exit is possible were shown to be: (1) the extent to which customers/members are willing to trade-off the certainty of exit against the uncertainties of an improvement in the deteriorated product, and (2) the estimate consumers-members have of their ability to influence the organisation.

The first factor is related to loyalty. Thus, even with a given estimate of one's influence, the likelihood of voice increases with the degree of loyalty. In addition, the two factors are far from independent. For example, a member with a considerable attachment to a product or organisation will often search for ways to make himself influential, especially when the organisation moves in the wrong direction. As a rule, loyalty holds exit at bay and activates voice. The intimation of some influence and the expectation that, over a period of time, the right turns will more than balance the wrong ones, distinguishes loyalty from faith.

When Is Loyalty Functional?

Loyalty can prevent exit. As a result of loyalty, potentially most influential customers or members will stay longer than they would ordinarily, in the hope that improvement or reform can be achieved 'from within'. A measure of loyalty to a firm or organisation has the function of giving it a chance to recuperate from a lapse in efficiency. Specific institutional barriers to exit can often be justified on the ground that they serve to stimulate voice.

Loyalty helps to redress the balance between exit and voice by raising the cost of exit, in situations where exit is seriously considered. In this redressing of balance, it pushes people into the alternative course of action from which they would normally recoil and performs a function similar to the underestimation of the prospective task's difficulties. Loyalty or specific institutional barriers to exit are therefore particularly functional whenever the effective use of voice requires a great deal of social inventiveness while exit is an available, yet not wholly effective, option. Second, the usefulness of loyalty depends on the closeness of the available substitute. Loyalty is at its most functional when it looks most irrational, for instance when loyalty means strong attachment to an organisation that does not seem to warrant such an attachment because it is so much like another one that is available. Such seemingly irrational loyalties are often encountered in relation to clubs, football teams and political parties.

The Loyalist's Threat of Exit

The flip side of loyalty is disloyalty, that is, exit. The chances of voice to function effectively as a recuperation mechanism are appreciably strengthened if voice is backed up by the threat of exit. The threat of exit will typically be made by the loyalist—that is, by members who care and who leave no stone unturned before they resign themselves to the painful decision to withdraw or switch.

Now it appears that the effectiveness of the voice mechanism is strengthened by the possibility of exit. The willingness to develop and use the voice mechanism is reduced by exit, but the ability to use it with effect is increased by it. Together, these two propositions spell out the conditions under which voice: (1) will be resorted to and (2) bids fair to be effective; there should be the possibility of exit, but exit should not be too easy (institutional constraints) or too attractive as soon as deterioration of one's own organisation sets in. The detail of institutional design can be of considerable importance for the balance of exit and voice, and this balance can help account for the varying extent of internal democracy in organisations.

Boycott

Boycott is another phenomenon on the border line between voice and exit, just like the threat of exit. Through boycott, exit is actually consummated rather than just threatened; but it is undertaken for the specific purpose of achieving a change of policy on the part of the boycotted organisation and is therefore a true hybrid of the two mechanisms. The threat of exit as an instrument of voice is here replaced by its mirror image, the promise of re-entry: for it is understood that the member/customer will return to the fold when certain conditions which have led to the boycott are remedied. Boycott is a temporary exit; it is costly for both sides.

Elements for a Model of Loyalist Behaviour

It is assumed that the normally bought product or the organisation to which one belongs begins to deteriorate. The focus will now be on organisations and their policies, rather than on firms and their products. Quality deterioration must therefore be redefined in subjective terms; from the member's viewpoint, it is equivalent to increasing disagreement with the organisation's policies. The loyal member doesn't exit, but something happens to her: she begins to be acutely unhappy about continuing as a member. She will intensify the use of voice and as the disagreement widens further, the member will have thoughts of exit, if that action can be at all expected to enhance the effectiveness of voice. Finally, loyalty reaches its breaking point and exit ensues.

Loyalist behaviour as sketched above leads to the break-up of economists' traditional demand curve which establishes a one-to-one relationship between price (or quality) and quantity brought into two distinct curves. When a loyalty-commanding product first deteriorates and then improves, there will be one demand schedule for the downward movement in quality, with low demand elasticities at the beginning and high ones eventually as intolerable deterioration finally does lead to exit of the loyalists, and quite another one as quality recovers. During the improvement phase, elasticities will be low in the low-quality ranges and will only become higher as improvement is confirmed. Demand is of course always likely to be a function not only of current but also of previous quality because of inertia and lags in perception. Loyalty strongly reinforces this influence of past performance of the firm, or organisation, on present behaviour of the customers or members.

There is also *unconscious loyalist behaviour*. The general difficulties of recognising change are a breeding ground for unconscious loyalist behaviour in case of deterioration, as well as for prolonged reluctance toward entry or re-entry in case the organisation improves. Since unconscious loyalist behaviour is by definition free from felt discontent, it will not lead to voice. The member is simply unaware of the degree of deterioration that is taking place.

Loyalist Behaviour as Modified by Severe Initiation and High Penalties for Exit

The opportunities for non-optimal outcomes are numerous. It is possible for loyalty to overshoot the mark and thus to produce an exit–voice mix in which the exit option is unduly neglected. Second, it must be realised that loyalty-promoting institutions and devices are not only uninterested in stimulating voice at the expense of exit: indeed they are often meant to *repress* voice alongside exit. High fees for entering an organisation and stiff penalties for exit are among the main devices generating or reinforcing loyalty in such a way as to repress either exit or voice, or even both.

There is often no clear dividing line between conscious and unconscious loyalist behaviour, because the customer or member of the organisation may have a considerable stake in self-deception; that is, in fighting the realisation that the organisation he belongs to, or the product he has bought, are deteriorating or defective. He will particularly suppress this sort of awareness if he has invested a great deal in his purchase or membership. By the same token, however, it may be expected that once deterioration is adverted, members of an organisation that requires severe initiation will fight hard to prove that they were right after all in paying that high entrance fee. Thus, while the onset of voice will be delayed by severe initiation, resort to it is likely to be more active than is ordinarily the case during a subsequent phase of loyalist behaviour.

A situation of dissonance may produce not only alterations of beliefs, attitudes and cognitions, but could lead to actions designed to change the real world when that is an alternative way of overcoming or reducing dissonance. One historical example: revolution devours its own children, as the saying goes. Why this should be so is now easily understood: in 'making revolution', revolutionaries have paid a high personal price in risk-taking, sacrifice and single-minded commitment. Once the revolution is over, a gap between the actual and the expected state of affairs is only too likely to arise. To eliminate the gap, those who have paid the highest price for bringing about the new reality will be strongly motivated to change it anew. In the process, they will take on some of their fellow revolutionaries who are now in positions of authority and a large number of the revolutionaries on either the one side or the other will come to grief in the engulfing fight.

A different kind of distortion of the model of loyalist behaviour occurs when an organisation is able to extract a high price for exit. Such a price can range from loss of lifelong associations to loss of life, with such intermediate penalties as excommunication, defamation and deprivation of livelihood. If an organisation has the ability to extract a high price for exit, it thereby acquires a powerful defence against one of the members' most potent weapons: the threat of exit.

What happens to voice in organisations where the price of exit is high? In situations where the price is high, voice will be delayed. These organisations (gangs, totalitarian parties) will often be able to repress both voice and exit. In the process, they will deprive themselves of both recuperation mechanisms.

The situation is quite different for traditional groups, such as family or nation, which extract a high price for exit, but not for entry. The high price or the 'unthinkability' of exit may not only fail to repress voice but may stimulate it. It is perhaps for this reason that the traditional groups which repress exit alone have proved to be far more viable than those which impose a high price for both entry and exit.

Loyalty and the Difficult Exit from 'Public Goods' (and Evils)

When loyalty is present, exit abruptly changes character: the applauded rational behaviour of the alert customer shifting to a better buy becomes disgraceful defection, desertion and treason. The penalty for exit is in most cases internalised. Loyalist behaviour may also be inspired by the anticipation that the organisation to which one belongs would go from bad to worse if one left. This latter observation is inspired by a somewhat strange assumption: the member continues to care about the activity and 'output' of the organisation even after she has left it. Of course, this in many instances is not the case. There are two conditions that underlie the special loyalist behaviour now under discussion: (1) exit of a member leads to further deterioration in the quality of the organisation's output, and (2) the member cares about this deterioration whether or not she stays on as a member.

Under condition (1) the consumer/member is a 'quality-maker', in the sense that her exit leads to further deterioration, which will lead to further exits and so on. In this situation, utter instability is once again avoided by the intervention of loyalist behaviour and particularly by members being aware of the prospective consequences of their exit. The only rational basis for such behaviour is a situation in which the output or quality of the organisation matters to one even after exit. An example: parents who plan to shift their children from a public to a private school may thereby contribute to further deterioration of public education. If they realise this prospective effect, they may end up by not acting on the plan for reasons of general welfare or even as a result of a private cost–benefit calculation: the lives of both parents and children will be affected by the quality of public education in their community.

The distinction made by economists between private and public goods is directly relevant. Public goods are defined as goods which are consumed by all those who are members of a given community, country or geographical area in such a manner that consumption or use by one member doesn't detract from consumption or use by another. The distinguishing character of these goods is not only that they can be consumed by everyone, but that there is no escape from consuming them unless one were to leave the community that provides them. It is easy to conceive of a public good turning into a public evil, for example if a country's foreign and military policies develop in such a way that their output changes from international prestige into international disgrace.

In some situations there can be no real exit from a good or an organisation so that the decision to exit, in the partial sense in which this may be possible, must take into account any further deterioration in the good that may result. The question is how a partial exit from such a good is possible. A private citizen can opt out of public education by sending his children to a private school, but at the same time he cannot opt out of the public education system, neither because his and his children's life will be affected by the quality of public education, nor because a portion of his taxes continue to support the system. Another example: if I participate in the formulation of a foreign policy of which I now disapprove, I can resign but cannot stop being unhappy as a citizen of a country which carries on with what seems to me an increasingly disastrous foreign policy. In this example, the individual is at first both producer and consumer of such public goods; he can stop being producer, but cannot stop being consumer.

The member of a society will compare the discomfort of remaining a member to the prospective damage that would be inflicted on her as a prospective non-member and on society at large by the additional deterioration that would occur if she were to get out. The avoidance of this hypothetical damage is now the benefit of loyalist behaviour, and if this benefit increases along with the cost of remaining a member, the motivation to exit need not become stronger as deterioration proceeds, although our member will become increasingly unhappy.

The decision to exit will become ever more difficult the longer one fails to exit. The conviction that one has to stay on to prevent the worst grows stronger all the time. The more wrongheaded and dangerous the direction of these states the more we need a measure of spinelessness among the more enlightened policymakers so that some of them will still be 'inside' and remain influential when the potentially disastrous crisis breaks out.

Organisations and firms producing public goods or public evils constitute the environment in which loyalist behaviour peculiarly thrives and assumes several distinctive characteristics. Moreover, when exit occurs its nature is different from the type of exit discussed up to now. In the case of public goods one continues to 'care' as it is impossible to get away from them entirely. To exit will now mean to resign under protest and to denounce and fight the organisation from without instead of working for change from within. The alternative is now not so much between voice and exit as between voice from within and voice from without (after exit). The exit hinges on a totally different question: At what point is one more effective in fighting mistaken policies from without than continuing to attempt to change these policies from within?

Exit and Voice in American Ideology and Practice

The United States owes its very existence and growth to millions of decisions favouring exit over voice. Why raise your voice in contradiction and get yourself into trouble as long as you can always remove yourself entirely from any given environment should it become too unpleasant? Those who departed from their communities had no thought of improving them or by fighting against them from the outside; they were immigrants rather than émigrés, and soon after their move 'couldn't care less' about the fate of the communities whence they came. The hippies would now fall into this category as well, be it that by making their exit so spectacular, they were actually closer to voice than was the case for their pilgrim, immigrant and pioneer forebears. Economically successful people leave their original social group behind; they exit from it, so to speak.

In the case of a minority that has been discriminated against, a further argument can be made: exit is bound to be unsatisfactory and unsuccessful even from the point of view of the individuals who acted on it. To some extent, exit is itself responsible for the emergence of its opposite. In leaving his country, the emigrant makes a difficult decision and usually pays a high price in severing many strong affective ties. Additional payment is extracted as he is being initiated into a new environment and adjusting to it. The result is a strong psychological compulsion to like that for which so large a payment has been made; hence, one has to be compulsively happy.

But if this is no longer the case, what then? Situations may then arise in which qualms can no longer be repressed. A number of reactions are then possible: (1) another exit may be attempted, but this time within the confines of the country, and (2) since clearly the country cannot be at fault, responsibility for unhappiness, qualms and so forth is assumed to lie with the person experiencing these sensations. Another 'dose' of adjustment is then in order: if the country is too obviously at fault after all, it has to be made into that ideal place that one wants it so passionately to be. Hence, voice will come into its own with unusual force. It will be animated by the typically American conviction that human institutions can be perfected and that problems can be solved.

Hirschman then noted the extreme reluctance of Americans in public office to resign in protest against policies with which they disagree. In this context, James C. Thomson coined the term 'domestication of dissenters'. These dissenters give up in advance their strongest weapon: the threat to resign under protest. Exit has an essential role to play in restoring quality performance of government, just as in any organisation. It will operate either by making the government reform or by bringing it down, but in any event the jolt provoked by a clamorous exit of a respected member is in many situations an indispensable complement to voice. A case in point was Senator Eugene McCarthy's decision to run for president, a decision which had a powerful influence on events at the time.

The Elusive Optimal Mix of Exit and Voice

This final chapter includes two quadrants. The first one classifies organisations whose members react strongly via either voice or exit. There are probably no organisations that are wholly immune to either exit or voice on the part of their members. The ones that have been listed in the column corresponding to that category are those that, in their intended structure, make no explicit or implicit allowance for either mechanism (see Table 5.1). Exit is here considered as treason—and voice as illegal and severely penalised—they will be engaged only when deterioration has reached so advanced a stage that recovery is no longer possible or desirable.

Moreover, at this stage voice and exit will be undertaken with such strength that their effect will be destructive rather than reformist. On the other hand, there is no implication in Table 5.1 that the organisations which are equipped with both feedback mechanisms are necessarily more advanced or viable than those which rely primarily on one alone. All depends on the responsiveness of the organisation to whatever mechanism or combination of mechanisms it is equipped with.

But what if an organisation is not sensitive to the particular reaction it happens to provoke or does not possess the mechanism to which it would be sensitive? A large part of this book has been devoted to such cases of inadequate or wrong responses and the argument can be summarised in Table 5.2.

The greatest interest-centres naturally are those 'perverse' cases where an organisation is in effect equipped with a reaction mechanism to which it is not responsive: those who are affected by quality decline do vent their feelings in one way or another, but management happens to be indifferent to their particular reaction and thus does not feel compelled to correct its course. Situations of this type involve organisations whose decline gives rise to exit that doesn't bother management nearly as much as might be the case for voice. In the previous chapter, however, a situation of the symmetrically opposite type was presented: an organisation—the Executive Branch of the United Sates government whose deteriorating performance under Lyndon Johnson led to numerous but futile manifestations of voice when exit might have been more effective.

5 The Return of Neoclassical Economics

Table 5.1 Organisational reactions to exit and voice

Organisations whose members react strongly via		Exit	
		Yes	No
Voice	Yes	Voluntary associations, competitive political parties and some business enterprises, e.g. those selling output to a few buyers	Family, tribe, nation, church, parties in non-totalitarian one-party systems
	No	Competitive business enterprise in relation to customers	Parties in totalitarian one-party systems, terrorist groups and criminal gangs

Table 5.2 Organisational decline in relation to exit and voice

		Exit	Voice
Organisation is sensitive primarily to:	Exit	Competitive business enterprise	Organisations where dissent is allowed, but is 'institutionalised'
	Voice	Public enterprise subject to competition from an alternative mode, lazy oligopolist, corporation–shareholder relations, inner cities etc	Democratically responsive organisations commanding considerable loyalty from members

Several conclusions follow from the general observation that an organisation may be arousing, through its decline, one kind of reaction from its members when its recovery would be more powerfully stimulated by another kind. One advantage of this formulation is that it points to a variety of remedies or a combination of them. Take the case where an organisation arouses primarily exit to which it is far more insensitive than it would be to voice. Corrective policies obviously include efforts to make the organisation more responsive to exit, but also efforts to have the members switch from exit to voice. A possible remedial measure, for example, is when railroads do not react vigorously to exit, that is, the loss of customers: the typical proposal is to introduce stringent 'financial discipline' in the hope that the railroad managers will then react to the loss of revenue like private enterprises threatened by bankruptcy.

It is clear that as an alternative or complementary step, it is worth looking into ways and means to strengthen voice on the part of the customers. This can be done directly by reducing the cost and increasing the rewards of voice, as well as indirectly by raising the cost of exit and even by reducing the opportunities for it. Similarly, when an organisation arouses but ignores voice while it would be responsive to exit, thought must be given both to making exit easier and attractive by appropriately redesigned institutions and to making the organisation more responsive to voice. The approach to the improvement of institutional design that is advocated here widens the spectrum of policy choices that are usually considered and it avoids the strong opposite biases in favour of either exit or voice.

What this approach fails to yield is that it doesn't present a firm prescription for some optimal mix of exit or voice, nor does it wish to credit the notion that each institution requires its own mix that could be gradually approached by trial and error. Each recovery mechanism is itself subject to the forces of decay which have been invoked in this book all along. As mentioned, the short-run interest of management in organisations is to increase its own freedom of movement. It will therefore strip the members/customers of the weapons which they can wield, be they exit or voice, and to convert what should be a feedback into a safety valve. Thus voice can become mere 'blowing off steam' as it is being emasculated by the institutionalisation and domestication of dissent which was described above.

To the extent that the game is played successfully by competing organisations or firms, exit, compensated by new entry, ceases to be a serious threat to the deteriorating organisations.

One will underestimate the effectiveness of voice when exit is dominant and vice versa. Once members have a slight preference for, say, voice over exit, a cumulative movement sets in which makes exit look less attractive and more inconceivable. As a result, voice will be increasingly relied on by members at a time when management is working hard to make itself less vulnerable to it. For these reasons conditions are seldom favourable for the emergence of any stable and optimally effective mix of exit and voice. Tendencies towards exclusive reliance on one mode and towards a decline in its effectiveness are likely to develop. Only when the dominant mode plainly reveals its inadequacy will the other mode eventually be injected once again. The invigorating results that can be achieved by the shock-effect of such an injection have recently been demonstrated when consumers' voice was suddenly introduced by Ralph Nader into an area where exit had long been the dominant and almost exclusive mode.

In the opposite case, when voice is the dominant reaction mode, exit can be similarly galvanising. Exit is not usually undertaken for the purpose of gaining more influence than one had as a member. That is nevertheless the way it often works out, especially when exit is a highly unusual event. Exit is unsettling to those who stay behind as there can be no 'talking back' to those who exited. The remarkable influence wielded by martyrs throughout history can be understood in these terms.

The critique of the optimal mix concept thus leads to a triple suggestion: (1) in order to retain their ability to fight deterioration, those organisations that rely primarily on one of the two reaction mechanisms need an occasional injection of the other; (2) other organisations may have to go through regular cycles in which exit and voice alternate as principal actors; and (3) an awareness of the inborn tendencies towards instability of any optimal mix may be helpful in improving the design of institutions that need both exit and voice to be maintained in good health.

Hirschman included five appendices to his book. Their purpose is to elaborate some of the aspects dealt with in the main text.

6

Capitalism Riding High

Introduction

During the Great Moderation, the triumph of neoclassical economics, including the functioning of the free market, was consolidated. Alternative economic systems were in short supply after the collapse of the Berlin Wall in 1989 and the Soviet Union's collapse in 1991. Of course there is China, still a socialist state, but it applies state capitalism.

The free-market ideology was also exported to many countries. Way back in 1986, sociologist Peter Berger published *The Capitalist Revolution* in which he presented 50 propositions about prosperity, equality and liberty. In his younger days Berger was open to the possibility that socialism might be a better form of economic and social organisation. However, empirical evidence led him to arrive at his pro-capitalist position. His turning point occurred when Berger saw the rapid economic growth of various East Asian societies.

But why didn't many Latin American and African countries enjoy growth? Their economies stagnated; quite a few even registered negative growth rates. Economists and other social scientists started to take a renewed interest in the factors explaining growth and stagnation. They discovered that developing countries had a different institutional environment than advanced capitalist economies. Theories about growth had to take into consideration endogenous institutional factors.

In the course of the 1980s new institutional economics became popular among economic historians, development economists and policymakers alike. Economic historian Douglass North published *Institutions, Institutional Change and Economic Performance* in 1990, wherein he presented an alternative to Robert Solow's growth model, in which technological progress, capital and labour, together, promote growth. North studied the influence of institutions in promoting or hindering economic growth in various development settings.

The biographies of Peter Berger and Douglass North are presented below, including summaries of the books just mentioned.

Biography: Peter Ludwig Berger (1929–)

Peter Ludwig Berger was born in Vienna, Austria, on 17 March 1929, the son of George William Berger and Jelka Loew. Young Peter migrated in 1946 to the United States, shortly after the end of WWII. In 1952 he became a naturalised American citizen. In 1959 he married Brigitte Kellner with whom he published various books.

Academic Career

Berger graduated from Wagner College with a BA and received his MA and PhD from the New School for Social Research, New York, in 1954.

In that same year Berger began his career as a sociologist at the University of Georgia. Over the next quarter century he held positions at numerous universities. In 1955 and 1956 he worked at the Evangelische Akademie in Bad Boll, Germany. He was appointed assistant professor at the University of North Carolina in 1956 for 2 years. Berger moved on to Hartford Theological Seminary where he was associate professor from 1958 to 1963. He held professorships at the New School for Social Research (1958–63), Rutgers University (1970–79), and Boston College (1979–81).

Since 1981 Berger has been University Professor of Sociology and Theology at Boston University. In 1985 he was also appointed Director of the Institute for the Study of Economic Culture, which was later transformed into the Institute on Culture, Religion and World Affairs. This institute studies the relation between economic development and sociological change on a global level.

Academic Thinking

Central to Berger's work is the relationship between society and the individual. In *The Social Construction of Reality* (1966) Berger and Luckmann presented a sociological theory: society as objective reality and as subjective reality. Subjective reality describes the process by which an individual's conception of reality is produced by his or her interaction with social structures. The authors proposed how new human concepts or inventions become a part of our reality through the process of objectivation. Often this reality is then no longer recognised as a human creation, through a process which the authors call 'reification'.

Berger's interest in the role of religion in society, being a powerful social force, is inspired by his Lutheran upbringing. He believes that humanity is God's reflection of the world. In this context Berger attempts to prove empirically that religion can provide true enlightenment beyond the simple, everyday experience. He predicted the secularisation of the world, as he initially believed that the process of modernisation and secularisation would go hand in hand. However, by the late 1980s he recognised that religion—both old and new—was not only still prevalent, but in many cases more vibrantly practised than in periods in the past, particularly in America. Berger co-authored with Dutch sociologist Anton Zijderveld *In Praise of Doubt: How to Have Convictions without Being a Fanatic* (2009).

Apart from the role of religion in society, Berger takes a keen interest in economic development. Max Weber's thinking about the role of religion—especially Protestantism—in economic development resonates clearly in *The Capitalist Revolution*. As for Berger's thinking in the domain of economics, he was particularly influenced by fellow Austrians Joseph Schumpeter and Friedrich Hayek, Hungarian-born Peter Bauer, and by Milton Friedman and Simon Kuznets.

The Capitalist Revolution intends to draw an outline of a theory concerning the relation between capitalism and society in the modern world. However, in the current state of the social sciences, it is not possible to present a full-blown theory. What Berger did was to suggest some building blocks for the endeavour at hand. Berger presents 50 propositions about prosperity, equality and liberty, which he wants the reader to accept as hypotheses within the ongoing enquiry about the pros and cons of capitalism. According to Berger, he did not write these propositions with a pro-capitalist bias, because in his younger days he was very open to the possibility that socialism might be a more humane form of economic and social organisation. However, the propositions contained in the book led Berger to conclude that capitalism was to be preferred.

Honours

Peter Berger was elected Fellow of the American Academy of Arts and Sciences in 1982. He is a doctor *honoris causa* of Loyola University, Wagner College, the University of Notre Dame, the University of Geneva and the University of Munich. In 1992 he was awarded the Manes Sperber Prize, presented by the Austrian government for significant contributions to culture. In 2010 he was awarded the Dr Leopold Lucas Prize by the University of Tübingen.

The Capitalist Revolution: Fifty Propositions About Prosperity, Equality, and Liberty

Introduction

The Capitalist Revolution, subtitled *Fifty Propositions about Prosperity, Equality, & Liberty*, was first published in 1986 by Basic Books.[1] The purpose of the book is to develop an outline of a theory in terms of the relationship between capitalism and society in the modern world.

---

[1] The edition used is published by Gower (Farnham), 1987.

This theory is based on hypotheses/propositions deduced from empirical evidence and which are subject to empirical testing and, as Berger insists, to *falsification*. Hence, further exploration may or may not sustain the empirical validity of these propositions.

Karl Marx integrated in a single theoretical construction the economic, social, political and cultural dimensions of capitalism. However, his theory is a mixture between science and prophesy. *The Capitalist Revolution* refers many times to Marxist interpretations of various phenomena in a critical manner. A serious weakness of Marxism has been its inability to explain the harsh realities of socialist regimes in the contemporary world, as well as the failure of the Marxist prediction that only socialism can generate successful development in the Third World.

Berger warned the reader that in the current state of the social sciences, no researcher is in a position to supply a full-blown theory. Not even Max Weber, Joseph Schumpeter or Friedrich Hayek were able to do so. What a researcher can do is to present a blueprint for the task at hand and to suggest some building blocks.

Berger's theory is built around the concept of economic culture. He wrote, 'An "economic culture" theory of capitalism (or, for that matter, of any other economic phenomenon) will explore the social, political, and cultural matrix or context within which these particular economic processes operate.'[2] No causality is assumed by this term. The concept 'economic culture' simply draws attention to the relationships that empirical enquiry must explore.

Berger presented 50 propositions which are to be understood as hypotheses within the ongoing empirical enquiry. These propositions are all included in this summary and are direct quotations from Berger's book. Each of these 50 propositions is, as noted, falsifiable. All of them are non-dogmatic, open-ended and hypothetical. Berger maintains that he doesn't hold a philosophical position that would lead him either to embrace or to reject capitalism. Yet, the book contains pro-capitalist conclusions. Most of the propositions are elaborated in the summary; others are self-explanatory.

---

[2] *The Capitalist Revolution*, 7.

The author didn't start his intellectual 'odyssey' with a pro-capitalist bias. However, the sheer pressure of empirical evidence led him to his pro-capitalist position. The turning point occurred in the mid-1970s when Berger noted the phenomenal growth of various East Asian societies, such as Japan, South Korea, Taiwan and the city-states of Hong Kong and Singapore. He realised that this experience made it difficult to remain even-handed between capitalist and socialist development models. The author analyses three imaginary gigantic 'test tubes', in each of which the process of 'modernisation' has reached a degree of high intensity. In other words, the image is that of a global laboratory in which the 'chemical reaction' of modernisation may be observed in a series of more or less complete experiments. The three 'test tubes' are: (1) Western industrial capitalism, (2) East Asian industrial capitalism and (3) industrial socialism.

Capitalism as a Phenomenon

The term capitalism refers to a set of economic arrangements. The citizens of a capitalist society encounter the economic arrangements as part of a much larger social world.

Capitalism is also a concept and a historical phenomenon. There is a remarkable agreement among historians of capitalism about certain features. The foundation of capitalism constitutes the expanding market economies of medieval Europe. Modern capitalism emerged between the sixteenth and eighteenth centuries. But a decisive leap forward came during the eighteenth century, released by the immense technological inventions that spawned the Industrial Revolution. The modern capitalist world system became established in the nineteenth century and was further consolidated in the twentieth century. Capitalism covered at first only a small part of Western economies. Gradually it became the basic organising principle of these economies as a whole.

The 'father' of capitalism, Adam Smith, did not use the term capitalism at all; he described the natural system of liberty. Karl Marx rarely used the term capitalism. It only became a common term after Werner Sombart published his magnum opus *Modern Capitalism* in 1902. By then it was seen as the opposite of socialism.

The term capitalism embodies some key elements: it is rooted in money, and it is a particular way of organising production. Modern industrial capitalism presupposes rational calculation through double-entry bookkeeping. Additional characteristics are the appropriation of all the material means of production as private property, a rational legal system, freedom of the market, rational technology geared to economic activity, free labour and the commercialisation of the economy.

Berger then presents a simple definition of capitalism: 'Production for a market by enterprising individuals or combines with the purpose of making a profit.'[3] Marx demonstrated how such a system generates vast and unprecedented productive power. This power has dramatically transformed the material conditions of human life, first in the capitalist 'core countries' and, later, increasingly throughout the world.

Initially, economic processes were determined by tradition. As the vast accumulation of productive resources, made possible by capitalism, merged with the quantum leap in technological power, this changed. The capitalist phenomenon in its full-blown form coincided with the phenomenon of industrialisation. Together, the new economic institutions and the new technology transformed the world.

As to economic arrangements, the basic option is whether economic processes are governed by market mechanisms or by mechanisms of political allocation. In simple terms, it is the option between market economies and command economies. As neither market nor command economies exist as pure forms in the real world, some critics noted that capitalist societies could be well on the way towards socialism. Regarding command economies, the question can be asked whether socialist economies could survive without some market mechanisms functioning there.

Economic institutions don't exist in a vacuum but rather in a context of social and political structures, cultural patterns and structures of consciousness (i.e. values, ideas, belief systems). An economic culture then contains a number of elements linked together. But which elements within a given matrix are intrinsically linked and which are merely linked extrinsically? An intrinsic linkage is one without which the phenomenon could not be imagined. Conversely, an extrinsic linkage can be ascribed

---

[3] *The Capitalist Revolution*, 19.

to this or that historical contingency and can therefore be 'thought away' from the phenomenon. An example: the linkage between modern technology and a rational engineering mentality appears to be intrinsic. On the other hand, the linkage of the engineering ethos with individualism may well be an accident of Western history. It may easily be hypothesised that it is an external linkage—that it can be 'thought away' in this or that highly collectivist society employing modern technology.

In its mature form, capitalism is linked to technology and thus to the vast transformations brought about by the latter in the material conditions of humans. Capitalism is also linked with a new stratification system based on class, a new political system, and a new culture. All of these new elements are intertwined within the economic culture of capitalism, experienced by ordinary people as a unity, and often conceptualised as such, both by advocates and by critics of capitalism.

A theory of capitalism will thus have to explain how these different elements are related to each other. Marxism has been the most ambitious effort to achieve such a theoretical integration. Berger added that perhaps the closest to an alternative paradigm is what has been called modernisation theory. This term is applied to a set of theoretical efforts to explain the rapid changes undergone by the developing societies of Africa, Asia and Latin America since WWII. The term can also be used to refer to a general view of modernity, emerging mostly from a central tradition of classical sociology. All told, one arrives at a synthetic paradigm in which the category of modernity is central and which differs in important aspects from the Marxist paradigm. *The Capitalist Revolution* stands within the sociological tradition; its argument is influenced by the Weberian approach to the modern world.

How is modernity different from all other periods of human history; what are the driving forces behind the modern world? According to Weber the most important was rationalisation, that is, the progressive imposition of rational thinking and rational techniques on every sector of society. He believed that specific features of Judaism and Christianity laid the groundwork of this rational transformation of the world. The French sociologist Emile Durkheim spoke of the shift from 'mechanical solidarity' to 'organic solidarity'. He felt that the change was for the better because it enhanced individual liberty. American sociologist Talcott

Parsons identified the phenomenon of differentiation: modern society segments, dividing up into distinct institutions, such as education, government, work and so forth, Segments which in earlier periods of history were integrated within the same institution.

The modernisation paradigm perceives capitalism as one of several causally central elements; in its more recent versions (particularly applied to Third World societies) technology tends to move to centre stage. These different emphases colour the perceptions of the other paradigm. Berger seeks to avoid the distortions of the convergence theory (which projects the converging of capitalist and socialist systems) which trivialises very important economic, social and political differences.

The theoretical challenge is to begin constructing a theoretical framework within which the linkages between economic, technological, social, political and cultural elements of the capitalist phenomenon can be adequately understood. This is a slow, painstaking, never fully completed enterprise. Berger concluded the chapter by stating that people kill each other for prophetic certainties, hardly for falsifiable hypotheses. The social scientist's insistence that he has no certainties to offer and that his hypotheses are falsifiable, therefore, has a moral as well as an intellectual justification.

Material Life: The Horn of Plenty

In the not too distant past material life was characterised by very high rates of infant mortality, low life expectancy, inadequate nutrition and frequent starvation, very high vulnerability to disease and pain, and a very high vulnerability to the ravages of nature. All this was sustained by a relatively unchanging technology and by a zero-growth subsistence economy. The arrival of modern technology radically changed this situation: the Industrial Revolution. Each of the mentioned characteristics changed dramatically; zero growth was replaced by sustained self-generating growth. The technological transformation of material life is at the core of what is meant by modernisation. The essential effect of the Industrial Revolution has been a vast increase in productivity. And this process is continuing at an accelerating pace. The Industrial Revolution was a historical achievement of capitalism. Yet, the two processes of capitalist development and technological modernisation are analytically distinct. Given the above, Berger presented two propositions (1, 2).

> 1. *Industrial capitalism has generated the greatest productive power in human history.*
> 2. *To date, no other socioeconomic system has been able to generate comparable productive power.*

An economy based on the production for market exchange on a large and expanding scale gives unprecedented opportunity for the unfolding of two representatives of human inventiveness: the entrepreneur and the engineer. Market forces provide the best incentive for ever-improving productivity. The engineer may be driven by different motives than profit; she simply may wish to improve her gadgets and see how they can be made to work more efficiently. But it is the market economy that provides the context in which her ingenuity can blossom. To the two propositions above, Berger added a third one (3).

> 3. *An economy oriented towards production for market exchange provides the optimal conditions for long-lasting and ever-expanding productive capacity based on modern technology.*

Berger analyses how industrial capitalism unfolded in England in terms of the condition of the working class. In this context, he referred to Friedrich Engels's book *The Condition of the Working Class in England* (1845) which he found 'highly partisan' and pessimistic. Nonetheless, he found merit in what Engels observed, although there is another school of historians that analysed the situation in a more optimistic way. There is reason to accept that the pessimist position, like the one Engels took, is more tenable for the earlier period of the English Industrial Revolution, but less so for the later period; that is after 1820.

> 4. *The early period of industrial capitalism in England, and probably in other Western countries, exacted considerable human costs, if not in an actual decline in material living standards then in social and cultural dislocation.*

Needless to say that there is no a priori warrant for proposing that the same costs will have to be borne by societies undergoing industrialisation today. In other words, there is no law of history by which all societies have to replicate the English experience. Since the middle of the nineteenth century there has been an immense increase in the material well-being of virtually all strata in Western societies, albeit with a short interruption in the 1930s.

5. Advanced industrial capitalism has generated, and continues to generate, the highest material standard of living for large masses of people in human history.

It may be that these standards of living may eventually be surpassed by societies operating under socioeconomic systems. But is there no guarantee that poor and rich will benefit equally under any system? Not necessarily. The economist Simon Kuznets introduced the so-called Kuznets Curve in 1955. It shows that income and wealth distribution follows a pattern: as modern economic growth continues over time, there occurs first a sharp rise in inequality and then, later, a levelling effect.

Although the Kuznets Curve appears to hold for both capitalist and socialist countries, it doesn't for Eastern Asia. There, the economic growth went hand in hand with decreasing inequality. It is plausible that growth rates per se may not be the cause of the Kuznets effects, but rather the extended duration of growth, with the technological and demographic consequences as a result of that extended growth. The Kuznets Curve primarily refers to income before taxes, without taking into account government-sponsored (re)distribution measures. Indeed, governmental redistribution measures strengthen and perhaps accelerate the levelling phase of the Kuznets Curve. However, strong redistributional policies, based on tax and transfer mechanisms, may well serve as a disincentive to productivity. There would then be a trade-off between equality and economic efficiency. In the long run this may lead to a lowering of living standards.

6. As technological modernisation and economic growth perdure over time, inequalities in income and wealth first increase sharply, then decline sharply, and then remain in a relatively stable plateau.

7. These changes are caused by the interplay of technological and demographic forces and are relatively independent of the forms of socioeconomic organisation.
8. The levelling phase of this process can be strengthened and accelerated by political interventions, but if these interventions exceed a certain degree (which at this time cannot be precisely specified), there will be negative consequences for economic growth and eventually for the standard of living.

Berger concluded this chapter by stating that if one wants to improve the material conditions of the people, especially the poor, one will do well to opt for capitalism. And if one wants to modernise, under any form of socioeconomic organisation, one will probably have to settle for a considerable measure of material inequality. If one wants to intervene politically to bring about greater material equality, one may eventually disrupt the economic engine of plenty and endanger the material living standards of the society.

Class: The Ladder of Success

The process of modernisation can be described as a revolution of rising expectations. However, this doesn't mean egalitarianism. All societies have been stratified. There are different ranks. The benefits of ranking are: (1) privilege, in the sense of access to material goods and services, (2) power and (3) prestige. These three benefits may go together but not necessarily so. And the different forms of ranking are likely to overlap or criss-cross in most societies.

The category of 'class' is understood as one of stratification but by no means the only one; therefore to speak of a 'class system' is to refer to a specific pattern of stratification that can be differentiated from other patterns.

Berger defined a class as a group deriving its privilege from its role in the production process. It is characterised by common interests and by common cultural traits. A class society is one in which class is the dominant form of stratification. Class has a political aspect, in that classes have vested interests that must be pursued against other interests. Berger's definition relates class to the production process. This implies that that occupation is of crucial importance in determining class position. There is the phenomenon of social mobility which cannot be answered by definition but must be explored empirically. Another aspect is the degree to which factors other than class affect an individual's or group's privilege. Factors such as race or gender are at play in this context.

9. Under industrial capitalism there has been the progressive displacement of all other forms of stratification by class.

The modern bourgeoisie, the class that carried capitalism, grew out of the old 'third estate', which consisted of tradesmen and artisans. It was very significant that this new class demanded legal equality for all. In other words, the relation of an individual to the order of privilege should no longer be determined by birth or by royal favour, but rather by his role and success in the production process. Class meant that 'money speaks loudest'. Although family origin remains an important variable in the individual's career within the class system, the educational level achieved is an increasingly more important variable in predicting social mobility.

Every existing class system is 'impure', in the sense that non-class factors interfere with the operation of the class system. An example is the way in which class and race have interacted in American society. In this case it can be argued that two distinct stratification systems have been superimposed on each other. It follows that one should never think of a class system in monolithic terms; one must always see such a system in relative terms, with class being the dominant but not the only form of stratification.

Industrial capitalism has a natural affinity to class. The market mechanism is the core of a capitalist economy. And just as the market determines the course of the production process, there is also a market in which privilege is obtained. In a 'pure' capitalist class system the two markets coincide: all privilege would be purchased by the income and wealth generated within the market economy.

One significant change has been the enormous expansion of the middle strata, triggered by technological development. After all, an ever-smaller portion of the labour force was required for the actual chores of material production, allowing the diversion of ever-larger numbers of workers into administrative and other white-collar activities. On top of this, growing businesses and government required more administrative officers.

The emergence of the large corporation was a formidable factor in the changes in economic organisation. An industrial working class took shape. Control over economic resources became more important than legal ownership (i.e. the manager replaces the entrepreneur). The old aristocratic upper class was replaced by a capitalist bourgeoisie. Industrialisation brings about an increase in social mobility. This mobility also applies to socialist economies. The basic engine of mobility is modified by social, political and—notably—demographic forces, so that demography ensures that there will be 'room at the top'.

> *10. Ongoing industrialisation, regardless of its sociopolitical organisation, is the basic determinant of social mobility.*
> *11. In all advanced industrial societies there have been moderate increases, but no dramatic changes, in the rates of upward mobility.*

This proposition could change if there is a continued shrinkage in the demand for unskilled manual labour.

> *12. In all advanced industrial societies, education has become the single most important vehicle of upward mobility.*

Especially in societies with an optimistic inclination (such as the American society) it is believed that hard work and getting an education are the major factors that determine whether an individual 'makes it' in terms of mobility.

> *13. Industrial capitalism, especially when combined with political democracy, is most likely to maintain openness in the stratification system of a society.*

Through the interaction of economic and political forces, Western societies have progressively removed traditional barriers to the advancement of individuals regardless of their social origin. The same opening-up of mobility opportunities can be observed today in Third World societies undergoing initial industrialisation.

Whenever industrial capitalism is combined with political democracy, the openness of the class system has invariably increased, not necessarily by improving income distribution or the overall amount of upward mobility, but by giving greater access to education to people of the less privileged classes. In this perspective the entire welfare state can be seen as a vast mechanism to further open up an already highly dynamic class system. Background does still count, but so does individual achievement and plain luck.

A new middle class, next to the already existing middle class, emerged, consisting of people whose occupations deal with the production and distribution of symbolic knowledge; the so-called knowledge class. Symbolic knowledge is knowledge that is not directly oriented towards material life. Tensions may occur between these two middle classes.

14. Contemporary Western societies are characterised by a protracted conflict between the two classes, the old middle class (occupied in the production and distribution of material goods and services) and a new middle class (occupied in the production and distribution of symbolic knowledge).

Where there are classes there tend to be conflicts between them. The new knowledge class tends to be politically and ideologically to the left of the old middle class, and *ipso facto* anti-capitalist in its orientation.

15. The new knowledge class in Western societies is a major antagonist of capitalism.

Why is that? It is because the livelihood of this knowledge class depends on government payrolls or subsidies. This suggests a vested interest in the expansion of the welfare state. Members of this class have an interest in the distributive machinery of government, as against the production system, and this pushes it to the left in the context of Western politics.

Berger concluded that industrial capitalism is one version of modernity. There are characteristics of Western societies that will probably have to be ascribed to their being modern societies and not to their being capitalist ones. Characteristics are income distribution and social mobility. On the other hand, what can be ascribed to capitalism are the productive power of these societies, as well as the relative openness of their class system.

Capitalism and Political Liberties

The overriding concern is to understand the manner in which economic arrangements, known as capitalism, interact and reciprocate with other processes and institutions in modern society. As noted above, the term 'economic culture' intends to suggest this concern. The most important of the relationships is between modern capitalism and the modern state. The latter attained its fullest development in tandem with the development of capitalism, and this modern state represents the most efficient and pervasive organisation of political power in history. Democracy developed precisely in the same Western countries in which modern capitalism unfolded. Modern democracy was one of the historical achievements of the bourgeoisie; the rising capitalist class.

Berger defined democracy as a political system in which governments are constituted by majority votes cast in regular and un-coerced elections. This definition does not touch upon suffrage and neither does it include the panoply of civil and human rights. Democracy constitutes an institutionalised limitation on the power of government. This presupposes that the political institutions of society are clearly differentiated from the other institutions and are not allowed to coalesce with them. Capitalism has been associated both with the greatest concentration of political power in history, but with the most intense effort to limit its power. Surely, the modern state can exist without capitalism. The question is whether modern democracy is possible without capitalism.

All democracies are capitalist but not all capitalist societies are democratic, and there are no socialist democracies. Schumpeter believed that, in principle, democracy is possible both under capitalism *and* socialism. He believed though that a socialist democracy would not be conducive to personal freedom.

There is the view, among others expressed by Milton and Rose Friedman, that economic freedom is necessarily linked to political freedom because both are expressions of one and the same impulse of individual autonomy against the coercive power of the state. They saw freedom as one whole; that is, that anything that reduces freedom in one part of our lives is likely to affect freedom in the other parts.

Socialism empirically means a vast expansion of state power. The zone of economic activity is incorporated in the sphere of the state in a much more complete manner. The term used often in this context is command economy. The socialist state functions as a monopoly of economic and political power. Property rights over the means of production are abrogated, which provides additional proof of its incompatibility with democracy.

> 16. *Capitalism is a necessary but not sufficient condition of democracy.*
> 17. *If a capitalist economy is subjected to increasing degrees of state control, a point will be reached at which democratic governance becomes impossible.*
> 18. *If a socialist economy is opened up to increasing degrees of market forces, a point will be reached at which democratic governance becomes a possibility.*

Berger noted that successful capitalism generates pressures towards democracy. And so-called development dictatorships work in the 'take-off' stages of capitalist development. Berger warns though that this doesn't mean that dictatorship is a necessary condition for capitalist take-off.

A distinction should be made between authoritarian and totalitarian regimes. An authoritarian regime does not tolerate political opposition. Nonetheless, it is prepared to allow institutions to function free of the state, provided they don't undertake activities of a political nature. Totalitarian regimes seek to impose state control over *every* institution of society. The socialist 'project' in itself contains a totalitarian tendency, since it necessarily precludes the autonomy of the economic sector of society vis-à-vis the political structure. Capitalism presupposes such autonomy and thereby inhibits totalitarian developments.

> 19. *If capitalist development is successful in reaching economic growth from which a sizeable proportion of the population benefits, pressures towards democracy are likely to appear.*

This development is very likely related to the emergence of a middle class, which wants political participation as one of the prizes of its economic success. Intermediate institutions, such as labour unions, cooperatives and occupational groups, are essential if democracy is not to degenerate into tyranny. The positive affinity between capitalism and mediating structures may serve to explain that successful capitalism creates pressures towards democracy. There is also a correlation between democracy and respect for human rights, but this is not logically necessary.

The modern democratic state is also a welfare state, which may imply 'creeping socialism'. There may well be a tipping point at which the expanding state might cease to be democratic. The state intervenes gradually more deeply in the economy so as to satisfy the demands of what Mancur Olsen called 'distributional coalitions', as described in *The Rise and Decline of Nations* (1982). So, there are built-in forces which may undermine capitalism and democracy. Neither can be indefinitely projected into the future as inevitable.

Capitalism and Personal Liberties

Western individualism is often castigated as selfishness, lack of community, lack of binding moral standards. Individualism is better captured by the term individual autonomy. This refers to a particular experience of identity. This term also refers to a set of institutions in society—those institutions that make the experience of individual autonomy possible, in particular legal and political institutions. Personal liberties require a liberating culture. Individualism may weaken authority. Karl Polanyi wrote in *The Great Transformation* (1944), 'To separate labor from other activities of life and to subject it to the laws of the market was to annihilate all organic forms of existence and to replace them by a different type of organisation, an atomistic and individualistic one.'

Historians now believe that it is not modernity that has promoted individualism. On the contrary, the individualistic patterns of medieval England made it possible for modernity to arise there. The roots of capitalism—and of the Industrial Revolution—must be sought in medieval English structures of ownership. The same applies to the roots of modern English history of equality and liberty. Berger goes even further back. Western individual autonomy finds its origin in ancient Israel and ancient Greece. The Israelite experience of the one transcendent and personal God almost inevitably created the counterpoint to the solitary human individual involved in a strange battle of wills with this God. The Hellenistic experience of individual autonomy was based on the discovery of the autonomous power of human reason.

20. The roots of individual autonomy in Western culture long antedate modern capitalism. Further, this premodern 'individualism' of Western culture engendered the particular 'individualism' associated with capitalism.

What is the relationship of modern autonomy to modern capitalism? The historic 'carrier' of capitalism is bourgeois capitalism and bourgeois culture, developed in tandem over the centuries. It can be argued that both developments were crucially related to the genesis of individual autonomy in its distinctive modern Western form. The bourgeoisie extolled rationality and an overall 'methodism', that is, both personal and social morality, of life, as opposed to the aristocrat's reliance on 'healthy instinct' and spontaneity. The bourgeois respected learning, whereas the aristocracy contained, well into the eighteenth century, many illiterates. The bourgeois emphasised personal responsibility, while the aristocrat relied on 'honour'.

Max Weber made a crucial contribution to the 'spirit of capitalism'. The Calvinist doctrine of 'double predestination', meaning that God has already determined before all time began who will be saved and who will be damned, led to a pervasive anxiety about one's own fate. To alleviate this anxiety, pious Calvinists led virtuous lives hoping to earn God's blessings on their activities in the world. For Weber the prototype of this Calvinist was the Puritan businessman who worked very hard, enjoyed himself very little and fashioned himself into a successful entrepreneur.

Weber believed that Eastern philosophies didn't promote a businesslike attitude. He interpreted Buddhism and Confucianism as not having the elements that Calvinist Protestantism had. He was proven wrong by Japan's rapid economic development as well as that of other East Asian countries.

21. Bourgeois culture in the West, especially in Protestant societies, produced a type of person strongly marked by both the value and the psychic reality of individual autonomy.

Western culture means an intensive interest in individual subjectivity; that is, a perception of the individual. This has roots in bourgeois culture. And because this culture is the product of the class that brought capitalism to power in Western societies, the emergence of individual autonomy is related to capitalism.

Berger identified the following elements of bourgeois culture that are directly related to its capital matrix: individualism, strong discipline, a sober, no-nonsense problem-solving attitude to economic life in particular, and ambition. However, the emergence of successful East Asian capitalism puts a question mark over the notion that the linkage between capitalism and individual autonomy holds cross-culturally. Take Japan: it has developed a highly successful capitalist economy on the basis of a non-individualistic culture. Moreover, there are the industrial socialist societies that simply deny individual autonomy both in theory and in practice.

> 22. Given the social and cultural bases of Western civilisation, capitalism is the necessary but not sufficient condition for the continuing reality of individual autonomy.
>
> 23. Certain components of Western bourgeois culture, notably those of activism, rational innovativeness and self-discipline, are prerequisites of successful capitalist development anywhere.

Human relations too become subject to the creative-destruction characteristics of capitalism. There is, therefore, a need for a world of 'warmth' to balance this 'coldness'. Family, church, friendships and freely formed associations have provided this balance throughout the development of bourgeois culture. They continue to do so today, despite contradictions within this culture.

> 24. Capitalism requires institutions that balance the anonymous aspects of individual autonomy with communal solidarity. Among these institutions are, above all, the family and religion.

Capitalism and Development

Capitalism has become an international system determining the economic fate of most of humankind and, at least indirectly, its social, political and cultural fate. In developing countries capitalist economics coexists with increasing poverty. The capitalist horn of plenty is an image of hope, a promise of wealth. But when the reality fails to catch up with this image, the dream easily turns into bitterness and hatred. Berger defines development as follows: 'Development is the process by which people in the poorer countries are to reach the levels of material life achieved in the countries of advanced industrial capitalism.'[4]

Economic growth is the condition of development. But growth per se doesn't necessarily constitute development. It is possible that a small minority of people benefit from this growth, while the mass of the population remains poor. The common-sense notion of development implies a distribution of the benefits of growth. So, development is a process of ongoing economic growth by which large masses of people are moved from poverty into an improved material standard of life. It should be noted that, in terms of social and economic indicators, every country of Europe and North America was poor 200 years ago.

The question about capitalism and development can be further refined: Is it plausible to assume that the story of development as it took place in Europe and North America can be replicated in the poor countries of the Third World? This optimistic outlook prevailed in the 1950s and 1960s. W.W. Rostow's five stages of economic growth implied that given sufficient technological and sociopolitical preconditions in place, economic growth and development would be brought about. This was exactly the same trajectory of development Third World countries could follow as, for example, Britain had taken in the past. Their economies would 'take-off' into a stage of maturity that could be reached in a period of, say, 60 years. Rostow's views were castigated as ethnocentric, reflecting a Western bias.

Berger felt that this criticism was unfair. Rostow's views were not so much ethnocentric as optimistic. His model assumed that the basic course of development was set and that, if due attention is paid to its inherent logic, the outlook for all developing countries was bright. A more balanced criticism would be that one could not equate modernisation with development. This relationship could have been proposed as a hypothesis, and not as an assumption that the technological and

---

[4] Ibid., 116.

economic transformations of modernity led in a more or less natural way to certain desired ends.

During the late 1960s, Rostow's approach to development came under fire and was increasingly replaced by much less optimistic views about the prospects of the Third World within the international capitalist system. Leftist views came to dominate the development debate. The so-called 'dependency theory' became fashionable. Not all of them are Marxist or socialist. Yet its basic conceptual apparatus does derive from Marxism, including its anti-capitalist stance.

Lenin maintained that imperialism was the necessary expression of capitalism at an advanced stage of its history. Capitalists started to look for fresh markets overseas and to invest their 'surplus capital'. Both were the result of the decline of competition due to the concentration of capital in giant corporations. The domestic market for goods and investments dries up. So, capitalists have to look abroad for new markets or investment opportunities. Imperialism is the political/military instrument to secure these economic goals. Lenin concluded that working for the revolution should be done in the periphery rather than in the centre of the capitalist world. However, the actual development of modern imperialism cannot be explained in terms of economic interests only. It must be explained in a combination of these with economically 'irrational' motives; after all, the colonial empires cost the mother countries more than they were worth in terms of economic advantage.

The dependency theory's central thesis is that the development of the periphery has been distorted or even prevented by the penetration of the forces of international capitalism. Berger asked then whether this dependent condition has been necessarily bad for the people of the periphery. Dependency adherents say yes. Foreign companies would dominate the national economy, national enterprises would be smothered, economic policies would be decided overseas and the indigenous population would be pauperised, with the exception of the so-called comprador class, that is, the local groups who become agents of foreign enterprise. André Gunder Frank coined the phrase 'development of underdevelopment'. The underdevelopment of the Third World is not a condition preceding the advent of international capitalism in those countries. It is a condition brought about by this international capital.

The dependency theory originated at a time when the colonisers had left and many new states had been established; nonetheless, the theory 'stuck'. Even non-radical economists felt that capitalism made Third World countries dependent and that it would perpetuate poverty. It became an important element in Third World ideology that the root causes of underdevelopment were to be found outside the national states. This prevented painful self-reflection. But this is not a correct reflection of realities. The economies of former colonial powers were much more geared to each other than to the 'periphery'. It is true that there were deliberate policies that harmed development. A few examples are the British policy that throttled the Indian textile industry to protect its own. A similar case can be made for the operation of some United States companies in Central America and for French capital in West Africa. On the other hand, Berger compared Ethiopia (least affected by colonialism) with Kenya (affected by it) and showed that Ethiopia is worse off than Kenya. The colonial powers left behind physical infrastructure and social institutions such as a modern bureaucracy and an educational system.

It is hard to believe that an international socialist system would be any more egalitarian. The Soviet Union and its industrialised allies in Europe have indeed established such an international socialist system in which both 'inequality' and 'dependency' are important features.

Multinational corporations are the most important vehicles for the transfer of capital and technology to Third World countries, for training of indigenous personnel in modern economic occupations and for reliable tax revenues into Third World treasuries. On the other hand, a large number of Third World governments are obstacles to development. Often their policies and actions perpetuate underdevelopment, such as destructive socialist experiments and regulations that favour urban population by artificially depressing farm prices, thus discouraging agricultural development. State ineffectiveness (Gunnar Myrdal invented the term 'soft state') is another characteristic of many Third World governments; corruption is yet another.

The development of the capitalist societies of East Asia is the most important empirical falsification of the dependency theory. One cannot be a supporter of the dependency theory and ignore this region of the world, not in the least because spectacular development cannot be explained by this theory.

> 25. *The inclusion of a Third World country within the international capitalist system tends to favour its development.*

This proposition doesn't imply that inclusion within the global capitalist system guarantees development. It only suggests that the inclusion releases forces that promote development. There is now widespread agreement in the world that an economy allowing market forces the fullest feasible sway will perform better than one in which all decisions are centrally administered.

> 26. *The superior productive power of capitalism, as manifested in the advanced industrial countries of the West, continues to manifest itself today wherever the global capitalist system has intruded.*

This proposition doesn't imply that only capitalism can generate economic growth. From 1950 to 1980 world output tripled in real terms. Capitalism alone could not have achieved this. Equity questions must be addressed as well, such as how the living standard of the mass of the population affects economic growth and how the benefits of growth are distributed.

An important element of 'Third Worldism' is the opinion that the condition of the poor in developing countries is deteriorating and the gap between rich and poor countries is widening. Berger's counter-arguments are that statistical data of Third World countries are not always reliable and one has to look at the 'physiology' of development: Are people better fed, do they live longer, what about infant mortality, and so forth? These indicators have improved almost everywhere. The reason lies in the modernisation as such, and not in any particular socioeconomic system.

As India and China demonstrated, the move from socialist to capitalist agrarian strategies greatly improved the condition of the rural poor. This is important in view of the widespread agreement that agriculture is the key to development and thus to the fate of the urban as well as the rural poor.

27. Capitalist development is more likely than socialist development to improve the material standards of life of people in the contemporary Third World, including the poorest groups.

Extreme inequalities in income tend to generate social and political tensions inimical to development. There is a trade-off between growth and equality. But is there? Economists believe that the Kuznets Curve holds in Third World countries today. Gustav Papanek studied relevant trends in three types of countries: 'populist' countries, 'modified capitalism' countries and 'growth-oriented private enterprise' countries. He concluded that the populist strategies are worst, modified capitalism is better and an all-out growth strategy is best for the poor. Berger argued that redistributionist government policies tend to make for inequality, not only because they inhibit growth, but because they introduce political distortions into the economic process. They tend to create a 'protected' sector (mostly consisting of urban skilled labour) that benefits from the policies but is likely to generate economic hardships in other sectors of society. The same government policies often set artificially low prices for agricultural products, thereby depressing the income of the rural population. However, government can also promote equality-inducing policies. Education is one such policy, asset ownership among the poor is another and fostering investment in labour-intensive industries is yet another.

28. Capitalist development leading to rapid and labour-intensive economic growth is more likely to equalise income distribution than strategies of deliberate, government-induced income redistribution.

Berger ended this chapter by underscoring that every development strategy is a gamble, but that capitalism is generally the better bet. He concluded that there is some reason to think that this insight is spreading in the Third World today.

East Asian Capitalism: A Second Case

One must try to understand East Asia in order to better understand the West. There are a few salient features that are common to East Asian societies. These societies have developed fully modernised industrial economies of a capitalist type. They have sustained high growth rates, even during periods of recession. Furthermore, these societies have succeeded in virtually eliminating poverty. They are export-oriented economies. The state plays a very active role in shaping the economic process. With the exception of education, they have an underdeveloped welfare state, although in Japan this is changing. And they have relatively low tax rates and high saving rates. Finally, the economies are highly productive and the work ethic is strong.

Japan's economy was back on its feet in 1953 when it reached its pre-WWII level. This was thanks to the experience gained during Japan's industrial revolution in the nineteenth century. Between 1890 and 1940, Japan's growth of 3.5 % per annum was among the highest in the world. Japan broke away from its traditional economic activities through the Meji Restoration. This was a bloodless coup which overthrew the Tokugawa regime. Fiefdoms and other feudal privileges were abolished. It formed the start of a hectic modernisation process. The Meji period was indeed a revolutionary period; a swift and deliberate move from feudalism to capitalism. Very interesting was the Tomomi Iwakura mission, which visited country after country (the USA, Britain, France, Germany) to see which institutions and production processes might be useful for Japan's development.

Land tenure was changed, realising that an agrarian society cannot modernise without changing its land tenure system. In the beginning the government established its own factories run by foreign managers. Once enough Japanese had been trained to operate the new industrial enterprises, the government sold them off to private entrepreneurs at very low prices. The new Japanese industrial corporation was born.

The government introduced a system of universal education. The emerging bourgeois ethos was derived from the traditional samurai code; an ethos of dedication and discipline transposed from a feudal-military to a capitalist-entrepreneurial class.

The recent history of South Korea, Taiwan, Hong Kong and Singapore, the 'Four Little Dragons' (as Berger called them), is one of spectacular economic and social success. As an example, Taiwan's population was 17.1 million in 1978 (1.8 % of mainland China's population), yet its per capita Gross National Product (GNP) was six times that of the People's Republic. All four Dragons developed increasingly high-technology economies. Land reform was one of the most important Taiwanese government policies. It created a new class of owner-farmers, with important consequences for the distribution of property and income. There is evidence that unskilled labour benefitted as much, if not more, than skilled labour from the upward movement of wages. In any event, income distribution became more equal in the process of growth.

> *29. East Asia confirms the superior productive power of industrial capitalism.*
> *30. East Asia confirms the superior capacity of industrial capitalism in raising the material standard of living of large masses of people.*
> *31. East Asia confirms the positive relation between industrial capitalism and the emergence of a class system characterised by relatively open social mobility.*
> *32. East Asia disconfirms the proposition that early economic growth under modern capitalist conditions must necessarily increase income inequality, though it confirms the proposition that income distribution stabilises as this economic growth continues.*

East Asian cultures, because of Confucianism and other religious traditions are peculiarly suited for modern development and East Asian societies do have very distinctive cultural characteristics. However, this does not mean that others cannot replicate the Asian miracle or a version thereof. There are good reasons to doubt that the East Asian experience is unique. Windows of opportunity in the world economy recur periodically, and other countries may take advantage of them. People in very different societies have managed to mobilise cultural traits of their own for successful economic performance or have changed their cultural traditions sufficiently to allow such performance. As for imperialist influences, the Meji Restoration was a direct reaction to Western imperialist intrusion.

> *33. The East Asian experience falsifies the proposition that successful development cannot occur in a condition of dependency upon the international capitalist system.*

East Asia was bad news for Marxists. But East Asia is also not very comforting for ideologists of capitalism who still adhere to some laissez-faire notions to the effect that state interventionism is bad for economic development. All successful East Asian nations are characterised by massive state interventions in economic life. They are heavily *dirigiste* and have been so from the beginnings of their respective modernisation process.

> 34. *The East Asian evidence falsifies the idea that a high degree of state intervention in the economy is incompatible with successful capitalist development.*

This proposition is not to be construed as an argument for a 'mixed economy', as advocated by Western social democrats. The East Asian economies are unambiguously capitalist. What is important is that the East Asian experience forces a modification of all theories of capitalism that seek to salvage a doctrinaire laissez-faire approach to the role of the state in a capitalist economy.

The East Asian experience raises the question whether successful capitalism generates pressures towards democracy. Japan has a democracy, albeit installed by the Americans after WWII. The Four Little Dragons do show signs of pressures towards democracy. Hence, any proposition has to be worded very cautiously.

> 35. *The East Asian evidence provides weak support for the thesis that successful capitalist development generates pressures towards democracy.*

A comparison between the 'spirit of Japanese capitalism' and the 'spirit' of Western capitalism shows differences. The most important similarity is what Weber called 'this-worldly asceticism', a combination of secularity with a morality of self-denial and discipline. In Japan this attitude has a much wider time horizon and it is combined with a non-individualistic ethos of service to others, and finally to the nation. This modification of the Western spirit of capitalism may account for the willingness of Japanese businessmen to tolerate low rates of profit for a long time with a future goal of success in mind.

36. The East Asian experience supports the hypothesis that certain components of Western bourgeois culture, notably activism, rational innovativeness and self-discipline, are necessary for successful capitalist development.
37. Specific elements of East Asian civilisation, be it in the 'great traditions' or in folk culture, have fostered these values and have consequently given the societies of the region a comparative advantage in the modernisation process.

The idea that economic and other social institutions are simply the result of historical circumstances, or can be freely constructed by a collective will, contradicts what the social sciences have discovered about the power of culture. Thus it is inherently implausible to believe that Singapore would be what it is today if it were populated, not by a majority of Chinese, but by Brazilians or Bengalis. Human beings' behaviour is indeed determined by their past, but they are also capable of changing their cultural inheritance. Culture is rarely changed as a result of deliberate acts, as in the application of legal, political or educational policies. Meji-Japan is a good example in this respect.

Another question is to what extent has East Asia succeeded in modernising itself under capitalist conditions without in the process becoming more 'individualistic'. There is widespread agreement that East Asia in general and Japan in particular are characterised by strong communal solidarities and, consequently, by resistance to Western-style individualism.

38. The societies of East Asia have succeeded for a long time in modernising under capitalist conditions without undergoing individualism along Western lines.

Cross-national evidence on individualising modernity is strong enough to make one very sceptical about the ability of East Asian societies to continue on their 'groupism' course.

39. The values of individual autonomy are undermining East Asian communalism and are likely to continue doing so.

It is likely that these societies sooner or later will face some problems both in the areas of economic productivity and political governability.

East Asia is acting in a capitalistic world system dominated by the West. Time will tell whether democratisation and individuation are intrinsic or extrinsic to the capitalist engine.

> 40. *The movements towards democracy and individualism in East Asia have been greatly strengthened by the adherence of these societies to an international capitalist system centred in the West.*

Industrial Socialism: A Control Case

Berger predicted that it might well be that China will be far more important than the Soviet Union in the long run. The comparison between advanced capitalist societies with the Soviet Union made more sense in 1987, as the Soviet Union was the 'lead society' in terms of modern socialism. The socialist model is centred around a highly centralised, planned economy from which market forces have been largely banned. Most observers of the Soviet economy have been struck by its inefficiency and low productivity, especially in agriculture and consumer industries. Yet, there has been economic growth and modernisation. The material standard of living of the population has been slowly but steadily improving. Berger argued that this is less a triumph of socialism than a consequence of the application of modern technology to economic production.

Centralised planning creates a vast bureaucracy, which—by its very nature—institutionalises inefficiency. It is intrinsically impossible to plan efficiently for the economy of a modern nation-state, especially if it is as vast as the Soviet Union. Most economists agree that this problem is built-in because the market has been eliminated and, therefore, cannot provide information about demand and supply, reflected in the price system.

> 41. *There is an intrinsic linkage between socialism and the pervasive bureaucratisation of the economy.*
> 42. *There is an intrinsic linkage between socialism and economic inefficiency.*

It is not possible to impose a socialist system without force, since those who are to be dispossessed will not accept their fate. Hence, as Marx argued, there must be dictatorship. And the need for dictatorship increases with the successful establishment of socialism. The degree of power required by 'the plan' requires dictatorial powers. The essential totalitarian features of a socialist regime are expressed in the fact that the political structure not only smothers all opposition, but continually seeks to control every institutional expression within the society, from the economy to the family. The 'totalitarian project' implies total integration of all societal institutions within the political structure.

> 43. *There is an intrinsic affinity between socialism and authoritarian governance.*
> 44. *There is an intrinsic affinity between socialism and the totalitarian project for modern society.*

In terms of social mobility in socialist societies, mobility rates and some of the mobility vehicles (education notably) are the same as in the West. There is the additional important vehicle of political mobility in socialist societies, that is, mobility via the apparatus of the party.

Socialist societies contain two different and interacting types of stratification. To the extent that they have modern industrial economies, they generate class systems similar to those existing in industrial capitalism. But superimposed on this class system is a quite different system of stratification, in which privilege as well as power and prestige are linked to political office. Max Weber called this a patrimonial system.

> 45. *Industrial socialism is characterised by the ongoing interaction of two distinct forms of stratification, a class system and a system of political patrimonialism.*

The New Economic Mechanism was introduced in Hungary as a result of the wish to diminish central control. Its central features were less centralised planning and control, partial price deregulation, greater reliance on a freer price system, incentive pay and greater decision-making powers for enterprise managers. Productivity went up, but so did central control and political obstruction by those who stood to lose.

Yugoslavia's experiment with 'market socialism' is somewhat older than the Hungarian one and had similar features. But there were additional aspects such as the institution of self-management and workers-management. As long as the basic socialist character of the economy is maintained, Soviet-style inefficiencies can only be mitigated to a limited degree. In these cases an 'artificial market' is instituted; artificial, that is, when compared with the manner in which the market operates in a capitalist economy.

In the end socialist bureaucracy, once established, will necessarily resist the diminishment of its power and privilege that will follow upon any expansion of market forces within the economy.

> 46. *A modification of industrial socialism through the introduction of market mechanism will encounter political limits, which are caused by the resistance of the patrimonial elite defending its vested interest.*
> 47. *A modification of industrial socialism through the introduction of market mechanisms will encounter economic limits, which are caused by the inability of the artificial market to replicate the efficiency of the capitalist market.*

Earlier in the book capitalism was defined in terms of the dominance of market forces rather than private ownership of the means of production. This definition has the advantage of allowing the relationship between the market and private ownership to be the subject of an empirical hypothesis rather than posited by definition. From the foregoing, the following proposition (48) can be made.

> 48. *There can be no effective market economy without private ownership of the means of production.*

At the current state of knowledge it can be stated with a fair degree of reliability that market forces almost always invigorate an economy and that socialism stultifies it.

Socialism is beset with contradictions. One such contradiction is between socialist collectivism and modern individualism. Modernisation brings about a weakening of traditional solidarities, and the process facilitates the emergence of modern individualism. And, as noted, there exists a particular affinity between capitalism and modern individuation. By contrast, socialism is an *ideal* of collective solidarity and unselfish morality.

There are two world systems. They are engaged in a political, economic and military struggle that is the major force dominating international relations since WWII. But the two systems are also engaged in what one may call a process of mutual contamination. Socialist ideas have penetrated the consciousness of significant strata in capitalist society. But Western ideas also continue to penetrate the socialist societies, creating comparable problems of legitimacy. The game of reciprocal subversion is likely to continue for a long time, barring the sort of military conflict that would eliminate one or both of the two contestants.

Capitalism and the Dynamics of Myth

A society is not held together simply by practical needs and interests but by beliefs that explain and justify its particular institutional arrangements. But there is a distinction between legitimations that sustain an institution in ordinary, everyday life and legitimations that command a high degree of commitment and sacrifice on the part of those who believe in them. It is a crucial distinction, between ordinary legitimations and the other ones, called myths. The genius of Marx was that he combined this emotionally, and indeed religiously, charged vision with a sober ideal of scientific inquiry. It is important that the ideas and images making up the myths are believed by people in the empirical situation and that these ideas and images inspire people to acts of commitment and sacrifice.

The importance of the distinction is that capitalism has been singularly devoid of plausible myths, whereas socialism has been singularly blessed with myth-generating potency. Modern Marxists explain away discrepancies between the theory and practice: if the Soviet Union could no longer be held up as the place of realised socialist ideals, then it had to be China; if not China, then Cuba or Vietnam or Mozambique or Nicaragua, and so on.

> 49. *Socialism, in addition to being a set of political programmes and the source of social-scientific interpretations, is also one of the most powerful myths of the*

contemporary era; to the extent that socialism retains this mythic quality, it cannot be disconfirmed by empirical evidence in the minds of its adherents.

Capitalism is mythically deprived. Adam Smith believed that the economic system he was describing was quite simply the natural ordering of things. Friedrich Hayek and Milton Friedman, probably the most prominent advocates of capitalism to date, would not agree with Smith's notions of what is natural; their defence of capitalism is indirect by reference to its linkage with liberty.

The mythic deprivation of capitalism is very likely grounded in the fact that capitalism is an economic system and nothing else. All economic realities are essentially prosaic. Economics is averse to myths.

Joseph Schumpeter believed that the very success of capitalism undermines the cultural foundations on which it rests. Capitalism doesn't legitimise itself. It depends for its legitimation upon traditional values. But the very dynamics of capitalism, its creative destruction, increasingly weakens all traditions and thus pulls the rug from under its own cultural credibility. However, when a society is more or less in a state of tranquillity, or when a social institution is functioning well, these very facts provide tacit legitimation for the status quo. This is the normal power of facticity.

> *50. Capitalism has a built-in incapacity to generate legitimations of itself, and it is particularly deprived of mythic potency; consequently, it depends upon the legitimating effects of its sheer facticity or upon association with other, non-economic legitimating symbols.*

The Shape and Uses of a Theory of Capitalism

This concluding chapter groups all 50 propositions under the following headings:

> Concerning capitalism and material life (propositions 1–8); concerning capitalism and class (9–15); concerning capitalism and democracy (16–19); concerning capitalism and the culture of individual autonomy (20–24); concerning capitalism and Third World development

(25–28); concerning capitalism in East Asia (29–40); concerning industrial socialism (41–48); concerning the legitimation of capitalism (49–50).

Social theorists sometimes use the language of architects. They talk of theoretical 'edifices' or 'constructions'; they describe their activities as 'theory building'. Berger's book has no pretence of proposing a complete theory. The purpose of the book's last chapter is twofold: (1) to take a look at the propositions as a whole and (2) to ask what practical use the emergent theory may have. Berger then observed,

> Simply taken as a body of empirical hypotheses, this emergent theory is neither pro- nor anticapitalist. Whether it is either will be determined not by the empirical support or falsification that it will eventually acquire but rather by the values to which it will be related. Again, simply taken as a social-scientific exercise, the emergent theory has no use at all, except for the use of reducing the intellectual perplexities of the theorist.[5]

However, values can be introduced. At the moment the most significant choice for most people is between capitalism and socialism. The values held by the majority of people in the world today—and relevant to this choice—are fairly limited in number. Therefore, the most reasonable clarifying exercise lies in the juxtaposition of this limited set of values and the capitalist–socialist alternative. What Berger then did was to look at the relevance of his 50 propositions in terms of seven commonly held values.

1. *The material well-being of people, especially the poor.* There is no question that capitalism, as against any empirically available alternatives, is the indicated choice.
2. *Equality.* It would be better to speak of equality in relation to specific purposes, such as equality before the law. As for income distribution, neither capitalism nor socialism come out very well.
3. *Political liberties and democracy.* This value clearly dictates a choice in favour of capitalism.

---

[5] Ibid., 216.

4. *Protection of human rights.* Empirically, democratic regimes have the best record on this value.
5. *Individual autonomy.* Again, capitalism offers the most plausible context for the realisation of this value.
6. *Preservation of tradition.* Neither capitalism nor any empirically available alternative appears conducive to this value.
7. *Community.* To some extent this value overlaps with the value of the preservation of tradition. For those who aspire towards some new, all-embracing community, transcending anything to be found in the world today, socialism will very probably continue to be the preferred choice.

In conclusion, in terms of the values, a choice in favour of capitalism is more plausible in light of the empirical evidence as currently available. Berger produced a set of hypotheses. He noted that the social sciences can never do more. All the empirical evidence that the social sciences can accumulate for the use of an actor in the end does no more than indicate which bets are likely to be safer. The empirical evidence presented is useful for the choice for or against capitalism as a form of socioeconomic organisation. It is probable that this choice will be decided on meta-empirical grounds. The Stoic maxim says that the most fundamental wisdom is to know the difference between what one can and what one cannot do.

The modern social scientist, probabilistic to the end, will modify this maxim only slightly: Wisdom is to know the difference between what one can probably do and what one can probably not do.[6]

Biography: Douglass Cecil North (1920–2015)

Douglass C. North was born on 5 November 1920 in Cambridge, Massachusetts. His father worked at Metropolitan Life Insurance Company (Metlife) in different locations, which meant that Douglass moved quite a few times during his youth to several cities and schools. He was educated at Ashbury College in Ottawa, Canada, and at the

---

[6] Ibid., 224.

Choate School in Wallingford, Connecticut. By the time Douglass was admitted to Harvard University, his father became head of Metlife on America's West Coast, so instead of going to Harvard, he enrolled in the University of California at Berkeley. He graduated with a BA in General Curriculum-Humanities in 1942.

During WWII North was a conscientious objector. He became a navigator in the Merchant Marine travelling between San Francisco and Australia, which allowed him to read economics when off-duty. During the final year of the war he taught navigation at the Maritime Service Officers' School in Alameda, California.

Academic Career

After the war the existential question came up, What to do now? Since he had meanwhile developed a love of photography, North hesitated between economics and photography, but in the end he decided to return to Berkeley to pursue a PhD in economics. His dissertation was a study on the history of life insurance in the USA. He received his degree in 1952. North began his career as assistant professor at the University of Washington in that same year. In 1960 he was promoted to a professorship in economics. He remained at the University of Washington until 1983. North then moved to Washington University in Saint Louis, where he initially occupied the position of Henry R. Luce Professor of Law and Liberty in the Department of Economics, and later as Spencer T. Olin Professor in Arts and Sciences. He combined his professorship with the position of Director of the Center for Political Economy from 1984 to 1990.

North held the position of Pitt Professor of American History and Institutions at Cambridge University in 1981. He contributed to the work of the Copenhagen Consensus (which seeks to advance global welfare using methodologies based on the theory of welfare economics) and advised governments of many countries around the world. He was appointed Bartlett Burnap Senior Fellow at the Hoover Institution at Stanford University. A collection of North's papers is housed at the Rubenstein Library at Duke University. In 1977, along with Ronald

Coase and Oliver Williamson, he founded the International Society for New Institutional Economics. The term 'new' suggests that there was also an 'old' variety of institutional economics before. In the past institutionalism flourished in America. Scholars such as Thorstein Veblen pointed to the dichotomy between business and industry on the one hand and institutional and technical aspects on the other. This would help explain societal and organisational constraints on—or reactions to—innovation and the diffusion of new technology. The old institutional economics maintained that economic systems evolved as a result of adjustments to existing institutions, triggered by technological change.

Major Publications

The Economic Growth of the United States, 1790–1860, published in 1961, formed the basis for much of North's later work, such as *Institutional Change and American Economic Growth* (1971), which he co-authored with Lance Davis.

A much-quoted work, written together with Robert Thomas, is *The Rise of the Western World: A New Economic History*, which came out in 1973. The same applies to *Structure and Change in Economic History*, published in 1981. This was followed by *Institutions and Economic Growth* in 1989. In the same year North also published *Constitutions and Commitment: The Evolution of Institutions Governing Public Choice in Seventeenth-Century England*. In 1990 appeared North's *Institutions, Institutional Change and Economic Performance*, probably his best-known book. In 1996 he edited, together with Lee Alston and Thrainn Eggertsson, a collection of essays entitled *Empirical Studies in Institutional Change*. And in 2005 North published *Understanding the Process of Economic Change*.

North continued to write well into his eighties. For example, in 2007 the World Bank published a Working Paper entitled 'Limited Access Orders in the Developing World', which he wrote together with John Joseph Wallis, Steven Webb and Barry Weingast. And North published in 2009, together with John Joseph Wallis and Barry Weingast, *Violence and Social Orders: A Conceptual Framework for Interpreting Recorded Human History*.

North's Academic Contributions

Douglass North is the economic historian who contributed to economic theory by revitalising and expanding the missing link in economic theory: the relevance of institutions in explaining stagnation and growth through time.

Economists, North argues, hang on to a body of theory developed to deal with advanced economies of nineteenth-century vintage when resource allocation was the dominant problem. That theory, which economists persist in trying to adapt to fundamental problems of development, is simply inappropriate to apply to issues of economic change and human choice. In *Institutions, Institutional Change and Economic Transformation* North observes that the challenge is to explain the widely diverging paths of historical change. This change is perplexing in terms of standard neoclassical and international trade theory, which implies that over time economies—as they traded goods, services and productive factors—would gradually converge. However, the gap between rich and poor nations is as wide today as it ever was.

Now, what North did was to build upon the neoclassical theory by refuting some of its assumptions while accepting two of its fundamental ones: scarcity and competition. In doing so, North tries to bridge the gap between the neoclassical theory and the real world. North was not fully successful in this attempt; nonetheless, he brings us a bit closer to an integral theory of economic growth. Deepak Lal argued that there is no hope of incorporating institutional development in economic growth theory, as the institutional dimension of economic growth has been mainly applied in descriptive historical studies.[7]

Neoclassical economics applies the theory of rational expectations. This assumes that 'agents' (i.e. decision-makers) form expectations based upon all available information about the future at the time they make decisions. Since markets always clear in the neoclassical theory, and since agents do not make systematic errors, full employment equilibrium is the

---

[7] Lal, D. (2000) Institutional Development and Economic Growth. In: *The Determinants of Economic Growth*. Ed. M. Oosterbaan, N. De Ruyter van Steveninck and N. Van der Windt. Boston: Kluwer Academic, 167.

economy's normal state of affairs. Prices will always adjust to ensure that there are neither unsatisfied buyers nor unsatisfied sellers in any market, including the labour market. The neoclassical theory reflects a mathematical precision and elegance and models a frictionless and static, but unrealistic, world; the theory doesn't explain the persistence of millennia of inefficient forms of exchange.

North's Critique of the Neoclassical Theory

The world portrayed by the neoclassical theory is frictionless, in which institutions don't exist, and all change occurs through perfectly functioning markets. In such an ideal situation, the costs of acquiring information and the costs involved in transactions don't exist. Ronald Coase had already argued in his essay 'The Problem of Social Cost' (1960) that when it is costless to transact, the efficient competitive solution of neoclassical economics obtains. This became known as the Coase Theorem, which is essentially the idea that freedom of exchange is the ultimate requirement to reach Pareto optimality, whereby no exchange will increase any party's welfare. But it isn't costless to transact in the real world, as elaborated below.

The neoclassical model says that even though the actors may initially have diverse and erroneous models, the informational feedback process will correct initially incorrect models, punish deviant behaviour and lead surviving players to the correct models. The implication is not only that institutions are designed to achieve efficient outcomes, but that they also can be ignored in economic analysis because they play no independent role in economic performance. Moreover, the neoclassical theory can't explain millennia of inefficient forms of exchange.

When applied to economic history and development, the neoclassical theory focused on technological development and, more recently, on human capital development. North concludes that the neoclassical analysis of economic performance through time contained two erroneous assumptions: (1) that institutions wouldn't matter and (2) nor would time. North demonstrated that it is institutions that constitute the underlying determinant of sustained economic growth of societies. North defines institutions as the constraints that structure human interaction.

These constraints can be formal (such as laws, rules, the Constitution) and informal (such as norms, beliefs and conventions), as well as their enforcement mechanisms. Together they define the incentive structure embodied in institutions of societies, which determines economic growth or stagnation. Institutions define the rules of the game, whereas firms and their managers are the players of that game.

Change may be of a revolutionary nature; however, as a rule, change is an incremental process. Hence institutions typically evolve in a gradual manner, while a certain path is being followed; economic development is path dependent. Institutions, and the technology employed, determine the transformation and transaction costs that add up to the production costs. Transaction costs are the costs of specifying what is being exchanged and of enforcing the terms of contracts. When it is costly to transact, institutions do matter. And it is indeed costly to transact: North calculated that 45 % of US GNP consisted of these transaction costs.

In economic markets the attributes of the value of goods and services are not only specified in their physical aspects but also in the form of property rights. Without these rights, people will not be prepared to invest, to apply new technologies; in short, to innovate.

Initially, North applied an evolutionary hypothesis about institutions, suggesting that ubiquitous competition would weed out inferior institutions and reward by survival those that better solve human problems. In *The Rise of the Western World: A New Economic History* (1973) North and Thomas made institutions the determinant of economic performance, and relative price changes the source of institutional change. As North later confessed, they had an essentially efficient explanation: changes in relative prices create incentives to construct more efficient institutions. The persistence of inefficient institutions, illustrated by the historical developments in Spain, was a result of fiscal needs of rulers that led to a disparity between private incentives and social welfare. However, such an anomaly didn't fit into the theoretical framework.

This anomaly was addressed in *Institutions, Institutional Change and Economic Performance*. North explains in this book why inefficient property rights can persist. The answer lies in the inefficiency of political markets. He argues that both high transaction costs and errors in the perceptions of participants in political markets can produce property rights that *hinder* economic growth. These property rights can result in the creation of new organisations designed to prosper under existing laws, which—consequently—have no incentive to create more efficient economic rules. Private gain is made at the cost of overall economic growth.

This is exactly the situation in many developing countries, which favours activities that promote redistributive rather than productive activities. The organisations that develop in this type of institutional framework will become more efficient in making the society even more unproductive, and the basic institutional structure even less conducive to productive activity.

If economies realise the gains from trade by creating relatively efficient institutions, it is because the private objective of those with the bargaining strength to alter institutions produces institutional solutions that evolve into socially and economically efficient ones. North notes, however, that the capture by organisations of the gains from trade for all parties to a transaction requires the development of a state as a coercive power, able to monitor property rights and the enforcement of contracts. However, the inability of most societies to develop effective, low-cost enforcement of contracts is the most important source of both historical stagnation and contemporary underdevelopment in the Third World.

North argues that the key to sustained economic growth is a flexible institutional matrix that will adjust to technological and demographic changes. Successful political/economic systems have evolved such characteristics over long periods of times. The critical issue is how to create such systems in short periods of time. North doubts whether the policies that will produce an efficient allocation are always the proper medicine for ailing societies.

A Typology of Societies

The World Bank Working Paper 'Limited Access Orders in the Developing World: A New Approach to the Problems of Development' (2007),[8] which North co-authored, analyses three types of societies in

---

[8] North, D. et al. (2007) World Bank Working Paper 4359 (2007) *Limited Access Orders in the Developing World: A New Approach to the Problems of Development.* Washington: World Bank.

historical perspective. The simplest type is the Primitive Order Society (POS, the hunter–gatherer one), followed by the Limited Access Order Society (LAOS) and the Open Access Society (OAS). Since humankind has left the POS behind it, the study focuses on the LAOS and the OAS.

The working paper was inspired by the realisation that most development policy today is based on donors' attempts to make developing countries look like the developed ones, while that doesn't seem to work. There is apparently a serious mismatch between theory and practice. The authors argue that the social and the political dynamics of developed countries are fundamentally different from those of developing countries. Development policies often fail because they try to transplant elements of the OAS—such as competition, markets and democracy—directly into the LAOS.

These policies threaten the privileged position of the elites in control, and challenge the very logic on which the LAOS is organised. Attempts to remove corruption, create the rule of law and institute democracy with competitive parties can destabilise an LAOS and generate resistance from those in control. Paradoxically, many who are exploited by these policies will hesitate to push for reform because they see disorder and violence as worse than being exploited.

The LAOS bars access to valuable political and economic functions to ensure income for the elites in control. The status quo is maintained by this privileged group through controlling violence (which otherwise undermines their power) and by maintaining stability. But there is more: the LAOS also frustrates the creation of organisations of potentially competing groups in society. The LAOS deliberately closes off political and economic possibilities for others than the happy few.

Relations between those in power and all others are personalised, such that the delivery of government services depends on to whom the recipient is connected. This insight was elaborated by Daron Acemoglu and James Robinson in *Why Nations Fail*.[9] The book is about the interplay between these political and economic institutions in the course of time. This interplay can result in extractive or inclusive institutions. Extractive

---

[9] Acemoglu, D., and Robinson, J. (2012) *Why Nations Fail: The Origins of Power, Prosperity and Poverty*. London: Profile Books.

institutions invite leaders to plunder. In such environments society's produce is captured by parasitical elites, which in turn discourage investment and innovation. These elites control a country's politics and the economy. Unfortunately, extractive institutions are the norm; failure is the rule.

But the interplay between political and economic institutions can also trigger dynamism and prosperity through a process of Schumpeter-like creative destruction. The institutions in this type of environment are inclusive: they protect individual property rights and, therefore, encourage investment. The political domain is not controlled by elites; no, other interest groups, such as the business community and those representing the interests of labour, have their say as well.

The OAS allows all citizens access to economic, political and social organisations. The OAS relies on competition, and on the free creation of organisations representing the interests of particular groups to hold the society together. The OAS uses competition and institutions (such as the rule of law applied to all) to make politicians realise that it is in their interest to observe constitutional rules. Economic dynamism is created by entrepreneurs.

Tackling the problem of development within the LAOS is unlikely to succeed simply by transplanting OAS institutional forms and mechanisms. But then the question is, What to do instead? Can the LAOS leap frog into an OAS? After all, many elites in an LAOS typically have been educated in Europe and North America, and they bring back ideas of institutional models from where they have studied. Modern technology (Internet, mobile phones, the social media) is available to them as well. However, corporations, parliaments and the judiciary in many developing countries operate differently when surrounding economic and cultural situations are different.

Many LAOSs have dualistic economies with a domestic economy governed by domestic rules and institutions on the one hand, and international enclaves run by OAS rules and institutions on the other. LAOS elites gain from this duality as it gives them the opportunity to prosper without having to bother about the development of their domestic economy. This doesn't imply that all LAOSs would be stagnant economies. The great civilisations of the past were all successful LAOSs before.

Tipping Points

In comparing the LAOS to the OAS, one can better understand what makes an LAOS evolve into an OAS; after all, that is what development is all about. The tipping point comes when open access in the economic or political domain results in sufficient power of the new entrants to press the elites, who are in control, to accept them. These elites give in when they see that their interests are better served by allowing the new entrants in. Once this stage is reached, history demonstrates that rapid changes occur, extending to ever-larger segments of society.

In a mature LAOS, sophisticated private organisations begin to emerge and their independence from the state becomes more clearly defined. A mature LAOS state must create new institutions that provide services (such as skills-training institutes) for these new organisations, including the protection—and enforcement—of their property rights. The tipping point comes when open access in one dimension (economic or political) commands sufficient power to press successfully for open access to the other dimension.

Honours

In 1991 North became the first economic historian to win the John R. Commons Award, a prize established by the International Honor Society for Economics in 1965. In 1993 he was awarded the Nobel Prize for Economics together with Robert Fogel; in the words of the Nobel Committee, 'For having renewed research in economic history by applying economic theory and quantitative methods in order to explain economic and institutional change.'

Institutions, Institutional Change and Economic Performance

Douglass North's book was probably the most-quoted volume on new institutional economics during the last decade of the twentieth century.[10]

---

[10] The edition used is the Cambridge University Press edition of 1990.

It is indeed a classic. It inspired many institutional economists, economic historians and political scientists to further explore the relevance of institutions in explaining the vastly different performances of economies in the long run.

Institutions, Institutional Change and Economic Performance is about institutions and time. The book does not provide a theory of economic dynamics comparable to the general equilibrium theory. What it does provide is the initial scaffolding of an analytical framework capable of increasing our understanding of the historical evolution of economies and a necessarily crude guide to policy in the task of improving the economic performance of economies. The analytical framework is a modification of neoclassical theory. What it retains is the fundamental assumption of scarcity, competition and the analytical tools of microeconomic theory. What it modifies is its rationality assumption, and it adds the dimension of time.

The specification of what exactly institutions are, how they shape incentives and how they influence transaction and production costs is the key to much of the analysis presented in this book. North's study is concerned as much with explaining the evolution of institutional frameworks that induce economic stagnation and decline as with accounting for growth and prosperity. The book consists of three parts, as its title suggests. Part I explains what institutions are. Part II deals with institutional change, while part III analyses economic performance.

Part I: Institutions

An Introduction to Institutions and Institutional Change

Institutions are the rules of the game in a society or, more formally, are the humanly devised constraints that shape human interactions. They structure incentives in human exchange, whether political, social or economic. Institutional change shapes the way societies evolve through time and, hence, constitutes the key to understanding historical change.

That institutions affect the performance of economies over time is not controversial. That the differential performance of economies over time is fundamentally influenced by the way institutions evolve is also not controversial. Yet neither current economic theory nor cliometric history shows many signs of appreciating the role of institutions in economic performance, because there is as yet no analytical framework to integrate institutional analysis into economics and economic history. The objective of *Institutions, Institutional Change and Economic Performance* is to provide such an underlying framework.

In the jargon of the economist, institutions define and limit the set of choices of individuals. Institutions include any form of constraint that human beings devise to shape human interaction. Institutions can be formal (such as rules that that human beings devise) or informal constraints (such as conventions and codes of behaviour). They are perfectly analogous to the rules of the game in a competitive team sport. An essential part of the functioning of institutions is the costliness of ascertaining violations and the severity of punishment.

There is a distinction between institutions and organisations. Like institutions, organisations provide a structure to human interaction. Organisations include political bodies, economic bodies, social bodies and educational bodies. They are groups of individuals bound by some common purpose to achieve objectives. Both how organisations come into existence and how they evolve is fundamentally influenced by the institutional framework. In turn they influence how the institutional framework evolves.

North argued that building a theory of institutions on the foundation of individual choices is a step towards reconciling differences between economics and the other social sciences. The strength of microeconomic theory is that it is constructed on the basis of assumptions about individual behaviour. Institutions are altered by human beings; therefore, according to North, his theory must begin with the individual. Integrating individual choices with the constraints institutions impose on choice sets is a major step towards unifying social science research.

Institutions affect the performance of the economy by their effect on the costs of exchange and production. An essential part of the functioning of institutions constitutes the costs of ascertaining violations and the severity of punishment. Together with the technology employed they determine the transaction and transformation (i.e. production) costs that make up total costs.

The major role of institutions in a society is to reduce uncertainty by establishing a stable (but not necessarily efficient) structure to human interaction. Institutions change incrementally rather than in a discontinuous fashion. Although formal rules may change overnight, as the result of political or judicial decisions, informal constraints are much more impervious to deliberate policies. These cultural constraints not only connect the past with the present and future, but provide us with a key to explaining the path of historical change.

The central puzzle of human history is to account for the widely diverging paths of historical change. This change is perplexing in terms of standard neoclassical and international trade theory, which implies that over time economies—as they traded goods, services and productive factors—would gradually converge. However, the gap between rich and poor nations is as wide today as it ever was and perhaps a great deal wider than ever before.

Now, what explains the difference? Which conditions either lead to further divergence or produce convergence? What accounts for societies experiencing long-term stagnation or an absolute decline in economic well-being? The answer hinges on the difference between institutions and organisations and the interaction between them that shapes the direction of international change. Institutions, together with the standard constraints of economic theory, determine the opportunities in a society. Organisations are created to take advantage of these opportunities and, as the organisations evolve, they alter institutions. The resultant path of institutional change is shaped by (1) the lock-in that comes from the symbiotic relationship between institutions and the organisations that have evolved as a consequence of the incentive structure, and (2) the feedback process by which human beings perceive and react to changes in the opportunity set.

What would the conditions be in many Third World countries, as well as those that have characterised much of the world's economic history? The opportunities for political and economic entrepreneurs overwhelmingly favour activities that promote redistributive rather than productive activity, that create monopolies rather than competitive conditions and that restrict opportunities rather than expand them. They seldom induce investment in education that increases productivity. The organisations that develop in this institutional framework will become more efficient—but more efficient at making the society even more unproductive and the basic institutional structure even less conducive to productive activity. Such a path can persist because the transaction costs of the economic and political markets of those economies, together with the subjective models of the actors, don't lead them to move incrementally towards more efficient outcomes.

Cooperation: The Theoretical Problem

Neoclassical theory does not explain the persistence for millennia of inefficient forms of exchange. The theory is based on the fundamental assumption of scarcity and competition. Its harmonious implications come from its assumptions about a frictionless exchange process in which property rights are perfectly and specified without cost, and information is likewise costless to acquire. What has been missing is an understanding of the nature of human coordination and cooperation. The British economist Ronald Coase discovered that when it is costly to transact, institutions matter. North—together with John Wallis—discovered that it is costly to transact in the US economy. They found out that transaction costs in the USA amounted to 45 % of the national income in 1986.

We usually observe cooperative behaviour when individuals repeatedly interact, when they have much information about each other and when small numbers characterise a group of players. However, the essence of impersonal exchange is the antithesis of game theoretic cooperation. The non-coincidence of wealth maximising behaviour and socially cooperative outcomes has been a key factor in the way game theory has evolved. The so-called prisoner's dilemma that has been a mainstay of game theory is clearly allied to Mancur Olsen's free-rider dilemma. Both suggest a discouraging perspective on the problems of human cooperation and coordination. Collective action depends not just on the size of the group, but also on the ratio of costs to benefits.

Under what conditions can voluntary cooperation exist without the Hobbesian solution of the imposition of a coercive state to create cooperative solutions? Historically the growth of economies has occurred within the institutional framework of well-developed coercive policies. There is no political anarchy in high-income countries. On the other hand, the coercive power of the state has been employed throughout history in ways that have been detrimental to economic growth. But it is difficult to sustain complex exchanges without a third party to enforce agreements.

Returning to Ronald Coase, he argued in his essay 'The Problem of Social Cost' (1960) that when it is costless to transact, the efficient competitive solution of neoclassical economics obtains. The neoclassical model says that even though the actors may initially have diverse and erroneous models, the informational feedback process will correct initially incorrect models, punish deviant behaviour and lead surviving players to the correct models. The implication is not only that institutions are designed to achieve efficient outcomes, but that they also can be ignored in economic analysis because they play no independent role in economic performance.

Institutions are not necessarily created to be socially efficient; rather they (or at least the formal rules) are created to serve the interests of those with the bargaining power to devise new rules. If economies realise the gains from trade by creating relatively efficient institutions, it is because under certain circumstances the private objectives of those with the bargaining strength to alter institutions produce institutional solutions that evolve into socially efficient ones.

The Behavioural Assumptions in a Theory of Institutions

All theorising in the social sciences builds upon conceptions of human behaviour. The neoclassical behaviour assumptions are the following: (1) the economic world is reasonably viewed as being in equilibrium; (2) individual economic actors repeatedly face the same choice situations or a sequence of very similar choices; (3) the actors have stable preferences and thus evaluate the outcomes of individual choices according to stable criteria; (4) given repeated exposure, any individual actor could identify and would seize any available opportunity for improving outcomes and, in the case of business firms, would do so on the pain of being eliminated by competition; (5) hence, no equilibrium can arise in which individual actors fail to maximise their preferences; (6) because the world is in approximate equilibrium, it exhibits at least approximately the patterns employed by the assumptions that the actors are maximising; and (7) the details of the adaptive process are complex and probably actor- and situation-specific.

By contrast, the regularities associated with optimisation equilibrium are comparatively simple; considerations of parsimony, therefore, dictate that the way to progress in economic understanding is to explore these regularities theoretically, and to compare the results with other observations. A fundamental assumption is that those who behave in a rational manner will survive, and those who do not will fail; and that therefore in an evolutionary, competitive situation the behaviour that will be continuously observed will be that of people who have acted according to such standards.

To explore the deficiencies of the rational choice approach as it relates to institutions we must delve into two particular aspects of human behaviour: (1) motivation and (2) deciphering the environment. Human behaviour appears to be more complex than that embodied in the individual utility function of economists' models. For example, our behaviour can be inspired by altruism. This is, among others, a facet of utility maximisation in which we get utility from the well-being of others. Thus we can build more elaborate models of complex human behaviour within the individual expected utility model, incorporating certain aspects of altruism. Research in experimental economics and a number of studies by psychologists point out that issues of free-riding, fairness and justice enter the utility function, and do not necessarily fit neatly with the maximising postulates in the narrow sense as described.

The evidence we have with respect to ideologies, altruisms and self-imposed standards of conduct suggests that the trade-off between wealth and these other values is a negatively sloped function. That is, where the price one pays for expressing one's own ideology, or norms, or preferences is extremely high, they will account much less for human behaviour than in the case when the price paid is low. Given this, North demonstrates that institutions basically alter the price individuals pay and this hence leads to ideas, ideologies and dogmas frequently playing a major role in the choices individuals make.

As regards the environment, the more complex and unique the issues we confront, the more uncertain the outcome. Subjective and incomplete processing of information plays a critical role in decision-making. It accounts for ideology, based upon subjective perceptions of reality, which plays a major part in human beings' choice. It brings into play the complexity and incompleteness of our information. It focuses on the need to develop regularised patterns of human interaction in the face of such complexities, and it suggests that these regularised interactions—which we call institutions—may be very inadequate or very far from optimal.

The behavioural assumptions of economists are useful for solving certain problems. However, they are inadequate to deal with many issues confronting social scientists and are the fundamental stumbling block to understanding of the existence, formation and evolution of institutions.

Institutions exist to reduce the uncertainties involved in human interaction. These uncertainties arise as a consequence of both the complexity of the problems to be solved and the problem-solving 'software' possessed by the individual. Uncertainties arise from incomplete information with respect to the behaviour of other individuals in the process of human interaction. The institutional framework limits the choice of individuals by structuring human interaction.

A Transaction-Cost Theory of Exchange

The costliness of information is the key to the costs of transacting, which consist of the cost of measuring the valuable attributes of what is being exchanged and the cost of protecting rights, policing and enforcing agreements. These measurement and enforcing costs are the sources of social, political and economic institutions. The classic economists didn't take into account the costliness of the exchange process. An exchange process involving transaction costs suggests significant modifications in economic theory and very different implications for economic performance. The resources of the economy consumed in transacting are of considerable magnitude and growing. As noted, transaction costs in the US amounted to 45 % of the national income in 1986. The cost of production is the sum of transformation and transaction costs.

Ronald Coase made clear that only in the absence of transaction costs did the neoclassical paradigm yield the implied allocative results; with positive transaction costs, resource allocations are altered by property rights structures. The transaction costs reflect the uncertainty by including a risk premium, the magnitude of which will reflect the likelihood of defection by the other party and the consequent cost to the first party. Throughout history the size of this premium has largely foreclosed complex exchanges, thereby limiting the possibilities of economic growth.

Institutions provide the structure for exchange and, together with the technology employed, determine the cost of transacting and the cost of transformation. Exchange in modern economies, consisting of many variable attributes extending over long periods of time, necessitates institutional reliability, which has only gradually emerged in Western economies. The kind of exchange that has characterised most of economic history has been personalised exchange, involving small-scale production and local trade. Under such conditions transaction costs are low. However, because specialisation and division of labour is rudimentary, transformation costs are high.

As the size and scope of exchange have increased, the parties have attempted to personalise exchange. But the greater the variety and number of exchanges, the more complex the kinds of agreements are, and, therefore, the more difficult to execute. As a result, a second general pattern of exchange evolved: impersonal exchange, in which the parties are constrained by kinship ties, bonding, exchanging hostages or merchant codes of conduct. They permitted a widening of the market and the realisation of the gains of more complex production and exchange. In early modern Europe these institutions led to an increasing role of the state in protecting merchants and to the adoption of merchant codes as the revenue potential of such fiscal activities increased.

The third form of exchange is impersonal exchange with third-party enforcement. It has been the critical underpinning of successful modern economies involved in the complex contracting necessary for modern economic growth. To develop a model of institutions, we must explore in depth the structural characteristics of informal constraints, formal rules and enforcement, as well as the way in which they evolve.

Informal Constraints

In all societies, from the most primitive to the most advanced, people impose constraints upon themselves to give a structure to their relations with others. Informal constraints come from socially transmitted information and are part of the heritage that we call culture. And culture can be defined as the transmission, from one generation to the next, via teaching and imitation, of knowledge, values and other factors that influence behaviour. Culture provides a language-based conceptual framework for encoding and interpreting the information that the senses are presenting to the brain. In this chapter the emphasis is on the way the cultural filter provides continuity so that the informal solution to exchange problems in the past carries over into the present and makes those informal constraints important sources of continuity in long-term societal change.

Informal constraints are pervasive features of modern economies as well. But how do we explain the emergence and persistence of informal constraints? One explanation is conventions that solve coordination problems. They are rules that have never been consciously designed and that are in everyone's interest to keep. A convention acquires moral force when almost everyone in the community follows it. In the short run, culture defines the way individuals process and utilise information and, thereby, affects the way informal constraints become institutionalised. Conventions are culture-specific, as are norms.

The striking decline in interest rates in the Dutch capital market in the seventeenth century, and in the English capital market in the early eighteenth century, provides evidence of the increasing security of property rights as a consequence of the effective interaction of a variety of both formal and informal institutional constraints.

It is impossible to make sense out of history (or contemporary economics) without recognising the central role that subjective preferences play in the context of formal institutional constraints that enable us to express our convictions at zero or very little cost. Ideas, organised ideologies and even religious zealotry play major roles in shaping society and economies. The long-term implications of cultural processing of information that underlies informal constraints is that it plays an important role in the incremental way in which institutions evolve and, hence, is a source of path dependence. Informal constraints that are culturally derived will not change immediately in reaction to changes in the formal rules. Tensions between altered formal rules and the persisting informal constraints produce outcomes that have important implications for the way economies change.

Formal Constraints

The difference between formal and informal constraints is one of degree. Formal rules can complement and increase the effectiveness of informal constraints. They may lower information, monitoring and enforcement costs and, hence, make informal constraints possible solutions to more complex exchange. Formal rules may also be enacted to modify, revise or replace informal constraints. A change in the bargaining power of parties may lead to an effective demand for a different institutional framework for exchange, but the informal constraints stand in the way of accomplishing it.

Formal rules include political and judicial rules, economic rules and contracts. Political rules broadly define the hierarchical structure of the polity, its basic decision structure and the explicit characteristics of agenda control. Economic rules define property rights, that is, the bundle of rights over the use and the income to be derived from property and the ability to alienate an asset or a resource. Contracts contain the provisions specific to a particular agreement in exchange.

Broadly speaking, political rules in place lead to economic rules, though the causality runs both ways. That is, property rights and individual contracts are specified and enforced by political decision-making, but the structure of economic interests will also influence the political structure. Changes in one will include changes in the other.

The simplest model of a polity is made up of a ruler and constituents. The ruler acts like a discriminating monopolist, offering to different groups of constituents protection and justice, or at least the reduction of internal disorder and the protection of property rights, in return for tax revenues. A democratic government gives a greater percentage of the population access to the political decision-making process, eliminates capricious capacity of a ruler to confiscate wealth and develops third-party enforcement of contracts with an independent judiciary. The result is a move towards greater political efficiency. Formal political rules, like formal economic rules, are designed to facilitate exchange. However, democracy in the polity is not equated with competitive markets in the economy. The distinction is important with respect to the efficiency of property rights.

Changes in the relative prices, or relative scarcities of any kind, lead to the creation of property rights when it becomes worthwhile to incur the costs of devising such rights. The efficiency of the political market is the key to this issue. If political transaction costs are low and the political actors have accurate models to guide them, then efficient property rights will result. But the high transaction costs of political markets and subjective perceptions of the actors more often have resulted in property rights that don't induce economic growth, and the consequent organisations may have no incentive to create more productive economic rules.

Looking only at the formal rules themselves gives us an inadequate and frequently misleading notion about the relationship between formal constraints and performance.

Enforcement

There are two reasons why enforcement is typically imperfect. The first has to do with the cost of measuring the multiple margins that constitute contract performance. The second rests in the fact that enforcement is undertaken by agents whose own utility functions influence outcomes.

Trade exists, even in stateless societies. Yet, the inability of societies to develop effective, low-cost enforcement of contracts is the most important source of both historical stagnation and underdevelopment in the Third World.

No institutions are needed in a world of complete information. With incomplete information, however, cooperative solutions will break down unless institutions are created that provide sufficient information for individuals to police deviations. There are immense scale economies in policing and enforcing agreements by a polity that acts as a third party and uses coercion to enforce agreements. But therein lies the fundamental dilemma of economic development. If we cannot do without the state, we cannot do with it either. The question then is, How does one get the state to behave like an impartial third party? There is a large difference in the degree to which we can rely upon contract enforcement between developed countries and Third World countries.

Third-party enforcement means the development of the state as a coercive force able to monitor property rights and enforce contracts effectively, but no one at this stage knows how to create such an entity. How does one create self-enforcing constraints in conduct? Part of the answer is that creating a system of effective enforcement and of moral constraints on behaviour is a long process that requires time to develop if it is to evolve.

Institutions and Transaction and Transformation Costs

It takes resources to define and protect property rights and to enforce agreements. As noted, institutions—together with the technology employed—determine transaction costs. It takes resources to transform inputs of land, labour and capital into the output of goods and services. That transformation is a function not only of the technology employed but also of institutions. Therefore, institutions play a key role in the cost of production. The relationships between rights and constraints in an exchange can be illustrated at three levels: (1) the level of a single straightforward exchange, (2) in a more complex relationship involved in the production process and (3) at the level of the economy as a whole.

As for the straightforward exchange, it is worth emphasising that uncertainties with respect to the security of rights are a critical distinction between the relatively efficient markets of high-income countries today and economies in the past, as well as those in the Third World today.

What about the relationship between institutions and transaction costs involved in the production of goods and services? We have only to contrast the organisation of production in a Third World country with that in an advanced economy to be impressed by the consequences of poorly defined and/or ineffective property rights. Not only will the institutional framework result in higher costs of transacting in the former, but insecure property rights will result in using technologies that employ little fixed capital and do not entail long-term agreements. Firms will typically be small. Moreover, such mundane problems as an inability to get spare parts, or a 2-year wait for a telephone line, will necessitate a different organisation of production than an advanced country requires.

The institutional structure in the Third World lacks the formal structure that underpins efficient markets. However, frequently in the Third World informal sectors exist that attempt to provide a structure for exchange. Such a structure comes at a high cost because the lack of formal property-right safeguards restricts activity to personalised exchange systems that can provide self-enforcing types of contracts. In addition, the institutional framework which determines this basic structure of production tends to perpetuate underdevelopment. Large firms with substantial fixed capital will exist only under the umbrella of government protection with subsidies, tariff protection and pay-offs to the polity—a mixture hardly conducive to productive efficiency.

The most important moral to be drawn from this chapter is that the institutional framework plays a major role in the performance of an economy.

Part II: Institutional Change

Organisations, Learning and Institutional Change

As Coase proposed, transaction costs are the basis for the existence of the firm. North focused on organisations as purposive entities designed by their creators to maximise wealth, income or other objectives defined by the opportunities afforded by the institutional structure of society. In the course of pursuing these objectives, organisations incrementally alter the institutional structure. They are not necessarily socially productive. Organisations are designed to further the objectives of their creators.

The incentives to acquire pure knowledge are affected not only by the structure of monetary rewards and punishments, but also by a society's tolerance of its development. A major factor in the development of Western Europe was the gradual perception of the utility of research in pure science. In the conversion of pure to applied knowledge, four points have to be noted: (1) in the absence of property-rights incentives, the size of the market was the most important single determinant of the rate of growth of innovation and technological change; (2) the development of an incentive structure through patent laws, trade secret laws and other laws raised the rate of return on innovation and also led to the development of the invention industry and its integration into the way economies evolved in the Western world; (3) the relationship between pure and applied knowledge is not a simple one. Pure knowledge is a prerequisite of applied knowledge, but developments of applied knowledge have opened up and suggested issues that should be further explored; and (4) the development of technology illuminates the path-dependent character of the way in which technologies change. Once technology develops along a particular path, given increasing returns, alternative paths and alternative technologies may be shunted aside and ignored, hence development may be entirely down a particular path.

The only function of management in the neoclassical form is to select profit-maximising quantities of outputs and inputs, which means determining the quantity and the consequent price that will be established. Because information for doing this is also freely at hand and the calculations are costless, the model strips from management any meaningful productivity in the performance of even those tasks.

This neoclassical approach came under critical evaluation, among others by Ronald Coase, who began to redirect the attention of economists looking at organisations. Coase introduced the concept of transaction costs, which began to make sense for the existence of the firm. In fact, the real tasks of management are to devise and discover markets, to evaluate products and product techniques, and to manage actively the actions of employees. These are all tasks in which there is uncertainty and in which investment in information must be acquired. The kinds of information the entrepreneur requires are a consequence of a particular institutional context.

Therefore, we need to examine the institutional context to see what kind of demand exists for different kinds of knowledge and skills. North gave the example of pirates: successful pirates will acquire the knowledge of naval warfare, trade routes of commercial shipping and the market for booty. He also gave a modern example of a chemical manufacturer. He requires knowledge of chemistry, potential uses of chemicals in different intermediate and final products, markets and problems of large-scale organisation. Successful chemical manufacturers give rise to a demand for both applied and pure chemical research as well as the study of markets and new forms of organisation to reduce production and transaction costs. These examples provide insight into the very different development of knowledge and skills. They typify much of economic history. The incentives that are built into the institutional framework play the decisive role in shaping the kinds of skills and knowledge that pay off.

It is the institutional framework that will shape the direction of the acquisition of knowledge and skills and, furthermore, that direction will be the decisive factor for the long-term development of a society. The USA has institutions that apply restrictions on output, make-work and crime, just as the country has institutions that reward productive economic activity. On balance, the latter have outweighed the former, but they have not done so through most of human history nor do they in many Third World countries today.

Maximising behaviour of economic organisations, therefore, shapes institutional change by: (1) the resultant derived demand for investment in knowledge of all kinds; (2) the ongoing interaction between organised economic activity; and (3) incremental alteration of the informal constraints as a by-product of maximising activities of organisations.

There are scholars who explore the most efficient governance structure and organisation within the existing institutional constraints. But an alternative is to devote resources to changing the institutional constraints. North concentrated on the incremental process of change that will result from the interaction between the economy and the polity. Organisations will also encourage society to invest in the kinds of skills and knowledge that indirectly contribute to their profitability. Such investment will shape the long-term growth of skills and knowledge, which are the underlying determinants of economic growth.

North illustrated this with an example from US history: the perceived rewards to increased knowledge and education in the nineteenth century induced public and private investment in formal education, on-the-job training and applied research, both in agricultural and industrial activities. The result was not only the gradual transformation of the economic organisations but also the evolving perceptions of politicians and voters of the value of such investment. The overall result reinforced the initial perception of the complementarity between economic performance and investment in the growth and dissemination of knowledge.

Throughout most history the institutional incentives to invest in productive knowledge have been largely absent. In Third World economies today the incentives are frequently misdirected. Why is there such a contrast with the US story? If the private market had been efficient, then the correct investment would have occurred through voluntary organisations. But if the market was imperfect so that the private rates of return were as low as not to make such private investment worthwhile, then the correct investment could have been undertaken by public investment, assuming members of the society appreciated that there was a large social rate of return on such investment. But the fact that such public investment was not undertaken suggests not only high transaction costs resulting in imperfect markets, but also that imperfect knowledge and understanding make up the subjective models of the actors.

In allocative efficiency, the standard neoclassical Pareto conditions obtain. Adaptive efficiency, on the other hand, is concerned with the kinds of rules that shape the way an economy evolves through time. It is also concerned with the willingness of a society to acquire knowledge and learning, to induce innovation, to undertake risk and creative activity of all sorts, as well as to resolve problems and bottlenecks of the society through time. The incentives embedded in the institutional framework direct the process of learning by doing and the development of tacit knowledge[11] that will lead individuals in decision-making processes to gradually evolve systems that are different from the ones that they had to begin with. A society that permits the maximum generation of trials will be most likely to solve problems through time. Adaptive efficiency, therefore, provides the incentives to encourage the development of

---

[11] Tacit knowledge, coined by Michael Polanyi, is acquired in part by practice and can only be partly communicated, unlike communicable knowledge. Different individuals have different innate abilities for acquiring tacit knowledge.

decentralised decision-making processes that will allow societies to maximise the efforts required to explore alternative ways of solving problems.

Competition, decentralised decision-making and well-specified contracts of property rights, as well as bankruptcy laws, are crucial to effective organisation. It is essential to have rules that eliminate failed economic and political organisations. The effective structure of rules, therefore, not only rewards success, but also vetoes the survival of maladapted parts of the organisational structure, which means that effective rules will dissolve unsuccessful efforts as well as promote successful efforts. North concluded that we are far from understanding how to achieve adaptively efficient economies because allocative efficiency and adaptive efficiency may not always be consistent. The very nature of the political process encourages the growth of constraints that favour today's influential bargaining group. But adaptively efficient institutional frameworks have existed, and do exist, just as adaptive inefficient frameworks have existed and do exist.

Stability and Institutional Change

The agent of change is the individual entrepreneur responding to the incentives embodied in the institutional framework. The sources of change are changing relative prices or preferences. The process of change is an incremental one. Change typically consists of marginal adjustments to the complex of rules, norms and enforcement that constitute the institutional framework. The overall stability of an institutional framework makes complex exchange possible across both time and space.

Relative price changes alter the incentives of individuals in human interaction; the only other source of such change is change in tastes. The process by which the entrepreneur acquires skills and knowledge is going to change relative prices by changing perceived costs of measurement and enforcement and by altering perceived costs and benefits of new bargains and contracts. We know very little about the sources of changing preferences or tastes. Changing prices may play some role in changes in taste.

Improved understanding of institutional change requires greater understanding than we now possess of what makes ideas and ideologies catch hold. Therefore, we are still at a loss to define, in very precise terms, the interplay between changes in relative prices, the ideas and ideologies that form people's perceptions, and the roles that the two play in inducing changes in institutions.

The process of institutional change can be described as follows: a change in relative prices leads one or both parties to an exchange, whether it is political or economic, to perceive that either or both could do better with an altered agreement or contract. Missing from this outline is the chief actor: informal constraints. Although changes in informal constraints, norms of behaviour, may very well evolve without any specific purposive activity by individuals or organisations, changes in formal rules and/or enforcement will usually require substantial resources or, at the very least, overcoming the free-rider problem. A major role of informal constraints is to modify, supplement or extend formal rules. A change in formal rules or their enforcement will result in a disequilibrium situation, because what makes up a stable-choice theoretic context is the total package of formal and informal constraints and enforcement aspects. Usually, the norms (informal constraints) that have evolved to supplement formal rules persist in periods of stability, but get overturned by new formal rules in periods of change.

The Path of Institutional Change

Two fundamental questions are: What determines the divergent patterns of evolution of societies, polities or economies over time? And, How do we account for the survival of economies with persistently poor performance over long periods of time?

Despite the immense decline in information costs and despite the implications of neoclassical international trade models that suggest convergence, there is still an enormous contrast between rich and poor economies. Now, what accounts for the survival of societies and economies that are characterised by persistent poor performance? If institutions existed in the zero transaction-cost framework, then history would not matter as a change in the relative process or preferences would induce an immediate restructuring of institutions to adjust efficiently. But if the process by which we arrive at today's institutions is relevant and constrains future choices, then not only does history matter but persistent poor performance and long-term divergent patterns of development stem from a common source.

There are two forces shaping the path of institutional change: increasing returns and imperfect markets characterised by significant transaction costs. With increasing returns institutions matter, as the interdependent web of an institutional matrix produces massive increasing returns. But if the markets are incomplete, the information feedback is fragmentary at best and transaction costs are significant, then the subjective models of actors modified both by very imperfect feedback and by ideology will shape the path. Then, not only can both divergent paths and persistently poor performance prevail, but also the historically derived perceptions of the actors shape the choices that they make.

North then described the story of institutional evolution occurring in Medieval and early modern Western Europe. The radical decline in population (as a result of the Black Death) in the fourteenth century altered the bargaining strength of peasants vis-à-vis lords and led to incremental alterations over time in the implicit contracts between them. Because competitive political forces and very slowly changing mental constructs of the status of both parties together produced more efficient outcomes, we tell it as a success story entitled, the Rise of the Western World. However, throughout most of history the experience of the agents and the ideologies of the actors, combined, did not lead to efficient outcomes.

The increasing returns characteristic of an initial set of institutions that provide disincentives to productive activity will create organisations and interest groups with a stake in the existing constraints. They will shape the polity in their interest. Such institutions provide incentives that may encourage military domination of the polity and economy, religious fanaticism, or plain, simple redistributive organisations, but they provide few rewards from increases in the stock of economically useful knowledge. As a result, the economy will evolve policies that reinforce the existing incentives and organisations.

What happens when a common set of rules is imposed on two different societies? North gave the example of the US Constitution which was adopted by many Latin American countries in the nineteenth century, and that of many of the property-rights laws of successful Western countries that have been adopted by Third World countries. Although the rules are the same, the enforcement mechanisms, the norms of behaviour and the subjective models of the actors are not. Hence, both the real incentive structures and the perceived consequences of policies will differ as well. Thus, a common imposition of a set of rules will lead to widely divergent outcomes in societies with different institutional arrangements.

North compared the evolution of North America and Latin America. In Britain, the Crown was losing power to Parliament. In North America the Navigation Act placed the colonies within the framework of overall British imperial policy. Yet, colonists were free to develop their own economy. British efforts to impose a very modest tax on colonial subjects, as well as to curb westward migration, produced a violent reaction. The subjective perception of many colonists was that the British navigation acts threatened the property of the colonies. This led to the Revolutionary War, the Declaration of Independence, the Articles of Confederation, the Northwest Ordinance and the Constitution. Yet although the revolution created the United States, post-revolutionary history is only intelligible in terms of continuity of informal and many formal institutional constraints carried over from before the revolution.

In the case of the Spanish Indies, conquest came at the precise time that the influence of the Castilian Cortes was declining; the conquerors imposed a uniform religion and a uniform bureaucratic administration on an already-existing agricultural society. Although efforts at reversing the centralised bureaucracy occurred under the Bourbons, the reversal was partial and quickly negated.

The control of agents was a persistent problem compounded by the efforts of the Creoles to take over the bureaucracy to pursue their own interests. The struggle for independence was imbued with the ideological overtones that stemmed from the US and French revolutions. As a consequence, independence brought US-inspired constitutions, but the results were radically different. In the case of Latin America, an alien set of rules was imposed on a long heritage of centralised bureaucratic controls and accompanying ideological perceptions of the issues. As a consequence, Latin American federal schemes and efforts at decentralisation did not work after the first few years of independence. The gradual reversion, country by country, to bureaucratic centralised control characterised

Latin America in the nineteenth and twentieth centuries. The persistence of the institutional pattern that had been imposed by Spain and Portugal continued to play a fundamental role in the evolution of Latin American policies and perceptions.

Technological and institutional change are the basic keys to societal and economic evolution and both exhibit the characteristics of path dependence. The increasing returns characteristics of the institutional matrix and the complementary subjective models of the players suggest that, although the specific short-run paths are unforeseeable, the overall direction in the long run is both more predictable and more difficult to reverse.

Part III: Economic Performance

Institutions, Economic Theory and Economic Performance

We cannot see, feel, touch or even measure institutions; they are the constructs of the human mind. Yet they play a very important role in society. They are the underlying determinants of the long-term performance of economies. If we are ever to construct a dynamic theory of change—something missing in mainstream economics and only very imperfectly dealt with in Marxian theory—it must be built on a model of institutional change. Although some of the pieces of the puzzle are still missing, the outline of the direction to be taken is clear. What follows will be dealing with: (1) a specification of what changes must be made in neoclassical theory to incorporate institutional analysis into that theory; (2) an outline of the implications for the static analysis of economic performance; and (3) an exploration of the implications of institutional analysis for the construction of a dynamic theory of long-term economic change.

The polity specifies and enforces the property rights of the economic marketplace. The characteristics of the political market are the essential key to understanding the imperfections of markets. What would make the political market approximate the zero transaction-cost model for efficient economic exchange? Legislation would be enacted which increased aggregate income in which the gainers would compensate losers at a transaction cost that is low enough to make it jointly worthwhile. The informational and institutional conditions necessary to realise such exchange are: (1) the affected parties must have the information and a correct model to know how the bill affects them and to know the amount of gains or losses they would incur; (2) the results can be communicated to their agent (the legislator) who will faithfully vote accordingly; (3) voters will be weighted by the aggregate net gains or losses so that the net result can be ascertained, and the losers appropriately compensated; and (4) this exchange can be accomplished at a low enough cost of transacting to make it worthwhile.

The institutional structure most favourable to approximating such conditions is a modern democratic society with universal suffrage. Vote trading, logrolling and the incentive of an incumbent's opponents to bring his or her deficiencies before constituents and hence reduce agency problems all contribute to better outcomes.

Agency theory has provided abundant, if controversial, evidence of the degree to which the legislator acts independently of constituent interests. And how often is there an incentive to compensate losers? There is a vast gap between better and efficient outcomes. It is necessary to emphasise two essential conditions that loom large, namely (1) the affected parties must both have the information and the correct model to accurately appraise the consequences and (2) all the affected parties must have equal access to the decision-making process. These conditions are not even approximately met in the most favourable institutional framework in all of history or in efficient political decision-making. Because polities make and enforce economic rules, it is not surprising that property rights are seldom efficient.

The consequences of institutions for contemporary economic analysis can be summarised as follows:

(1) economic (and political) models are specific to particular constellations of institutional constraints that vary radically both through time and cross-sectionally in different economies. Even more important, the specific institutional constraints dictate the margins at which organisations operate and, hence, make intelligible the interplay between the rules of the game and the behaviour of the actors.

Third World countries are poor because the institutional constraints define a set of pay-offs to political/economic activities that do not encourage productive activity.

(2) A self-conscious incorporation of institutions will force social scientists in general, and economists in particular, to question the behavioural models that underlie their disciplines and, as a consequence, to explore much more systematically the implications of the costly and imperfect processing of information for the consequent behaviour of the actors. The preoccupation with rational choice and efficient market hypotheses has blinded us to the implications of incomplete information and the complexity of environments and subjective perceptions of the external world that individuals hold. Social scientists would then understand not only why institutions exist, but also how they influence outcomes.

(3) Ideas and ideologies matter, and institutions play a major role in determining just how much they matter. Ideas and ideologies shape the subjective mental constructs that individuals use to interpret the world around them and make choices. A key characteristic of formal institutions is mechanisms, like voting systems in democracies or organisational structures in hierarchies, that enable individuals who are agents to express their own views and to have a very different impact upon outcomes than those implied in simple interest-group modelling that has characterised so much of economic and public-choice theory.

(4) The polity and economy are interlinked in any understanding of the performance of an economy and, therefore, we must develop a true political economy discipline. Modern macroeconomic theory, for example, will never resolve the problems that it confronts, unless its practitioners recognise that the decisions made by the political process critically affect the functioning of economies. This can be done by a modelling of the political-economic process that incorporates the specific institutions involved and the consequent structure of political and economic exchange.

Integrating institutional analysis into static neoclassical theory entails modifying the existing body of theory. But devising a model of economic change requires the construction of an entire theoretical framework, because no such model exists. Path dependence is key to an analytical understanding of long-term economic change.

The promise of this approach is that it extends the most constructive building blocks of neoclassical theory—both the scarcity/competition postulate and incentives as the driving force—but modifies that theory by incorporating incomplete information and subjective models of reality and the increasing returns characteristic of institutions. The result is an approach that offers the promise of connecting micro-level economic activity with the macro-level incentives provided by the institutional framework. The source of incremental change is the gains to be obtained by organisations and their entrepreneurs from acquiring skills, knowledge and information that will enhance their objectives. Path dependence comes from the increasing-returns mechanisms that reinforce the direction once on a given path. North described England's and Spain's evolution regarding their influence on, respectively, North America and Latin America's evolution, and concluded as follows:

> The divergent paths established by England and Spain in the New World have not converged despite the mediating factors of common ideological influences. In the former, an institutional framework has evolved that permits the complex impersonal exchange necessary to political stability and to capture the potential economic gains from modern technology. In the latter, personalistic relationships are still the key to much of the political and economic exchange. They are a consequence of an evolving institutional framework that produces neither political stability nor consistent realisation of the potential of modern technology.[12]

Stability and Change in Economic History

What combination of institutions permits capturing the gains from trade inherent in the standard neoclassical model at any moment of time? The argument advanced by North is that the current forms of political, economic and military organisation and their maximising directions are

---

[12] *Institutions, Institutional Change and Economic Performance*, 117.

derived from the opportunity set provided by the institutional structure that, in turn, evolved incrementally.

It all began with the simple exchange within the village or even with the simple exchange of hunting and gathering. Self-sufficiency is the rule. A small step is trade expansion beyond a single village, in which some small specialisation occurs. As the market extends to regional trade, it not only implies the growth of multilateral trade and the creation of specialised marketplaces, but it also sharply increases the number of trading partners. Then long-distance trade developed which entailed some substantial specialisation in the exchange process of individuals whose livelihood was confined to trading. It implies the early development of trading centres. Geographical specialisation begins to emerge as a major issue and some occupational specialisation occurs as well.

The next stage in the expansion of the market entails more specialised producers. Economies of scale emerge with full-time workers working either in a central place or in a sequential production process. Towns and some central cities emerge, and occupational distribution of the population now shows, although the population is predominantly agricultural. It also reflects a significant shift towards urbanisation of the society. In the present stage, specialisation has increased, agriculture is a small percentage of the labour force, and gigantic national and international markets characterise economies. The occupational distribution of the labour force gradually shifts from dominance by manufacturing to dominance by services. It is an overwhelmingly urban society.

This evolutionary process required institutions necessary to enable the cost of transacting and transforming to reach a level that permitted the increasing specialisation and division of labour to occur. As the size of markets grew, regional trade resulted in sharply higher transaction costs; hence, more resources were devoted to measurement and enforcement.

The creation of capital markets and the development of manufacturing firms with large amounts of fixed capital entailed some form of coercive political order. Secure property rights require political and juridical organisations that effectively and impartially enforce contracts across space and time. In the final stage, specialisation entails that increasing percentages of the resources of the society be engaged in transacting, so that the transaction sector accounts for a large percentage of GNP.

However, history demonstrates that there is not such a logical sequence in economic evolution. Some primitive forms of exchange still exist today. The beginning of long-distance trade initiated a sequel of more complex forms of organisation. It induced, through information costs, some economies of scale and the development of local enforcement of contracts. By examining in more depth primitive forms of exchange, and then Western European development, North focused on the contrasting forces that produced institutional and organisational stability in the first instance and dynamic economic exchange in the second.

Deviance and innovation are viewed as a threat to the group in primitive societies, as flouting of generally accepted standards is tantamount to a claim to illegitimate power and becomes part of the evidence against one. In the *suq* innovation is also seen as a threat to survival; yet it is hard to understand why these inefficient forms of bargaining in the *suq* would continue. Missing in the *suq* are the underpinnings of legal institutions and judicial enforcement that would make such voluntary organisations viable and profitable. In their absence, there is no incentive to alter the system.

In contrast, the history of long-distance trade in early modern Western Europe led to a rise of the Western World. Various innovations lowered transaction costs. These innovations occurred at three cost margins: (1) those that increased the mobility of capital, (2) those that lowered information costs and (3) those that spread risk. The mobility of capital was promoted by techniques that evaded usury laws. Also, the evolution of the bill of exchange promoted the mobility of capital.

A major development that lowered information costs was the printing of prices of various commodities as well as the printing of manuals that provided information about weights, measures, customs, brokerage fees and, in particular, the complex exchange rates between monies in Europe and the trading world. These developments were a function of the volume of international trade and, therefore, a consequence of economies of scale. The final innovation was the transformation of uncertainty of the cost of risk. Marine insurance was one example of the development of actuarial, ascertainable risk.

The specific innovations and particular institutional instruments evolved as a result of the interplay of two fundamental economic forces: (1) economies of scale associated with a growing volume of trade and

(2) the development of improved enforcement mechanisms that made possible the enforcement of contracts at lower costs. The gradual blending of the voluntaristic structure of enforcement of contracts via internal merchant organisations with enforcement by the state is an important part of the story of increasing the enforceability of contracts.

The evolution of capital markets was critically influenced by the policies of the state, because of the extent to which the state was bound by commitments that it would not confiscate assets or in any way use its coercive power to increase uncertainty in exchange. This made possible the evolution of financial institutions and the creation of more efficient capital markets. The shackling of the arbitrary behaviour of rulers and the development of impersonal rules that successfully bound both the state and voluntary organisations was a key part of this institutional transformation.

> It was in the Netherlands—and Amsterdam specifically—that these innovations and institutions were put together to create the predecessor of the efficient modern set of markets that made possible the growth of exchange and commerce. An open immigration policy attracted businessmen; efficient methods of financing long-distance trade were developed, as were capital markets and discounting methods in financial houses that lowered the costs of underwriting this trade. The development of techniques for spreading risk and transforming uncertainty in actuarial risks, the creation of large-scale markets that allowed for lowering the costs of information and the development of negotiable government indebtedness, all were part of this story.

The Netherlands and England were the carriers of institutional change. The characteristics of path dependence set within the context of the constraining initial conditions produced the divergent stories of England and Spain.

Incorporating Institutional Analysis into Economic History: Prospects and Puzzles

Incorporating institutions into history allows us to tell a much better story than we otherwise could; that is, to attempt to explain the diverse patterns of growth, stagnation and decay of societies over time, and to explore the way in which the frictions that are the consequences of human interaction produce widely divergent results. Karl Marx attempted to integrate technological change with institutional change. Marx's elaboration of the productive forces (by which he usually meant the state of technology) with the relations of production (he meant aspects of human organisation and particularly property rights) was a pioneering effort to integrate the limits and constraints of technology with those of human organisation.

Pre-cliometric economic historians placed technology on centre stage. The story of the Industrial Revolution as the great watershed in human history is built around a discontinuous rate of technological change occurring in the eighteenth century. Technology is the creator of human well-being and posits utopia to a simple story of increasing productive capacity.

What was left out of the analysis of productivity growth, developed by Simon Kuznets, Robert Solow and others, was why the productive potential wasn't realised in most countries. Neoclassical theory does not deal directly with the issues of growth itself. Recent neoclassical models of growth built around increasing returns and physical and human capital accumulation crucially depend upon the existence of an implicit incentive structure that drives the model.

What is yet to be undertaken is systematic empirical work that will identify the costs and underlying institutions that make economies unproductive. North concluded that then we will be in a position to ascertain the sources of these institutions. The analytical framework will have answered some of the questions raised in earlier chapters, and will offer the promise of answering unresolved ones.

North then drew some final conclusions: Bringing incentives up front puts the attention where it belongs: on the key to performance of economies. The central argument advanced in the foregoing chapters is that incentives have varied immensely over time and still do. Institutions determine the performance of economies, but what creates efficient institutions? The answer may be found in the informal constraints and the transaction costs inherent in the political process. Fundamental changes in relative prices will gradually alter norms and ideologies. The lower the costs of information are, the more rapid the alterations will be.

The political actor throughout history, as in the Third World and Eastern European polities, has been far less constrained by constituent interests. The key is the incentives facing the politicians that make some of the constituents—those willing to undertake change—more important than others. The political actor, then, is in the position of being able to initiate more radical change. One gets efficient institutions by a polity that has built-in incentives to create and enforce efficient property rights. But it is hard to model such a polity with wealth-maximising actors unconstrained by other considerations. Informal constraints matter. We need to know much more about culturally derived norms of behaviour and how they interact with formal rules to get better answers.

North ended his book as follows: 'We are just beginning the serious study of institutions. The promise is there. We may never have definite answers to all our questions. But we can do better.'[13]

---

[13] Ibid., 140.

7

The Great Recession

Introduction

It isn't entirely correct that economists did not see the Great Recession coming. Hyman Minsky predicted what happened in the build-up to the Great Recession, 22 years before the event, but no one listened. Another example: the 2005 annual economic policy symposium of the Federal Reserve Bank of Kansas City, held in Jackson Hole, Wyoming, was devoted to the lessons of the Greenspan era. Raghuram Rajan, then chief economist of the IMF (and now Governor of the Bank of India), said in his speech there that the financial system had taken on more risks than before, which exposed the system to large systematic shocks. Cheap money encourages banks and hedge funds to borrow more and place bigger bets. When credit would stop suddenly, this would do great damage to the economy; this is what Rajan said in Jackson Hole. He proved to be right a few years later, but when he delivered his speech in August 2005, the audience wasn't amused. Others may have issued warnings as well, but they were a minority and lacked the political clout to have impact.

John Cassidy wrote *How Markets Fail: The Logic of Economic Calamities* (2009). It is a comprehensive analysis of the Great Recession—the factors that made it happen and what was done about it. He put a large part of the blame on neoclassical economics (which he called utopian economics) for neither predicting nor preventing the Great Recession. Cassidy pitted utopian economics against reality-based economics that attempts to capture how an economy really functions and how human beings make economic choices.

How Markets Fail traces the rise and fall of free-market ideology, which is more than just a set of opinions: it is a well-developed and all-encompassing way of thinking about the world. The author presents a combination of a history of ideas, a sobering narrative of the financial crisis and a call to action. After all, one cannot comprehend recent events without taking into consideration the intellectual and historical context in which the events unfolded. Cassidy investigated the underlying economics of the crisis to explain how the rational pursuit of self-interest created and prolonged the crisis. This chapter includes a summary of *How Markets Fail*.

John Cassidy is a *New Yorker* staff-writer and a contributor to the *New York Review of Books*. He wrote *Dot.con: The Greatest Story Ever Told* (2002). Cassidy received his undergraduate education at University College, Oxford. He holds a master's degree in journalism and in economics from Columbia University and New York University, respectively. In writing *How Markets Fail* Cassidy drew on his vast knowledge of America's financial and stock-exchange markets.

How Markets Fail: The Logic of Economic Calamities

Introduction

Even in the summer of 2007, just before the collapse, the vast majority of analysts, including former Fed chairman Ben Bernanke, thought worries of a recession were greatly overblown.[1] However, in many parts

---

[1] The edition used of John Cassidy, *How Markets Fail: The Logic of Economic Calamities*, was published by Allen Lane (London) in 2009.

of America home prices had started falling and the number of families defaulting on their mortgages was rising sharply. But among economists there was still a deep faith in the vitality of American capitalism, and the ideals it represented.

For decades, economists had been insisting that the best way to ensure prosperity was to scale back government involvement and let the private sector take over. In the late 1970s this conservative counter-revolution was led by Ronald Reagan and Margaret Thatcher, inspired by the theories of Friedrich Hayek and Milton Friedman, both widely seen as representatives of—as Cassidy calls it—utopian economics. By the 1990s, Bill Clinton and Tony Blair, and other progressive politicians, had adopted the language of the Right. In America deregulation started out modestly, with the Carter Administration's abolition of restrictions on airline routes. In 1999, President Clinton signed into law the Financial Services Modernization Act, which allowed commercial and investment banks to combine and form vast financial supermarkets.

The generally accepted opinion was that no single firm could corner the market or determine the market price. In other words, Adam Smith's invisible hand of the market transmuted individual acts of selfishness into socially desirable collective outcomes. If this argument didn't contain an important element of truth, the conservative movement would not have enjoyed the success it did. Properly functioning markets reward hard work, innovation and the provision of well-made, affordable products. They punish firms and workers who supply overpriced or shoddy goods.

But to claim that free markets always generate good outcomes is to fall victim to the illusion of harmony. The period of conservative dominance lasted one decade—from 1997 to 2007. Even so, during this period there were three speculative bubbles: in technological stocks, real estate and in oil. But they were regarded as aberrations. Once bubbles begin, free markets can no longer be relied on to allocate resources sensibly and efficiently. By holding out the prospect of quick and effortless profits, they provide incentives for people and firms to act in ways that are individually rational but very damaging. The problem of distorted incentives is perhaps the most acute in financial markets. Market failure is not an intellectual curiosity. In many areas of the economy such as healthcare, high technology and finance, it is endemic.

For some reason, the economics of market failure has received minor attention. Reality-based economics is less unified than utopian economics because the modern economy is labyrinthine and complicated, and it encompasses many different theories, each applying to a particular market failure. These theories are not as general as the invisible hand, but they are more useful.

The emergence of reality-based economics can be traced to two sources. Within the orthodox economics, beginning in the late 1960s, a new generation of researchers began working on a number of topics that did not fit easily within the free-market model—information problems, monopoly power and herd behaviour. At about the same time, two experimental psychologists, Amos Tversky and Daniel Kahneman, were analysing rational economic man—*homo economicus*—and found that humans don't act in an economically rational way when faced with complicated choices. Human beings often rely on rules of thumb, or on our instinct, and we are greatly influenced by the actions of others. These new developments merged into behavioural economics. However, reality-based economics is broader than that.

Special attention is also devoted to the causes of the financial crisis and ensuing deep recession. New York bankers faced the so-called prisoner's dilemma: if they wouldn't have reacted as they did, their business would have been taken over by other bankers, and they would lose their job.

Part I: Utopian Economics

Warnings Ignored and the Conventional Wisdom

As early as 2002 some commentators, including the author, were saying that in many parts of the country real-estate values were losing touch with incomes. In June 2005 *The Economist* wrote that the worldwide rise in house prices was the biggest bubble in history. The 2005 annual economic policy symposium of the Federal Reserve Bank of Kansas City was devoted to the lessons of the Greenspan era. Raghuram Rajan, then chief economist of the IMF, warned that the risks that the financial system was taking on exposed it to large systematic shocks; that is, large shifts in asset prices or changes in aggregate liquidity. Since the returns are correlated with risks, there are perverse incentives for managers and firms to take even more risks. The tendency for investors and traders to ape each other's strategies (i.e. herding) was another destabilising factor. Taken together, incentive-based compensation and herding constitute a volatile combination. If herd behaviour moves asset prices away from fundamentals, the likelihood of large realignments—precisely the kind that trigger losses—increases. Low interest rates add to the volatility. Cheap money encourages banks and hedge funds to borrow more and place bigger bets. When followed by a 'sudden stop', great damage to the economy can be done. Rajan predicted what indeed happened a few years later.

Adam Smith's Invisible Hand

Market systems have proved to be durable for several reasons. In allowing individuals, firms and countries to specialise in what they are best at, they expand the economy's productive capacity. In providing incentives for investment and innovation, they facilitate a gradual rise in productivity and wages, which compound into improved living standards.

One of the first economists to put these arguments together was Scotsman Adam Smith. His great work *The Wealth of Nations* appeared in 1776. He invented the term the invisible hand, which to date remains central to any discussion of how markets operate. Smith described how specialisation, through the division of labour, greatly improves productivity and thus wealth.

The market system is efficient in that human and physical resources are directed to where they are most needed and prices are tied to costs. It is also self-correcting. If a shortage develops, prices rise and supply expands while, if a glut occurs, prices fall and production contracts until supply and demand come into balance. Each businessman is only interested in his own gain, and thereby promotes that of society; and does so more efficiently than if he were only intent on promoting society's gain.

As for the role of government, Smith felt that with a few exceptions, such as providing for national defence and making sure that laws are properly enforced, it should confine itself to clearing away outmoded conventions that prevent competitive markets from operating. Smith's economy is a self-regulating mechanism that stimulates technological innovation, satisfies human wants, minimises wasteful activity, polices rapacious businessmen and enriches the population. Most remarkable is that the system is fed by human selfishness. A well-known quotation from Smith is, 'It is not from the benevolence of the butcher, the brewer, or the baker that we expect our dinner, but from their regard to their own interest.'

Smith's opinion about the role of government is best expressed in his own words:

> Erecting and maintaining certain public works and certain public institutions, which it can never be for the interest of any individual, or small number of individuals, to erect or maintain, because the profit could never repay the expense of any individual or small number of individuals, though it may frequently do much more than repay it to a great society.

Economists in the classical tradition, such as David Ricardo and John Stuart Mill, were less dogmatic than some of their twentieth-century followers on the role of government. Within confines, they saw a legitimate role for government programmes. Smith and his successors believed that the government had a duty to protect the public from financial swindles and speculative panics. Mill traced most economic downturns to disturbances that emerged from the financial system, as—later—did Alfred Marshall in his classic *Principles of Economics* (1890). He wrote that reckless inflations of credit were the chief cause of economic malaise. The monetary authorities should prevent them.

The notion of financial markets as rational self-correcting mechanisms is a fairly recent notion. Before that (i.e. in the 1930s and 1940s) capitalism was seen to be floundering and many economists were wondering whether central planning wouldn't be a better option.

Friedrich Hayek's Telecommunications System

The Great Depression of the 1930s didn't do the laissez-faire, small government and low taxes philosophy of classical economists any favours. In America the industrial production had dramatically dropped and the unemployment rate had reached 25 % of the working population. Most economists agreed with John Maynard Keynes that the only way to prevent mass unemployment was for the government to manage the level of demand in the economy, through investing heavily in public works.

The Soviet Union and its satellites replaced the market by central planning and boasted that they had fully eradicated unemployment and mass poverty. When the Soviets launched their first satellite, Sputnik I, into the stratosphere, some observers concluded that the Communist empire had moved ahead of the United States in the race for military and economic domination. Even before WWII some economists tried to construct a middle way between laissez-faire and communism. They advocated market socialism, which would combine state ownership of major industries with a modified price system: the central planner would determine some prices, the free market others.

In such environments free-market economists were relegated to the role of preachers of an obscure sect. Two men stood out: Vienna-born Friedrich Hayek and Brooklyn-born Milton Friedman, who later would be the most prominent representative of the Chicago School of economists.

Hayek was influenced by his teacher Ludwig von Mises, a staunch free-marketer who in his *Socialism: An Economic and Sociological Analysis* (1922) dismissed collectivist planning as impractical. During the 1920s Hayek studied the causes of business cycles, formulating the view that slumps were the inevitable result of prior booms, during which growth had become unbalanced, with investment in industrial capacity outstripping the supply of savings. Recessions, in his view, were a way of restoring the balance between savings and investments.

This was not the view that Keynes and his young Cambridge pupils were developing, which held that it was a lack of overall demand in the economy that caused recession, and that the increase in government spending could restore prosperity. Keynes's views were adopted as the guiding policy framework by governments the world over.

Hayek and Keynes differed substantially as to what was to be done in addressing recessions. Even before the publication of *The General Theory* in 1936, Hayek had lambasted Keynes's *A Treatise on Money* in 1931, saying that the book lacked a proper theory of capital investment and interest rates. Keynes returned fire by describing Hayek's *Prices and Production* (1931) as one of the most 'frightful muddles' he had ever read.

Hayek was suspicious about collective planning. In the absence of genuine competition, how would the government know what prices to set and how would factory managers know which goods to produce and in what quantities? Hayek believed that many critics of the free market ignored the role it played in coordinating the actions of millions of individual consumers and firms, each with different wants and capabilities. As early as 1933, Hayek referred to the market as an immensely complicated mechanism that worked to solve problems. In 1937 he published a paper entitled 'Economics and Knowledge', which was the first appearance of his most lasting contribution to economics: the suggestion that market prices are primarily a means of collating and conveying information. Centralised systems may look attractive on paper but they can't deal with the 'division of knowledge' problem, which Hayek described as 'the really central problem of economics as a social science'.

The great advantage of organising production in a market system is that firms don't need to go out and ask consumers what things to manufacture and how many to make; prices transmit that information. Hayek introduced the metaphor of the market as a system of telecommunications. Markets work via transmission of price signals. He wrote, 'The most significant fact about the [market] system is the economy of knowledge with which it operates, or how little the individual participants need to know in order to be able to take the right action.' Later in life Hayek told an interviewer that the utilisation of knowledge was the basis of his economic *and* of his political views.

During WWII Hayek became concerned about the future of the free-market philosophy. He published *The Road to Serfdom* in 1944 in defence of the values of free-market liberalism. Hayek believed that the market was the only effective guarantor of individual freedom. He repeated his views on the inadequacy of planning, including its political implications. He wrote, 'Planning leads to dictatorship, because dictatorship is the most effective instrument of coercion and enforcement of ideals and, as such, essential if central planning on a large scale is to be possible.' Hayek didn't have the Soviet Union in mind. His concerns were the developments in Britain, France and other European democracies, and even the United

States, who were only a step away from totalitarianism. Hayek's views coincided with Schumpeter's *Capitalism, Socialism and Democracy* (1942).

Meanwhile preparations for the creation of a welfare state in Britain were underway, and President Roosevelt had created the New Deal well before WWII. Both didn't impinge upon the industrial and financial core of the free enterprise system. Hence, Hayek's interpretation of what was going on in the Western world was lopsided. He neglected to account for some serious flaws of the market system; not only in *The Road to Serfdom* but also in his other works. In the 1930s and 1940s it became glaringly obvious that ordinary people needed decent medical care, breathable air and money to retire on. The market had failed to provide these things. Why was that? Hayek did not provide an answer.

The Road to Serfdom was a smashing success in America. The Book-of-the-Month Club edition sold 600,000 copies. In Britain, where there was widespread support for the welfare state, the reception was lukewarm.

During the 1930s and 1940s Hayek had been teaching at the London School of Economics. His American success prompted him to decide to migrate to the United States. In 1950 he was offered a position at the University of Chicago. It was in Chicago that Hayek published *The Constitution of Liberty* in 1960, by many considered his finest work. When the Berlin Wall fell in 1989, he remarked to his son Laurence, 'I told you so.'

The Perfect Markets of Lausanne

How can we be sure that the price signals the market sends are the right ones? As long as each industry contains many competing suppliers, and firms aren't able to lower their unit costs merely by raising output, it can be mathematically demonstrated that a market clearing of set prices exists. Once these prices are posted, supply will equal demand in every industry, and no resources will be idle. At this equilibrium set of prices, labour, land and other inputs will be directed to their most productive uses. It won't be possible to produce more output. Moreover, it won't be possible to make anybody better off without making somebody else worse off. In short, competitive markets are efficient.

The branch of economics that generated these findings is known as the general equilibrium theory. An attractive aspect of this theory is its mathematical elegance. In the course of the nineteenth century some economists started to translate economics into mathematical terms. In Germany, Johann Heinrich von Thunen devised an equation for the rent that land yielded. And in France, Antoine Augustin Cournot invented a mathematical theory of monopoly and duopoly. In Britain, William Stanley Jevons, Francis Ysidro Edgeworth and Alfred Marshall began to apply the methods of calculus in a systematic fashion, developing models of how consumers and firms behave.

Leon Walras and Vilfredo Pareto, who both taught at the University of Lausanne, set out to create a coherent mathematical theory of the entire economy. Joseph Schumpeter, inspired by Walras's treatise *Elements of Pure Economics* (1884), called him the greatest of all economists. Walras developed the Theorem of Maximum Utility, or the 'marginal condition' as economists call it, meaning equality between the satisfaction of two people involved in barter-trading two items.

Walras recognised that individual markets cannot be studied in isolation, as they are all interconnected. For each industry in the economy Walras wrote down two equations: one for demand and one for supply. Then he asked if there was a set of prices that would satisfy the system of simultaneous equations. If such a solution existed, it would equate supply and demand in every market and that would result in a general equilibrium. After counting the number of equations in the system and showing that it was equal to the number of prices to be determined, Walras claimed that such a solution did indeed exist and was unique. So he concluded that the price system worked.

Pareto elaborated on Walras's Theorem of Maximum Utility, in that he realised that some people will fare better than others. How then do we decide which economic outcome is preferable? And, who gets to decide? But, how can one measure a person's happiness, especially compared to others? Pareto developed the Pareto-efficient situation, which means that in that particular situation it is impossible to make anybody better off without making somebody else worse off. However, Pareto failed to deal with issues of equality, as an economy can be Pareto-efficient even when some people are rolling in luxury while others are near starvation as long as the latter cannot be made better off without cutting into the pleasure of the rich.

Perhaps the best thing about free markets is that they enable people to make mutually advantageous deals. Some economists have argued that markets ensure that all such trades take place, which implies that every free-market outcome is Pareto-efficient. This idea is the first fundamental theorem of welfare economics. Pareto was the first economist to spell out that markets facilitate mutually advantageous trading.

Later, Abba Lerner and Oskar Lange, two leftist economists, were concerned with the question how to combine equity and efficiency. Lerner showed that in a competitive market the fear of rivals stealing their market would force firms to follow the efficient pricing rule. The profits firms make, which can be regarded as part of their production, should not exceed the level needed to pay their debtors and investors. To the extent that firms exchanged prices that exceeded their marginal costs, and made excess profits, they were exploiting monopoly power, which wasn't consistent with the Pareto-efficient situation.

Oskar Lange developed the mathematical conditions for Pareto-efficiency in a planned economy. It turned out to bear a remarkable similarity to the conditions for competitive equilibrium. Wages had to be set in proportion to the productivity of the workers and, as Lerner's paper stipulated, firms had to charge prices that covered their marginal costs, and consumers had to distribute their spending so they couldn't make themselves any happier by buying a bit less of one good and a bit more of another. Lange assumed, unlike Hayek, that the planner had at his disposal all the information he needed. There would be differences in a socialist planned economy. Much of the industry would be publicly owned, and any economic surplus would be distributed more equitably than they would be in a competitive system. A logical question would be if competition enforces the same rules of allocating resources, as in a rationally conducted socialist economy, why bother about socialism? Lange's answer was that capitalism fosters inequality and an assortment of other ills.

The Mathematics of Bliss

It was time to pull the different strands together regarding attempts to formalise the theory of the invisible hand. The American Alfred Cowles, a rich investor, established the Cowles Commission, which set itself the task to advance the scientific study and development of economic theory in its relation to mathematics and statistics. The Cowles Commission moved to the University of Chicago in 1936 and would stay there for the next 20 years.

Kenneth Arrow, who at the time was a research associate at the Cowles Commission, turned his mind to the thorny issue of general equilibrium. In 1950 he presented a paper in which he proved that competitive equilibriums are also Pareto-efficient: at the equilibrium prices the market will deploy the economy's resources in such a way that it is impossible to make a single person better off without making somebody else worse off. Arrow's result became known as the first fundamental theorem of welfare economics. Arrow also dealt with the problem of equity. As long as the government redistributes resources in an appropriate manner—by taxing people and giving lump-sum payments to others—society can select the specific Pareto-efficient solution it prefers, and the free market will generate the prices needed to support such an outcome. Not just one but any optimal point can be achieved by a suitable choice of prices under a competitive system. This result is the second fundamental theorem of welfare economics. This theorem suggests that a society can redistribute resources in a just manner and then rely on the market to ensure an efficient outcome.

But one big task remained: proving that there was a set of prices that equated supply and demand *throughout* the economy. If such a solution could *not* be found, then all of the work that had been done on general equilibrium theory would amount to nothing.

Arrow, now supported by Gerard Debreu, a French-born economist, had another go at the problem. The two presented a paper in 1952, entitled 'Existence of an Equilibrium for a Competitive Economy'. Its readers agreed that the Walras problem had finally been solved, and the case for competitive markets had been placed on a sound analytical foundation; at least so it seemed. However, the idea that general equilibrium amounts to a scientific endorsement of laissez-faire is a product of later popularisers. The theorists were perfectly open about the fact that their results depended on a number of restrictive assumptions, one being that economies of scale—the ability of firms to reduce their unit costs simply by ramping up production—are everywhere absent. But this isn't realistic. In real life the market outcome may very well be inefficient.

The answer to the question of whether general equilibrium theory can serve as a useful guide to policy is negative. Apart from the fact that the economy's equilibrium is not unique, there is the problem of time, which Arrow and Debreu didn't deal with. Furthermore, the theory of the invisible hand holds that markets are stable. But markets can behave in all sorts of ways. If a rise in demand generates more demand, markets can be prone to wild ups and downs of varying lengths and amplitudes, which mathematicians refer to as chaos. The axioms of individual rationality and perfect competition simply are not sufficient to determine what would happen. One should thus be suspicious of models which are always stable.

The Evangelist

To Milton Friedman the efficacy of free markets was self-evident. Friedman did more than anybody else to revive laissez-faire ideas. His *Capitalism and Freedom* (1962) and *Free to Choose* (1980), which he wrote with his wife Rose, furnished conservative politicians like Ronald Reagan and Margaret Thatcher with a consistent and well-articulated set of ideas and policy proposals.

Friedman made four major contributions to the rehabilitation of market economics. He championed cutting government programmes, reducing taxes and deregulating industries; he provided a revisionist explanation of the Great Depression, describing it as an example of government failure rather than market failure; he critiqued Keynesian demand management and supplied an alternative policy framework—monetarism; and reminded Americans of the connection that John Stuart Mill had stressed between economic and political freedom.

In many ways *Capitalism and Freedom* was an American version of Hayek's *The Road to Serfdom*. Friedman conceded that some government activities are required, such as national defence and law enforcement. But he questioned government's involvement in public projects such as highway construction and the provision of public education. He also felt that government's intervention in regulating the banking sector was unnecessary. In fact, he opposed almost all types of regulation, and his attitude towards government was one of unremitting scepticism. He insisted that the expansion of government posed a fundamental threat to America's civil liberties.

Arguably, the most urgent task facing conservatives in the post-WWII world was confronting the consensus that unregulated capitalism had failed during the global slump of the 1930s. Before laissez-faire policies could again be taken seriously, something else would have to be blamed for the Great Depression. Friedman's candidate was the Federal Reserve Board which had been mandated to stabilise the economy and prevent financial panics.

In 1963, Friedman, together with Anna Schwartz, published *A Monetary History of the United Sates*, wherein they argued that the real culprit of the Great Depression was a sharp decline in the country's money stock. Between the summer of 1929 and the spring of 1933, the total amount of currency in circulation and demand deposits at banks fell by almost a third. The authors said that if the Fed had pumped more money into the economy, disaster could have been avoided.

Friedman was well aware of the dangers that can arise in an unregulated financial system. For example, in *Capitalism and Freedom* he explained how a bank faced with demands for money from its depositors and creditors will put pressure on other banks by calling loans or selling investments or withdrawing deposits and that these other banks will in turn put pressure on still others. This is a succinct description of contagion.

Friedman argued that the best way to stabilise the financial sector, and indeed the entire economy, was not by beefing up regulation. Rather Congress should pass a law instructing the Fed to achieve a specified growth rate of the money stock—somewhere between 2 % and 5 % a year—and leave things at that. Targeting the money supply would both keep inflation in check and maintain economic stability—thus the doctrine of monetarism.

Friedman invented the term natural rate of unemployment, recognising that there would always be some people out of work. Now, if government brought unemployment down below its natural rate, workers would bid up wages and firms would raise prices. Economists believed that there was an inverse relationship between inflation and unemployment. But the experience of the 1970s demonstrated otherwise. Stagflation emerged: high inflation combined with unemployment. Keynesians didn't have an explanation for stagflation. Friedman did and he paved the way for the revival of conservative economics.

By the early 1990s the traditional distinction between monetarism and Keynesianism had been blurred. Many economists who were nominally associated with the Keynesian tradition were strong supporters of the free-market ideas that Friedman had devoted his life to espousing.

The Coin-Tossing View of Finance

What determined a country's prosperity was how effectively it mobilised its natural resources, the commitment it made to educate its workers and the fruits of its investments in science and technology. The financial system was merely a 'veil' covering the real economy. Monetarists and Keynesians shared this way of looking at things. However, economic development is a process of capital accumulation, and financial markets play a key role in distributing investment capital among competing projects. Hence if financial markets work properly, they help the economy to prosper.

The efficient market hypothesis, which Friedman's pupil Eugene Fama popularised, states that financial markets always generate the correct prices, taking into account all the available information. In short, financial prices are tied to economic fundamentals: they don't reflect any undue pessimism or 'irrational exuberance'. However, predicting what financial markets will do next is extremely difficult.

Louis Bachelier was the first person to write a theory of speculation in 1900. He concluded that investing in the markets is just like tossing a coin. The outcomes will be governed by luck rather than skill. Bachelier's findings are known by the term 'random walk'. Fama, who did his PhD on the behaviour of stock prices, pointed out that any analyst has a 50 % chance of being right, even if his powers of analysis are completely non-existent. Fama's key innovation was that the stock market was efficient, in the sense that prices reflected all the available information.

So, the efficient market hypothesis was up and running. Burton Malkiel, a Princeton economist, published in the late 1960s *A Random Walk Down Wall Street*, which became a bestseller, in which he showed that most Wall Street earnings forecasts were hopelessly off the mark and that most of the mutual funds failed to outperform the market.

Bachelier's insight was that daily movements in a stock in the course of time, reflected on a bar chart, would look like the famous Bell Curve. Hence most movements would be mild; and large ones, positive and negative, would be at both extremes of the curve. The likelihood of an extreme outcome was thus small. Cassidy asked, Is that not a measure of risk? It points to the possibility of designing a portfolio to minimise a big loss, or to maximise returns given a certain willingness to accept losses. So, risk can be managed scientifically, or so it appears. In the following three decades an enormous risk management industry developed.

However, as far back as the 1960s and 1970s, some academics and Wall Street practitioners didn't buy into the coin-tossing view of finance. Sanford Grossman and Joseph Stiglitz published a paper in 1975 in which they claimed that the efficient market hypothesis was based on a logical inconsistency. If stock prices at every moment reflected all of the available information about the economic outlook and other factors pertinent to individual companies, investors wouldn't have any incentive to search out information and process it. But if nobody finds and processes information, stock prices won't reflect that information, and the market won't be efficient. So, for the market to work at all there must be some level of inefficiency. Their paper didn't have much influence on Wall Street. Benoit Mandelbrot was another sceptic of the efficient market hypothesis. He studied cotton prices over the long term and concluded that the price pattern didn't look like a Bell Curve at all.

On Wall Street, the tendency for big moves to occur more often than the Bell Curve suggested (as demonstrated in Mandelbrot's research) became known as the phenomenon of 'fat tails'. Mandelbrot's data showed that markets are characterised by long periods of relative calm, during which prices don't move very much, interspersed with short periods of frantic activity, when prices zigzag dramatically. This pattern, which became known as 'volatility clustering', suggests that financial markets contain an element of predictability. However, it also raises the possibility that the causal relationships that determine market movements aren't fixed, but vary over time. Yet, the economics profession didn't exactly embrace Mandelbrot's criticism. By the 1980s, many MBA students were being taught that the efficient market hypothesis was a description of reality.

The Triumph of Utopian Economics

Robert Lucas did read Paul Samuelson's *Foundation of Economic Analysis* (1947) with appreciation. He said,

> I internalized its views that if I couldn't formulate a problem in economic theory mathematically, I didn't know what I was doing. I came to the position that mathematical analysis is not one of many ways of doing economic theory: it is the only way.[2]

However, there was one area that remained largely beyond the purview of rationality and individual choice—economic policy. In *The General Theory* (1936), Keynes had emphasised that the logic of individual behaviour often doesn't apply to the entire economy, as evidenced by the 'paradox of thrift'. To avoid this type of problem, Keynes focused on aggregate concepts such as the economy-wide level of consumption, investment and government spending. Using this macro-framework, he was able to explain how economies could get stuck in a depressed state, and—along the way—invented macroeconomics.

Some economists were uncomfortable with the failure to integrate the two sides of their subject, and Lucas was one of them. He was determined to develop Samuelson's idea of constructing theories from the ground up.

Lucas's idea was to assume that everybody knows exactly how the economy works. People aren't merely aware that unemployment is somehow linked to inflation, which is linked to interest rates: they all have the same (correct) mathematical model of the economy in their heads, which they use to form expectations of wages, prices and other variables. This is the 'rational expectations hypothesis'. Lucas could simply write down some equations to describe how workers, firms and the government behave,

---

[2] Cassidy, *How Markets Fail*, 98.

put a mathematical expectation operator in front of them and derive a solution that was consistent with the decision rules of everybody in the economy. But this wasn't realistic.

One of Lucas's predictions was that anticipated changes in monetary policy wouldn't have any impact on output or employment. Robert Barro, one of Lucas's followers, purported to show that changes in taxes, a favoured Keynesian practice, wouldn't be any more effective than changes in the money supply.

The economic framework Lucas used was the idealised general equilibrium world of Arrow and Debreu. Lucas assumed that all of the conditions necessary for the attainment of general equilibrium were satisfied and, further, that the equilibrium was unique and stable. In such a setup, supply always equals demand throughout the economy, which also means that unemployment is always at or close to Friedman's natural rate of unemployment. Lucas and his followers claimed that a slightly modified version of the Arrow–Debreu model could be used to represent reality. It is in this sense that Lucas adapted the efficient market hypothesis to the entire economy. However, in the world of Arrow–Debreu, firms are merely shells that react to market prices by transforming inputs into outputs. There is no room for innovation. There are no monopolists. Financial markets exist, but only in a very abstract form. People are assumed to plan ahead for every possible state of the world and make contingency plans for each of them. There is no place for stock market bubbles, banking crises or lending crunches. The typical ups and downs of a modern credit-driven economy are nowhere to be seen.

Although they had failed the test of reality, Lucas's theories remained extremely influential with academia. During the 1980s and 1990s his followers extended the rational expectations approach in various ways and marketed it under a new name: new classical economics. The high point was the construction of 'real business cycle' models of the economy, which retained the assumptions of individual optimisation and rational expectations, but added richer dynamics, such as random fluctuations in productivity growth. The empirical evidence has proved no kinder to real business-cycle theory than it was to the original rational expectation theory.

The rational expectation approach was just another incarnation of utopian economics. It relied on the ancient notion of the free-market economy as a stable self-equilibrating mechanism, and ignored many of the problems and pathologies that the history of capitalism had thrown up. In the middle of the twentieth century, the most important of these appeared to be mass unemployment: Keynesian economics was explicitly designed to prevent a repeat of the 1930s. During the 1970s, inflation emerged as a major problem, and the Keynesian models faltered, presenting the opportunity that Friedman, Lucas and others had been looking for.

Chicago School economics, and the ultimate expression in the form of the efficient market and rational expectations theories, could never have achieved the success it did if its promulgations hadn't coincided with a period of economic turmoil. Once the counter-revolution had taken place, history continued to run in favour of the heirs of Adam Smith. Following the steep recession of 1981–1982, the US economy went 25 years without entering another prolonged downturn. When things are going well, it is much easier to ignore inconvenient issues, such as rising inequality, chronic budget deficits, gaps in the healthcare system and the potential for financial instability. During his speech to the American Economic Association in 2003, Lucas concluded that macroeconomics in its original sense had succeeded: its central problem of depression-prevention had been solved, for all practical purposes, and had in fact been solved for many decades.

Part II: Reality-Based Economics

The Prof and the Polar Bear

In October 2006, Sir Nicholas Stern issued an official report on the economics of global warming which raised the spectre of major disruption to economic and social activity, later in this century and in the next, on a scale similar to those associated with the great wars and the economic depression of the first half of the past century. Polar bears setting out for the coast as a result of the shrinking ice cap illustrates climate change. And climate change, concluded Stern, presents a unique challenge for economists. It is the greatest and widest-ranging market failure ever seen.

The key to global warming and the source of market failure is the presence of something that economists call negative 'spillovers' or 'externalities'. For instance, when a power plant is burning coal, their polluting social costs diverge from the private costs involved in generating electricity. Stern concluded that it is not corrected through any institution or market, unless policy intervenes.

The first economist to examine spillovers in modern terms was Arthur Cecil Pigou (1877–1959), a prolific and somewhat tragic English scholar (he lived in the shadow of his contemporary Keynes) who, for many years, was the forgotten man of economics. Pigou helped to define a pragmatic middle ground between laissez-faire and collectivism. Pigou supported private enterprise and limited government. Still he believed that careful analysis of the economy revealed a number of areas where a policy of laissez-faire could not be justified. He said that even in the most advanced states there are failures and imperfections.

Pigou's greatest contribution was to take some of the failures and imperfections of the market and develop them into a systematic case for public intervention. The key step in his argument was the distinction between the private and social value of economic activity. Where the two differ, because of the presence of spillovers, markets can no longer ensure an ideal allocation of resources, and certain acts of interference with normal economic process may be expected not to diminish but to increase overall welfare.

From the point of view of society, what is needed is a balancing of social costs and social benefits. Free markets don't lead to such a balancing. Whenever spillovers are present, the prices that Hayek's supercomputer spits out reflect only private costs and benefits, and the overall outcome that the market economy produces is neither efficient nor socially desirable. Pigou advocated the use of taxes and subsidies to address the imbalances.

Ronald Coase, a British economist, who was teaching at the University of Chicago, was wondering in 1960 whether the presence of spillovers justified government intervention. He argued that the problem came down to an issue of conflicting property rights. For example, if a chemical factory releases noxious fumes into a nearby housing development, the factory's right to carry out its business is ranged against the right of the people who live nearby to breathe clean air. Providing that property rights were well specified and laws were enforced effectively, Coase argued, private bargaining between the affected parties would ensure an economically effective outcome. This is known as the Coase Theorem. To supporters of laissez-faire its appeal is obvious: if Coase was right and Pigou was wrong, there were solid grounds for questioning a whole litany of government policies. Many Chicago-leaning economists argue that the only policy necessary to deal with spillovers is the adequate formulation and enforcement of property rights. Coase himself acknowledged that when an activity inflicted harm on many different people, getting all the interested parties to agree on an efficient solution might be difficult and costly.

Global warming is just one of many damaging spillovers, and spillovers are just one of many types of market failures. Others include anticompetitive behaviour, the refusal of health insurers to offer insurance to some of those who need it most and the repeated emergence of speculative bubbles. In the early part of Pigou's *The Economics of Welfare* (1920) he compares economists to doctors who are interested in scientific knowledge of the healing which that knowledge may help to bring. To a doctor the key thing about treating a disease is not the elegance and internal consistency of the analysis, but whether the treatment he recommends works.

A Taxonomy of Failure

Francis Bator, emeritus Harvard professor, was the author of a couple of articles on the limits of free-market economics. In *The Anatomy of Market Failure* (1958) Bator examines the circumstances in which the theories of the free market didn't apply. He began by pointing out that the world is full of things that violate the assumptions of the Arrow–Debreu model: imperfect information, inertia and resistance to change, businessmen's desire for a quiet life, the vagaries of aggregate demand and so forth. Uncertainty and imperfect information are indeed fundamental features of any economy.

Even in a world of perfect foresight, Bator argued, there would be at least three other sources of market failure. One is monopoly or oligopoly power. The second is that businesses may have little incentive to produce some things that people value highly, such as bridges, hospitals and parks, because they can't charge enough for them to make it worthwhile. The third market failure which Bator mentioned was the phenomena of spillovers or 'externalities' (in fact, he invented the term). Bator's article had an impact on modern economic textbooks, in that they contain chapters on uncertainty, imperfect information, monopoly, public goods and spillovers, albeit by way of annexes to the main body, which is devoted to the classical free-market model. The subprime crisis started out as a micro failure but then it developed into a global recession. Slumps of this nature are obviously macro-level market failures, but they have their roots in uncertainty and coordination problems at the micro level, especially in the financial sector.

The role of the state has continued to expand, as John Kenneth Galbraith already noted in *The Affluent Society* (1958). A highly important public good that largely escaped the attention of economists until quite recently is scientific knowledge. Back in the 1950s Robert Solow, an MIT economist, calculated that between 1909 and 1949 technical progress accounted for about 51 % of the annual growth in America's GDP. In the early 1980s Paul Romer, a Stanford economist, turned his attention to the forces that drive technical change. Romer realised that knowledge is non-real and largely non-excludable, that is, once a piece of technical knowledge has been invented, preventing other firms from copying it is extremely difficult. The result being that the originators of new technologies often don't receive any benefits from them. Such knowledge is non-rivalrous and non-excludable and creates substantial problems for a market economy. As a result, market economies with competitive firms will be reluctant to produce enough research and development.

One way to tackle the problem is, of course, to strengthen patent rights; another option is government-funded scientific research. Giving universities and other publicly funded institutes the right to patent their inventions would create financial incentives for academic researchers to team up with businesses and venture capitalists. US universities have created more than 4500 companies and signed more than 40,000 licensing deals. This strategy signals that the key to creating a successful economy is finding a middle ground between laissez-faire and state control.

The Prisoner's Dilemma and Rational Irrationality

Rational irrationality one finds in a situation in which the application of rational self-interest in the market place leads to an inferior and socially irrational outcome. John von Neumann and Oskar Morgenstern invented game theory, which they explained in their *Theory of Games and Economic Behavior* (1944). Most of their methods applied were zero-sum games. But many types of economic activity, such as international trade and investing in the stock market, involve the possibility of cooperation and mutual gains—or positive-sum games. During the late 1940s, some progress was made in tackling this broader category when John Nash, a Princeton mathematician, introduced a general method for solving non-zero-sum games.

Robert Axelrod organised a prisoner's dilemma tournament to find out how the players would decide their choice. The outcome of repeated games was: cooperate in the first round and then in consecutive rounds, copy what your opponent did in the previous round. As long as the opponent cooperates, such a strategy can sustain cooperation indefinitely. Axelrod's findings have received a lot of attention, and they may well help to explain how cooperation is sustained in many areas of human society.

Regarding sustainability, the question becomes one of figuring out how to preserve the 'commons' for future generations, or, where that is not possible, how rapidly to deplete it. Free-market economists often argue that privatising common resources would ensure that they were used more responsibly. In some cases, this may be true—many historians believe that the enclosure of common lands in the fifteenth- and sixteenth-century England helped to raise agricultural productivity and stimulate economic growth. But privatising doesn't remove the conflict between private benefits and social benefits that defines the 'commons' problem. Specifying property rights may well be a necessary part of tackling these enormously complex issues, but blind reliance on self-interest and on the market is a recipe for further environmental catastrophes. The first step in preventing such an outcome is recognising the pervasive nature of rational irrationality and how difficult it is to overcome.

Hidden Information and the Market for Lemons

George Akerlof believed that a major reason why people preferred to buy a new car rather than a used one was their suspicion of the motives of the sellers of used cars. Horse traders and other dealers in second-hand goods of questionable quality have been dealing with this type of dilemma for centuries. Economists now refer to it as the problem of 'adverse selection', but 'hidden information' is equally accurate. Akerlof discovered that bad cars tend to drive out good ones. Why is that? It is because buyers won't buy the higher-priced good cars because they suspect that there may be something wrong with them. So, the good cars are taken off the market, while the bad ones remain. Akerlof wrote an article in 1967 about his findings, entitled 'The Market for Lemons: Quality Uncertainty and the Market Mechanism'. It is still one of the most widely referenced articles in all of economics.

The problem of hidden information arises in many areas other than the market for used cars. In the labour market, employers know much less about the skills and diligence of job applicants than the applicants themselves. In banking, lenders know less about borrowers' ability to repay their loans than borrowers do. In healthcare, the providers of medical insurance know less about the health of their customers than the customers do. This goes in fact for most markets.

Hidden information doesn't always prevent the market from operating. This is partly because of the product warranties and money-back guarantees. The point is that many free-market theories ignore this sort of problem. Hidden information creates market failures which only government intervention can correct. The American health insurance market has 'lemons' characteristics. The American healthcare system is chronically inefficient. Despite the fact that America spends roughly twice as much per person on healthcare than Canada, Britain and France, life expectancy in America is consistently lower than in those three countries.

Insurance removes the incentive on the part of individuals, patients and physicians to shop around for better hospitalisation and surgical care, said Kenneth Arrow in 1963 in an article in *The American Economic Review*. Economists now refer to the phenomenon of insurance changing people's behaviour as 'moral hazard'. Arrow concluded in an interview in 2005 on the argument about healthcare reform that it

> ... really comes down to the fact that the government is better than the private sector at keeping costs down for insurance purposes. This isn't true in any other industry. If, for example, you are trying to produce electronics, you could hardly do worse than the government to run such an industry. But, in an insurance program, it's a different matter.[3]

Orthodox economics cannot be applied to banks and other financial institutions. One example concerns the American savings and loans (S&L) scandal in the 1980s. President Reagan deregulated the S&L (also known as thrifts) industry, allowing them to offer higher interest rates and to expand their lending to riskier areas, such as commercial real estate junk bonds. At the same time the limit on insured deposits at S&Ls was raised from $40,000 to $100,000. It resulted in reckless lending, much of it related to the real estate boom and bust across the Sunbelt. By the mid-1980s, many of the thrifts were insolvent and should have been closed down. In 1989 Congress set up the Resolution Trust Corporation, giving it the power to take over troubled thrifts, fire their managers and sell their assets. More than 700S&Ls went out of business. None of the depositors lost money, but the total cost to the taxpayers of cleaning up the mess was about $125 billion.

In many ways, the S&L scandal was a rehearsal for the subprime crisis. The central causes of the two financial calamities were the same: a misguided faith in the free market, deregulation that was heavily influenced by industry lobbyists and the unsustainable real estate boom. The lesson that should have been learned is that orthodox economics cannot be applied to banks and other financial institutions. Even Adam Smith recognised that banking is different.

Joseph Stiglitz showed how information issues are key to many different types of market failure, such as unemployment, credit rationing and financial blow-ups. His key insight was that information is not, as Hayek suggested, fully revealed by market prices. Nor is it, as George Stigler and

---

[3] Ibid., 159.

other Chicago economists suggested, just another input to the productive process, akin to labour or capital. Information is more like air: Its adequate provision is a precondition for other things to happen. And when information is lacking, or hidden, the standard theories of economics, such as those of Arrow and Debreu, often don't apply.

By the late 1980s, the new paradigm of hidden information had been widely accepted in the economics profession. It complements and extends the older analysis of market failure provided by Pigou. In those areas of the economy devoted to the production of consumer goods and the provision of personal services, private enterprise does a highly effective job of providing what people want to buy. Generally speaking, where brand names and reputations are important, they can serve to mitigate some of the problems caused by hidden information. In many areas of the economy, however, the hidden information problem is acute.

Alan Greenspan acted as if he would have been happy to see the SEC and other regulatory agencies closed down, leaving Wall Street to its own devices. The reality economics that Akerlof, Stiglitz and others developed tells a different story. Yet, proposed government solutions to market failures need to be examined critically. There is no general theorem on which one can base the conclusion that markets are necessarily the most efficient way of allocating resources.

Keynes's Beauty Contest

John Maynard Keynes was a sceptic. He didn't believe in the corrective functioning of the market. He was of the opinion that investing and most economic activities are carried out on the basis of information that is limited and unreliable. He wrote that the market will be subject to waves of optimistic and pessimistic sentiment, which are unreasoning, and yet in a sense legitimate where no solid basis exists for a reasonable calculation. Keynes also gave short shrift to the Chicago idea that when prices of financial assets depart from economic fundamentals, professional speculators can be relied on to restore the correct prices. A more likely outcome, Keynes argued, was that they would add to mispricing. On Wall Street investing is a 'battle of wits', the primary aim being 'to outwit the crowd, and to pass the bad, or depreciating, half-crown to the other fellow'.

If at the first sign of an economic downturn people start saving more, the construction, automobile and hospitality industries will be forced to lay off workers. Unemployment will rise. People will become more concerned about the future and even more reluctant to spend. When these knock-on effects are taken into account, an initial rise in savings of, say, $100, can generate a fall in spending of $200 or $300. This is Keynes's famous multiplier, and it helps to explain how relatively small shocks to the economy can lead to recessions. In contemporary language, Keynes was pointing out that market economies are subject to positive feedback: downturns have a tendency to feed on themselves and get amplified, with the level of spending spiralling down. The only way to reverse the process is for somebody, somewhere, to spend more. Since consumers and firms are unwilling to do this, for reasons that make sense to them, the burden has to fall on the government, in the form of increased outlays in public works and other programmes. This is the central tenet of Keynesianism: the most reliable cure for a deep recession is a big government stimulus package.

In Keynes's time and today, some economists have argued that using fiscal policy is unnecessary because the central bank can cut interest rates and revive the economy that way. Keynes was dubious of this argument. When the economy enters a slump, he noted, people of wealth tend to flee from risky financial paper, such as stocks, switching their portfolios to cash. This rise in the propensity to hoard short-circuits the free-market recovery mechanism which involves a fall in interest rates and a rise in business and residential investment. Even if the central bank prints more money, the typical response to a downturn, people and businesses will simply hold on to the extra cash rather than spend it. The economy will get stuck in a 'liquidity trap', with further increases in the money supply having little or no impact on interest rates or spending. Keynes conceded that liquidity traps were rare, but he claimed that one had occurred in the United States during the financial crisis of 1932, when a large number of banks failed and scarcely anyone could be induced to part with holdings of money on any reasonable terms.

In switching the level of economic analysis from the individual to the economy as a whole, and in discrediting some extremely misleading free-market doctrines, Keynes made a major contribution not just to economics but to history.

Keynes said that 'animal spirits', or the spontaneous urge to action rather than inaction, play an important role in economic behaviour. Most people occupy the middle ground between rational and irrational behaviour; a realm of purposeful but constricted decision-making, of limited information, of action motivated by careful forethought and rules of thumb.

The Rational Herd

In 1990, David Scharfstein and Jeremy Stein published 'Herd Behaviour and Investment' in *The American Economic Review*. They said about this behaviour that 'The underlying idea is that if you do something dumb, but everybody is doing the same dumb thing at the same time, people won't think of you as stupid, and it won't be harmful to your reputation.'[4] It was the dot-com bubble which discredited the idea that rational investors would never invest in stocks they considered overvalued.

In the efficient market view of finance, speculators play a stabilising role, purchasing undervalued assets and selling short overvalued ones; it is this arbitrage activity that keeps prices tied to economic fundamentals and prevents bubbles from developing. During the dot-com era, though, speculators played a destabilising role, buying overvalued stocks and pushing prices farther and farther away from the fundamentals. The sight of sophisticated investors knowingly helping to pump up a bubble was doubly destructive to the efficient market hypothesis and to the Chicago project generally.

In the presence of naïve investors (aka noise traders), some of whom may react to rising prices by buying more stocks, selling overpriced stocks is risky. Instead of trying to counteract the activities of noise traders, and pushing prices back towards fundamental levels, it may well pay to trade alongside the noise traders. Rational arbitrage can stabilise security prices. Rather than bucking the trends, smart investors might rationally choose to jump on the bandwagon.

---

[4] Ibid., 177.

On a short-term basis—days, weeks or months—stocks do tend to follow trends: winners keep winning; losers keep losing. But over the long term (several years, say) the high fliers tend to fall back to earth, and 'the dogs get up and bark'. Statistically speaking, stocks display short-term momentum and long-term mean reversion.

Herd behaviour can be explained as the tendency to conformity being so strong that reasonably intelligent and well-meaning people are willing to call white black. Economists refer to the tendency to infer information from the actions of others as 'social learning'. Stock markets and other financial markets may adhere to economic fundamentals. However, it is more likely that they will be the subject of frequent bubbles and crashes.

Psychology Returns to Economics

In eighteenth- and nineteenth-century Britain, economics and psychology were two branches of the same subject: moral philosophy. Adam Smith was a moral philosopher. Prior to *The Wealth of Nations*, Smith published another well-known work: *The Theory of Moral Sentiments* (1759).

John Stuart Mill also demonstrated a keen interest in psychology. He put forward a theory of 'mental chemistry', which compared creative thinking to combining chemical elements in compounds. And Alfred Marshall discussed the impact of social conventions on the demand for prestige goods such as silk hats and big houses. Arthur Pigou iterated Smith's point that people prefer instant satisfaction to deferred pleasure, noting that 'our telescopic faculty is defective'.

It was in the aftermath of WWII that economists began to focus almost exclusively on the *homo economicus*, elevating rationality to a near-sacred principle. But Daniel Kahneman and Amos Tversky broke this rationality preoccupation. They studied how people choose between uncertain outcomes; a subject that economists regarded as having been settled in the 1940s, when John Von Neumann and Oskar Morgenstern put forward the expected utility hypothesis. According to their game theory, decision-makers weigh possible outcomes according to how likely they are. Kahneman and Tversky found that when people are faced with problems involving uncertain outcomes, most of them don't even attempt to do what von Neumann and Morgenstern proposed, but instead would fall back on rules of thumb (heuretics) and/or unsubstantiated beliefs. To the man in the street, this view of human behaviour might seem like merely acknowledging the obvious, but it challenged the very foundations of economics.

Confronted with a given piece of evidence or sample, people usually assume it is representative of reality. Kahneman and Tversky cited evidence that many of their fellow research psychologists had on occasion 'put too much faith in the results of small samples and grossly overestimated the replicability of such results'. Given the law of probability, extreme outcomes are much more likely to occur in small samples than in large ones, but even people familiar with statistics tend to ignore this fact. Once people are convinced that a small sample is representative of reality, they place unwarranted faith in their ability to forecast the future.

Another trap that people fall into is putting too much weight on their own experiences. If asked about the risk of having a heart attack, they answer differently depending on whether somebody they know has suffered a coronary. Another trap is that people often ignore the fact that outliers in one period—for example stocks—are likely to fall back into the pack during subsequent periods; a phenomenon known to statisticians as 'regression to the mean'.

Kahneman, Tversky and Richard Tahler, with whom the former two collaborated in the 1970s, laid the groundwork for behavioural economics. In 2002 Kahneman was awarded the Nobel Prize in Economics, being the first non-economist to receive it.

Often echoing the insights of Keynes and other economists of earlier generations, the best papers in behavioural economics start with a seemingly minor psychological quirk and examine how, in a competitive setting, it can scale up into a significant market failure. One example is the erstwhile popularity of takeovers. Many empirical studies indicate that they rarely deliver the financial benefits that bidders hope to reap. They are inspired by overconfidence on the part of top executives.

Evidently, economic reasoning is not something that comes naturally to people. Perhaps this is the way the human brain is wired. In recent years, many behavioural economists have adopted Plato's idea that human beings have two distinct decision-making systems: one is intuitive and the other deliberative. Kahneman elaborated on Plato's insight, by developing two systems of thinking, leading to yet another branch of specialised economics: neuro-economics, which studies two distinct patterns in the brain's function. When people are engaged in a complicated thought processes, such as working out a mathematical problem, most of the activity takes place in the prefrontal cortex, an area at the front of the brain that is much larger in humans than in animals. When people get excited or emotional, there is a lot more activity in the limbic region, which is located deep inside the brain.

The rise of behavioural economics and neuro-economics has presented a direct challenge to the concept of rationality that underpins much of economics. Some representatives of these new fields of research believe that the entire rational choice paradigm needs replacing. Others are more cautious. They say that it is just a recognition of the fact that decision-making is not always perfect: people try to do the best they can, but they sometimes make mistakes.

People are often subject to rival impulses. One part of the brain says that it is wise to save for one's retirement, the other part says that it is better to enjoy life now. At the same time, as Keynes emphasised, people's knowledge about the future is often limited. Even if they sit down and try to calculate all the pros and cons of a certain purchase or investment, the figures rarely give an unequivocal answer. In this sort of environment it is hardly surprising that rational irrationality is often the problem.

Hyman Minsky and Ponzi Finance

Minsky predicted the banking crisis of 2007/08 more than two decades before it occurred. Minsky was a Keynesian who taught for many years at Washington University in St Louis. He advanced the view that free-market capitalism is inherently unstable, and the primary source of its instability is the irresponsible actions of bankers, traders and other financial types. Minsky warned that it would be subject to periodic blow-ups, some of which could plunge the entire economy into lengthy recessions.

Although Keynes in *The General Theory* demonstrated how a free-market economy could get stuck in a slump, he didn't explain how booms and busts developed. His followers, such as Alvin Hansen and Paul Samuelson, also largely ignored this problem. Their brand of Keynesianism concerned itself mainly with exploring how monetary and fiscal policy could be used to stabilise the economy in the face of exogenous shocks. The mainstream Keynesian framework treated the financial sector in a cursory manner. It had no place for stock market bubbles or credit crunches. That was the gap that Minsky set out to fill. In 1986, he wrote *Stabilizing an Unstable Economy*, which went unnoticed at the time.

As the future is inherently uncertain, there is no way to predict if investments will lead to favourable outcomes. Therefore, Minsky pointed out, the expansion of the economy depends on the willingness of people and institutions with money to speculate on future cash flows and financial market conditions. In an economic upswing, borrowed money is easy to come by, investment spending rises and so do stock prices and corporate profits. This reinforces business demand for credit and the willingness of bankers and other lenders to supply.

Minsky stressed that this process doesn't depend on any external precipitating event, such as the invention of an exciting new technology. The primary incentive came from competitive forces at work within the financial sector. Any period of economic stability leads to an expansion of debt-financing; weak at first, but triggered by new financial assets it will lead to an investment boom. In other words—stability is destabilising. As the boom proceeds, competition between lenders increases, and their innate sense of caution diminishes. Many of them make loans to borrowers who can meet only the interest payments; repaying the principal would be beyond their means. Loans of this nature have to be rolled over at regular intervals. Eventually, banks start extending credit to people and firms that can't even afford to make regular interest payments. On each repayment date, the portion of the interest due gets added to the principal, meaning the longer the loan lasts, the more money they end up owing. Technically, loans with this feature are called negative amortisation loans. Minsky referred to them as 'Ponzi finance'. These types of loans are particularly prevalent in the real estate industry.

No credit boom lasts forever. At some point lenders get nervous about the dubious credit they extended. This prompts them to call back and restrict issuance of new ones. Where money was flowing freely, it is suddenly much harder to obtain, even for financially sound creditors. This is a 'Minsky moment'. And this is likely to lead to a collapse of asset values, as Minsky projected, which in turn can lead to a spiral of declining investment, declining profits and declining asset prices. Unless the financial authorities intervene, lending public money freely to whomever needs it will lead to traumatic debt deflation and deep depression.

Minsky wrote in his thesis that capitalist economies inevitably progress from conservative finance to reckless speculation. He called it the 'financial instability hypothesis'. He mentioned Keynes's General Theory, as well as Joseph Schumpeter for influencing his views. Although he didn't state it as such, Minsky's is a theory of rational irrationality, with the individual rational actions of banks and other financial institutions serving to destabilise the entire system. Capitalist financial processes have endogenous destabilising forces within them.

Apart from the government, banks are the only institutions in the economy with the ability to create money, and this is what makes them so important. The level of bank lending that makes sense for individual banks doesn't necessarily make sense for the country. Banks also borrow in a variety of ways. They issue long-term and short-term bonds; they take out overnight loans and occasionally they borrow from the Fed. While some of these loans are lent to individuals and businesses, the rest are invested in financial assets. If the returns a bank receives on its financial investments exceed its own borrowing costs, it makes money. Banks borrowed ever-larger percentages of money which they lent out. In technical terms this is called 'leveraging'. Minsky concluded that the increase in bank leverage ratios was part of the process that moved the economy towards financial fragility.

Another shortcoming in the traditional view of banking that Minsky highlighted was its failure to take adequate account of financial innovation. The recent key development was securitisation. With the development of a secondary market in mortgages and other types of credit, banks were able to sell many of the loans they made. The 'originate-to-distribute' model of banking gradually replaced the 'originate-to-hold' model. If a mortgage holder whose loan has been securitised falls behind on her monthly payments, it is the buyers of the mortgage securities who lose out rather than the bank that issued the loan. Securitisation enabled banks to move many of their loans off their balance sheets. This meant that they didn't have to keep as much capital in reserve to satisfy the regulators, which boosted their profits. They also set up special-purpose vehicles, also known as Structured Investment Vehicles (SIVs). Thus conceived, the so-called shadow banking system would grow to enormous proportions while remaining largely beyond the purview of regulators, bank stockholders and reporters.

At the beginning of this century almost half of the loans that US banks initiated had been transferred to nonbank entities, mostly through securitisation. The downside of this shift in the source of bank profits from interest earnings to originating and servicing fees was that bank loan officers did not worry as much about the creditworthiness of borrowers as long as there was a strong market for these loans. This is a strong incentive for bank loan officers to become loan pushers.

Minsky concluded in the early 1980s that countering financial instability was becoming a major task of economic policy. Between 1980 and 2000, financial industry profits rose from $32.4 billion to $195.8 billion, and the financial sector's share of all domestically produced profits went from 19 % to 29 %. In this type of economy the only way to prevent rampant instability is for the government to play a more active role. In addition to opposing efforts to weaken the financial statutes that had been created during the Great Depression, Minsky favoured much stricter supervision of financial institutions by the Fed; another idea that only became popular well after his death in 1996. Minsky argued that the Fed needs to guide the evolution of financial institutions by favouring stability-enhancing and discouraging instability-augmenting institutions and practices.

Part III: The Great Crunch

Greenspan Shrugs

The economic historian Charles P. Kindleberger divided the evolution of a typical bubble into five stages: displacement, boom, euphoria, peak and bust. The most recent displacement came in the form of a drastic reduction in interest rates. From a peak of 6.5 % in 2000, the Fed cut the federal funds rate to 1.25 % in November 2002. It went further down to 1 % in 2003; well below the inflation rate of 2 %. The result was a borrowing binge on the part of homeowners, consumers, businesses and speculators. The biggest rise in borrowing came in the financial sector, the equivalent of 117 % of GDP in 2007, creating a giant credit bubble. The Bank for International Settlements warned against the excessive leverage and risk-taking of American banks. The Fed chairman had fallen victim to disaster myopia and the illusion of stability. Greenspan's 18.5-year tenure at the Fed provides a classic confirmation of Minsky's financial instability hypothesis: the forces of leverage and financial innovation gradually built up until they were on the verge of overwhelming the system.

John Taylor, inventor of the Taylor Rule (an equation that shows what interest rate the Fed should set depending on the level of inflation and unemployment), was Undersecretary of the Treasury from 2001 to 2005. He held Greenspan responsible for the financial crisis. He said that the Fed caused it by deviating from historical precedents and principles for setting interest rates which had worked well for 20 years. Other critics of Greenspan pointed at his support for deregulation. It was the twinning of the two that was to prove so disastrous. In a modern economy with a large financial sector, the combination of cheap money and lax oversight, if maintained for years on end, is sure to lead to trouble. The gains of financial innovation and speculation are privatised, with the bulk of them going to a small group of wealthy people who sit at the apex of the system. Many of the losses are socialised, that is, the tax payers have to foot the bill.

The Lure of Real Estate

What was new about the real estate boom that ended in 2006 was its geographic spread from coast to coast. House prices started to appreciate at an unprecedented rate in the mid-1990s. Overall, between the end of 1996 and the end of 2006, average house prices nationwide rose by 129 %. In real estate bubbles particularly, monetary policy is key.

Low interest rates provide the helium that inflates the bubble. The majority of homebuyers were taking out adjustable-rate mortgages, which offered even lower fixed rates for a specified period. The boom was also promoted by the political body. The Clinton Administration introduced the National Home Ownership Strategy, which was aimed specifically at minority groups. Both the Clinton and Bush Administration pressed Fannie Mae and Freddie Mac, the two government-sponsored mortgage giants, to increase funding of home loans to middle-income and low-income borrowers.

Financial innovation was the second integral element of speculative bubbles. More home financing models came about—interest-only loans, stated-income loans and option ARMs. They had one aspect in common: a borrower could purchase a more expensive property than he would have been able to afford under the conditions of a conventional loan.

The primary driver of this deterioration in credit standards was the buoyant mortgage securitisation market. Rather than encouraging lenders to allocate capital wisely, the market was sending signals that greatly distorted their behaviour. If mortgage lenders had been forced to keep some of the loans they originated on their books, they would have been a lot more careful, but there was no such requirement. Companies who stuck to the old ways lost market share.

The third factor in speculative bubbles is crowd psychology. The spirit at the time was, If we don't buy now, prices will just keep going up and we will never be able to afford a house. And this spirit was underscored by reports of prestigious institutions, such as the Federal Reserve Bank of New York, which wrote in the spring of 2005, '[O]ur analysis reveals little evidence of a housing bubble. In high appreciation markets like San Francisco, Boston, and New York, current housing prices are not cheap, but our calculations do not reveal large price increases in excess of fundamentals'.

The Subprime Chain

The birth of the modern subprime industry can be dated to the 1980 passage of the Depository Institutions Deregulation and Monetary Control

Act, which allowed banks and thrifts to charge borrowers what rates they wanted. The Alternative Mortgage Transaction Parity Act of 1982 further loosened restrictions on lenders. The home loan industry got another boost in the Tax Reform Act of 1986, which eliminated the tax deduction for interest on consumers and car loans but kept it for mortgages. However, during the 1980s and 1990s most mortgage-issuing institutions did not lend to people with poor credit histories.

In the early 1990s a cheaper source of finance arrived in the form of warehouse loans from Wall Street banks that were entering the business of cobbling together subprime mortgages and transforming them into residential mortgage-backed securities (RMBSs) and collateralised debt obligations (CDOs). The securitising of prime mortgages was already a big business, since its introduction by Solomon Brothers in the 1970s.

This is how it works: investment banks lent money to mortgage companies at a rate of 6 % or 7 %. These companies passed the money on to subprime borrowers, charging them a substantially higher rate (10 % or more). Once the loan agreements had been signed, the mortgage company sold the loans to a Wall Street firm, often the same one that had extended the credit in the first place, for securitisation. As the Wall Street traders had predicted, hedge funds and other investors were eager to buy new subprime mortgage bonds, which were known as 'private label' mortgage-backed securities, to distinguish them from 'public label' mortgage bonds that had the backing of Fannie and Freddie. Politically this was an attractive model as people with limited means could now afford a house; at least that is what everybody thought. The first wave of defaults came in 1997/98 when subprime borrowers failed to honour their obligations. When the Fed slashed interest rates in 2001/02 the market for subprime mortgage securities bounced back.

In the old days, hard-money lending had been a simple but labour-intensive business, based on a direct long-term relationship between the borrower and the lender. Now, nowhere in the lengthy mortgage chain did anybody play the role of an old-fashioned bank loan officer, screening borrowers to ensure they could afford the loans they had applied for, and then monitoring their behaviour.

As long as house prices were going up, the only checks on the growth of subprime lending were the rating agencies and the government regulators, both of which are supposed to prevent market failures. The rating agencies, however, received generous fees for their rating activities from the lenders, thereby undermining objectivity in the rating.

The regulation of subprime lenders was also weak. Instead of the different regulators concerned coming together, they engaged in turf wars which allowed the financial institutions to play one off against the other.

In the Alphabet Soup

The continuing rise in house prices disguised the rot. As a previous financial crisis recedes in time, it is quite natural for bankers, businessmen, government officials and even economists to believe that a new era has arrived. There was also the belief that advances in financial technology had enabled banks to manage the hazards of their business more effectively. By securitising loans rather than keeping them on their balance sheets, they could distribute credit risks to investors. And, added Fed chairman Bernanke, lending had become more routinised as banks had become increasingly adept at predicting default risk by applying statistical models to data such as credit scores; they had made substantial strides in their ability to measure and manage risks.

However, these models obscured what should have been obvious: too many financial institutions were lending heavily to an overheated property market. Even when house prices started to fall by late 2006, firms like Citigroup, Merrill and UBS refused to scale down their mortgage business.

Risk-management techniques were further developed. One of them was the value-at-risk (VAR) model, which followed a fairly straightforward series of steps, on the basis of which the market-risk department of a bank could provide senior management with an exact dollar estimate of the firm's losses under a worst-case scenario.

Under the old system, governments had simply ordered banks to maintain a certain level of capital. Now the regulators allowed firms to carry less capital if their VAR models suggested they weren't carrying a lot of risk. Unfortunately, VAR was ill-suited to the task its promoters had apportioned for it—preventing financial calamities. By the turn of the century, most economists had accepted Mandelbrot's argument that big movements in financial markets are more frequent than the Bell Curve predicts.

When investors panic, they will sell many different types of assets at the same time. When this happens, even a bank that appears to be well diversified can suffer losses much bigger than a VAR model would have predicted. The use of VAR models also contributed to rising leverage levels. As the stock and bond markets entered a period of unusual tranquillity, market-based VAR estimates fell sharply, encouraging banks to run down their capital.

Then there were the credit default swaps (CDSs), developed by J.P. Morgan in the realm of credit insurance. CDSs are not really swaps; they should be called credit insurance contracts. What is at stake is that a bank puts some loans it had issued in a special purpose vehicle (SPV) and distributes tranches of it to investors. Now, the investors don't get to own the loans, which remain on the bank's books; they agree to take on the risk of the bank's borrowers defaulting. In return, the bank agrees to pay the investors what is effectively an insurance premium. The result is that the bank can remove a part of its credit risk from its balance sheet, freeing up capital which the bank can use elsewhere. Moreover, it transferred the risk to the financial institutions that had more of an appetite for them; and it created securities that could be traded. To a traditional banker, the idea of separating risk from lending seemed revolutionary—for the first time in history banks would be able to make loans without carrying all of the risks involved themselves. And CDSs were not regulated.

By the end of 2005, virtually every big firm on Wall Street was heavily involved in the credit insurance market. So were big commercial banks, such as Citigroup and Bank of America and top insurance companies, such as AIG. Already in 2003 Warren Buffett warned that the trouble with CDSs was that one could quickly infect the others, and central banks had so far found no effective way to control or even monitor the risks posed by these CDSs. Buffett concluded that derivatives are weapons of mass destruction, carrying dangers that, while now latent, could be potentially lethal.

In increasing financial firms' liabilities without bolstering their capital reserves, the growth of the CDS market effectively added even more leverage to the system. Given the chain-link structure of many CDS transactions, issuers and buyers were indirectly exposed to problems at firms several links down the chain, creating an additional layer of network risk.

In October 2006 the Financial Services Regulatory Relief Act was adopted which allowed banks to keep even less capital in reserve.

A Matter of Incentives

Economics is largely about incentives. Communism collapsed because it failed to encourage innovation, enterprise and hard work. Capitalism promoted all these things. The market system is heartless and unforgiving, but, as Marx and Engels pointed out, it is uniquely productive.

In the 1970s, the resurrection of free-market economics was based largely on the argument that high taxes and excessive regulation were stifling the economy. But markets can create damaging incentives. The financial market was humming away funnelled by distorted market incentives. Unfortunately, this was an outbreak of rational irrationality. The outcome was a ruinous housing and credit bubble. The long period of relative stability, aka the Great Moderation, triggered disaster myopia. During the period interest rates were typically low and deregulation was pressed too far. The banks were inclined to take too many risks, also promoted by the perverse incentive packages that many traders and senior executives on Wall Street received. The book contains detailed information of what some CEOs earned during 2006. For example, Lloyd Blankfein, Goldman Sachs's CEO, earned $54.72 million, including a cash bonus of $27.2 million, $15.7 million in restricted stock and $10.5 million in options. When the markets are rising, bankers are paid magnificently; when things go wrong, the shareholders of the firms, and in extreme cases the taxpayers, suffer the bulk of the losses. In banking, the CEO incentive problem is even more severe than in other industries. This is partly because the existence of deposit insurance, securitisation and the widespread assumption that some institutions are 'too big to fail' induce moral hazard, but the speculative nature of finance also plays a role. CEOs of big banks had no choice but to take more and more risks;

if not, the banks' shares would plunge and the CEO's career would hang in the balance. As Chuck Prince, CEO of Citigroup, commented in a famous interview in the *Financial Times* in July 2007, '[A]s long as the music is playing you've got to get up and dance'.

Prince conceded that a full-scale blow-up in subprime could cause liquidity to dry up in other asset-backed securities markets, leaving Citi and other banks saddled with numerous loans of questionable value that they couldn't sell. Prince was openly acknowledging the possibility of a catastrophe and saying that despite it all, he and Citi would continue to surf the bubble, hoping to get out before they came a cropper. The logic of rational irrationality had rarely been spelled out more clearly.

London Bridge is Falling Down

As long as liquidity remains above a certain level, markets enable people to spread risks and invest in long-term assets, such as real estate, with confidence. But if liquidity falls below a certain threshold, all the elements that formed a virtuous circle to promote stability now will conspire to undermine it. The financial markets can become highly unstable, and in a worst-case scenario they can cease to operate at all. And that started to happen on 9 August 2007 when the large French bank BNP Paribas announced that it was suspending redemptions from three of its investment funds that had substantial holdings in American mortgage securities. Citing evaporation of liquidity in certain segments of the US securitisation market, BNP said that it was impossible to value certain assets fairly regardless of their quality or credit rating. A month earlier, Standard & Poor and Moody's had unnerved subprime investors by announcing they were reviewing the credit ratings of almost $18 billion worth of mortgage bonds. After that, the subprime markets were in turmoil. BNP's announcement sent stocks tumbling. In the interbank lending market, where banks extend credit to one another on a daily basis, lending activity dried up—something that hadn't happened since the global financial crisis of September 1988.

The European Central Bank (ECB) made €95 billion available in emergency credits, and the Fed pumped more cash into the system.

The next day, things got worse; the ECB was forced to inject another €61 billion into the system and the Fed assured the markets that it would supply big banks with as much short-term credit as they needed. The mortgage securities market had frozen up. Banks and other lenders had no way to estimate how exposed to it other financial institutions might be. Rather than extending credit to a rival firm that could turn out to be insolvent, they opted to hoard their capital, forcing the ECB and the Fed to step in as lenders of last resort. The information problem was so bad that many financial institutions didn't know what their own subprime holdings were worth. Hayek's telecommunications system was no longer emitting any price signals: the market had failed, and the great credit crunch of 2007–2009 had begun.

Fannie Mae and Freddie Mac were understandably hard hit by the housing and mortgage crisis. Their stock prices dropped. For the Bush Administration, allowing the mortgage companies to default was not an option. America's foreign debtors, especially China, were heavy holders of their bonds. If Fannie and Freddie had defaulted, the creditworthiness of the United States would have been called into question, and the dollar might have collapsed. The government pumped money into both institutions and nationalised them.

Then Lehman Brothers collapsed. It is still unclear why the US government let Lehman Brothers go; there was no rescue like the Bear Stearns rescue operation. The government, however, shortly after Lehman's collapse, rescued AIG. The source of AIG's problems turned out to be roughly $400 billion in credit protection it had provided to banks and other financial institutions, much of it in the form of credit default swaps on subprime mortgage bonds. AIG's balance sheet was much bigger than Lehman's, and so were its off-balance-sheet commitments.

The situation worsened. There were rumours that Goldman Sachs and Morgan Stanley were also having trouble raising money. Their stock prices dropped. Depositors started to withdraw their money. Bernanke and the Secretary of the Treasury, Hank Paulson, asked Congress to approve a huge rescue plan to the tune of some $700 billion, to buy up toxic assets, and Congress complied.

Realising that purchasing assets at low prices would force banks to shoulder even more losses, Paulson shelved the plan and switched to recapitalising the banks directly through the purchase of preference shares. The Troubled Asset Relief Program (TARP) was established. Having allowed global capitalism to move to the cliff's edge, terrifying their electors, the politicians finally pledged to do whatever was necessary to prevent it from toppling over. This alone was enough to restore a semblance of order. Only the government could overcome the threat of rational irrationality and get private decision-makers to coordinate a more favourable outcome. Government also adopted a Temporary Liquidity Guarantee Program that guaranteed debts issued by big financial institutions, thereby transferring the credit risks involved in lending to these companies from investors to the American taxpayers.

As far as financial stabilisation policy was concerned, the accession to the White House of Barack Obama, in January 2009, changed little. Timothy Geithner moved from the New York Fed to the Treasury Department and continued the policies he, Paulson and Bernanke had designed.

In April 2009, the IMF put a price tag on the efforts Western governments had taken to shore up their financial systems: roughly $10 trillion was spent. Was it worth it? It came too late to prevent the sharpest economic downturn since the 1930s. Between September 2008 and June 2009, more than 5 million jobs were lost in the USA, and the unemployment rate jumped from 6.2 % to 9.5 %. Between April 2008 and March 2009, world industrial production fell by almost 15 %. The recession was on a global scale.

By the summer of 2009 there was evidence that the lending crunch had eased. In early June, the Treasury Department announced that ten big banks would be allowed to repay $68 billion in loans they had obtained through the TARP programme. In short, the American financial markets and the economy at large showed signs of improvement.

Banks across the Atlantic were affected as well. The British bank Northern Rock, which didn't have any direct connection to the US subprime market, got into trouble. Its practice was, among others, to raise large amounts of money from other financial institutions. This raised questions about its viability. In the middle of September there was a run on the bank and the British government had to step in to rescue it.

Fed chairman Bernanke thought that it was a temporary liquidity crisis that caused the problem, and that it would fairly quickly resolve itself; Bernanke was under the illusion of stability. And, after all, the spreading of risk was purported to be the greatest benefit of securitisation; it was the very reason Alan Greenspan had supported the concept in the first place. But far from distributing the risks associated with subprime, securitisation and the construction of the shadow banking system helped to concentrate it at the heart of the financial world, in Citigroup, J.P. Morgan Chase, HSBC and others.

In November 2007 these big banks accepted reality and incorporated SIVs into their balance sheets. The implosion of the shadow banking system was just one of several factors that amplified the subprime bust, elevating it into the worst financial breakdown since the 1930s. With the market for securitised products frozen, banks were forced to sell many other types of financial assets, causing their prices to fall and the crisis to intensify. So, the initial disturbance fed on itself. A compounding factor was that the leverage practices the banks applied now magnified the problem. By late 2007, many financial firms were trapped in a loss spiral: banks sell so prices fall! In the slumping housing market, foreclosures were rising sharply, causing a glut of forced sales and adding to the pressure on prices. Between August 2007 and October 2008 more than 936,000 homes were foreclosed on. The slump in the housing market was doing serious damage to the rest of the economy, especially to the construction industry, which had been a major source of economic growth.

Attention focused on Wall Street firms. Unlike commercial banks, such as Citigroup, two financial institutions, Lehman Brothers and Bear Stearns, didn't have access to the Fed's lending facility. Their finances were precarious. Both Bear and Lehman had leverage ratios at the end of 2007 of more than 30 to 1. With this sort of leverage, a mere 4 % drop in the value of a firm's assets can wipe out its entire capital base. Bear faced a run on its bank. In March 2008 the Fed announced that it would provide temporary help to Bear, with J.P. Morgan Chase acting as the conduit, as Bear's possible bankruptcy would result in an 'chaotic unwinding of positions in an already damaged market', according to the Secretary of the Treasury. Bear was too interconnected to fail. A few days later, J.P. Morgan Chase purchased Bear.

Socialism in Our Time

When big banks collapse, there are enormous spillovers that policymakers have to take into account, even if they don't like it. History demonstrates that in such circumstances the only way for policymakers to get ahead of the problem is to acknowledge its scale, excise some of the bad debts and recapitalise the banks deemed able to survive. As a senior IMF official said, one cannot rely on the private sector or markets alone to solve systemic banking problems. However, the American political system was designed to prevent effective government action rather than to facilitate it, and many senior congressmen remained wedded to the nostrums of Milton Friedman.

During an economic crisis, when markets fail, even many conservative economists are relieved to see the government step in: practically nobody is willing to risk creating another Great Depression by relying on free enterprise. But that, surely, raises the question of why anybody believed in utopian economics to begin with.

Conclusion

As Keynes once said, ideas matter. Indeed, the world is ruled by little else. When historians come to write about the 'Greenspan bubbles', they will do so with good cause: more than any other individual, the former Fed chairman was responsible for letting the hogs run wild. But even if Greenspan hadn't been at the Fed, history would have proceeded in the same general direction: the free-market counter-revolution would have continued, and so would have the rapid growth of the financial sector. Nevertheless, misguided ideas were largely responsible for setting the US economy on its disastrous trajectory. Between the collapse of communism and the outbreak of the subprime crisis, an understandable and justified respect for market forces mutated into a rigid and unquestioning devotion to a particular, and blatantly unrealistic, adoption of Adam Smith's invisible hand. A new way of thinking about the economy has to be articulated as a replacement of utopian economics—an economic philosophy that acknowledges the usefulness of markets but also their limitations, that recognises the existence of Hayek's telecommunications system but also its tendency to break down. If further calamities are to be avoided, policymakers need to make a big mental shift and embrace this eminently practical philosophy.

The biggest lesson we have learned is that Wall Street needs taming, as Minsky already suggested in the 1980s. Regulators should impose maximum leverage ratios on banks and other financial firms, and they should also oblige them to hold more than adequate levels of liquidity and capital in reserve. In addition, banks should be prevented from hiding liabilities and risks in SIVs. The same principles that govern financial institutions should be applied to derivatives and other complex financial products. Executive pay is yet another issue that needs to be addressed. The Fed's mandate which is now ensuring maximum sustainable employment and price stability should be extended with the preservation of financial stability.

Economic research tended to be motivated by the internal logic, intellectual sunk capital and aesthetic puzzles of established research programmes rather than by a powerful desire to understand how the economy works. So the economics profession was unprepared when the crisis struck. And yet, some prominent economists still say that despite the enormity of recent events, the principles of economics are largely unchanged. In the world of utopian economics, the latest crisis was always a blip. Before the political will for reform dissipates, it is essential to put Wall Street in its place and confront utopian economics with reality.

8

Inequality Revisited

Introduction

Inequality has been around for most of humankind's history. Adam Smith published the *Wealth of Nations* in 1776. His analysis of economic development was about the creation of wealth through the efficient division of labour. As for labour, Smith presented the subsistence theory of wages, allowing workers to survive. He died before the Industrial Revolution brought about a very wide gap between rich industrialists and poor workers. Karl Marx predicted that capitalism, which created wealth and poverty, would collapse. As we know, his prediction was wrong. Nonetheless, inequality between capital and income remained on the agenda. However, it did not always get the attention it deserves, as inequality is obviously more than an economic issue; it is a political and moral issue as well. Thomas Piketty brought inequality back on top of the agenda, thanks to his monumental work *Capital in the Twenty-First Century*,[1] which instantly became a bestseller.

---

[1] Piketty, T. (2014) *Capital in the Twenty-First Century.* Cambridge, MA: The Belknap Press of Harvard University Press.

As regards some of the economists presented in this book, Keynes also dealt with inequality in *The General Theory*. In the chapter dealing with observations on the nature of capital he wrote that in a situation where capital goods would be so abundant that the marginal efficiency of capital would drop to zero, this might be the most sensible way of gradually getting rid of many of the objectionable features of capitalism. One consequence would be, in Keynes's own words, the 'euthanasia of the rentier', and, consequently, the euthanasia of the oppressive power of the capitalist to exploit the scarcity-value of capital. Keynes concluded,

> For a little reflection will show what enormous social changes would result from a gradual disappearance of a rate of return on accumulated wealth. A man would still be free to accumulate his earned income with a view to spending it at a later date. But his accumulation would not grow.[2]

That Keynes wasn't insensitive about income and wealth distribution also shines clearly through in yet another observation: he argued that the outstanding faults of the economic society in which we live are its failure to provide for full employment and its arbitrary and inequitable distribution of wealth and incomes.[3]

Friedman also analysed the inequality issue from a societal efficiency point of view; yet he wasn't entirely insensitive about the plight of the lowest-income earners. In *Capitalism and Freedom* he presented his negative income tax proposal, meaning that income earners below a certain minimum level should receive a subsidy from the government to make both ends meet. Hayek argued in *The Road to Serfdom* that governments' income redistribution policies will only put a brake on economic growth, as the rich will have less incentive to invest; the fruits of their efforts will be taken away by high taxes, reminiscent of the initial stages of the Kuznets Curve.

Simon Kuznets introduced the Kuznets Curve during his 1954 Presidential Address at the American Economic Association's meeting in Detroit. Kuznets argued that inequality follows a u-shaped path. Inequality will increase during the initial stages of industrialisation and

---

[2] Keynes, J.M. (1964) *The General Theory of Employment, Interest, and Money.* San Diego, New York and London: Harcourt Brace & Company, 221.
[3] Ibid., 372.

then decrease over the course of the industrialisation process. Once industrialisation is maturing, the demand for specialised knowledge will increase, resulting in higher wages for those who can offer special skills. So, first there will be a widening gap between the various income groups, which will be followed by sharply decreasing inequality.

Piketty begged to differ with the economic automatism implied in the Kuznets Curve. The reduction in inequality between 1914 and 1945 was due not to the evolution of the economy, said Piketty, but to the two world wars and the Great Depression. In an article published in 2011, written by Piketty, Anthony Atkinson and Emmanuel Saez, they explained why inequality first rose, then dropped, but subsequently rose again.[4] This article was a harbinger of what Piketty would present a couple of years later in *Capital*. Now, who is Thomas Piketty? The following brief biographical sketch attempts to answer this question.

Biography: Thomas Piketty (1971–)

Thomas Piketty is in his mid-forties and has already gained world fame; he is a celebrity. His *Capital in the Twenty-First Century* appeared just at the right time. After the Great Recession many people wondered—as they did after the Great Depression—whether capitalism was the right system after all. Joblessness, poverty and a widening gap between rich and poor were the issues people were concerned—if not angry—about. The capitalist system was blamed. The financial sector, including greedy bankers, lost credibility. Piketty argued that capitalism is good for the wealthy, but not necessarily for the less well-off. There is no corrective automatism within the capitalist system to keep the gap between the rich and the rest within manageable proportions. This, according to Piketty, can only be done through state intervention. Young Thomas had visited the Soviet Union in 1991 and he saw there that central planning didn't work. He became a believer in capitalism, private property and the market. However, checks and balances had to be applied by the state, to keep the system in check.

---

[4] Atkinson, A., Piketty, T. and Saez, E. (2011) Top Incomes in the Long Run of History. *Journal of Economic Literature*, Vol. 49 (March), 3–71.

Thomas Piketty was born on 7 May 1971 in Clichy, France. His parents had left-leaning sympathies. Thomas's brilliance came to light at an early age. He entered the prestigious École Normale Supérieure (ENS) at the age of 18. He studied economics and mathematics and earned his PhD when he was only 22 years old. He wrote his thesis at the École des hautes études en sciences sociales (EHESS) and the London School of Economics; it dealt with wealth distribution and won the award for the best thesis from the French Economics Association.

From 1993 to 1995 Piketty held the position of associate professor in the Economics Department of the Massachusetts Institute of Technology at Cambridge, Massachusetts. In 1995 he returned to France to take up a research position at the French National Centre for Scientific Research and in 2000 he became professor at the EHESS. In 2006, Piketty was instrumental in founding the Paris School of Economics, and was its director until he became economic advisor to the French Socialist Party's presidential candidate Ségolène Royal. However, she lost the election and Piketty returned to the Paris School of Economics to resume teaching and to work for long years on his 'chef-d'oeuvre' *Capital au XXIe siècle*, which did not receive an overwhelming reception when the Seuil edition came out in 2013 in France. One year later, it was Arthur Goldhammer's English translation, *Capital in the Twenty-First Century*, that catapulted Piketty to world fame.

He remained loyal to the Parti Socialiste and publicly supported François Hollande's candidacy for the French presidency. However, he became disappointed in Hollande's tenure as president. This may have influenced his rejection of the Légion d'Honneur which he was offered in 2015. He said that he did not want the nomination because governments cannot establish who is honourable.

Honours

In 2002 Piketty won the prize for best young economist in France, comparable to the American John Bates Clark Medal.[5] In 2013 Piketty received the Yrjö Jahnsson Award for the economist under the age of 45

---

[5] There is a striking similarity between Piketty's career and that of his compatriot Esther Duflo. Both studied at the ENS and Esther Duflo is now Abdul Latif Jameel Professor of Poverty Alleviation and Development Economics at MIT. In 2010, she received the John Bates Clark Medal.

Academic Work

Looking at his publications, Piketty is an economist specialising in public finance, and issues of inequality with a heavy emphasis on long-term trends, supported by statistical data. Some of his best works were co-authored by Emmanuel Saez, a French-American economist who is Professor of Economics at the University of California, Berkeley. Piketty and Saez were both influenced by Sir Anthony Barnes Atkinson, the *éminence grise* of inequality and poverty at Nuffield College, Oxford, and the London School of Economics.

Capital in the Twenty-First Century provides an impressive historical analysis, spanning three centuries, of income and wealth data across the countries that had collected statistical and other economic data (such as tax declarations). Piketty used them to underscore his concern about the growing inequality in income and wealth. During the belle époque (i.e. the end of the nineteenth century) the richest people controlled 90 % of all wealth in Europe. Piketty coined this period 'patrimonial capitalism'. He argues that a similar situation is emerging once again in Europe:

In the years after WWII many people thought capitalism had been almost eradicated. Yet, at the beginning of the twenty-first century Europe seems to be in the avant-garde of the new patrimonial capitalism, with private fortunes once again surpassing US levels. This is fairly explained by the low rate of economic and especially demographic growth in Europe compared with the United States.[6]

The essence of *Capital* can be captured by the formula $r > g$. As long as the return on capital (r) is higher than the percentage of economic growth (g), while taking into consideration that the wealth distribution is (very) uneven, it can be projected that inequality will increase. Once constituted, capital reproduces itself faster than output increases. Even a

---

[6] Piketty, *Capital*, 154.

small gap between the return on capital and the rate of growth can—in the long term—have powerful and destabilising effects on the structure and stability of societies.

Reactions to *Capital in the Twenty-First Century*

Understandably, there were many reactions and reviews on *Capital*. Self-respecting journalists, bloggers and columnists felt that they had to vent their opinions about the book everybody was talking about. The same applied to the academic community. Most reviews were favourable; all authors were impressed with *Capital*'s wide scope, going back to the time of the French Revolution, supported by an overwhelming wealth of data. Surely, there were also critical observations; yet, all in all, the book was praised. Given the enormous flood of reactions, I have chosen three types of reactions which, I believe, are fairly representative. The first type is about Piketty's statistical data. The second represents observations about the book's perceived weak theoretical underpinning, and the lack of a distinction between capital and wealth, while the third type draws attention to the missing institutional dimension of inequality.

Bloomberg View's Clive Crook wrote on 20 April 2014 that Piketty's data would be shaky and that, based on the data, he drew far-reaching conclusions that are not justified. And *Financial Times* economics editor Chris Giles published an article on 23 May 2014 criticising Piketty for constructing some of his numbers 'out of thin air'. Once corrected, some of Piketty's central findings no longer seemed to hold, concluded Giles. However, *The Economist*'s Free Exchange column of 31 May 2014 supported Piketty:

> All told, Mr. Piketty is guilty of sloppiness (certainly in his notation), and perhaps of some errors. But there is little evidence, so far, to support the serious charge of cherry-picking statistics. Nor have his findings that wealth concentration is, once again, rising, been fatally undermined.[7]

Piketty reacted to these criticisms by putting all his data online, and he explained which methodologies he applied. He added that it would

---
[7] *The Economist*, 31 May 2014, 66.

surprise him if improvements as suggested by Crook and Giles would alter his main conclusions.

Regarding the weak theoretical underpinning, Harvard professor Dani Rodrik's *Project Syndicate* article of 13 May 2014 had this to say. On the one hand, Rodrik found *Capital* a fantastic read, but on the other he blamed Piketty for not paying more attention to formal theory. Piketty is not, and I quote Rodrik, 'beyond sprinkling an occasional equation or Greek letters throughout the text'. Rodrik also argued that Piketty's extrapolations are dangerous. After all, r could go down in a situation when there is too much capital relative to labour and other inputs, or when the pace of innovation slows down. Moreover, the world economy may be growing faster than Piketty anticipates. Hence, Piketty's formula $r > g$ may not be applicable throughout the remainder of this century.

In a blog, Australian economist Joshua Gans referred to a long article that Solow published in the 22 April 2104 issue of *New Republic*, about *Capital*.[8] In that article Solow admitted that in a situation—as presented by Piketty—wherein $r > g$, income and wealth of the rich will grow faster than the average income from labour. Solow calls this a 'rich-get-rich dynamic'. Piketty's prediction of where inequality is heading is not based upon a solid theoretical model; it is speculative and based on the rich-get-rich dynamic. Yet, Solow underscored that this insight is one that no one before Piketty discovered. Solow concluded that the economy apparently has been able to absorb increasing quantities of capital that did not result in a decreasing rate of return on capital.

This absorption ability must have been done by 'capital creators', as Gans calls them. But wouldn't these capital creators also be able to further promote economic growth? If so, this would not justify Piketty's low economic growth projections. Gans is critical of Piketty for not having referred to older theories, including Solow's, on the basis of which Solow proposed the same sort of taxes Piketty proposes, so as to bring about a more equal income and wealth distribution.

Dutch economist Bas Jacobs argues that the problem with Piketty's rate of return on capital r and the savings rate s are both determined by economic circumstances; both are, in economists' language, endogenous,

---

[8] *Digitopoly, Capital Creators, Piketty and the Growth Theory*, 23 April 2014.

and cannot be determined by simply extrapolating historical trends. Jacobs—like Solow—concludes that Piketty doesn't present a theory of the workings of capital markets and saving and investment behaviour, based on which the outcome would be $r>g$.[9]

Regarding capital and wealth, Piketty does not make a clear distinction between them, while the two differ in their respective role in the productive process. The term capital encompasses means of production, such as machinery, buildings, equipment and the like. The term wealth is used to express what someone owns, such as a house, a building, pieces of art, shares and so forth, minus his or her debts. Capital wields a far larger socio-economic influence than wealth. The issue is thus how much influence a rich person can exert. That influence is concretised through the productive capital he or she invests. However, Piketty's main objective is to analyse the distribution of wealth. He analysed the evolution of wealth and the development of the ratio between wealth—in general terms—and income. The influence that wealth in the form of capital can wield as explained above is—strictly speaking—another subject matter. Piketty analysed the development of the growth of wealth and how this impinged upon the concentration of wealth in fewer hands. In doing so he escaped the need to clearly distinguish between capital and wealth.

Now we turn to inequality's institutional dimension. Daron Acemoglu and James Robinson wrote *Why Nations Fail* (2013), in which they argued that institutions play a crucial role in the development of economies. In an interview Harvard professor James Robinson criticised Piketty for his disregard of the role of institutions.[10] Robinson said that limiting inequality is not determined by Piketty's formula $r>g$ but by changes in the political domain and through government intervention in the economy.

In *Why Nations Fail* a distinction is made between extractive and inclusive institutions. The more inclusive institutions are, the greater the chance that economic development unfolds. Institutions that provide incentives for people to develop play a fundamental part in overcoming inequality, argued Robinson. In the interview he gave a few examples

---

[9] Jacobs, B. (2015) *De Prijs van Gelijkheid*. Amsterdam: Prometheus/Bert Bakker, 250.
[10] *NRC Handelsblad*, 3–4 September 2014, W8–9.

to underscore his point. Sweden is one of them: the social-democratic government there had more influence on the distribution of income and wealth than a supposedly autonomous development of r and g. Another example is South Korea. During General Park's autocratic rule in the 1960s, the country was characterised by extractive economic growth. But growth continued throughout the next two decades because South Korea adopted democratic rule and thus transformed itself into an inclusive political system.

Capital in the Twenty-First Century

Inequality tends to evolve pro-cyclically, that is, it moves in the same direction as the economic cycle.[11] One of its consequences is that during the Great Recession, the purchasing power of the lower and middle classes stagnated or even diminished, which was not helpful in overcoming the recession. From a political view point, the super-rich wield more and more political influence, including over their own remuneration packages. Piketty believes that large and increasing inequality, which we now witness, triggers political instability. He argues that our democracies rest on a meritocratic worldview; a belief in a society that is based more on merit rather than on kinship and rents.

As regards the high remuneration of 'supermanagers', which contributes to widening the gap, Piketty questioned the justification for such high levels of compensation. There is none; empirical studies revealed that there is no relation between very high salaries of these 'supermanagers' and their performance. Now, what can be done about increasing inequality? Piketty suggests investing more in education, as better-educated people can get better-paid jobs. However, his central proposal is taxing the (very) wealthy by introducing a global wealth tax. As this isn't easy to achieve, he proposes a gradual approach towards this goal.

Capital in the Twenty-First Century provides an impressive historical analysis, spanning three centuries of income and wealth data across the

---

[11] The edition used is the 2014 edition of Belknap Press of Harvard University Press.

countries that had collected statistical and other economic data (such as tax declarations). Piketty used the data to underscore his concern about the growing inequality in income and wealth, and his proposed response.

A 685-page long book, like *Capital in the Twenty-First Century*, can either be summarised in an expanded manner or by way of capturing the essence of *Capital*'s analysis and message. I have chosen the latter option, as—in my opinion—this contemporary book, given its large political influence, should be read in full by students and the general readership alike. To underscore my choice, I quote *New Yorker* staff writer John Cassidy: 'Piketty has written a book that nobody interested in a defining issue of our era can afford to ignore.'

Apart from an introduction, the book consists of four parts. Part I is about income and capital. The second part is entitled 'The Dynamics of the Capital/income Ratio.' Part III deals with the structure of inequality, and part IV includes proposals regarding the regulation of capital in the twenty-first century. The book ends with a concluding chapter.

Introduction

'[C]apitalism automatically generates arbitrary and unsustainable inequalities that radically undermine the meritocratic values on which democratic societies are based.' This memorable sentence in *Capital*'s introduction sets the book's tone. Piketty describes the thinking of the 'classics', starting with Adam Smith, and how they valued the role of capital in the process of economic development. The possession of land embodied wealth until the Industrial Revolution. Since then, capital took the upper hand. More and more capital was concentrated in the hands of a few industrialists. Labourers received very low wages triggered by an oversupply of workers who had left the countryside to look for work in industrial cities.

Once the industrialisation process matured, the demand for specialised skills increased, resulting in higher wages for workers who could offer the required skills. As a result, the gap between the owners of capital and those who acquired their income through work diminished. This is what Simon Kuznets observed. The Kuznets Curve is a reflection of the same.

But was Kuznets right? No, says Piketty. The reason being that Kuznets developed his curve during the middle of the past century, when capital had dramatically diminished as a result of the two world wars (during which much installed capital was destroyed), the decolonisation process that started after WWII, the nationalisation of some industries and the improved bargaining position of labour. So, not only economic factors, but also institutional and political factors played their part. The capital–income ratio changed in favour of income. This explains why the role of capital in the analysis of inequality lost the interest of economists at the time.[12]

> One important reason for my choice [to return to France] has a direct bearing on this book: I did not find the work of US economists entirely convincing. To be sure, they were all very intelligent, and I still have many friends from that period of my life. But something strange happened: I was only too aware of the fact that I knew nothing at all about the world's economic problems… I quickly realized that there had been no significant effort to collect historical data on the dynamics of inequality since Kuznets, yet the profession continued to churn out purely theoretical results without even knowing what facts needed to be explained… When I returned to France, I set out to collect the missing data.[13]

This lack of interest was unjustified, as the situation changed in the second half of the past century. Private capital resumed its prominent place. Thanks to higher wages, people were able to save and invested their savings in capital (such as real estate); others gained a lot of money in private business, sports and entertainment. The income from capital also increased substantially.

The capital–income ratio (β) is simply related to the share of income from capital in the national income, denoted as α, and r is the rate of return on capital, so: $\alpha = r\,\beta$. Piketty calls $\alpha = r \times \beta$ the first fundamental law of capitalism, which links the stock of capital to the flow of income

---

[12] Perhaps illustrative is the title of professor Jan Pen's book, published by Penguin in 1971: *Income Distribution*. Pen put the emphasis on income, while Piketty emphasised the role of capital in the title of his book.

[13] Piketty, *Capital*, 31–2.

from capital. The author gives an example: if β is 600 % and $r = 5$ %, then $\alpha = r \times \beta = 30$ %. In simple terms, if national wealth represents the equivalent of 6 years of national income, and if the rate of return on capital is 5 % per year, then capital's share in national income is 30 %. It expresses a transparent relationship among the three most important concepts for analysing the capitalist system: (1) the capital–income ratio, (2) the share of capital in income and (3) the rate of return on capital. The capital–income ratio is, as noted, changing again in favour of capital. Piketty calculates that in most developed countries capital represents four to six times the national income of these countries.

To summarise: towards the end of the belle époque, capital provided the largest contribution to total income. This contribution diminished during, roughly, the first half of the twentieth century. As of the second half of the twentieth century, the role of capital is increasing again.

> Piketty also analysed the development of the return on capital r. He writes,
> More important, there is a set of forces of divergence associated with the process of accumulation and concentration of wealth when growth is weak and the return of capital is high. This second process is potentially more destabilizing than the first [i.e. top earners who quickly separate themselves from the rest], and it no doubt represents the principal threat to an equal distribution of wealth over the long run.[14]

In a situation as described in the above quote—'when the return of capital is higher than economic growth'—concentration of wealth will be in the hands of an ever-smaller number of individuals. This is contrary to what the standard economic theory tells us. The theory suggests that the return of capital would be dependent on the level of economic growth: when g (economic growth) would drop, so would r (return on capital). Piketty analysed the historical trend of r in relation to g, and concluded that r, including return on inherited wealth, grew *faster* than g. And in a situation where g drops, r diminishes less. So, all told: $r > g$. Some say that Einstein's $E = Mc2$ is for physics what Piketty's $r > g$ is for economics.

---

[14] Ibid., 23.

He warns the reader that one should interpret his findings with care. He based his insight partly on estimates and on extrapolations. And we know from history that economic extrapolations are not necessarily in conformity with what will happen. Moreover, he only took the developments in France and Britain as the basis for a global trend.[15]

Piketty expects that the average r to be 4–5 % per annum, based upon the average growth in the period 1900–2010. Given the low economic growth percentages prevailing in the developed world, r will remain larger than g in the foreseeable future.

Forces of convergence also exist, and in certain countries at certain times, these may prevail, but the forces of divergence can at any point regain the upper hand, as likely decrease in the rate of growth of both the population and the economy in coming decades makes this trend all the more worrisome.[16]

Historically speaking, economic growth has been low. Before 1750 the percentage was on average below 1 % per annum, and after 1750 it rarely was higher than 2 %. This doesn't mean that there was hardly any economic progress. The law of accumulated growth has it that an average growth of 1 % per year results in 35 % growth of the economy in a period of 30 years. Average growth percentages should not be confused with those of exceptional periods, such as Europe's reconstruction period after the end of WWII, Japan's phenomenal growth in the same period or China's during the past few decades. Nonetheless, Piketty estimates that economic growth during this century will be between 1 % and 2.5 %.

Now, given the trends of (1) the return of capital r has historically been higher than g and (2) wealth as a source of income is growing again, this leads to the insight that inequality will be increasing again. The rich will see their income and wealth grow faster than people who do not posses capital and only receive a salary for the work they do.

---

[15] Piketty's main data source is the World Top Income Database (WTID), the establishment of which he participated in. Twenty-seven countries are included in this database; it is debatable whether this group of 27 is representative enough for the entire world. For example, no data are included from Russia, neither from most African countries and some emerging economies. Apart from WTID, Piketty also used data from tax declarations, data on wage and price developments, capital and household enquiries, as well as wealth rankings from *Forbes Magazine*.

[16] Piketty, *Capital*, 27.

A country that saves a lot and grows slowly will over the long term accumulate an enormous stock of capital relative to its income, which can in turn have a significant effect on the social structure and distribution of wealth. Piketty then introduced the second fundamental law of capitalism: $\beta = s/g$, wherein β is the capital–income ratio, s the savings rate and g the economic growth rate. Again, Piketty provides an example on page 170: if a country is saving 12 % of its income every year, and if its initial stock is equal to 6 years of income, then the capital stock will grow at 2 % per year,[17] thus at exactly the same rate as the national income, so that the capital–income ratio will remain stable. In a quasi-stagnant society, wealth that was accumulated in the past will inevitably acquire disproportional importance.

Part III of *Capital* is devoted to the structure of inequality. The question is, What does inequality look like worldwide? And how did it evolve across time? Piketty analysed how capital and income have been distributed through time. In almost every country there has always been a more unequal distribution of capital than income. In his own words,

> The first regularity we observe when we try to measure income inequality in practice is that inequality with respect to capital is always greater than inequality with respect to labor. The distribution of capital ownership (and of income from capital) is always more concentrated than the distribution of income from labor.[18]

This goes for all parts of the world and for each historical period. He then analysed, for different periods and for different countries, how much capital or income would go to the top 10 % and, subsequently, to the very top 1 %. In some cases Piketty analysed the share that goes to the 0.1 % of the population.

Looking at the distribution of income from labour, one sees that the top 10 % earns between 25 % and 30 % of the total labour income. As regards capital, the picture is as follows: through time the top 10 %

---

[17] Twelve per cent of income gives 12 divided by 6, or 2 per cent of capital. More generally, if the savings rate is s and the capital–income ratio is β, then the capital stock grows at a rate equal to s/β.
[18] Ibid., 244.

owns 50 % of total capital. In short, capital is, generally speaking, more concentrated in the hands of a smaller percentage of the population than income. There were exceptions though. During the French belle époque, the richest 10 % of the French population owned 90 % of all capital. Between 1910 and 1970, however, their share dropped to 60 %. As noted, the two world wars and France's loss of its colonies explain, to a large extent, this fall in capital.

As regards the poorest 50 % of the population, they owned on average at most 5 % of the capital stock, again through time. This even goes for the past century, despite the fact that there was a convergence between rich and poor during a considerable period of the twentieth century. True, everybody benefited from the economic growth; however, the distribution of the fruits of this growth did not change much; the 50 % poorest section of the population didn't see their capital share increase.

Looking at France's total income, since 1910 the share of the top 10 % fell considerably: dropping from close to 50–35 %. Given the fact that the share of income from labour of the top 10 % remained more or less stable, this implies that their share of income from capital must have decreased considerably. The trend in America was quite different: the share of the richest 10 % measured in income terms—while it had dropped during the middle part of the twentieth century—increased sharply since the 1980s. To date the richest 10 % owns 45 % of America's total income. This sharp increase can be explained by the equally sharp increase in top salaries.

The history of the distribution of capital and income in Europe is different from that of the United States. Up to the beginning of WWI the distribution in Europe was very uneven. That was not the case in America; the gap between rich and poor was smaller. Europe had larger inequalities around the turn of the nineteenth century than America today. The USA at that time was still a young society that needed time to catch up with the richest European sections of society. Land was available in abundance—the population was still relatively small especially in comparison with the enormous landmass available to them.

In the years after WWII many people felt that capitalism was done for. Yet, at the beginning of this century Europe is in the avant-garde of the new patrimonial capitalism, as Piketty coins it, with private fortunes once again surpassing US levels. This can be explained by Europe's lower economic and demographic growth compared with America's, automatically leading to increased influence of wealth accumulated in the past. The author concluded that European countries have never been so rich. And then Piketty made a political statement:

> What is true and shameful, on the other hand, is that this vast national wealth is very unequally distributed. Private wealth rests on public poverty. And one particularly unfortunate consequence of this is that we currently spend far more in interest on the debt than we invest in higher education.[19]

What happened, not only in Europe, but throughout the developed world? At the beginning of the 1970s the total value of private wealth (net of debt) stood between 2 and 3.5 years of national income in all the countries studied by Piketty. Since then, there is a strong comeback of private capital in the rich countries, and that is how this new patrimonial capitalism came about.

There are three factors that explain why. The first one is a slower growth in the long term, especially demographic growth, which, together with a high savings rate, automatically gives rise to a structural increase in the long-term capital–income ratio, owing to the above-mentioned $\beta = s/g$. The second is the gradual privatisation and transfer of public wealth into private hands, and the third is a long-term catch-up phenomenon affecting real estate and stock market prices, since the 1980s and 1990s in a more conducive political environment than that of the postwar decades.

Inequality really took off in America as of the 1980s. Capital played its part, but not the most important part. In particular income inequality has exploded in America. Piketty introduced the term 'supermanagers'. They didn't exist yet when Honoré de Balzac's novel *Le Père Goriot* came out in the early part of nineteenth century. The novel's main theme is what

---

[19] Ibid., 567. In fact his book is to some extent also a political treatise. That is not surprising; the author writes on page 574: 'Everyone is political in his or her own way. The world is not divided between a political elite on one side and, on the other, an army of commentators and spectators whose only responsibility is to drop a ballot in a ballot box once every 4 or 5 years. It is illusory, I believe, to think that the scholar and the citizen live in separate moral universes.'

the best way would be to climb the social ladder. Would it be working hard, or to find a rich marriage partner? At the time, the latter option was preferred, as working hard for a salary wouldn't make one rich, let alone add to one's prestige.

Today's 'supermanagers' have grown rich during their own lifetime. Think of Bill Gates, Mark Zuckerberg, Jeff Bezos and the like. Sky-high remunerations are a reflection of the social and political changes since the 1980s. The average CEO salary of a firm whose stock is traded on the stock exchange was around $2 million at the end of the 1980s. In 2007, it had risen to $16 million. CEO salaries in the financial sector are even higher (see the summary of *How Markets Fail* in Chap. 7). On the other hand, the salaries of mid- and lower-income earners hardly rose; at best by a few per cents per year. This explains the rapidly widening divide between the top earners and the rest. The top earners are in a position to put aside a large part of their income to add to their own capital.

Piketty fears that this large and increasing gap between the super-rich and the rest, which we now witness, triggers political instability. He wrote, 'Inequality is not necessarily bad in itself: the key question is to decide whether it is justified, whether there are reasons for it.'[20] He argues that our democracies rest on a meritocratic worldview; a belief in a society that is based more on merit and effort than on kinship and rents. As regards the high remuneration of 'supermanagers', Piketty wonders what the justification is for such high levels of compensation, which he described as meritocratic extremism. Is it a reward for their exceptional contribution to a firm's productivity and profitability? No, he responds, as empirical studies have found that there is no relation between the very high salaries of these 'supermanagers' and their performance. Some firms that are managed by managers who earn less than their peers perform even better. The author also observed that the reduction of top marginal income tax rates and the rise of top incomes do not seem to have stimulated productivity or at any rate did not stimulate productivity enough to be statistically detectable at the macro level.[21]

---

[20] Ibid., 19.
[21] Ibid., 150.

Another reason why top salaries have risen so much is that tax tariffs in the US for these salaries has fallen from 90 % in 1970 to 30 % in 1990. Even more important is the manner in which the salaries are being established. Managers establish the salary levels for their employees, but their own salaries are established by compensation committees whose members are appointed by the firm's management.

There are additional factors that add to growing inequality. One factor is that a large capital fund grows faster than a small one. Large funds yield higher returns, which can be reinvested, and so on. Moreover, owners of a small capital fund have to manage it themselves and, thus, cannot benefit from professional advice. Piketty provides an example of fast-growing large capital funds:

> The only way to make sense of these wealth rankings is to examine the evolution of the amount of wealth owned by a fixed percentage of the world's population, say the richest twenty-millionth of the adult population of the planet: roughly 150 people out of 3 billion adults in the late 1980s and 225 people out of 4.5 billion in the early 2010s. We then find that the average wealth of this group has increased from just over $1.5 billion in 1987 to nearly $15 billion in 2013, for an average growth rate of 6.4 percent above inflation.[22]

It is not easy to do research on capital investments and their returns; after all, people aren't eager to share this very personal information. However, Piketty identified one source that could be researched: university endowments. Based on the investment results of these funds, he was able to confirm that large endowments yielded more returns than small ones. Harvard's endowment, for example, amounts to roughly $30 billion. Princeton's and Yale's follow with $20 billion and $15 billion, respectively. Their average annual return on capital was 10.2 %. Endowments of less than $100 million were doing not so well; their annual return was 6.2 %.

The author wondered whether educational institutions promote social mobility. After all, the better a child is educated the greater the chance that he or she will get a well-paid job. This will contribute to limiting the gap

---

[22] Ibid., 434.

between the rich and not-so-rich. Even with the considerable increase in the average level of education during the twentieth century, earned-income inequality did not diminish. Qualification levels have shifted upwards, which partly explains why inequality did not diminish. Tuition fees rose sharply in America in the period 1990–2010, which contributed to reduced social mobility. Only well-off parents could afford to send their children to the best American universities. Research demonstrates that the proportion of college degrees earned by children whose parents belong to the bottom quartiles of the income hierarchy stagnated at 10–20 % in 1970–2010, while it rose from 40 to 80 % for children with parents in the top quartile.

The main forces of convergence, the author notes on page 21, are the diffusion of knowledge and investment in training and skills. But he also realises that achieving real equality of opportunity in higher education is not easy. Nonetheless, it is an important policy challenge to overcome this barrier, as it would contribute something positive to counter the threat of more income inequality in the future.

A person inheriting a large sum of money on top of what that person already owns results in faster growth of the total capital sum. Capital that was generated by past generations is now going to play an important role. If one takes into consideration a lower population growth rate, this leads to more capital for each inheritor and the inherited capital will constitute an important factor in the total capital sum.

Piketty shows that the capital owned by a person at the time of the person's death is on average 20 % larger than the capital owned by a living person. If one would include the spectacular rise in capital transfers of parents to their children (e.g. to help them buying a house) during their life time, then the capital owned at the time of death would be twice as high compared to the average capital of a person still alive. This may suggest that we are moving into a situation that existed during the belle époque. This, however, is not the case; income from labour is still the most important source of income, and this also goes for the top 10 %. For the very top 1 % the situation is different; capital eclipses income as the most important source of income. 'Supermanagers' salaries make it now possible to reach the exclusive league of the super-rich. In the nineteenth century, this wasn't possible, says Piketty, as during that time only *rentiers* belonged to the top.

What will the situation be towards the end of this century? Piketty estimated that global output will gradually decline from the current 3 % a year to 1.5 % in the second half of this century. The savings rate will stabilise at about 10 %, in the long term. With these assumptions, including a slowing-down of demographic growth, $\beta = s/g$ implies that the global capital–income ratio will continue to rise and could approach 700 % before the end of this century, or approximately the level observed in Europe from the eighteenth century to the belle époque.

> Piketty pays attention to the so-called Two Cambridges Debate, about the question of capital accumulation and a possible dynamic equilibrium, on pp. 230–2. From the outset he notes that the national accounts and other statistical data available in the late nineteenth and early twentieth centuries were inadequate for a correct understanding of the dynamics of the capital–income ratio. By the middle of the twentieth century, following the shocks of 1914 and 1945, the reverse was true. This explains why this question of capital accumulation and a possible dynamic equilibrium continued to feed controversy, hence the Cambridge capital theory controversy, or the Two Cambridges Debate. The two Cambridges involved were Cambridge, England, and Cambridge, Massachusetts, USA. The former was represented by, among others, Joan Robinson and Piero Srafa; the latter by Paul Samuelson and Robert Solow.
>
> First, a bit of history: Harrod and Domar had introduced the formula $\beta = s/g$, after which it was common to be inverted as $g = s/\beta$. Harrod argued that β was *fixed* by the available technology, so that g was entirely determined by the savings rate. Suppose that the savings rate is 10 % and a capital–income ratio of 5, then the growth rate g of the economy's productive capacity is 2 % per year. However, since the growth rate must be equal to the population's growth rate (and of productivity, which, as Piketty added, at the time was still ill-defined), it follows that g is an intrinsically unstable process (in line with Keynes's thinking). There is either too much or too little capital, which gives rise to excess capacity and speculative bubbles or else to unemployment, or perhaps both at once. Remember, Harrod was writing during the time of the Great Depression, an obvious sign of macroeconomic instability. The conclusion then was that growth was a highly volatile process. To bring savings into line with investment decisions is difficult, as decisions about savings and investments are made by different people, especially since it is difficult in the short term to alter the capital intensity and organisation of production. Piketty observed that in the long term the capital–income ratio is relatively flexible, together with the fact that the elasticity of substitution of capital for labour has in actual fact been greater than one (1) over a long period of time.

In 1956, Robert Solow introduced a production function with substitutable factors, which made it possible to invert the formula and thus write $\beta = s/g$. In the long term, the capital–income ratio adjusts to the savings rate and the economy's structural growth rate rather than the other way around. So, the two Cambridge schools differed about the equation, in that, as the Americans suggested, that growth would always be balanced, contrary to the British emphasis on the Keynesian importance of short-term fluctuations.

Solow's neoclassical growth model called the shots as of the 1970s, when Keynesianism was in retreat (see Chap. 5). The British suspicion of the Americans not being sensitive to short-term fluctuations was unfounded, says Piketty, as both Samuelson and Solow understood that short-term growth was unstable and that, consequently, the economy would require Keynesian policies; they viewed $\beta = s/g$ as a long-term law only.

Long-term growth does not guarantee a harmonious distribution of wealth and in no way implies the disappearance or even reduction of inequality in capital ownership. Furthermore, $\beta = s/g$ does not preclude very large variations in the capital–income ratio over time and between countries. Piketty argued that

> the virulence of the Cambridge capital controversy was due in part to the fact that the participants in the debate on both sides lacked the historical data needed to clarify the terms of the debate. It is striking to see how little use either side made of national capital estimates prior to World War I...The two world wars created such a deep discontinuity in both conceptual and statistical analysis that for a while it seemed impossible to study the issue in a long-run perspective, especially from a European point of view.[23]

What Can Be Done to Limit the Gap?

After the wide-ranging analysis of capital and income trends through time, Piketty proposes measures to 'regulate capital in the twenty-first century', the title of part IV of his book. His overall conclusion is as follows:

> ...a market economy based on private property, if left to itself, contains powerful forces of convergence, associated in particular with the diffusion of knowledge and skills; but it also contains powerful forces of divergence,

---

[23] Ibid., 232.

which are potentially threatening to democratic societies and to the values of social justice on which they are based.[24]

His historical analysis suggests that a new belle époque is beckoning, wherein a small section of the population owns almost all capital. Can something be done to prevent such a situation from emerging? Yes, says Piketty.

First, the fact that history tells us that r was larger than g does not necessarily imply that it will be like this forever; it may be a historical fact but it is not a logical necessity. Trends like this one—which the author finds worrying for the reasons explained above—can be adjusted through the adoption of economic and fiscal policies.

Piketty noted that the influence of the state is much greater now than it was in the past. Indeed, it is greater than it has ever been. Tax income increased through time and so did the state's social expenditures.[25] Education, for example, is now much more important than in the eighteenth century.

To prevent a global trend of growing inequality, Piketty proposes the introduction of a global progressive tax on capital (but not on the income generated by this capital). As regards the annual percentages to be applied, Piketty suggests: (1) 0.1–0.5 % for capital between €1 and €5 million; (2) 2 % for capital between €5 and €10 million; (3) 5–10 % for capital more than €10 million; however, applied progressively (i.e. the higher the capital the higher the tax percentage).

The effect of this global capital tax would be to have a dampening effect on the income from capital. And through the introduction of such a global tax, tax havens will be something of the past, which—in turn—would promote efficient capital investments. Transparency of where capital is moving to and who owns it will be enhanced as well. Tax evasion will also be curbed, and international financial stability will be improved.

---

[24] Ibid., 571.

[25] Regarding the role of the state in poor and emerging countries Piketty observed that 'The development of a fiscal and social state is intimately related to the process of state-building as such. Hence, the history of economic development is also a matter of political and cultural development, and each country must find its own distinctive path and cope with its own internal divisions.' *Capital*, 491.

The author realises that his proposed global capital tax is a utopian ideal, yet it might be introduced regionally, for example in the European Union and in America. Piketty concludes,

> But if the idea is utopian, it is nevertheless useful, for several reasons. First, even if nothing resembling this ideal is put into practice in the foreseeable future, it can serve as a worthwhile reference point, a standard against which alternative proposals can be measured.[26]

---

[26] Ibid., 515.

Erratum to: From Keynes to Piketty

Peter de Haan

Erratum to:

Bibliography from letter S-Z which was missing has been updated in the printed version.

DOI 10.1057/978-1-137-60002-8.

The online version of the original book can be found under
DOI 10.1057/978-1-137-60002-8

© The Editor(s) (if applicable) and The Author(s) 2016
P. de Haan, *From Keynes to Piketty*,
DOI 10.1057/978-1-137-60002-8_9

Epilogue

The past century was a turbulent one, politically and economically. The Keynesian revolution shattered the belief that neoclassical economics could address recessions. Keynes provided the analytical framework—and the tools—to overcome the crisis and restore full employment. However, Keynesianism wasn't equipped to address stagflation; neoclassical economics was better suited to do so. The popularity of economic schools of thought apparently depended on what was happening in the real world. One of the two main schools—Keynesianism or neoclassical economics—flourished when the time was ripe for it. Robert Solow once observed that the questions keep changing and the answers to even old questions keep changing as society evolves. After the outbreak of the Great Recession, neoclassical economics lost credibility because it hadn't predicted, nor could it explain, the recession. There was a re-appreciation of what Keynes had proposed in dealing with recessions. His prescriptions, this time promoted by New Keynesians, were again widely applied.

This does not imply that sensible economists don't recognise useful insights in both the neoclassical school and the New Keynesian school of thought. A merger of the two is underway. Robert Waldmann, a University of Rome economics professor, provided a succinct explanation of this development in America. Waldmann coined the terms 'freshwater economists' for neoclassical economists, and 'saltwater economists' for New Keynesians.[1]

Freshwater economists, typically trained at the University of Chicago, consider general equilibrium models, with well-functioning markets and symmetric information of buyers and sellers, to be reflective of reality; they don't like government intervention much. At the same time, saltwater macroeconomics, or New Keynesianism, is to be found at East Coast universities in America, like at the Massachusetts Institute of Technology, Harvard and Princeton, as well as at the IMF and the Fed. Not surprisingly, New Keynesians portray a Keynesian vision of what should be done with recessions. Yet they accept the neoclassical rational expectations hypothesis. But their models don't exclude the possibility of frictions, resulting from—among other things—market imperfections. Their practitioners allow policy intervention in the short term if there is a crisis. New Keynesians propose effective demand management. This is necessary—underscoring what Keynes argued before—because demand has to be stimulated to pull the economy out of a crisis, while freshwater economists maintain that in a crisis situation, market forces, and the central bank printing money, will in the long term re-establish economic equilibrium.[2]

Now, the philosophies of the saltwater and freshwater economists are translated into Dynamic Stochastic General Equilibrium (DSGE) top-down models. They are dynamic in nature as they study how the economy evolves over time. The term stochastic is included as the models take into account random shocks ranging from technological progress to changes in macroeconomic policymaking. There are two distinct schools of thought that each present their particular model.

Real Business Cycle (RBC) theory, which is based upon the neoclassical growth model, assumes flexible prices and studies how real shocks to the economy may cause business-cycle fluctuations. The freshwater

---

[1] Skidelsky, R. (2009) *Keynes: The Return of The Master*. London: Allen Lane, 30.

[2] This is what Skidelsky wrote about the past crisis and symmetric information: 'It is a crisis of symmetric ignorance, not asymmetric information … If only one person were perfectly informed there could never be a general crisis. But the only perfectly informed person is God, and he does not play the stock market.' *The Return of the Master*, 45.

DSGE model is based on this theory. Then there are the saltwater-New Keynesian DSGE models, building on a structure that resembles the RBC models, but assuming prices set by monopolistically competitive firms that cannot be immediately adjusted. These DSGE models are not perfect; that is, they have not proven useful in analysing the recent financial crisis, because they accept the view that there is some equilibrium in the economy to which all prices converge. Nonetheless, the applicability of the models is improving, in the sense that there is consensus among economists that the models should incorporate the phenomena of price stickiness and frictions in financial markets, so as to better reflect what can happen in the real economy.

There are also bottom-up models: the agent-based models (ABM) that analyse the economy from the micro-level point of view. ABMs don't assume that the economy can achieve an equilibrium; large fluctuations and even crashes are not excluded in these models. No order or design is imposed on the economy from the top down. The agents involved do not belong to the one-size-fits-all category; no, some agents may think that prices reflect fundamentals, while others may base their decisions on observations of price trends. The models also allow for interactions between agents; hence, phenomena such as herding and panic (leading to bubbles or crashes) can be simulated; ABMs can run computer simulations to see what comes out, not hindered by top-down assumptions. These ABMs may evolve into reliable early crisis warning systems. Perhaps with the help of improved DSGE and ABM models, economists will be able to better *predict* in which direction the economy is heading.

Karl Marx observed that economists are like theologians. Every religion, other than their own, is a human invention, whereas their own brand of religion is an emanation from God. In time, the economic science, supported by for example DSGE or ABM models and subdisciplines such as behavioural economics, may be able to adequately explain what happened in the past and predict the future course of economies. Such a great achievement wouldn't necessarily give economists a God-given aura, but it would at least give them back the pride and confidence with which they held sway during the time of the Great Moderation.

References

Acemoglu, D., & Robinson, J. (2012). *Why nations fail: The origins of power, prosperity and poverty*. London: Profile Books.

Adelman, J. (2013). *Worldly philosopher: The Odyssey of Albert O. Hirschman*. Princeton: Princeton University Press.

Arrow, K. (1963). *Social choice and individual values*. New York: Wiley.

Atkinson, A., Piketty, T., & Saez, E. (2011). Top incomes in the long run of history. *Journal of Economic Literature, 49*, 3–71.

Berger, P. L., & Luckmann, T. (1966). *The social construction of reality*. New York: Anchor Books.

Berger, P. L. (1987). *The capitalist revolution: Fifty propositions about prosperity, equality, & liberty*. Aldershot: Gower.

Berger, P. L., & Zijderveld, A. (2009). *In praise of doubt: How to have convictions without being a fanatic*. New York: Harper Collins.

Bernanke, B. (2000). *Essays on the great depression*. Princeton: Princeton University Press.

Bomhoff, E. J. (1982). *Government is not the solution: It's the problem* (Economen over crisis). Amsterdam, Brussels: Uitgeverij Intermediair.

Cassidy, J. (2009). *How markets fail: The logic of economic calamities*. London: Allen Lane.

Centraal Bureau voor de Statistiek. Statistics on Unemployment in The Netherlands.

Chang, H.-J. (2010). *23 things they don't tell you about capitalism.* London: Penguin.
Chang, H.-J. (2014). *Economics: The user's guide.* London: Pelican Books.
Churchill, W. S. (2000). *My early life.* London: Eland.
Coase, R. (1960). The problem of societal cost. *Journal of Law and Economics, 3,* 1–44.
Davenport-Hines, R. (2015). *Universal man: The seven lives of John Maynard Keynes.* London: William Collins.
De Beus, J. W. (1982). *The enemy of the market is not ideology but the engineer* (Economen over crisis). Amsterdam, Brussels: Uitgeverij Intermediair.
Drucker, P. F. (2007). *Adventures of a Bystander.* New Brunswick/London: Transaction.
Easterly, W. (2006). *The White Man's Burden: Why the West's efforts to aid the rest have done so much ill and so little good.* New York: Penguin.
Eatwell, J., Milgate, M., & Newsman, P. (Eds.). (1998). *The new Palgrave: A dictionary of economics* (Vol. 2, E to J). London: MacMillan Reference.
Ebenstein, L. (2007). *Milton Friedman: A biography.* New York: Palgrave Macmillan.
Eichengreen, B. (2015). *Hall of mirrors: The great depression, the great recession, and the uses – and misuses – of history.* New York: Oxford University Press.
Fitzgerald, F. S. (1974). *This side of paradise.* Harmondsworth: Penguin.
Friedman, M. (1953). *The methodology of positive economics* (Essays in positive economics). Chicago: University of Chicago Press.
Friedman, M. (1957). *Theory of the consumption function.* Princeton: Princeton University Press for the National Bureau of Economic Research.
Friedman, M. (1978). *From Galbraith to economic freedom.* Occasional paper 49. London: The Institute of Economic Affairs.
Friedman, M., & Friedman, R. (1990). *Free to choose.* New York: Hartcourt.
Friedman, M., & Friedman, R. (1998). *Two lucky people: Memoirs.* Chicago: University of Chicago Press.
Friedman, M., & Friedman R. (2002). *Capitalism and freedom.* Fortieth Anniversary Edition. Chicago: University of Chicago Press.
Friedman, M., & Kuznets, S. (1945). *Income from independent professional practice.* New York: National Bureau of Economic Research.
Friedman, M., & Schwartz, A. J. (1963). *A monetary history of the United States, 1867–1960.* Princeton: Princeton University Press for the National Bureau of Economic Research.

Galbraith, J. K. (1952). *A theory of price control.* Cambridge: Harvard University Press.
Galbraith, J. K. (1954). *The great crash.* Boston: Houghton Mifflin Company.
Galbraith, J. K. (1967). *The new industrial state.* Boston: Houghton Mifflin Company.
Galbraith, J. K. (1983). *A life in our times: Memoirs.* London: Corgi Books.
Galbraith, J. K. (1987). *Economics in perspective: A critical history.* Boston: Houghton Mifflin.
Galbraith, J. K. (1999). *The affluent society.* Fortieth Anniversary Edition. London: Penguin Group.
Galbraith, J. K. (2011). *American capitalism: The concept of countervailing power.* New Brunswick/London: Transaction.
Gans, J. (2014). Capital creators: Piketty and the growth theory. *Digitopoly*, April 23.
Greenspan, A. (2007). *The age of turbulence.* London: Allen Lane.
Groenewegen, J. (1982). *Capitalism is change* (Economen over crisis). Amsterdam, Brussels: Uitgeverij Intermediair.
Grunwald, M. (2012). *The new new deal: The hidden story of change in the Obama Era.* New York: Simon & Schuster.
Haffner, S. (2000). *Geschichte eines Deutschen: Die Erinnerungen 1914–1933.* Stuttgart/München: Deutsche Verlags.
Hayek, F. A. (1933). *Monetary theory and the trade cycle.* London: Jonathan Cape.
Hayek, F. A. (1945). The use of knowledge in society. *American Economic Review, 35*(4), 519–530.
Hayek, F. A. (1973). *Law, legislation and liberty* (Vol. I, II, and III). Chicago: Chicago University Press.
Hayek, F. A. (1976). *Law, legislation and liberty* (Vol. I, II, and III). Chicago: Chicago University Press.
Hayek, F. A. (1979). *Law, legislation and liberty* (Vol. I, II, and III). Chicago: Chicago University Press.
Hayek, F. A. (1988). *The fatal conceit: The errors of socialism.* Chicago: Chicago University Press.
Hayek, F. A. (2006). *The constitution of liberty.* London/New York: Routledge Classics.
Hayek, F. A. (2010). *The road to serfdom.* London: The Institute of Economic Affairs.

Heilbroner, R. (1995). *The worldly philosophers: The lives, times and ideas of the great economic thinkers*. London: Penguin Group.
Hirschman, A. O. (1945). *National power and the structure of foreign trade*. Berkeley/Los Angeles: University of California Press.
Hirschman, A. O. (1958). *The strategy of economic development*. New Haven: Yale University Press.
Hirschman, A. O. (1970). *Exit, voice and loyalty: Response to the decline in firms, organisations and states*. Cambridge, MA: Harvard University Press.
Hirschman, A. O. (1977). *The passions and the interests: Political arguments for capitalism before its triumph*. Princeton: Princeton University Press.
Hirschman, A. O. (1991). *The rhetoric of reaction: Perversity, futility, jeopardy*. Cambridge: Belknap Press of Harvard University Press.
Hirschman, A. O. (1998). *Lemma on Hirschman* (The new Palgrave: A dictionary of economics, Vol. 2, E to J). London: MacMillan Reference.
Jacobs, B. (2015). *De Prijs van Gelijkheid*. Amsterdam: Prometheus/Bert Bakker.
Keynes, J. M. (1919). *The economic consequences of peace*. London: Macmillan and Co.
Keynes, J. M. (1926). *The end of laissez faire*. London: Hogarth Press.
Keynes, J. M. (1930). *A treatise on money*. London: Macmillan and Co.
Keynes, J. M. (1931a). *The economic consequences of Mr. Churchill* (Essays in Persuasion). London: MacMillan.
Keynes, J. M. (1931b). *Economic possibilities for our grandchildren* (Essays in Persuasion). London: MacMillan and Co.
Keynes, J. M. (1964). *The general theory of employment, interest, and money*. San Diego/New York/London: Harcourt Brace & Company.
Krugman, P. (2009). *The return of depression economics and the crisis of 2008*. New York: W.W. Norton & Company.
Krugman, P. (2013). *End this depression now*. New York: W.W. Norton & Company.
Lal, D. (2000). Institutional development and economic growth. In M. Oosterbaan, N. De Ruyter van Steveninck, & N. Van der Windt (Eds.), *The determinants of economic growth*. Boston: Kluwer Academic.
Maddison, A. (2003). *The world economy: Historical statistics*. Paris: OECD Development Centre Studies.
Marshall, A. (1977). *The principles of economics*. London: The English Language Book Society and Macmillan.
McCraw, T. K. (2007). *Prophet of innovation: Joseph Schumpeter and creative destruction*. Cambridge, MA: Harvard University Press.
McFadden, D. L. (2013). *The new science of pleasure*. NBER working paper 18687. Cambridge: National Bureau of Economic Research.

Minsky, H. (1986). *Stabilizing an unstable economy*. New Haven/London: Yale University Press.
Mises, L. V. (1951). *Socialism: An economic and sociological analysis*. New Haven: Yale University Press.
Mises, L. V. (1990). *Economic calculation in the socialist commonwealth*. Auburn: Ludwig von Mises Institute.
Myrdal, G. (1944). *The American dilemma*. New York: Harper and Brothers Publishers.
Nagy, A. (1999). The memoirs of a 'Proud Hungarian'. *The Hungarian Quarterly*, *40*(Autumn).
Naim, M. (2013). *The end of power*. New York: Basic Books.
Nasar, S. (2011). *Grand pursuit: The story of economic genius*. London: Fourth Estate.
Nentjes, A. (1982). *The system is not self-adjusting* (Economen over crisis). Amsterdam, Brussels: Uitgeverij Intermediair.
North, D. C., & Thomas, R. P. (1973). *The rise of the Western world: A new economic history*. Cambridge: Cambridge University Press.
North, D. C. (1977). Markets and other allocation systems in history: The challenge of Karl Polanyi. *Journal of European Economic History*, *6*(Winter).
North, D. C. (1989). Institutions and economic growth: A historical introduction. *World Development*, *17*(9), 1319–1332.
North, D. C. (1990). *Institutions, institutional change and economic performance*. Cambridge: Cambridge University Press.
North, D. C. (2005). *Understanding the process of economic change*. Princeton: Princeton University Press.
North, D., et al. (2007). *Limited access orders in the developing world: A new approach to the problems of development*. World Bank working paper 4359. Washington, DC: World Bank.
Olsen, M. (1982). *The rise and decline of nations: Economic growth, stagflation and social rigidities*. New Haven: Yale University Press.
Pen, J. (1971). *Income distribution*. Harmondsworth: Penguin.
Pen, J. (1983). *Keynes, Keynes, Keynes*, June 3.
Piketty, T. (2014). *Capitalism in the twenty-first century*. Cambridge, MA: The Belknap Press of Harvard University Press.
Polanyi, K. (Ed.). (1957). *Trade and market in the early empires*. Glencoe: Free Press.
Polanyi, K. (2001). *The great transformation: The political and economic origins of our time*. Boston: Beacon Press.

Pressman, S. (2014). *Fifty major economists*. London: Routledge Key Guides.
Pyka, A., & Fagiolo, G. (2005). Agent-based modelling: A methodology for Neo-Schumpeterian economics. *Volkswirtschaftliche Dioskussionsreihe*, Beitrag Nr. 272.
Reinhart, C., & Rogoff, K. (2009). *This time is different: Eight centuries of financial folly*. Princeton/Oxford: Princeton University Press.
Robinson, J. (1974). *Economic philosophy*. Harmondsworth: Penguin.
Rodrik, D. (2014). Piketty and the Zeitgeist. *Project Syndicate*, May 13.
Samuelson, P. (1947). *Foundations of economic analysis*. Cambridge, MA: Harvard University Press.
Schumpeter, J. A. (1934). *The theory of economic development*. Cambridge: Harvard University Press, Harvard Economic Studies.
Schumpeter, J. A. (1939). *Business cycle: A theoretical and statistical analysis of the capitalist process*. New York: McGraw-Hill Book Company.
Schumpeter, J. A. (1954). *History of economic analysis*. London: Oxford University Press.
Schumpeter, J. A. (1970). *Capitalism, socialism and democracy*. London: Unwin University Press.
Scitovsky, T. (1951). *Welfare and competition: The economics of a fully employed economy*. Chicago: R.D. Irving.
Scitovsky, T. (1958). *Economic theory and Western European integration*. Stanford: Stanford University Press.
Scitovsky, T. (Ed.). (1970). *Industry and trade in some developing countries*. London: Oxford University Press.
Scitovsky, T. (1992). *The Joyless economy: The psychology of human satisfaction*. New York/Oxford: Oxford University Press.
Scitovsky, T. (1999). The memoirs of a 'Proud Hungarian'. *The Hungarian Quarterly*, 40(Autumn).
Sedlacek, T. (2011). *Economics of good and evil: The quest for economic meaning from Gilgamesh to Wall Street*. New York: Oxford University Press.
Shiller, R. (2000). *Irrational exuberance*. Princeton: Princeton University Press.
Sint, M., & Verbruggen, H. (1982). *Economen over crisis*. Amsterdam, Brussels: Uitgeverij Intermediair.
Skidelsky, R. (2004). *John Maynard Keynes 1883–1946: Economist, philosopher, statesman*. London: Pan Books.
Skidelsky, R. (2009). *Keynes: The return of the master*. London: Allen Lane.
Skidelsky, R., & Skidelsky, E. (2012). *How much is enough? Money and the good life*. New York: Other Press.

Solow, R. (2014). Thomas Piketty is right. Everything you need to know about capital in the twenty-first century. *New Republic*, April 22.
Stedman Jones, D. (2012). *Masters of the universe: Hayek, Friedman, and the birth of neoliberal politics*. Princeton: Princeton University Press.
Stiglitz, J. (2012). *The price of inequality: How today's divided society endangers our future*. New York: W.W. Norton & Company.
Taylor, F. (2013). *The Downfall of money: Germany's hyperinflation and the destruction of the middle class*. New York: Bloomsbury Press.
US Department of Labor: Industrial Bureau of Labor Statistics. Statistics on Unemployment in the USA.
Veblen, T. (1899). *The theory of the leisure class*. New York: MacMillan.
Verbon, H. (2013). De Late Ekenning Van De Zwarte Zwaan Door Paul Samuelson. *ESB, Jaargang 98* (4664 and 4665), July 12.
Wapshott, N. (2011). *Keynes–Hayek: The clash that defined modern economics*. New York: Norton & Company.
Went, R. (Ed.). (2014). *Waarom Piketty Lezen?* Amsterdam: Amsterdam University Press.
Wolf, M. (2014). *The shifts and the shocks: What we've learned – and have still to learn – from the financial crisis*. London: Allen Lane.
Zweig, S. (1945). *The world of yesterday*. New York: The Viking Press.

Index

A
Abenomics, 33
Abe, Shinzo, 33
academic freedom, 275
Acemoglu, Daron, 393, 478
adaptive efficiency, 411–12
Adelman, Irma, 206
Adelman, Jerry, 309, 310, 312, 314–16
adverse economic policies, 38
affluence, 13–14
The Affluent Society (Galbraith), 14, 181–3
   conventional wisdom, 183–4
   dependence effect, 189–90
   divorce of production from security, 198
   economics and tradition of despair, 184–5
   economic security, 187–8
   imperatives of consumer demand, 189
   inequality, 186–7
   inflation, 192–3
   investment balance, 196–7
   labour, leisure and new class, 199
   Marxian Pall, 186
   monetary illusion, 193–4
   paramount position of production, 188–9
   position of poverty, 198–9
   production and price stability, 194
   redress of balance, 198
   on security and survival, 199–200
   social balance theory, 195–6
   transition, 197–8
   uncertain reassurance, 185
   Veblen's observations, 185–6
   vested interest in output, 190–1

Note: Page number followed by "n" refers to footnotes.

African economies (1980–2002), 21
agency theory, 417
agent-based models (ABM), 497
Age of Liberalism, 294
The Age of Turbulence (Greenspan), 12, 22
aggregate demand, 7, 99
aggregate demand function, 75, 77–79
agriculture and natural resources
　direct controls of production, 272
　shrinking consumption, 271
AIG. *See* American International Group (AIG)
Akerlof, George (The Market for Lemons: Quality Uncertainty and the Market Mechanism), 448–50
Alternative Mortgage Transaction Parity Act, 461
American Capitalism: The Concept of Countervailing Power (1952) (Galbraith), 178
American Constitution, 252
American constitutionalism, 252
American Economic Association (AEA), 19, 23, 118, 155, 290, 292, 443
American International Group (AIG), 27, 463, 466
American Revolution, 253
anti-capitalist policy, 128
anti-stagflation policy, in *Bestek 81*, 16
appeasement, 9
Arendt, Hannah, 309
Aristotle, 251
Arrow–Debreu model, 442, 445

Arrow, Kenneth, 202, 203, 287, 436, 437, 442, 448–50
Atkinson, Anthony, 473, 475
Austria, inflation in, 5–6
authoritarian state systems, 106
autocratic rule, 479
　Russia, 1
　Western democracies, 9
automatism, economic, 473
Axelrod, Robert, 447

B

Bachelier, Louis, 439, 440
Bank of England, 45, 56
Baptiste, Jean, 73
Barro, Robert, 442
Bator, Francis, 445, 446
Bauer, Otto, 113
Bauer, Peter, 292, 353
Becker, Gary, 321
Bell Curve, 440, 463
Bentham, Jeremy (Utilitarians), 251, 293
Berger, Peter Ludwig (1929–)
　academic career, 352–3
　academic thinking, 353–4
　The Capitalist Revolution: Fifty Propositions about Prosperity, Equality, & Liberty, 19, 351, 353–6
　capitalism and development, 370–5
　capitalism and dynamics of myth, 383–4
　capitalism and personal liberties, 368–70
　capitalism and political liberties, 366–8

capitalism as phenomenon,
356–9
class system, 362–5
East Asian capitalism, 375–80
individualism, 368–9
Industrial Revolution,
359–60
industrial socialism, 380–3
shape and uses of a theory of
capitalism, 384–6
honours, 354
The Social Construction of Reality
(1966), 353
Berlin, Isaiah, 40
Bernanke, Ben, 4, 27–8, 38, 290,
426, 462, 468
Essays on the Great Depression,
2000, 4
Bestek 81, anti-stagflation policy
in, 16
Bezos, Jeff, 487
Blair, Tony, 427
Blankfein, Lloyd, 464
Bloomberg View (Crook), 476
Boody, Elizabeth, 119
bourgeois culture, 369, 369n21,
370
bourgeois stock, 146
Breton, André, 309
Bretton Woods
agreement, 13, 19, 55–6
monetary system, 38, 225
and UN, 13
Buchanan, James, 52, 53
Buffett, Warren, 463
Burns, Arthur, 278
Bush (president), 237, 460
business incentives to liquidity,
88–90

C

capital asset, 84, 93, 94
capital–income ratio, 481, 482, 484,
486, 490–1
Capital in the Twenty-First Century
(Piketty), 471, 473,
476–93
first fundamental law of
capitalism, 481
freshwater economists, 496
limiting the gap, 488
New Keynesian school of thought,
495
patrimonial capitalism, 485–6
progressive global tax on capital,
492
saltwater economists, 496
second fundamental law of
capitalism, 484
supermanagers, 486–9
Two Cambridges debate, 490
capitalism, 9–11, 109, 118, 473,
480
civilisation of, 134–5
and development, 370–5
and discrimination, 301
and dynamics of myth, 383–4
East Asian, 375–80
economic culture theory of, 355
Great Moderation period, 18–20
industrial, 357, 360, 363, 365,
371, 381
labourist, 157
new institutional economics,
20–1
patrimonial, 475, 485–6
and personal liberties, 368–70
as phenomenon, 356–9
and political liberties, 366–8

Capitalism and Freedom (Friedman), 17, 472
  alleviation of poverty, 306–8
  distribution of income, 304–5
  flat income tax, 305
  monopoly and social responsibility, 302–3
  negative income tax, 287, 307, 472
  occupational licensure in medicine, 303–4
  Smoot–Hawley Tariff Act of 1930, 297
  social welfare measures, 305–6
  voucher system, 300
Capitalism, Socialism and Democracy (Schumpeter), 9–10
  capitalism survive, 126–7, 135–7
    civilisation of capitalism, 134–5
    creative destruction process, 129–30
    decomposition, 139–40
    growing hostility, 137–9
    monopolistic practices, 130–1
    plausible capitalism, 128–9
    rate of increase of total output, 127–8
    vanishing investment opportunity, 133–4
  Marxian doctrine
    Marx the economist, 123–5
    Marx the prophet, 121
    Marx the sociologist, 121–3
    Marx the teacher, 125–6
  socialism and democracy
    classical doctrine of democracy, 149–51
    inference, 152–5
    march into socialism, 155–8
    setting of the problem, 149
    theory of democracy, 151–2
  socialism work
    blueprints comparison, 144–5
    clearing decks, 140–1
    human element, 145–7
    socialist blueprint, 141–3
    transition, 147–9
capitalist economy, 116, 124, 363, 370, 378, 382
  uncertainty in, 144
capitalist process, 118, 122, 124–5, 133, 135, 137
The Capitalist Revolution: Fifty Propositions about Prosperity, Equality, & Liberty (Berger), 19, 353–6
capitalism
  and development, 370–5
  and dynamics of myth, 383–4
  and personal liberties, 368–70
  as phenomenon, 356–9
  and political liberties, 366–8
  class system, 362–5
  East Asian capitalism, 375–80
  individualism, 368–9
  Industrial Revolution, 359–60
  industrial socialism, 380–3
  shape and uses of a theory of capitalism, 384–6
capitalist system, 122–3
Carnegie, 136, 174, 185
Cassidy, John, 11, 234, 440, 480
  How Markets Fail: The Logic of Economic Calamities (2009), 24, 226, 425–6
CDSs. *See* credit default swaps (CDSs)

Chagall, Marc, 309
Chang, Ha-Joon, 17, 25
Chaplin, Charlie (*Modern Times*), 3
Chenery, Holllis, 312
China, GDP in, 32
Churchill, Winston, 2, 45, 109
Cicero, 251
Civilian Conservation Corps, 8
civilisation
    of capitalism, 134–5
    creative powers of free, 240–6
Clark, Kenneth, 40
classical economics, 442
    postulates of, 71–3
    See also neoclassical economics
classical theory
    of employment, 71
    rate of interest, 88
    on unemployment, 96
Clemenceau (president), 37, 59, 65, 298
Clinton (president), 25, 427, 460
Coase, Ronald, 388, 390, 399, 400, 403, 408, 409, 444
    Coase Theorem, 390, 445
Cold War, 11, 237
collateralised debt obligations (CDOs), 461
colonial powers, 9, 373
command economy, 257, 367
commercial society, 140, 141, 145
commodities
    fictitious, 167, 168
    money-rate of interest, 91–2
    rates of interest for different, 92
Commons, John R., 395
communism, 11, 120, 171, 202, 310, 464, 469
Communist Manifesto, 4

conservatism, 276, 277
The Constitution of Liberty
    employment and independence, 247–8
    free civilisation, creative powers of, 240–6
    freedom and the law
        American Constitutionalism, 252
        coercion and the state, 248–9
        Law, Commands and Order, 249–50
        origins of the Rule of Law, 250–1
    freedom and the state
        American constitutionalism, 252
        cicero, modern liberalism, 251
        coercion and state, 248–9
        decline of the law, 257–9
        economic policy and the rule of law, 255–7
        individual liberty, safeguards, 254–5
        law, commands and order, 249–50
        liberalism and administration, 252–4
        origin of rule of law, 250–1
    freedom in the welfare state
        decline of socialism and rise of welfare state, 259–61
        labour union and employment, 261–3
        monetary system, 268–70
        social security, 263–7
        taxation and redistribution, 267–8
    majority rule, 246–7
    The Value of Freedom, 239–40

consumer demand, 179, 182, 189, 193, 230
Corn Laws in 1846, 169
Cournot, Antoine Augustin, 434
Cowles, Alfred, 435
Cowles Commission, 436
credit default swaps (CDSs), 27, 463, 464, 466
creeping socialism, 368
Crook, Clive, 476
Crossman, R., 260

D
Darwin, 114, 248
Davenport, John, 233
de Balzac, Honoré, 486
Debreu, Gerard, 436, 437, 442, 450
decision-making process, 411–12
deflation, 31
 of effective demand, 100
democracy, 246–7
de Montaigne, Michel, 309, 311, 314
 Essais, 309
dependency theory, 372–4
Depository Institutions Deregulation and Monetary Control Act, 460–1
de Soto, Hernando, 293
de Tocqueville, 248
Director
 Aaron, 233, 279, 285
 Rose, 279
dirigisme, 257
dirigiste, 378
discrimination, capitalism and, 301

distribution of income, 50, 58, 79, 103, 105, 127, 131, 257, 264, 266, 267, 304–5, 479, 484
Dodd–Frank Act of 2010, 27
Dodd–Rank Wall Street Reform and Consumer Protection Act, 27
Domar, 490
The Downfall of Money (2013) (Taylor), 5
Draghi (ECB president), 30–1
Drucker, Peter, 158–60, 168
Duchamp, Marcel, 309
Duflo, Esther, 474n5
Durkheim, Emile, 358
Dutch
 anti-stagflation policy in *Bestek 81*, 16
 stagflation and Dutch disease, 16
Dynamic Stochastic General Equilibrium (DSGE)
 top-down models, 496, 497

E
East Asian capitalism, 375–80
Ebenstein, Lanny, 288
École des hautes études en sciences sociales (EHESS), 474
Econometric Society, 118
economic automatism, 473
Economic Calculation in the Socialist Commonwealth (von Mises), 228
The Economic Consequences of Peace (Keynes), 2, 37, 42–4, 57–69
 Marshall Plan in, 11–13

Economic Cooperation
    Administration (ECA), 309
economic culture theory of
    capitalism, 355
economic imperialism, 169–70
Economic Philosophy (Robinson), 51
economic policy and rule of law,
    255–7
economic security, 187–8
Economics in Perspective (Galbraith),
    15n13
The Economist (Yellen), 28
ECSC. *See* European Coal and Steel
    Community (ECSC)
Edgeworth, Francis Ysidro, 434
education and research, 197, 248,
    273–5
    compulsory education, 273
    The Constitution of Liberty
        (Hayek), 275
    cost of, 273
    subsidising higher education, 274
education, government and, 300–1
effective demand, 77, 90, 96, 98–9
    deflation of, 100
    moderate change in, 101
    principle, 73–5
    quantity of, 101, 102
efficient market hypothesis, 439–42,
    452
EFSF. *See* European Financial
    Stability Facility (EFSF)
EFSM. *See* European Financial
    Stability Mechanism
    (EFSM)
Eichengreen, Barry, 4, 26, 30, 33
    depression's causes analysis, 4
    monetary policy, 30

Ellington, Duke, 3
employment
    classical theory of, 71
    dealing with theory of, 76
    equilibrium level of, 74
    expectation as determining output
        and, 76–7
    and independence, 247–8
    labour unions and, 261–3
Engels, Friedrich, 360, 464
entrepreneur's income, 77
equilibrium level of employment, 74
Erhard, Ludwig, 12
    Wirtschaftswunder, 235
Ernst, Max, 309
European Central Bank (ECB), 22,
    30, 32, 465
European Coal and Steel
    Community (ECSC), 12
European Financial Stability Facility
    (EFSF), 30, 31
European Financial Stability
    Mechanism (EFSM), 30, 31
European Stability Mechanism
    (ESM), 31
exchange, transaction-cost theory of,
    402–3
Exit, Voice and Loyalty (1970)
    (Hirschman), 18, 226
    command economy, 367
    The elusive optimal mix of exit
        and voice, 346–9
    Emile Durkheim, 358
    Eugene McCarthy, 345
    Harold Hotelling, 336
    Mancur Olsen *The Rise and
        Decline of Nations* (1982),
        368

Exit, Voice and Loyalty (cont.)
   Ralph Nader, 330, 349
   Talcott Parsons, 358–9
   voice, 326–7
   voice as an alternative to exit, 328–31
   voice as a residual of exit, 327–8
   Werner Sombart (*Modern Capitalism*), 356–7
expenditure on consumption, 77

F

Fabians: Sydney and Beatrice Webb, 184, 227
Fama, Eugene (efficient market hypothesis), 439
fascism, 9, 171, 258
Federal Home Loan Mortgage Corporation, 26
Federal National Mortgage Association, 26
Federal Reserve Act, 297
Federal Reserve System, 297, 298
Ferguson, Niall, 44, 243
feudalism, 260
fictitious commodities, 167, 168
financial instability hypothesis, 459
Financial Modernization Act, 25
Financial Services Regulatory Relief Act, 464
financial stabilisation policy, 467
Financial Times (Giles), 476
fiscal policy, 79, 127, 194, 287, 299, 300, 451, 456
Fisher, Irving, 4
Fitzgerald, F. S (*This Side of Paradise*, 1974), 278
flat income tax, 305

Fogel, Robert, 395
Ford, Henry, 3
Foundation of Economic Analysis (1947) (Samuelson), 441
France, Anatole, 258
Frank, André Gunder (development of underdevelopment), 372
free-market economics, 160, 445, 464
free-market ideology, 351, 426
free-market model, 428, 446
French Revolution, 253, 257–8, 415, 476
freshwater economists, 496
Freud, Sigmund, 159
Friedman, Milton (1912–2006), 15, 18, 39, 52, 178–80, 226, 233, 236, 262, 273, 281n24, 290–2, 300–2, 306–8, 353, 366, 384, 427, 431, 437, 439, 443
   academic work
      economics as a science, 282
      inflation and unemployment, 289, 291
      influential role in policy making, 281
      MA economics, 281
      natural rate of unemployment, 290
      permanent and transitory incomes, distinction between, 281
      quantity theory of money, 288
      role of money in business cycles, 288
      supply-sider, 287
      Taxing to Prevent Inflation, 284

A Theory of the Consumption Function (1957), 282
Two Lucky People, 287
wartime advice of raising taxes, 284
worked for American Armed Forces, 284
capitalism and discrimination, 301
Capitalism and Freedom, 17, 277–8, 438, 472
  concentrating power in political hands, 293
  equality of opportunity and material inequality, 293
  libertarian school of thought, 293
career, 279–80
  attribution to Chilean inflation, 280
  economic adviser, 280
  writer, 279–80
distribution of income, 304–5
economic and political freedom, relation between, 294–5
fiscal policy, 300
government's role and education
  approved nationalised schools, 300–1
  minimum degree of literacy for stable and democratic society, 300
  public expenditure on higher education, 301
government's role in a free society, 295–6
Great Depression, 17
honours
  awarded Nobel Prize for Economics, 292
  Cato Institute established Friedman Prize for advancing liberty, 292
  elected president of the American Economic Association, 292
  John Bates Clark Medal, 292
  National Medal of Science, 292
  Nobel Prize for Economics, 292
  Presidential Medal of Freedom, 292
Incomes from Independent Professional Practice (1945), 281
International financial and trade arrangements, 299
life history, 278–9
The Methodology of Positive Economics (1953), 282, 283
Monetary History of the United Sates, 438
money, control of
  economic stability, 297
  Federal Reserve Act, 297
  Federal Reserve System (Fed), 297
  Great Depression, 298
  limit government's powers that tend to weaken society, 297
  reforms, 298
monopoly and social responsibility
  government monopolies, 302–3
  industrial monopolies, 302
  monopoly in labour, 302
  private sector monopolies, 302

Friedman, Milton (*cont.*)
  occupational licensure in
    medicine, 303–4
  permanent income hypothesis,
    282
  poverty alleviation, 307–8
    construction of highways, 307
    negative income tax, 307
    private charity, 307
    state action towards
      ameliorating poverty, 307
  sequential analysis, 284
  social responsibility, 303
  social welfare measures, 305–6
Friedman on Pinochet, 280
Friedman, Rose, 279–80, 281n24,
  286, 366, 437
Frisch, 131
Fry, Varian, 309

G
Galbraith, John Kenneth (1908–
  2006), 174
  The Affluent Society, 14, 181–3,
    289, 446
    conventional wisdom, 183–4
    dependence effect, 189–90
    divorce of production from
      security, 198
    economics and tradition of
      despair, 184–5
    economic security, 187–8
    imperatives of consumer
      demand, 189
    inequality, 186–7
    inflation, 192–3
    investment balance, 196–7
    labour, leisure and the new
      class, 199
    Marxian Pall, 186
    monetary illusion, 193–4
    paramount position of
      production, 188–9
    position of poverty, 198–9
    production and price stability,
      194
    redress of balance, 198
    on security and survival,
      199–200
    social balance theory, 195–6
    transition, 197–8
    uncertain reassurance, 185
    Veblen's observations, 185–6
    vested interest in output,
      190–1
  *American Capitalism: The Concept
    of Countervailing Power*
    (1952), 178–9
  democrat, 176–7
  Democratic Party and, 176–7
  Economics in Perspective, 15n13
  economist, 178–81
  education, 175
  A Life in Our Times (1983), 174,
    202
  Modesty is a vastly overrated virtue,
    174
  The New Industrial State (1967),
    10, 179
  The New York Times Book Review
    (1965), 54
  radio and TV, 177
  A Theory of Price Control (1952),
    178
  Washington D.C., 175–6
Gans, Joshua, 477
Gates, Bill, 487
GDP. *See* Gross Domestic Products
  (GDP)

Geithner, Timothy, 467
General Agreement on Tariffs and Trade, 13
general equilibrium theory, 434
General Motors, 289
The General Theory of Employment, Interest, and Money (1936) (Keynes), 7, 38, 46–55, 69–70, 103–7, 231, 281, 441, 456, 472
general theory, rate of interest, 87–8
George, Lloyd, 38, 60, 62, 65, 184
Germany
　agricultural production in, 66
　hyperinflation, 5
　Nazism in, 201
　tariff systems, 61
　war bonds, 4
Gerschenkron, Alexander, 309
Geschichte Eines Deutschen (2000) (Haffner), 5
Giles, Chris, 476
Glass–Steagall Act of 1933, 8
global warming, 445
Glorious Revolution, 251
Golden Age, 13, 14
Goldman Sachs, 27, 464, 466
gold production, 132
government and education, 300–1
Grand Pursuit (2011) (Nasar), 55
Great Depression, 3–8, 69, 109
　Great War (1914–1918) and, 2, 37
　Keynesian approach, 7
　Milton Friedman, 17
　and WWII, 157
Great Moderation period, capitalism, 18–20
Great Recession, 22–33, 70, 425–69

The Great Transformation: The Political and Economic Origins of Our Time (Polanyi), 10, 164–72, 368
　international system, 165
　rise and fall of market economy, 166–70
　transformation in progress, 170–2
Great War (1914–1918), 42, 59
　and Great Depression, 2, 37
Greenspan, Alan, 16, 24, 110, 450, 468
　The Age of Turbulence, 12, 22
Gross Domestic Products (GDP)
　1921–1927, 3
　1928–1942, 6
　China, 2013, 32
Grossman, Sanford, 440
Grunwald, Michael, 28

H

Haberler, Gottfried, 227
Haffner, Sebastian (*Geschichte Eines Deutschen*, 2000), 5
Hansen, Alvin, 54, 456
happiness, income and, 216–17
Harlem Renaissance, 3
Harriman, 187
Harrod, 490
Hawtrey, Ralph, 215
Hayek, Friedrich August (1899–1992), 18, 46, 52, 159, 353, 355, 384, 427
　academic career and publications, 227–9
　as army fighter, 227
　Austria and Germany, 235
　booms and depression, United States, 229–30

Hayek, Friedrich August (*cont.*)
  British citizenship, 230
  coercion, 239
  composition of demand, 230
  The Constitution of Liberty, 17, 234, 237–8, 275, 293
  dampening effect on consumer demand, 230
  final years, 236
  free civilisation, creative powers of, 240–6
  government intervention in the economy, 232
  government policy with warning, 231
  Hayek's Austrian School theory, 45
  honours, 236–7
  Monetary Theory and the Trade Cycle, 229
  money, role of, 230
  The Mont Perelin Society, 232–4
  Nobel Prize in Economics, 236
  opposite views to Keynes, 227
  postscript, *Why I am Not a Conservative*, 276–7
  Prices and Production, 229
  problems of economic policy, 238
  rent policy, 229
  The Road to Serfdom, 10, 231–3, 237, 294–5, 432–3, 437, 472
  Socialism: An Economic and Sociological Analysis (1922), 431
  telecommunications system, 233, 430–3, 466, 470
  as Tooke Professor of Economic Science and Statistics, 230
  The Treatise in *Economica*, 52
  A Treatise on Money, 45
  University of Chicago, 236
  The Use of Knowledge in Society, 232
  value of freedom, 239–40
  Vienna to London and Cambridge, 230–1
Hazlitt, Henry, 232, 233
Heilbroner, Robert (*The Worldly Philosophers*), 55, 110, 117
Herfindahl–Hirschman Index, 311
Herfindahl, O.C., 311
Hicks, 131
high-income economies, 34
Hirschman, Albert Otto (1915–2012)
  economic advisor, National Planning Council (NPC), 310
  Economic Cooperation Administration (ECA), 309
  Exit, Voice and Loyalty: Responses to the Decline in Firms, Organisations and States (1970), 18, 226, 312, 313, 317
  combining exit and voice, special difficulty, 331–3
  competition as collusive behaviour, 325–7
  The elusive optimal mix of exit and voice, 346–9
  enter, exit, voice, 319
  exit, 323–5
  exit and voice as impersonations, 322–3
  introduction and doctrinal background, 318–19

latitude for deterioration and slack, 319–22
voice as an alternative to exit, 328–31
voice as a residual of exit, 327–8
honours
annual prize in honour of Hirschman, 317
Benjamin E. Lippincott Award, 317
strings of honorary doctorates, 317
job at Commerce Department, 309
joined in Spanish Civil War (1936–1939), 308
London School of Economics, 308
monopoly comforted by competition, 333–5
National Power and the Structure of Foreign Trade, 309, 311
The Passions and the Interests: Political Arguments for Capitalism before Its Triumph (1977), 315, 316
philosophy, 311
The Principle of the Hiding Hand (1967), 312
Rhetoric of Reaction: Perversity, Futility, Jeopardy (1991), 315
Rockefeller Fellowship at the University of California, 309
social sciences, contributions to disequilibria, 311
spatial duopoly and dynamics of two-party systems, 335–7
The Strategy of Economic Development (1958), 310, 311
theory of loyalty
activation of voice as a function of loyalty, 337–8
boycott, 339
exit and voice, elusive optional mix, 346–9
exit and voice in American ideology, 344–5
loyalist behaviour by severe initiation and high penalties for exit, 340–2
loyalist's threat of exit, 339
loyalty and difficult exit from public goods, 342–4
loyalty, functional, 337–8
model of loyalist behaviour, elements for, 339–40
University of Trieste, 308
victims of McCarthyism, 310
Hitler, Adolf, 8, 9, 160
homo economicus, 23, 52, 70, 428, 453
Hoover, Herbert, 66, 297
Hotelling, Harold, 336
housing and town planning
rent restriction, 270
side effects, 270
How Markets Fail: The Logic of Economic Calamities (2009) (Cassidy), 24, 225, 425–8
Benoit Mandelbrot, 440
conclusions, 469–70
Daniel Kahneman, 453–5
efficient market hypothesis (Barro, Robert), 442
Eugene Fama (efficient market hypothesis), 439

How Markets Fail (cont.)
　The Great Crunch, 458–69
　John von Neumann and Oskar Morgenstern: *Theory of Games and Enomic Bahaviour*, 447
　rational expectations hypothesis, 441
　reality-based economics, 443–5
　　The Anatomy of Market Failure (1958), 445–6
　　Herd Behaviour and Investment, 452–3
　　Hyman Minsky and Ponzi finance, 455–8
　　psychology returns to economics, 453–5
　　rational irrationality, 447
　　The Market for Lemons: Quality Uncertainty and the Market Mechanism, 448–50
　　Richard Tahler, 454
　utopian economics, 428–9
　　Adam Smith's invisible hand, 429–30
　　coin-tossing view of finance, 439–41
　　evangelist, 437–9
　　Friedrich Hayek's telecommunications system, 430–3
　　mathematics of Bliss, 435–7
　　perfect markets of Lausanne, 433–5
　　triumph of, 441–3
　　warnings ignored and conventional wisdom, 428–9

Hume, David, 213, 243
Humphrey, Hubert, 176
Hungary, The New Economic Mechanism in, 381
hyperinflation, 5, 8, 42, 227

IMF. *See* International Monetary Fund (IMF)
imperialism, 372
　economic, 169–70
　Marxian theory of, 126
income
　consumer, 78
　definition, 77
　distribution of, 50, 58, 79, 103, 105, 127, 131, 257, 264, 266, 267, 304–5, 479, 484
　entrepreneur, 77
　and happiness, 216–17
income redistribution policies, 231
income tax, 267
　negative, 287, 307, 472
　rate, 305, 487
individualism, 106, 134, 294, 358, 368–70, 379, 382
inducement to invest
　essential properties of interest and money, 91–3
　general theory of employment restated, 93–4
　long-term expectations, 85–6
　marginal efficiency of capital (mec), 84–5
　psychological and business incentives to liquidity, 88–90

Index 521

rate of interest
  classical theory, 88
  general theory, 87–8
  sundry observations on nature of capital, 90–1
industrial capitalism, 357, 360, 363, 365, 371, 381
industrial monopolies, 302
Industrial Revolution, 116, 164–6, 356, 359–60, 368, 376, 423, 471, 480
industrial socialism, 380–3
inequality, 186–7, 471
  reduction in (1914 and 1945), 473
inflation, 192–3
  in Austria, 5–6
  discourages savings, 270
  government financial policy, 269
  and unemployment, 289, 291
inflationism, 170
institutional economics, new, 20–1, 352, 388, 395
Institutions, Institutional Change and Economic Performance (North), 21, 395–6
  economic performance, 416–24
    incorporating institutional analysis into economic history, 422–4
    institutions, economic theory and economic performance, 416–19
    stability and change in economic history, 419–22
  institutional change, 408–16
    organisations, learning and, 408–12
    path of, 413–16
    stability and, 412–13

institutions, 396–408
  behavioural assumptions in theory of, 400–2
  cooperation, 399–400
  enforcement, 406–7
  formal constraints, 405–6
  informal constraints, 404–5
  and transaction and transformation costs, 407–8
  transaction-cost theory of exchange, 402–3
Institutions, Institutional change and economic transformation (North)
  enforcement, 406–7
  formal constraints, 405–6
  informal constraints, 404–5
  institutions and transaction and transformation costs, 407–12
  Michael Polanyi, 411n11
  the path of institutional change, 413–19
  stability and change in economic history, 419–22
  stability and institutional change, 412–13
  a transaction cost theory of exchange, 402–3
interest and money, 91–3
international financial and trade, 299
International Monetary Fund (IMF), 13, 55, 425, 428, 467
international monetary stability, 13
international trade theory, 389
investment balance, 196–7
investment, definition, 77–8
investment multiplier, 48, 82, 95

involuntary unemployment, 53, 71–2
isonomia, 251

J

Jacobs, Bas, 477
Jawaharlal Nehru, 177
Jenks, Jeremiah Whipple, 229
Jevons, William Stanley, 434
John R. Commons Award, 395
The Joyless Economy: The Psychology of Human Satisfaction (Scitovsky), 14, 201, 203, 205–8
   the American way of life, 217–23
      disdain for culture, 220–1
      specialisation, 221–3
   the psychology and economics of motivation, 208–17
      comfort *vs.* pleasure, 211–13
      economic activity, 213–16
      income and happiness, 216–17
      personality, 209–10
      pursuit of novelty, 210–11

K

Kahneman, Daniel, 23, 428, 453–5
Kahn, Richard, 82
Kant, Immanuel, 253
Karolyi, Michael, 159
Kennedy (president), 176–7
Keynesian economics, 15n13, 443
Keynesianism, 18, 115, 158, 225, 234, 278, 288, 293, 439, 451, 456, 491, 495, 496
Keynes, John Maynard, 38–56, 103–7, 231, 247, 286, 431, 441, 450–2, 456

The Economic Consequences of Mr. Churchill, 45
The Economic Consequences of Peace, 2, 37, 42–4, 57–69, 163, 231
Economic Possibilities for our Grandchildren, 173
Eton, 39
The General Theory of Employment, Interest, and Money (1936), 7, 38, 46–55, 69–70, 103–7, 281, 282, 441, 456, 472
Indian Currency and Finance, 42
India office and back to Cambridge, 42
Keynesian Revolution, 7, 47, 69, 184, 495
Keynesian-style stimulus programme, 33
King's college, 40–1
liquidity trap, 50
The Road to Serfdom, 232
scepticism, 41
A Tract on Monetary Reform (1923), 42
A Treatise on Money, 44–6
Treaty's negotiations, 2
Keynes, John Neville, 283
Kindleberger, Charles P., 458–9
Klimt, Gustav, 159
Knight, Frank, 281, 291
Kokoschka, Oskar, 159
Kondratiev cycle, 115–16
Krugman, Paul, 29, 178
Kuznets Curve, 35, 361, 375, 472–3, 480, 481
Kuznets, Simon, 279, 281, 282n25, 353, 361, 423, 472, 480

L

labourist capitalism, 157
labour union and employment, 261–3
   Friedman and real wages, 262
   and higher wages, 262
   inflation and wages, 263
laissez-faire policies, 438
Lal, Deepak, 389
Lange, Oskar, 435
legal positivism, 258
legal theories, 253, 257
Lehman Brothers, 22, 26, 466, 468
Lenin, 148, 372
Lerner, Abba, 435
liberalism, 246, 251, 276, 277
   and administration, 252–4
   market, 162, 168
liberty, 239, 243, 250
A Life in Our Times (1983)
   (Galbraith), 174, 202
Limited Access Order Society
   (LAOS), 393–5
liquidity, 87, 103
   psychological and business
     incentives to, 88–90
liquidity trap, 50
Locke, John, 251, 293
   *Second Treatise on Civil
   Government*, 251
London School of Economics (LSE),
   230, 231
long-run monopolies, 131
Long-Term Refinancing Operations
   (LTROs), 30
Lopokova, Lydia, 44, 44n5
Lucas, Robert, 19, 52, 53, 441–3
Luce, Henry R., 387
Luckmann, 353
Lukács, Georgy, 159

M

MacArthur, Douglas, 13
Mac, Freddie, 460, 461, 466
Machiavelli, 309, 311
Machlup, Fritz, 227, 232, 233, 235
macroeconomics, 19, 25, 52, 321
macroeconomic theory, modern, 418
Mae, Fannie, 26, 460, 461, 466
Mahler, Alma, 309
Malkiel, Burton (*A Random Walk
   Down Wall Street*), 440
Malthus, Thomas, 105, 168, 184–5
Mandelbrot, Benoit, 440
   criticism, 441
Mandeville, Bernard (*Fable of the
   Bees*), 105
Mannheim, Karl, 159
Mann, Heinrich, 309
marginal efficiency of capital (mec),
   74, 82, 84–5, 88, 472
marginal propensity to consume, 75,
   82–4, 94, 282
market liberalism, 162, 168
market socialism, 382, 431
Marshall, Alfred, 69, 181, 198,
   283n26, 434, 453
   Principles of Economics, 39, 185, 430
Marshall Plan, 11–13, 235, 309
Marxian theory, 416
   of imperialism, 126
Marxism, 121, 137, 159, 355, 358
Marx, Karl, 38–9, 114, 120, 121,
   133, 185, 248, 355, 356,
   423, 464, 471, 497
Marx's theory, 122, 126
   accumulation, 124
   concentration, 124–5
   exploitation, 123
   Verelendung, 125, 132

Maynard, Young, 38–9
McCarthy, Eugene, 345
McCraw, Thomas, 118
McGovern, George, 176
Meji Restoration, 1, 376, 377
mercantilism, 104
microeconomics, orthodox, 15n13
microeconomic theorem, 321
Mill, John Stuart, 166, 245, 267, 291, 430, 453
Minsky, Hyman, 23, 110, 425, 455–8
Molotov–Ribbentrop Pact 1939, 9
monetarist approach, 52
monetary authority, 14, 45, 89, 263, 269, 298, 310, 430
monetary policy, 29, 48, 97, 193–4, 269, 284, 289, 297
monetary system
    Bretton Woods, 38, 225
    by central bank, 269
    inflation, 269, 270
    reasons for, 269
    spontaneous fluctuations in money supply, 269
Monetary Theory and the Trade Cycle (Hayek), 229
money policy, 98
money, quantity theory of, 100–1
money-rate of interest, 91–3
money-wages, 72, 92
    effect of reduction in, 97
money-wages and prices, 96–8
    employment function, 98–100
    theory of prices, 100–2
Mont Perelin Society, 157, 232–4, 282, 285
Moore, G.E., 39
    Principia Ethica, 41

Morgan, J.P., 187, 463, 468
Morgan Stanley, 27, 466
Morgenstern, Oskar, 227, 447, 453–4
My Early Life (1930) (Churchill), 2
Myrdal, Gunnar, 51, 174, 236
    The American Dilemma (1944), 174
    cumulative causation, 174

N

Nader, Ralph, 330, 349
Naim, Moises (*The End of Power*), 181
Nasar, Sylvia (*Grand Pursuit*), 55, 233
Nash, John, 447
National Bureau of Economic Research (NBCR), 279
National Resource Committee (NRC), 279, 282, 284
natural rate of unemployment phenomenon, 290
nature of capital, sundry observations on, 90–1
Navigation Act, 415
Nazism, in Germany, 201
negative income tax, 287, 307, 472
neoclassical economics, 17–18, 225–349, 351, 389, 495
    neoliberalisation, 225
    policies, 225
    principle, 88, 178
    stagflation, 14–15
    technological and human capital development, 226
neoclassical economists, 12, 24, 194, 228n3, 496

Index   525

neoclassical growth model, 491
neoclassical theory, 6, 47, 72, 96,
    226, 291, 389–92, 396,
    399, 418–19, 423
neoliberalism, 225
neoliberal policies, 225
neuro-economics, 455
New class, 199
The New Deal, 7, 28, 117, 165, 170,
    188, 281n24, 299, 433
New Economic Mechanism, 381
New Keynesian school of thought, 495
The New New Deal (Grunwald), 28
New York Stock Exchange, 3
Nineteen Eighty-Four (Orwell), 231
Nixon (president), 19, 286
North America the Navigation Act,
    415
North, Douglass Cecil (1920–), 161,
    226, 386–7, 408, 419
  academic career, 387–8
  academic contributions, 389–90
  critique of neoclassical theory,
    390–2
  honours, 395
  *Institutions, Institutional Change
    and Economic Performance*,
    21, 352, 395–6
  economic performance, 416–24
  institutional change, 408–16
  institutions, 396–408
  publications, 388
  typology of societies, 392–4

O

Obama, Barack, 467
October Revolution of 1917, in
    Russia, 1, 38

oil shock of 1973, 13
Olin, Spencer T., 387
Olsen, Mancur, 368, 399
Open Access Society (OAS), 393–5
orthodox economics, 428, 449
orthodox microeconomics, 15n13
Orwell, George, 231
Outright Monetary Transactions, 31

P

Papanek, Gustav, 375
Pareto, Vilfredo, 434
Parker, Dorothy, xii, 42
Parsons, Talcott, 358–9
paternalism, 296
patrimonial capitalism, 475, 485–6
Paulson, Hank, 466, 467
Paulson, Henry, 26–7
Pen, Jan, 56, 481
Phelps, Edmund, 290
Phillips, Bill, 290
Phillips Curve, 15, 290
Pigou, Arthur Cecil, 444, 445, 450,
    453
Piketty, Thomas (1971–)
  academic work, 475–6
  *Capital in the Twenty-First
    Century*, 34, 471, 473,
    479–93
    capital and income analysis,
      491–3
    capital and income in Europe,
      485
    capital funds, 488
    capital–income ratio, 481, 486
    capitalist system, 482
    first fundamental law of
      capitalism, 481

Piketty, Thomas (*cont.*)
  income from labour, 484–5
  limiting the gap, 35, 305, 488–9
  patrimonial capitalism, 475, 485, 486
  progressive global tax on capital, 492
  reactions to, 476–9
  second fundamental law of capitalism, 484
  supermanagers, 479, 486, 487, 489
  Two Cambridges debate, 490
  World Top Income Database (WTID), 483n15
  capitalism, 473, 480
  École des hautes études en sciences sociales (EHESS), 474
  honours, 474–5
Plato, 251, 454–5
Polanyi, Karl (1886–1964), 158–61, 275
  double movement, 168–9
  The Great Transformation: The Political and Economic Origins of Our Time, 10, 163–72
  and Keynes, 162–3
  moralist, 163
  themes, 161–2
  Viennese period, 159–60
Polanyi, Michael, 250, 275, 411n11
Poor Law Reform of 1834, 169
Popper, Karl, 159, 233, 282, 283, 285

price
  money-wages and, 96–8
  theory of, 100–2
price rigidity, 131
Prices and Production (Hayek), 229
price stability, production and, 194
price–wage interaction, 193
Primitive Order Society (POS), 393
Prince, Chuck, 465
Project Syndicate (Rodrik), 477
propensity to consume, 79–80
  subjective factors, 81–2
proportional taxation, 267, 268
protectionism, 169
psychological incentives, to liquidity, 88–90

Q
Quantitative Easing (QE) measures, 27
quantity theory of money, 100–1
Quesnay, 123

R
Raghuram Rajan, 425, 428, 429
rate of interest
  classical theory, 88
  for different commodities, 92
  general theory, 87–8
  policy of autonomous, 105
rational choice approach, 401
rational expectation approach, 442–3
rational expectation hypothesis, 441, 496
Reagan, Ronald, 15, 225, 234, 237, 238, 280, 286, 293, 427, 437, 449

Index 527

real business cycle (RBC)
  models of the economy, 442
  theory, 496–7
reality-based economics, 428, 443–58
Rechtsstaat, 252–4
The Recovery Act, 28, 29
Recovery and Reinvestment Act, 28
redistribution, 267
Reith, John, 177
Renner, Karl, 113
Reparation Commission, 63, 67
residential mortgage-backed securities (RMBSs), 461
Reversal Paradox, 203, 204
Ricardian Bank Charter Act of 1844, 169
Ricardo, David, 123, 166, 184–5, 430
rigidity of prices, 131
The Road to Serfdom (1944) (Hayek), 10, 472
Robbins, Lionel, 230, 233, 234, 285
Robinson, James, 393, 478
Robinson, Joan, 40, 51, 204, 490
Rockefeller, 136, 185, 187, 229n5
  fellowship, 309
Rodrik, Dani, 317, 477
Romer, Paul, 446
Roosevelt (president), 54, 55, 184
  New Deal, 7, 175–6
  Tennessee Valley Authority, 8
  war and, 9
Roosevelt, Eleanor, 176
Rostow, W.W., 371, 372
  stages of economic growth, 312, 371

rule of law
  decline of the law, 257–9
  economic policy and, 255–7
  origin of, 250–1
Russell, Bertrand, 227
Russia, October Revolution of 1917 in, 1, 38

S

Saez, Emmanuel, 473, 475
saltwater economists, 496
saltwater macroeconomics, 496
Samuelson, Paul, 10, 54, 110, 290, 441, 456, 490
  on Friedman's assumptions, 283
Say's law, 74, 190
scepticism, 41, 438
Scharfstein, David, 452
Schiele, Egon, 159
Schliemann, 248
Schnitzler, Arthur, 159
Schumpeter, Joseph Alois, 110–11, 353, 355, 384, 434
  academic work, 114–19
  Business Cycles: A Theoretical and Statistical Analysis of the Capitalist Process (1939), 115, 116
  Capitalism, Socialism and Democracy, 9–10, 115–18, 120–58
  The General Theory, 116
  History of Economic Analysis (1954), 119
  legacy, 119–20
  life, 111–14
  socialist system, 10

Schwartz, Anna Jacobson, 288, 290, 438
Scitovsky, Tibor (1910–2002)
    academic career, 203
    academic work, 203–6
    Capital Accumulation, Employment and Price Rigidity (1941), 204
    Economic Theory and Western European Integration (1958), 205
    Industry and Trade in Some Developing Countries, 205
    The Joyless Economy: The Psychology of Human Satisfaction, 14, 173, 201, 203, 205–8
        the American way of life, 217–23
        the psychology and economics of motivation, 208–17
    A Reconsideration of the Theory of Tariffs (1942), 204
    Welfare and Competition: The Economics of a Fully Employed Economy (1951), 205
Second Treatise on Civil Government (Locke), 251
Senate Finance Committee, 284
Shaw, George Bernard, 46
The Shifts and the Shocks (Wolf), 31n36
Shiller, Robert, 22, 291
Simon, H.A., 321
Simons, Henry, 291
sinking funds, 80
Skidelsky, Robert, 40, 43, 45, 50, 57
Smith, Adam, 18, 166, 184, 243, 255, 293, 303, 315, 356, 384, 427, 429–30, 443, 449, 453, 469, 471, 480

Smoot–Hawley Tariff Act of 1930, 297
social balance theory, 195–6
social Darwinism (Spencer, Herbert), 186
socialism, 9–11, 140–9, 260, 264, 367, 469
    and democracy
        classical doctrine of democracy, 149–51
        inference, 152–5
        march into socialism, 155–8
        setting of the problem, 149
        theory of democracy, 151–2
    industrial, 380–3
Socialism: An Economic and Sociological Analysis (von Mises), 228
socialist bureaucracy, 382
socialist society, 141, 146, 147
    social mobility in, 381
social security, 263–7
    aims of, 264
    compulsory membership in state organisation, 264
    free health service, 265
    reasons for, 263
    unemployment compensation, 266
social welfare measures, 305–6
Solow, Robert, 290, 423, 446, 477, 490, 491, 495
    model, 352
Sombart, Werner (*Modern Capitalism*), 356–7
Spencer, Herbert (social Darwinism), 186
Stabilizing an Unstable Economy (1986) (Minsky), 23
stagflation, 14–15, 225, 237

anti-stagflation policy in *Bestek 81*, 16
and Dutch disease, 16
Stanley, Morgan, 27
Statistical Research Group (SRG), 279
Stedman Jones, Daniel (*Masters of the Universe*, 2012), 225
Stein, Jeremy, 452
Stern, Nicholas, 443–4
Stevenson, Adlai, 176
Stigler, George, 279, 285, 449
Stiglitz, Joseph, 18, 23, 29, 29n32, 34–5, 164, 233, 288n32, 291n35, 440, 450
Strachey, Lytton (Bloomsbury Group), 40, 42
supermanagers, 479, 486–489
Supreme Economic Council, 57, 58
Sweezy, Paul, 110

T

Tahler, Richard, 454
Takahashi, Korekiyo, 8
TARP. *See* Troubled Asset Relief Program (TARP)
taxation
  progressive taxation, 267, 268
  proportional taxation, 267, 268
  and redistribution, 267–8
  revenue from, 267
Tax Reform Act of 1986, 461
Taylor, John, 459
Taylor Rule, 459
technostructure, 179
telecommunications system (Hayek), 233, 430–3, 466, 470
Temporary Liquidity Guarantee Program, 467

Tennessee Valley Authority establishment, 8
Thatcher, Margaret, 15, 225, 234, 237, 286, 293, 427, 437
Theorem of Maximum Utility, 434
Theory of Games and Enomic Bahaviour (von Neumann and Morgenstern), 447
A Theory of Price Control (1952) (Galbraith), 178
Thomson, James C., 345
Tinbergen, Jan, 53, 131
totalitarian rule, 231
A Tract on Monetary Reform (1923) (Keynes), 42
transaction-cost theory of exchange, 402–3
A Treatise on Money (Keynes), 44–6, 230
Treaty of Versailles, 2, 11, 43, 57
Troubled Asset Relief Program (TARP), 27, 28, 467
Tullock, Gordon, 314
Tversky, Amos, 23, 428, 453, 454
Two Cambridges debate, 490

U

uncertainty, in capitalist economy, 144
unemployment, 128, 145, 266, 290
  classical theory on, 96
  development, 1928–1938, 7
  inflation and, 289, 291
  involuntary, 72
United Nation, Bretton Woods and, 13
United Nations Relief and Rehabilitation Administration, 13

US Congressional Oversight Committee, 24
utopian economics, 24, 428–41

V
value-at-risk (VAR) model, 462, 463
Vanderbilts, 136
vanishing investment opportunity, 133–4
Veblen, Thorstein, 175, 182, 185–6, 388
Vietnam War, 18–19, 176, 289, 313
Viner, Jacob, 281, 291
volatility clustering, 440
Volcker, Paul, 15–16, 28n30
Volker Fund, 233
volume of employment, 78, 79
von Böhm-Bawerk, Eugen, 112
von Mises, Ludwig, 141, 159, 160, 228, 229, 231, 233, 285, 294, 431
von Neumann, John, 447, 453–4
von Thunen, Johann Heinrich, 434
von Wieser, Friedrich, 227–8
voucher system, 300

W
wage policy, 97, 98
Waldmannm, Robert, 495–6
Wallis, John, 399
Walras, Leon, 434
Walras's treatise *Elements of Pure Economics* (1884), 434
Wapshott, Nicholas, 46, 237

Wassenaar Agreement, 17
Waxman, Democrat Henry, 24
Wealth of Nations in 1776 (Adam), 471
Webb, Beatrice, 184, 227
Weber, Max, 353, 369, 381
Western democracies, autocratic rule, 9
White, Harry Dexter, 56
Why I am Not a Conservative (Hayek, F.A.), 234, 238, 276–7
Why Nations Fail (2013) (Acemoglu and Robinson), 478
Williamson, Oliver, 388
Wilson (president), 37, 59–62, 65
Wittgenstein, Ludwig, 159, 227
Wolf, Martin, 32, 34
The Shifts and the Shocks, 31n36
world economy, 34
Woolf, Leonard, 40, 42
The World of Yesterday (1945) (Zweig), 5–6
World Top Income Database (WTID), 483n15

Y
Yellen, Janet, 28

Z
Zijderveld, Anton, 353
Zuckerberg, Mark, 487
Zweig, Stefan, 159
  economy's self-correcting mechanism, 6
  The World of Yesterday (1945), 5–6

The manufacturer's authorised representative in the EU is Springer Nature Customer Service Centre GmbH, Europaplatz 3, 69115 Heidelberg, Germany. If you have any concerns regarding our products, please contact ProductSafety@springernature.com

Printed and bound by CPI Group (UK) Ltd, Croydon, CR0 4YY
23/03/2026
02076734-0007